DATE DUE

DEMCO 38-296

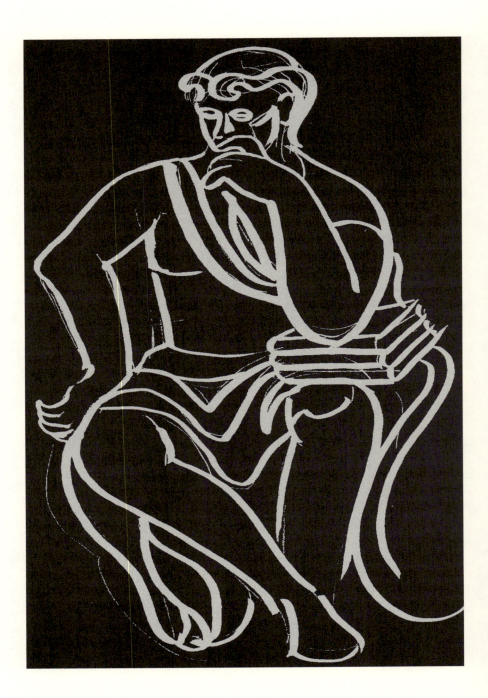

Consumer Protection and the Law

A Dictionary

12

CONTEMPORARY LEGAL ISSUES

Consumer Protection and the Law

A Dictionary

Lauren Krohn

ABC-CLIO

Santa Barbara, California
Denver, Colorado
Oxford, England

Library of Congress Cataloging-in-Publication Data
Krohn, Lauren.
      Consumer protection and the law : a dictionary / Lauren Krohn.
         p.   cm.
      Includes bibliographical references and index.
      1. Consumer protection—Law and legislation—United States—
   Dictionaries.   I. Title.
      KF1607.5.K76   1995   343.73'071'03—dc20   95-36285
                           [347.3037103]

ISBN 0-87436-763-8 (alk. paper)

01 00 99 98 97 96   10 9 8 7 6 5 4 3 2   (cloth)

ABC-CLIO, Inc.
130 Cremona Drive, P.O. Box 1911
Santa Barbara, California 93116-1911

This book is printed on acid-free paper ∞.
Manufactured in the United States of America

For my parents,
Edmond A. Krohn and Evelyn Pellillo Krohn

Contents

Preface, xv

Consumer Protection and the Law, 1

ABSOLUTE LIABILITY, 15
ACTION, 15
ADULTERATION, 16
ALTERATION OF PRODUCT, 17
AMERICAN COUNCIL ON SCIENCE AND HEALTH, 18
ANTITRUST LAW, 19
ASSUMPTION OF THE RISK, 21
AUTOMOTIVE CONSUMER ACTION PROGRAM, 22

BAIT-AND-SWITCH ADVERTISING, 25
BALLOON PAYMENT, 26
BANKCARD HOLDERS OF AMERICA, 27
BAXTER V. FORD MOTOR COMPANY, 27
BETTER BUSINESS BUREAU, 28
BLUE SKY LAW, 30
BULK SUPPLIER DEFENSE, 31

CAVEAT EMPTOR, 33
CAVEAT VENDITOR, 34
CENTER FOR SCIENCE IN THE PUBLIC INTEREST, 34
CHASE, STUART (1888–1985), 36
CIPOLLONE V. LIGGETT GROUP, INC., 37
CIVIL LAW, 39
CIVIL LAW SYSTEM, 40
CLASS ACTION, 40
CLAYTON ANTITRUST ACT, 42
CLOSE-CONNECTEDNESS DOCTRINE, 42
COLLATERAL SOURCE RULE, 43
COMMERCIAL CREDIT COMPANY V. CHILDS, 44
COMMON LAW, 45
COMPARATIVE FAULT, 48
CONFLICT OF WARRANTIES, 49

CONSUMER, 50
CONSUMER BOYCOTT, 51
CONSUMER CREDIT PROTECTION ACT, 53
CONSUMER CREDIT TRANSACTION, 53
CONSUMER EXPECTATION TEST, 54
CONSUMER FEDERATION OF AMERICA, 56
CONSUMER INFORMATION CENTER, 57
CONSUMER LEASING ACT, 58
CONSUMER PRODUCT, 59
CONSUMER PRODUCT SAFETY ACT, 59
CONSUMER PRODUCT SAFETY COMMISSION, 60
CONSUMER REPORT, 62
CONSUMERS' RESEARCH, 63
CONSUMERS UNION, 64
CONTEST, 66
CONTRACT, 70
CONTRIBUTORY NEGLIGENCE, 72
COSMETIC, 74
CREDIT CARD, 76
CREDIT INSURANCE, 78
CREDIT PRACTICES RULE, 80
CREDIT REPORTING AGENCY, 81
CREDITOR, 83
CRIMINAL LAW, 84
CUSTOM SPECIFICATIONS DEFENSE, 85

DAMAGES, 87
DECEIT, 90
DECEPTIVE PRICING, 92
DECEPTIVENESS, 95
DEFECTIVENESS, 100
DEFERRAL CHARGE, 101
DELANEY CLAUSE, 102
DELINQUENCY, 103
DEMONSTRATION, 104
DESIGN DEFECT, 105
DISCLAIMER OF WARRANTY, 107
DIVISION OF MARKETS, 111
DOOR-TO-DOOR SALE, 112
DRUG, 113
DUTY OF CARE, 116

ELECTRONIC FUND TRANSFER ACT, 119
ENDORSEMENT, 122
ENHANCED INJURY DOCTRINE, 124
EQUAL CREDIT OPPORTUNITY ACT, 125

EXCLUSIVE DEALING, 127
EXPRESS WARRANTY, 127
EXPRESS WARRANTY BY DESCRIPTION, 133
EXPRESS WARRANTY BY MODEL, 134
EXPRESS WARRANTY BY SAMPLE, 135

FAILING COMPANY DEFENSE, 137
FAIR CREDIT AND CHARGE CARD DISCLOSURE ACT, 137
FAIR CREDIT BILLING ACT, 138
FAIR CREDIT REPORTING ACT, 138
FAIR DEBT COLLECTION PRACTICES ACT, 140
FAIR PACKAGING AND LABELING ACT, 144
FALSE ADVERTISING, 145
FEDERAL CIGARETTE LABELING AND ADVERTISING ACT, 147
FEDERAL TRADE COMMISSION, 148
FEDERAL TRADE COMMISSION ACT, 150
FLAMMABLE FABRICS ACT, 152
FOOD, 153
FOOD AND DRUG ADMINISTRATION, 154
FOOD, DRUG & COSMETIC ACT, 157
FOREIGN-NATURAL TEST, 158
FORESEEABILITY, 159
FRAUD, 160
FTC V. SPERRY & HUTCHINSON COMPANY, 161
FURNESS, ELIZABETH MARY (BETTY) (1916–1994), 162

GARNISHMENT, 165
GENERALLY RECOGNIZED AS SAFE, 166
GREEN SEAL, 166
GREENMAN V. YUBA POWER PRODUCTS INC., 167
GRIMSHAW V. FORD MOTOR COMPANY, 168
GUARANTY, 170

HAZARDOUS SUBSTANCES ACT, 171
HENNINGSEN V. BLOOMFIELD MOTORS, INC., 171
HOLDER-IN-DUE-COURSE DOCTRINE, 173
HYPERSENSITIVE CONSUMER DEFENSE, 175

IMPLIED WARRANTY OF FITNESS FOR A PARTICULAR PURPOSE, 177
IMPLIED WARRANTY OF GOOD AND WORKMANLIKE PERFORMANCE, 179
IMPLIED WARRANTY OF HABITABILITY, 181
IMPLIED WARRANTY OF MERCHANTABILITY, 183
IMPLIED WARRANTY OF TITLE, 187
INHERENTLY DANGEROUS PRODUCT, 188
INJUNCTION, 189
INTERLOCKING LOAN, 189

Interstate Land Sales Full Disclosure Act, 191
Intervening Cause, 193

Joint and Several Liability, 195

Lanham Trademark Act, 197
Lemon Law, 197
Limitations of Warranty Remedies, 199
Loan Flipping, 202

MacPherson v. Buick Motor Company, 203
Magnuson-Moss Warranty Act, 204
Mail-Order Rule, 207
Manufacturing Defect, 208
Market Share Liability, 208
Medical Device, 210
Meeting-the-Competition Defense, 212
Merger, 213
Misbranding, 214
Misrepresentation, 215
Misuse, 217
Monopolization, 218
Muckrakers, 220

Nader, Ralph (1934–), 223
National Consumers League, 226
National Highway Traffic Safety Administration, 227
National Traffic and Motor Vehicle Safety Act, 228
Negligence, 228
Negligence *Per Se*, 231
Nondisclosure, 232
Notice in Warranty, 234
Nutrition Labeling and Education Act, 236

Open and Obvious Danger, 239
Ordinary Useful Life, 240

Pertschuk, Michael (1933–), 241
Peterson, Esther (1906–), 243
Poison Prevention Packaging Act, 244
Predatory Pricing, 244
Preemption, 245
Preservation of Defenses Rule, 246
Price Discrimination, 247
Price Fixing, 248
Printer's Ink Model Statute, 250

Private Right of Action, 251
Privity of Contract, 251
Products Liability, 254
Proximate Cause, 255
Prudent Manufacturer Test, 257
Public Citizen, 258
Puffery, 260
Pyramid Sales, 261

Real Estate Settlement Procedures Act, 265
Reasonable Person Test, 266
Referral Sales, 268
Refusal To Deal, 268
Reliance, 269
Rent-To-Own Contract, 271
Res Ipsa Loquitur, 273
Resale Price Maintenance, 275
Rescission, 276
Restitution, 277
Restraint of Trade, 278
Risk-Utility Test, 278
Rule of Reason, 280

Sales Law, 281
Schlink, Frederick John, (1891–1995), 282
Sealed Container Defense, 283
Securities and Exchange Commission, 284
Seller, 285
Sherman Antitrust Act, 286
Sinclair, Upton Beall (1878–1968), 288
Standard of Care, 290
State-of-the-Art Defense, 291
Statute of Limitations, 292
Statutes of Repose, 293
Statutory Law, 294
Strict Tort Liability, 295
Subsequent Remedial Measures Rule, 297
Sulfanilamide Tragedy, 298

Tarbell, Ida Minerva (1857–1944), 301
Thalidomide Incident, 302
Time-Price Doctrine, 303
Tort, 304
Truth in Lending Act, 306
Truth in Savings Act, 309
Tying Agreement, 309

UNAVOIDABLY UNSAFE PRODUCT, 311
UNDERWRITERS LABORATORIES INC., 311
UNFAIR OR DECEPTIVE ACTS OR PRACTICES STATUTE, 314
UNIFORM COMMERCIAL CODE, 315
UNITED STATES RULE, 316
UNITED STATES V. STANDARD OIL COMPANY, 316
UNKNOWABLE DEFECT, 318
UNREASONABLY DANGEROUS CONDITION, 319
USED CAR RULE, 320
USED GOODS, 320
USURY, 322

WAIVER OF DEFENSE CLAUSE, 325
WAIVER OF TORT LIABILITY, 325
WARNE, COLSTON E. (1900–1987), 327
WARNING DEFECT, 328
WARRANTY, 330
WILEY, HARVEY WASHINGTON (1844–1930), 332
WOLFE, SIDNEY (1937–), 334

For Further Reading, 337

Table of Cases, 343

Index, 345

Preface

Lawyers today are criticized for many transgressions. One of the least just complaints is that they can't give a straight answer about what the law is. It is easy to understand why a nonlawyer is frustrated by waffling responses from lawyers to straightforward questions. After all, the law is all written down in a lot of big books, isn't it? Shouldn't someone who has passed a rigorous bar examination and hung out a shingle for clients be able to state clearly whether something is legal or not?

Not necessarily. In truth, when examined closely, the law resembles the physical world of quantum mechanics where everything is uncertain, relative, and changeable depending on the questions asked. Of course, some broad rules about the law may be stated, but their proper application to a given case will often depend on a host of variables that must be decided first. These variables in turn may depend on the answers to other questions—and so on. Moreover, more than one general rule of law may be appropriate in a given case, leading to conflicting outcomes.

No area of the law illustrates this confusion better than laws dealing with the rights of consumers. First, there is no single body of law devoted to consumer issues. Consumer law is a pastiche drawn from every major branch of the law: criminal, civil, administrative, common, statutory, etc. These laws may be valid for the entire nation, within a single state, or just in a single town. Sometimes the provisions of the laws of these various jurisdictions conflict. In that case, there are complicated rules to determine which law will prevail.

Second, many different laws and legal theories may apply to a particular consumer problem. Depending on the specific facts of a case, one or the other theory might be more likely to result in a positive outcome from the consumer's point of view.

Third, the law is constantly changing. The entire kaleidoscope of laws concerning consumers is continually shifting, with new rules coming into prominence and old ones vanishing. And, to make matters worse, amidst this undulating landscape a rich lava of legal jargon flows this way and that, ready to totally envelope the uninitiated in a thick magma of confusion.

In spite of this complexity, however, the most astonishing thing about the law is that—stripped of its peculiar incantations—it is really good old common sense prancing around in disguise. Without its fancy wraps, baubles and gewgaws, the law is accessible to anyone with a sensible mindset. This is not to say that the law is any less uncertain, merely that it is uncertainty in which all may partake.

And therein lies the purpose of this book: to explain in common sense terms some of the concepts and jargon that underlie the law pertaining to consumers. While consumer law is the chosen subject, it is hoped that the discussion will shed some light on the way the American legal system works in general. This book is not intended to give legal advice, nor is it a self-help book for consumers with specific problems. It is not exhaustive. Many concepts that affect consumers have necessarily been left out for reasons of space. While the overview and some entries are embellished with historical narrative, the book is also not intended to be a history of the consumer movement. Nevertheless, the general trend of American law towards increased protection for consumer rights should be apparent.

The book is organized as an alphabetical encyclopedia of commonly-used legal terms, concepts, practices, and major legislation in the field of consumer protection law. Also included are short entries on prominent individuals in the consumer movement and important consumer organizations. Bold-faced terms within an entry indicate that the term is defined elsewhere in its own entry. A table of cases cited, with their respective legal citations, is also included.

By the time it reaches publication, every book represents the collective efforts of many minds. This book is no different. I wish to express my gratitude especially to Mr. Henry Rasof of ABC-CLIO, Inc., who conceived of the idea of a series of books on contemporary legal issues for nonlawyers. His confidence in my ability to contribute this work to the series is largely responsible for bringing that ability into being. And his expert editorial advice is behind every passage that makes this arcane subject intelligible. I also am grateful to my friend Mark Arnest for his excellent editorial assistance, computer knowledge, and encouragement and support throughout the project.

Consumer Protection and the Law

THE ORIGINS OF CONSUMER LAW

Laws specifically intended to protect consumers are very recent in the United States, dating back only to the closing days of the nineteenth century. The reason such laws began to appear at that time, rather than another, can plausibly be traced to two converging historical developments. The first was the Industrial Revolution. While this development made it possible to create abundant and varied products at affordable prices, it also had the consequence of making it less likely that sellers would care about the quality of those products. The second development was philosophical: the trend in legal thought away from strict liability towards liability based on fault, and away from societally imposed rules towards allowing people to create their own rules through the medium of contracts. There is much speculation that these two trends are causally related, though it is impossible looking through the far reaches of time to say for sure. Because American law continued and elaborated on the common law of England, an examination of these developments must start there.

The Consequences of the Industrial Revolution

In the earliest days of the common law in England, roughly before 1200, there was hardly any need for laws to protect consumers. First, there were hardly any consumers. Most people lived off the land and made or grew most of the goods they needed themselves. To the extent that ready-made products were sold, there were very strong incentives for their sellers to be honest and committed to quality. The biggest incentive was personal

1

accountability. A tradesman in a small village had to look his customers in the eye day after day. They were his neighbors and very likely his kin, by birth or marriage. If there was not already a genuine concern for the welfare of these customers, there was at least the realization that shoddy, unwholesome, or short-weighted goods would be discovered and one's business reputation would be ruined. Indeed, ready-made goods of the day were likely to be simple—either raw bulk products or very basic processed goods. A buyer of such goods usually could easily ascertain their qualities before buying them. If this were not enough, there was the added incentive of religious teachings against cheating and theft that put the seller's very soul on the line. Of course, in every society there are always a few totally unprincipled individuals who will not heed any incentives to be honest. Thus, even in the earliest days one can find laws on the books prohibiting the sale of adulterated foods or cheating in the weighing of bulk goods. However, there were relatively few of these laws—far fewer than the blizzard of laws and regulations we have today.

One additional reason for the lack of consumer protection laws in the early days of the common law should be mentioned. The problems of the common people of the time, who were often mere tenants bound to a lord's land, were not really considered important enough to be the subject of legislation or lawsuits. Local magistrates or ecclesiastical courts decided disputes in a relatively summary manner. Additionally, rural village folk were likely to settle with a suspected cheater themselves—without the sanction of law.

In the late 1700s, the Industrial Revolution changed this static picture. As it literally "picked up steam" in the 1800s, the Industrial Revolution began to chip away at the incentives that sellers of goods had to be honest and careful. First, transportation technology had improved so that goods could be sold at far distances from their points of origin. This meant that the seller no longer even knew the people who would be buying his or her goods, let alone felt any kinship with them. Moreover, the sale of shoddy or unwholesome goods in one distant market would not ruin the seller's reputation in other far-flung markets. The seller no longer had to fear ruination because word of the bad quality of his or her goods had gotten around.

Another way the Industrial Revolution lessened the sense of responsibility for the quality of goods came through the invention of mass production. The people who made the goods for sale now worked at an assembly line and were personally responsible for only one small component of the finished product. The sense of pride and personal identity in crafting a whole, integrated article was harder to evoke. Moreover, the people who worked on the assembly lines were mere hired hands. Their reputations and identities were not instilled in the goods that came from the factories. They worked for their pay and had little reason to care about the quality of the goods they made.

Nor could the consumer easily inspect the products before purchase. First, products were frequently manufactured at a great distance from the consumer and were ordered sight unseen. Second, they frequently were delivered in sealed containers. Third, the products were becoming more complex. Food products now contained mixtures of unfamiliar chemicals. Articles might be manufactured by complicated machinery that was powered by electricity, neither of which the average person understood. Moreover, consumers remained isolated individuals, while sellers now were incorporated—often conglomerates of conglomerates with massive financial power and the single goal of amassing more.

Another blow to the incentive to provide quality products occurred with the invention of the corporation. This happened in the late part of the nineteenth century. The corporate form of organization has two features that tend to destroy a sense of accountability for the quality of products. First, ownership is divorced from management. The owners of a corporation are its shareholders. They put money into the company in exchange for a share of its profits and a voice in its governance. Frequently, they are investing in many companies. They may not even know what products are produced by the companies they invest in, let alone anything about the methods of making the products or the quality of the final results. So long as dividends on shares are paid and the value of the company does not fall, the shareholders are content. The managers of the corporation also have little reason to involve their personal identities in the quality of the product. They are paid by the shareholders, not to ensure a high quality product, but to maximize profits. They have incentive to care about the quality of the product only to the extent that it will help produce profits. Additionally, in the latter half of the nineteenth century, large corporations began to combine to create even larger corporations that encompassed all or most of the producers of certain products. These were the infamous *trusts* that could use their monopoly powers to keep prices high. They had even less reason to care about the quality of the products they produced because they did not have to face much competition for customers.

A second way in which the corporate system operates to destroy accountability for the quality of products is the feature of limited liability.

Limited liability means that each shareholder in a corporation can only lose as much money as he or she has invested in the company. He or she will not normally be required to use personal funds to compensate anyone who has been injured or suffered losses because of something the corporation did. Similarly, the managers of the corporation normally are risking only their jobs. They will not be required to take personal responsibility for any decisions they make on behalf of the corporation. The feature of limited liability has advantages. Because personal risk is limited, people are willing to invest in unusual ventures that can pay off with big benefits for everyone. Great leaps in technological progress have been made by corporations precisely because of limited liability. On the other hand, once again, the fact that one will not be held personally responsible if the products of the corporation are defective is a disincentive to care about them.

Finally, with the rise in nationwide advertising, consumers could be manipulated to desire products that rational human beings would not consider worthy of purchase. The individual consumer, himself or herself probably working on an assembly line for a mere paycheck, was somehow brought to believe that the fulfillment that eluded him or her at work resided now in the acquisition of an article made without care by another distant, faceless worker in the same position. In an odd way, the product itself had become devoid of value, except as a vehicle to shift money around.

The Consequences of Changes in Legal Thought

In the early days of the common law in England, roughly before 1200, a system of so-called *strict liability* regulated legal responsibility. This meant that if one caused harm, one paid compensation for it, regardless of how the harm came about. Payment was required whether the harm was intentional or purely accidental. No inquiry was made as to whether the conduct that caused the harm was somehow "immoral" or "blameworthy." The person who caused the harm was required to pay a set sum both to the injured party and to the King's treasury to atone for the breach of the peace caused by the incident. Gradually, the obligation to pay the King came to depend on whether the harm was intentional. If the harm was caused accidentally or if there was some moral justification for it, the person who caused the harm could avoid paying the sum to the King's treasury. This was the beginning of the criminal law system.

By contrast, the payment made to the injured party or his or her family continued to be required regardless of how or why the harm was caused.

This obligation to pay the injured party developed into the law of torts, or private compensable wrongs. As the centuries passed, the law of torts acquired a messy, scaly accretion of rules and their exceptions. Particularly in the area of unintentional harm, legal responsibility began to depend on the status of the individuals involved or whether the harm could be characterized as *direct* or *indirect*. These categories were difficult to recognize and were subject to a myriad of definitions and distinctions. Civil lawsuits were so complicated that success or failure could turn on fine distinctions in characterizing the nature of the suit and the filing of it in an appropriate court of law. It was clear that reform was needed. In response, courts grasped at a heretofore little-used basis for liability: negligence. By the mid-1800s, the tort of negligence was the primary way of imposing liability for unintentional harm both in England and the United States. Negligence liability was revolutionary because it introduced the concept of "fault"—or "blameworthy" conduct—into the determination of whether compensation was required for unintentional injuries. In this respect it resembled criminal law, which had been based on "fault" for a long time. Strict liability was gone. From now on it would be necessary to prove that one who had unintentionally caused injury had acted carelessly before compensation would be exacted from him or her.

Another change in legal thought was taking place at the same time as tort law was developing. This was the rise of private contracts as a way for people to regulate their own affairs. In the earliest days, the conduct of private citizens was regulated by public norms. Agreements between individuals may exist, but the law would not involve itself with them. Gradually, as the feudal system broke down and classes of merchants, tradesmen, and artisans grew, the idea that free men (women were still restricted in their legal rights) could regulate their own affairs took hold. Agreements that could be made enforceable by law were beneficial for the expansion and stability of trade. One of the consequences of this new outlook was the shift of the concept of a warranty from a static rule to a flexible agreement resulting from bargaining between free parties. In the earliest days, the law required that goods conform to their sellers' statements about them. If the goods did not conform, the seller had to pay compensation for a breach of warranty. Liability was strict. Later, however, warranties became part of the new idea of contracts. Henceforth, a warranty would arise only if it was bargained for and made part of the agreement between the parties to a contract. Moreover, as part of the agreement between contracting parties, a warranty could only be enforced by a party to the contract. Someone who was not a party to the contract who was harmed because the warranty was breached had no legal recourse.

The Collision of Consequences

By the late 1800s, the consumer was confronted by these two historical developments: the Industrial Revolution and the introduction of fault-based and contractual liability. Thus, at the same time that sellers had less and less incentive to make quality products, the consumer who had suffered injury or loss because of bad products had to prove more and more in order to receive compensation. He or she could no longer rely on the rule of strict liability: that is, that one who causes harm must pay regardless of how the harm came about. Now, it was necessary to show that, at the very least, the seller had acted carelessly in making or marketing the product. This was difficult to do because the average consumer had no idea how the increasingly complex products were made, so he or she had no idea about what degree of care was necessary to make a good product. In addition, the average consumer had limited funds to hire lawyers and specialists to investigate the matter and take it to court. By contrast, the ever larger corporations had vast financial resources to fend off any claims. As if this were not enough, new legal rules made it even harder to recover for injuries with the introduction of the concept of contributory negligence. Under this rule, if the carelessness of the injured consumer had contributed to causing the injury or loss in even the least degree, the injured consumer could not recover anything from the seller.

Some historians believe that the invention of fault-based civil liability was a result of the Industrial Revolution. They reason that the new corporations would have been ruined if strict liability was applied to require automatic compensation for the many accidents caused by the new machinery and products that were appearing. Demanding that an injured party show that the one who caused injury had acted carelessly would cut down on the number of adverse judgments these companies would have to pay. Others point out that the old system of strict liability had been so undermined by the time that negligence appeared as a basis for liability that it did not make any difference. An injured consumer would have had a hard time under either system.

The consequences of warranties having become part of contract law were also hard on the consumer. This was particularly true as advertising became more widespread. Now sellers could make all sorts of claims for their products in advertisements without having to make good on them at all. After all, an advertisement was not a contract. A consumer who purchased an item because of statements made in an advertisement was, therefore, without a remedy if the statements were false. Other avenues provided by the common law for redress of injury caused by false statements were equally unavailing. For example, in order to prove fraud or deceit, a consumer was required to show that the seller not only knew the statements were false, but made them with the intent of inducing the consumer to act on them. Proving intent is one of the most difficult undertakings in the law. Recovery in such a suit was rare.

While it is plausible to assume that changes in the law and the Industrial Revolution are causally connected, other reasons might be cited for the particular affinity of Americans for the negligence theory of liability and for the movement to private contracts as a way of running society. First is the negligence theory's inherent appeal to fairness: After all, why should one whose conduct was in no way deficient have to pay for injuries that were purely accidental? Negligence seems to be a far more just and more civilized basis for legal responsibility than the primitive idea of liability without fault. Second, the idea of free agents, equally matched in knowledge and power, being left alone to hammer out their own agreements appealed to young America's idealization of the rugged individualist. The slogan of *caveat emptor* ("let the buyer beware") was embraced in America in the mid-1800s as nowhere else before or since.

Yet despite the enormous advances in living standards brought by the Industrial Revolution, under the hum of the industrial engines all was not well. Against the massive financial power of the corporations, the individual consumer was not a free agent with equal bargaining power. The small business person also was feeling the pressure of large trusts that could undercut prices, commandeer raw materials, and drive him or her from business. Moreover, in order to successfully market the goods made plentiful by the Industrial Revolution, banks began to invent ways of extending credit to people of little means. This opened up yet another way to extract money from consumers in the form of usurious interest rates or confusing borrowing terms that hid the real cost of the transaction. In addition, legal doctrines such as the holder-in-due-course rule allowed sellers to make the consumer's obligation to pay back borrowed money absolute. Increasingly common in the twentieth century, these types of practices allowed sellers to collect money from purchasing consumers regardless of whether the products delivered to them were of any value—or in some cases, whether they were delivered at all. In the face of these developments, public sentiment was rising for laws to regulate the behavior of sellers in favor of fair competition and fairness to the consumer.

THE DEVELOPMENT OF CONSUMER LAW

By the late nineteenth century it was clear that the golden age of laissez-faire capitalism would have to come to an end. Some balance of power between sellers and consumers would have to be struck in order to maximize the good of both. Too many small producers had been driven from business by large trusts. Too many individual consumers had been injured or lost their hard-earned money because of goods that were defective or did not live up to claims made about them. Even business people themselves realized that the bad apples among them were hurting those companies that continued to maintain high standards of quality and accountability.

The law responded on numerous fronts. First, legislatures of the various states passed statutes in an attempt to force sellers to deal honestly. These laws concerned matters such as fraudulent selling practices, false advertising, adulterated food products, and harmful patent medicines. Unfortunately, these laws were not very effective because of varied standards from state to state and the fact that many mass-produced products were being sold across state lines. The Commerce Clause of the U.S. Constitution forbids the states from burdening interstate commerce with restrictive laws, such as those imposing standards for products.

Pressure grew for a legislative response at the federal level. First to appear, in 1890, was the Sherman Antitrust Act. This law pledged fidelity to the preservation of competition among numerous sellers as the key to national prosperity. Then came the federal Pure Food and Drug Act of 1906 that forbade the adulteration of foods and drugs. Federal agencies were set up to administer these laws. The Bureau of Chemistry, which later became the Food and Drug Administration, began operations under Dr. Harvey Wiley to monitor and regulate the purity and cleanliness of food products. In 1938, the Food, Drug & Cosmetic Act was passed to strengthen the old 1906 law and increase the Food and Drug Administration's power to enforce it.

The Federal Trade Commission (FTC) was formed in 1914 in order to enforce the Sherman Antitrust Act and prohibit unfair competition among sellers. In 1938, the FTC's authority was expanded to prohibit unfair practices that injured consumers as well. Today, that authority includes evaluating product advertisements for truthfulness and banning those found to be deceptive.

The 1960s and 1970s saw increased activity on the federal level, largely in response to the prodding of consumer groups under the leadership of Ralph Nader. During that period the federal government passed a spate of laws aimed at unfair and deceptive practices with regard to credit transactions. It created the National Highway Traffic Safety Administration and the Consumer Product Safety Commission to set safety standards for automobiles and other products.

Many of the statutory responses to consumer problems over the last century have been directed at providing consumers with unbiased information about products and services so that consumers can make rational purchasing choices. Laws requiring accurate labeling, warnings, and instructions on products are common at both the federal and state levels. Most states have passed their own versions of the Federal Trade Commission Act, commonly known as unfair or deceptive acts or practices statutes. Among the many types of practices these statutes are intended to address are deceptive credit policies and false advertising.

At the same time that lawmakers were passing statutes to deal with rising fraud by sellers, the courts of many states began to chip away at the special common-law rules that prevented consumers from recovering compensation for injuries or losses caused by defective products. Throughout the 1920s and 1930s, judges were increasingly willing to interpret statements made by sellers about their products as enforceable warranties. Even when a seller had made no statements about a product at all, some courts were willing to find implied warranties that the product would be reasonably useful. They reasoned that the mere act of putting a product on the market is an implicit statement that it is of reasonably sound quality.

Judges also began to do away with the old rule that a warranty could only be enforced by the person who bought the product against the person who sold the product. This paved the way for lawsuits against distant manufacturers who had sold their products through middlemen and distributors. It also made it possible to find warranties arising from statements made in advertisements. In addition, nonpurchasers who were injured because a product did not conform to a warranty were able to sue to recover compensation.

In the twentieth century, courts also began to knock down some of the rules regarding lawsuits based on negligence. Judges or state legislatures abolished the rule of contributory negligence in favor of more liberal rules that allowed injured consumers to recover some compensation even if their own behavior had contributed to the accident that injured them. The definition of *seller*, for purposes of imposing legal responsibility for defective products, was expanded to include anyone in the chain of distribution of a product. In 1962, a landmark case, *Greenman v. Yuba Power Products Inc.*, even succeeded in resurrecting the concept of strict liability as a basis for imposing legal responsibility on sellers of products that cause loss or injury. The newly rediscovered theory was quickly adopted by most states. While it resembles the strict liability of old, the newly minted *strict liability in tort* is slightly less favorable to consumers. Under ancient strict liability rules, a seller of a product that caused harm was required to pay compensation—period. Under the modern version of strict liability in tort, the seller of a product that causes harm is required to pay compensation only if the product is defective. Various objective tests have been developed by courts to determine if a product is so unreasonably dangerous as to be found legally defective. The development of strict liability in tort represents a philosophical shift away from placing the risk on each individual consumer that products they purchase will prove unsafe in favor of placing the risk on society as a whole. Making sellers answerable to consumers for defects in their products through the mechanism of lawsuits encourages sellers to raise the prices of their products to offset the costs of making them safer. Of course, this means that society as a whole ends up paying for the increased safety and effectiveness of the products and services it demands. In the late twentieth century most have viewed this as a desirable trade-off.

In addition, courts over the past century have relaxed procedural rules to admit more types of evidence of negligence in the manufacture of products or of defects in the products themselves. They even have allowed consumers who do not know who sold the product that injured them to sue sellers that might not have even been responsible—on the chance that such a seller *might* have sold the product. In addition, courts have enforced the rules of joint and several liability that allow an injured consumer to collect the entire amount of compensation due him or her from any one single seller among several who caused the harm. Judges also began to require payment of large sums from sellers as punitive damages in an effort to deter them from unconscionable practices.

At the same time that statutes and judge-made law have introduced standards for product safety and effectiveness, forbidden unfair selling practices, and knocked down barriers to consumers' recovery of compensation for injuries caused by defective products, many extralegal responses to consumer concerns percolated up through the grass roots of society. Consumer protection organizations were formed to pressure lawmakers and sellers to adopt more stringent product standards. The first of these to appear on the national level was the National Consumers' League, founded in 1899. In the first decade of the twentieth century, the activities of a small band of investigative journalists known as the "muckrakers" helped stoke public passions against unsafe foods, shoddy merchandise, and the overweening bullying of small businesses by large conglomerates.

A lull in consumer protection activity during World War I and the relative prosperity of the "roaring" 1920s was followed by increased concern during the Great Depression in the 1930s that consumers "get their money's worth" for the few products they could now afford to buy. The 1927 bestseller *Your Money's Worth*, by Stuart Chase and Frederick Schlink, ignited consumer demand for unbiased, objective information regarding the quality of goods and services for sale. The response was the formation of Consumers Research and Consumers Union in the late 1920s and early 1930s. The latter became the largest and best-known independent product evaluation organization in the nation. It is still in operation.

World War II and the unprecedented prosperity its ending brought to the United States in the 1950s again resulted in a quiescence in consumer protection activity. However, the stillness was broken in 1965 with the publication of *Unsafe at Any Speed*, by Ralph Nader. Then a young lawyer, Nader had painstakingly assembled damning evidence of the callous disregard for human life displayed by the automobile industry in its quest for profits.

In the 30 years since that fateful publication, Ralph Nader has almost single-handedly shaped the modern consumer protection movement in the United States. Today, consumer protection is almost an industry in itself; the tactics, organization, and structure of which has largely been inspired by Ralph Nader. Nader himself has been involved in founding more than 40 separate consumer organizations. His umbrella group, Public Citizen, is looked to by dozens of national, state, and local consumer organizations for ideas and support. Large alliances of these many grassroots organizations have increased their influence as a counterbalance to the power of large corporate organizations in the marketplace. The Consumer Federation of America is a good example of such an alliance.

The era of activism symbolized by Nader has, of course, brought many other concerned citizens to the fore, many of whom have gone on to make their life's work the exposing of unfair corporate practices and the connections between corporate and political power. Uncounted thousands of private citizens have been educated and empowered by Nader's movement to address consumer problems in their own neighborhoods with creative solutions. New issues are constantly arising that require consumer vigilance, such as the availability of credit, access to telecommunications media, and the provision of services of all types.

Finally, in the twentieth century, sellers—seeing that their own best interests lie in satisfying their customers—have formed their own trade associations to promote high standards of quality and service among their members, as well as to provide alternative, impartial dispute resolution services for consumers. The good faith of increasing numbers of sellers to provide quality products and services should not be overlooked as a reason for the vast improvement in the status of the consumer in the modern era.

As the twentieth century draws to a close, it is not an exaggeration to say that the United States has come full circle from *caveat emptor* (buyer beware) to *caveat venditor* (seller beware). Indeed, some critics contend that the pendulum has swung too far. In their view, overly litigious consumers, believing that life owes them safety and satisfaction, are hurting the ability of businesses to be innovative by demanding huge settlements for small injuries. A movement is afoot to restrict damage awards in civil products liability lawsuits, to institute a rule that the loser pay the winner's legal fees in such suits, and to abolish the rule of joint and several liability so that losing defendants pay only according to their degree of fault in causing harm. At the same time, sentiment is growing to cut back on government-imposed regulations benefiting consumers on the grounds that they are so burdensome as to harm the ability of many sellers to survive.

Whatever side of the debate one supports, however, one thing is clear: The amassing of laws and regulations, both to protect consumers from unscrupulous sellers and to defend sellers from overreaching consumers, is only a Band-Aid for the ills begotten by our own material progress. The divorce of personal accountability from the production and sale of our products and services has also contributed to skewed values among those who buy them. The only real, systemic way to stem abuse of consumer protection laws by both sides is through the redevelopment of a sense of personal ethics. This will be the challenge of the twenty-first century. Like water pressure behind a leaky dike, the will to cheat will always find a way to flow through even the most impermeable wall of laws. Rather than continuing to shore up the dike with layer upon layer of laws, regulations, judge-made precedent, and injunctions, we must find a way to lessen the pressure on the dike.

HOW THE LAW PROTECTS CONSUMERS

It is important to realize that there is no special set of laws, or branch of law, specifically devoted to solving every consumer protection problem. Consumer law is actually a collage of laws from all different fields: criminal, civil, and administrative. There are, however, two main avenues that can be identified. The first is the making of rules for safety and fairness for prospective implementation. The second is private lawsuits for compensation if products or services do not prove as safe and effective as the law, or society, says they should be.

The first avenue is traveled mainly by state and federal legislatures and regulatory agencies. Operating under the authority of broadly phrased statutes, the regulatory agencies set standards for the safety and effectiveness of products and services and for the truthfulness of advertisements and warranties made for them. These agencies also monitor the compliance of sellers with laws mandating informative labeling and disclosures. In addition, agencies enforce the antitrust principles of the Sherman Antitrust Act and other laws. The regulatory agencies can seek injunctions to stop unfair practices or impose fines and sanctions on companies who violate their rules. Generally, these administrative avenues do not help compensate individual consumers who have been injured by products, services, or unfair sales practices. However, some consumer laws enforced by government agencies do give injured consumers a right to sue violators directly for compensation.

The second legal avenue providing protection for aggrieved consumers is through resort to the civil law. In order to receive compensation for injuries or losses caused by a defective product or service, an injured consumer may need to bring a civil lawsuit against the seller. Such a lawsuit will usually be based on a tort, or private wrong, such as deceit, misrepresentation, negligence, or strict liability in tort. Or the consumer's lawsuit may be based on the theory that the seller breached a warranty for the product or service. Courts will decide the issue and the judgment will have the force of the law.

These are the main ways that the legal system protects consumers. However, it is important to inject a note of caution for consumers anxious to try out the many legal vehicles on the consumer protection lot. Anyone trained in the law has learned its first and most important lesson: Lawsuits are expensive, time-consuming, and aggravating. They should be avoided whenever possible. Visions of riches and vindication at the end of the lawsuit line that are lavishly painted by some lawyers should be viewed with the most jaundiced gaze. Instead, a consumer contemplating a lawsuit should heed the ancient maxim "litigator beware." By far the best way to settle most disputes with sellers is through informal means, either by appealing to the seller's sense of fairness and concern for maintaining customer goodwill or through one of the many systems of alternative dispute resolution offered by neutral consumer protection organizations.

ate adulteration of any type of product is generally unfair to consumers and is illegal.

The **Food and Drug Administration** (FDA), which is the federal agency in charge of ensuring that the nation's **food** and **drug** supply is safe and fairly marketed, has adopted a very broad definition of *adulteration* when it refers to food or drugs. A food or drug product will be found to be *adulterated* under FDA rules regardless of whether the presence of an unexpected substance was intentional or accidental. Illegal adulteration occurs whenever a food or drug:

- contains poisonous or harmful substances, including pesticides on raw foods;
- contains impermissible amounts of approved food additives;
- is putrid or in any way decomposed, or contains any decomposed substances;
- is contained in any unhealthy or unsafe packaging; or
- has been irradiated in contravention of rules established by the FDA.

In addition, food or drug products that are manufactured under unsanitary conditions are also considered adulterated even though they may have escaped contamination. Economic adulteration of foods and drugs is also forbidden by the FDA. The FDA may seize any product that it finds to be adulterated or order a recall and obtain an **injunction** forbidding its further sale. See also **Delaney Clause.**

ALTERATION OF PRODUCT   A defense in a **products liability** lawsuit based on the argument that a **seller** should not be liable for harm caused by alterations in products that were made after the products were sold.

This defense is raised most often in cases based on **strict tort liability.** However, it is relevant in all **tort** cases because it is a variation of a fundamental tenet of fairness in American law: One should only be held responsible for harm that one actually causes. If a product is altered after it is sold, the seller cannot be said to cause any injuries that might result from the alterations. See **proximate cause.**

In order for this defense to be successful it must first be shown that the alterations made to the product were substantial. If the alterations were very minor, the seller will still be responsible for injuries caused by the product. For example, replacing the brake shoes on a car is probably not such a substantial alteration as to preclude recovery of compensation for injuries caused by a failure of the brakes.

Second, the alteration of the product must be unforeseeable to the seller [see **foreseeability**]. If the alteration is predictable, the seller of the product may be liable for injuries caused by the product unless a specific warning was given against making the particular alterations at issue. For example, removing the safety guard from a table saw is a substantial alteration of the machine. However, if the saw makes better angular cuts with the guard removed, it may be expected that a certain number of consumers will remove the guard in order to increase the machine's effectiveness to make those types of cuts. The seller may be held liable for injuries caused by removal of the safety guard.

Third, the alteration in the machine must have been the cause of the consumer's injuries. The fact that an automobile was altered by painting it a different color would not have affected its drivetrain. If injury is caused by a defective drivetrain, the seller of the automobile may be liable. Similarly, in the table saw example, removal of the saw's safety guard would not have affected the wiring. If the saw's user was electrocuted by an ungrounded wire in the machine, the seller could not use the fact that the product was altered by removal of a safety guard as a defense. See also **intervening cause; misuse.**

AMERICAN COUNCIL ON SCIENCE AND HEALTH   Founded in 1978, the American Council on Science and Health (ACSH) represents an inevitable and beneficial development in **consumer** protection: a consumer watchdog group that watches other consumer groups. The ACSH was founded by scientists and policy advisers concerned that the true state of the nation's health was being distorted by sloppy or even pseudoscientific studies put out by the mass media. The ACSH aims to apply mainstream science and peer-reviewed analysis to allegedly scientific claims made by other consumer groups about products and policies. It then attempts to debunk reports it believes to be flawed or inaccurate.

The council unabashedly declares its belief in the free enterprise system that has led to many advancements in the standard of living for Americans. Thus, it aims to ensure that **seller**s get a fair hearing when attacked by other consumer groups for deleterious products and practices. To this end, ACSH brings to bear the scientific scrutiny of over 250 of the nation's most prestigious and influential scientists to provide an unbiased review of studies put out by other groups that criticize new or existing technologies and products. The ACSH then publishes its findings in numerous books, pamphlets, and a periodical magazine, *Priorities.* Hotly disputed topics such as the health effects of pesticides, low-level radiation, and secondhand smoke are all researched and discussed by the council's experts. It should be noted that the resulting reports do not always disagree with the finding of other consumer organizations. In particular, ACSH blasts the cigarette industry for continuing to market a product of known addictive and deleterious effects on the body.

The ACSH is a nonprofit organization. Its funding derives from contributions of individuals, foundations, corporations, and trade associations. Despite its corporate support, the ACSH maintains that it is unbiased and avoids influence by any special interest group. The organization's list of contributors is available annually. The ACSH is based in New York City.

Antitrust Law   A law, or the branch of law, that is concerned with preventing concentrations of economic power in a single **seller** or small groups of sellers and with promoting competition among sellers.

Rapid industrialization after the Civil War and the invention of new types of business organizations created a climate in the late nineteenth century that encouraged groups of sellers to act together to curb competition, restrict production, and raise prices. The term *trust* was invented to describe any type of combination of sellers, from loose confederations to tightly formed business units of a single corporation. Trusts could be used to acquire a *monopoly* for a single seller [see **monopolization**] or to create an *oligopoly,* in which a small number of sellers controlled the entire market.

The perceived evils of the trusts were many and went far beyond mere economic harm caused by the higher prices monopolies and oligopolies charge. A trust with sufficient economic power could not only drive its rivals out of business but could dictate the behavior of its own suppliers and customers as well. Even noncompeting businesses could come under the influence of large trusts, since many of them would have dealings with either the trust itself or with the trust's suppliers and customers. Individuals too would be affected, because employment opportunities would be restricted. Massive economic power could ultimately translate into political power and threaten the foundations of American democracy itself.

As more and more key industries fell under the control of trusts, the public clamored for antitrust legislation. The states were the first to respond, passing laws to restrict business combinations. However, the state laws were relatively ineffective. First, they were inconsistent. Second, the federal rules of interstate commerce required states to allow companies chartered in other states to do business within their borders.

Under pressure, the federal government passed the **Sherman Antitrust Act** in 1890. This simply worded law became, in effect, the "economic constitution" of the country. It set forth the principles of free competition that— as interpreted by the courts over the past century—have become the hallmark of American capitalism. The Sherman Act was supplemented and extended by the **Clayton Antitrust Act** in 1914. Also in that year, the **Federal Trade Commission Act** was passed to prevent "unfair methods of competition," and the **Federal Trade Commission** was formed to enforce it. Together, these three federal laws and their amendments form the pillars supporting the edifice of competitive free enterprise in the United States. There are also numerous state laws that may be applicable in certain cases. Today, American-style antitrust restrictions have been adopted by developed nations throughout the world.

The business practices prohibited by the antitrust laws are varied. Generally, each suspect business arrangement is evaluated for any anticompetitive intent and effect. If there is no overriding legitimate business reason for a practice that injures competition, it may be found illegal. Common business practices that require application of this **rule of reason** are **price discrimination, mergers,** and **resale price maintenance.** Some other practices are so pernicious in terms of their injury to competition that they are *per se* illegal regardless of either the intent of the seller involved or their actual effect on competition. Among these are **price fixing, division of markets,** and **refusal to deal.**

Certain businesses and organizations are specifically excluded from the nation's antitrust laws. Among the most significant are labor unions, insurance companies, export associations, agricultural cooperatives, and Major League Baseball.

Antitrust laws are of great benefit to the **consumer.** First, by preventing monopolies and encouraging competition, they ensure that prices paid by consumers for goods and services will be fair: that is, that they will bear a reasonable relationship to the costs of producing them. An unregulated monopoly or oligopoly can raise prices at will. Second, vigorous competition promotes innovation and the development of new and improved products, including improved product safety. Monopolies feel little pressure to innovate, since they can already sell as much as they wish.

ASSUMPTION OF THE RISK   A voluntary and deliberate decision to encounter a known risk, which serves to relieve the creator of the risk of legal responsibility for harm that might result. Assumption of the risk is usually raised as a defense in **tort** cases involving **negligence.** However, it may also arise in **contract** cases, in which the seller of a dangerous product makes clear to the buyer that the seller will not be responsible for injuries. See **waiver of tort liability.**

Assumption of the risk and **contributory negligence** are similar and, therefore, frequently confused. One who is contributorily negligent is merely careless or thoughtless in failing to see a risk that he or she ought to appreciate. By contrast, one who assumes a risk is fully aware of the danger and proceeds to encounter it anyway. For example, A negligently fails to unload his pistol before lending it to B. B, thinking the gun is unloaded, uses it to play Russian roulette. B is contributorily negligent in causing his own gunshot injuries because (1) reasonable people do not play Russian roulette, and (2) if they do, they check to make sure the gun is unloaded first. By contrast, C knows that A's pistol contains a bullet when he borrows it. Nevertheless, he proceeds to play Russian roulette. He has assumed the risk of injury.

Assumption of the risk also differs from contributory negligence in that it is determined subjectively, from the point of view of the person involved. By contrast, contributory negligence is determined from an objective standpoint, with reference to how most reasonable people would think and act in the situation under review [see **reasonable person test**]. For example, a person who approaches a stray ocelot on the street may well be negligent, because most reasonable people seeing a very large, unfamiliar type of cat on the street would react with caution. However, unless that person were personally familiar with ocelots and the dangers they pose, he or she could not be said to have assumed the risk of injury from approaching the animal.

In practice, however, this rule is sometimes overlooked. If evidence shows that nearly everybody would recognize danger in a particular situation, the adult victim of harm who protests that he or she really did not see it simply may not be believed. For example, approaching an ocelot when one is unfamiliar with that type of animal may only be negligent. However, approaching an unfamiliar stray dog that is snarling, growling, and foaming at the mouth probably would be found to be assumption of the risk merely because it cannot be believed that a normal adult person would not see the danger in the situation.

Importance to Consumers

A consumer who brings a **products liability** lawsuit to recover for injuries caused by a defective [see **defectiveness**] product may be barred from compensation if the seller can prove that the consumer assumed the risk of injury presented by the product. However, this defense is not often successful. The dangers associated with defective products are usually not readily apparent. Therefore, it is difficult to prove that a consumer not only discovered that the product was defective, but also that he or she fully understood the type and degree of the risk posed by the defect and then voluntarily proceeded to use the product anyway. In rare instances, however, the danger posed by a defective product may already be known to a consumer, so that he or she assumes the risk of using it. For example, a product may be defective because it is sold in dangerous aerosol cans instead of safer pump bottles. However, the label on the can warns that it should not be exposed to heat because it may explode. If a consumer reads the label and nevertheless throws the can into an open incinerator, he or she may have assumed the risk of injury.

AUTOMOTIVE CONSUMER ACTION PROGRAM   An organization affiliated with the National Automobile Dealers Association that resolves disputes between consenting **consumer**s and participating automobile dealers. The Automotive Consumer Action Program (AUTOCAP) differs from traditional consumer organizations in that it is sponsored by the **sellers** of a product (in this case, automobiles) rather than consumers or neutral parties. Founded in 1973, AUTOCAP represents a type of consumer service that is increasingly finding a place within industry trade associations. Sellers in many fields are realizing the increased customer goodwill that may be gained by dealing fairly and impartially with customer complaints.

Headquartered in McLean, Virginia, the AUTOCAP organization has subsidiaries in 23 states. In 1994, 36 separate car dealer associations were members. Each AUTOCAP office provides a staff skilled in mediation. If a dispute has reached an impasse between a consumer and one of its members, AUTOCAP can be a satisfactory alternative to a lawsuit for both parties.

Most disputes that come to AUTOCAP are resolved in an informal process by which an AUTOCAP representative works with each side to resolve differences. In cases in which informal mediation is unsuccessful, however, the organization offers formal review of the case by an impartial panel. The panel usually consists of six members, half of whom must be consumer representatives. After hearing the two sides' arguments and considering the evidence, the panel recommends a solution. However, the disputing parties are not legally bound to accept the ruling. Most of the disputes handled by AUTOCAP involve **warranty** issues or **products liability** matters. AUTOCAP cannot resolve disputes if either party has already taken legal action or if the seller is not a member of the organization.

In addition to its mediation activities, AUTOCAP compiles statistics on the most frequent types of consumer complaints. AUTOCAP's services are free.

 **BAIT-AND-SWITCH ADVERTISING**   A tactic used to lure **consumers** by means of an attractive offer to sell a product or service that the **seller** does not, in fact, intend to sell. Rather, after the consumer has been enticed in by the advertised item, the intention is to induce him or her to purchase another product at a higher price or on terms more favorable to the seller.

Bait-and-switch advertising is considered unfair to consumers for two reasons. First, consumers are inconvenienced merely to find out that the advertised offer is not genuine. Second, consumers may actually end up paying more for a product to which they are switched than they would have paid if they had not been deceived. Having once decided to make a purchase, a consumer frequently is reluctant to leave a store without buying something.

The use of bait-and-switch advertising is proscribed by the **Federal Trade Commission Act** as well as many state **unfair or deceptive acts or practices statutes**. A consumer who has been the victim of a bait-and-switch scheme may seek relief by suing the advertiser under a state statute that prohibits the tactic, or on the basis of a number of common-law theories [see **common law**].

How does a consumer know when a bait-and-switch technique is in play? Two factors are: (1) refusing to sell the advertised item, and (2) attempting to sell the consumer another product on less advantageous terms.

However, instances of bait-and-switch tactics are rarely so obvious. Other, subtler behavior designed to discourage the consumer from wanting the advertised product is more common; for example, failing to have sufficient quantities of the advertised product on hand or refusing to deliver the item in a reasonable time. However, if the advertiser plainly states in the advertisement that supplies of the product are limited or only available at certain locations, there may be no deception intended.

The refusal of the advertiser to demonstrate the advertised product, the showing or demonstrating of a defective or broken sample of the product, or the making of disparaging comments about the advertised product are also indicators of an intent to bait and switch. The advertiser may tell the consumer that the product is unsuitable for his or her needs or that the consumer would be better served by buying a more expensive product.

Because bait-and-switch advertising is characterized by hidden motives on the part of the seller, it is frequently difficult to prove. A consumer who suspects having been the victim of such a scheme may have to delve behind the scenes to find evidence of the advertiser's hidden intent; for example, finding that the advertiser penalized salespeople who actually sold the advertised product or that a large budget was spent on advertising an item that resulted in relatively few sales in comparison to a large number of sales of more expensive items.

BALLOON PAYMENT   A payment on an installment loan that is significantly larger than other payments. Balloon payments usually are made at the end of the loan period in order to pay off the debt quickly. However, the parties can schedule them to come due at any time during the repayment of the loan. Balloon payments are useful because they allow **consumer**s with unsteady incomes to make the largest contribution towards repayment of their loans at those times when they believe they will have the most financial resources.

Balloon payments can also be abused by unscrupulous lenders. Consumers may be enticed to take out a loan on the promise of very small payments in the initial repayment period, only to be overwhelmed by the size of the later installments. Even worse is the case in which the small initial payments are not sufficient even to cover the interest due on the loan. This unpaid interest continues to accumulate so that the consumer is forced to pay interest upon interest, in addition to the principal part of the loan. This is known as *negative amortization.*

In order to prevent these practices, the federal **Truth in Lending Act,** as well as many state laws, require disclosure of the amounts of all of the payments due on an installment loan, as well as when they are due. Some laws allow a consumer automatically to refinance any balloon payment that is more than twice as large as the average of the other payments. The refinancing terms must be essentially the same or better for the consumer. This is to prevent lenders from knowingly scheduling balloon payments that are beyond the means of the borrower and then offering to refinance them at a higher interest rate. Other practices regarding balloon payments may be regulated by a state's **unfair or deceptive acts or practices statute.**

BANKCARD HOLDERS OF AMERICA A national nonprofit organization dedicated to educating **consumer**s of credit services about their legal rights and the wise use of credit in general. The Bankcard Holders of America (BHA) is also engaged in advocacy before Congress for lower credit rates and fees and increased protection for the privacy rights of credit consumers.

The BHA publishes a bimonthly newsletter and numerous lists and pamphlets on consumer credit issues. Most are available at nominal cost and address issues ranging from managing debt and securing credit to spotting fraud and whether to lease rather than buy an automobile. The organization offers its members help in finding credit cards with the lowest interest rates or those that provide rebates and other incentives. It also helps locate banks offering secured credit cards for consumers who have had trouble obtaining credit. New members may receive application forms for low-rate or no-fee credit cards. The group runs a free credit card registration service to help prevent fraud caused by lost or stolen cards. For a small fee the organization will provide personalized counseling for members having trouble managing debt. In addition, the BHA advises members on how they may obtain copies of their credit reports and medical records and on how they may have their names removed from mailing and telemarketing lists.

The BHA is headquartered in Herndon, Virginia. Founded in 1980, its estimated membership was approximately 100,000 in 1994.

BAXTER V. FORD MOTOR COMPANY The first case to hold that a manufacturer's statements made in advertising directed at a mass audience may be an enforceable **warranty** for the benefit of **consumer**s who purchase the advertised products.

The plaintiff in *Baxter v. Ford Motor Company* [168 Wash. 456, 12 P.2d 409 (1932)] lost an eye when a pebble shattered the windshield of his automobile. He sued the manufacturer, claiming that he had relied on the manufacturer's widely distributed advertisements touting the car's shatterproof windshields when he purchased it. The manufacturer defended itself by invoking the rule requiring **privity of contract,** or direct contractual relations, between parties to a sale before a warranty would arise. Since the plaintiff in *Baxter* did not buy the car directly from the manufacturer, the manufacturer claimed it was immune from suit.

The court disagreed, noting that ways of doing business had changed since the early days of the *caveat emptor* rule:

> Radio, billboards, and the products of the printing press have become the means of creating a large part of the demand that causes goods to depart from factories to the ultimate consumer. It would be unjust to recognize a rule that would permit manufacturers of goods to create a demand for their products by representing that they possess qualities which they, in fact, do not possess, and then, because there is no privity of contract existing between the consumer and the manufacturer, deny the consumer the right to recover if damages result from the absence of these qualities. . . . [*Baxter v. Ford Motor Company,* 168 Wash. at 462–463, 12 P.2d at 412]

The rule announced in *Baxter* was gradually adopted in other states. Today, statements made in mass advertising are considered to be express warranties [see **express warranty**] created in favor of the buyer of the product advertised, whether the buyer purchases the product directly from the maker of the warranty or from someone else in the chain of distribution.

BETTER BUSINESS BUREAU   A private, nonprofit organization providing assistance to **consumer**s and businesses in their relations with each other through voluntary, self-regulated programs.

The Better Business Bureau system grew out of efforts by representatives of business early in the twentieth century to promote honest advertising and selling practices. Concerned that rampant **deceit** by **seller**s was eroding consumer confidence and hurting business for everyone, these business people founded numerous private "vigilance committees" and "advertising clubs" to monitor the content of advertising and create standards for truthfulness.

One of these organizations, founded in Boston in 1912, took the name National Better Business Bureau in 1921. A contemporary but separate group developed in Chicago with a similar name. In 1970, the groups merged into the Council of Better Business Bureaus, Inc. Today there are approximately 175 Better Business Bureaus nationwide, with a national headquarters in Arlington, Virginia.

The Better Business Bureau assists consumers by collecting and disseminating information about local businesses so that prospective buyers of goods and services can make informed decisions. Typically, the information available to an inquiring consumer consists of the length of time a company has been in business, whether the Bureau has received any complaints from consumers about the business, and whether the complaints have been resolved.

In addition to providing information, the Better Business Bureau offers dispute resolution services to consumers and businesses who cannot work out their differences by themselves. Typically, a consumer will call the Bureau with a complaint about a company. The Bureau may then act as a go-between to resolve the issue with the company. If informal methods do not work, either party may request a formal procedure. This may involve mediation, in which a Bureau representative meets with the parties to help them come to an agreement, or full-blown arbitration. In an arbitration proceeding, the consumer and the seller may present evidence before a neutral third party—usually a certified arbitrator—who will make the final decision to end the dispute.

Participation in any Better Business Bureau program is entirely voluntary. The Bureau does not have the power to force businesses to adopt any practice or to abide by any decision in a dispute resolution procedure. However, in rare cases the Bureau may give its file on a company to law enforcement authorities if it appears that a pattern of **fraud** by the company is occurring. The Bureau does not give legal advice, make recommendations, or compare one company with another. It does not evaluate the quality of goods or services, make endorsements, or give credit information.

The Better Business Bureau is supported almost entirely by dues from businesses and professionals that have become members. Despite the source of its funding, the Bureau is pledged to remain neutral in handling information and complaints about members and nonmembers alike.

In addition to the services the Bureau provides directly to consumers, the organization is active in promoting ethical advertising and selling practices among its members and businesses in general. It monitors advertisements for truthfulness and may advise businesses on how to ensure that their advertising is truthful before it is published or broadcast. The Bureau alerts consumers to fraudulent marketing schemes, provides news media with information on consumer problems, and publishes numerous pamphlets and books on issues of concern to the consuming public.

BLUE SKY LAW   A name given to state laws that regulate the sale of financial securities, such as stocks and bonds, in an effort to protect small investors from **fraud**. The term *blue sky* is a reference to the abuses the laws were designed to correct; namely, the sale of shares in worthless ventures that had no more monetary value than "so many feet of blue sky." [*Hall v. Geiger-Jones Company*, 242 U.S. 539 (1917)]

The first blue sky law was passed in Kansas in 1911. Evidence suggests that the law's main promoters were state financial institutions that were more concerned about the flight of capital from themselves to speculative new investment companies than they were about small investors being fleeced by con artists selling worthless stock. Indeed, while it is undoubtedly true that there were many instances of fraud in the early days of American financial markets, it is likely that most ventures that were the targets of blue sky legislation were actually legitimate, though highly risky, enterprises.

Today, most states have some sort of blue sky law. Generally, such laws require the **seller**s of financial securities to register with a state regulatory agency before they may do business in the state. Registration requires the disclosure of information both about the seller and about the financial health and status of the companies whose stocks and bonds are for sale. Most states consider this sufficient to allow individual **consumer**s to make their own informed decisions about whether or not to buy the stocks and bonds on the register. However, under some blue sky laws, a state agency actually judges the soundness of the various securities for sale. If a security does not pass the agency's test for a "good" investment, it may not be sold. This is known as *merit regulation*. Critics of merit regulation charge that it is overly protective and paternalistic. Provided there is no outright fraud involved, these critics contend that the sale of even the most speculative and risky stocks and bonds should be allowed. These arguments are gaining acceptance, and merit regulation is declining.

Up until the passage of the federal Securities Exchange Act in 1934, blue sky laws were the primary way in which the sale of financial securities was regulated. Thereafter, both the federal law and state blue sky laws applied to the sale of securities. However, over time the federal regulatory scheme has prevailed. Today, there are a growing number of exemptions from state blue sky laws. For example, stocks and bonds of companies that are listed on the major stock exchanges, such as the New York Stock Exchange, the American Stock Exchange, and the NASDAQ exchange, are exempt from state regulation. In spite of the declining influence of blue sky laws in favor of federal rules, it is likely that they will continue to be important in some areas, especially the investigation and prevention of small-scale fraudulent investment schemes occurring at local levels.

BULK SUPPLIER DEFENSE   A defense sometimes available to a **seller** of products in bulk who is defending against allegations in a **products liability** lawsuit that the product reached the ultimate **consumer** without the proper warnings or instructions [see **warning defect**]. The defense is based on the argument that there is no practical way to affix warning labels to products sold in bulk to ensure that the information reaches the ultimate consumer.

Typically bulk products are in liquid, particulate solid, or even gaseous forms. In such situations, it is impossible to affix a label to the product itself. Moreover, the bulk product typically will be repackaged and relabeled by intermediate distributors for sale to consumers. Bulk sellers usually have no control over the labeling of retail containers once the product is delivered to an intermediate or retail dealer.

The bulk supplier defense evolved through the **common law** to remedy the unfairness of holding a bulk supplier responsible for a retail seller's failure to provide proper warnings and instructions to the ultimate consumer of the product. In order to invoke the defense successfully, a bulk seller must prove that he or she supplied an intermediate buyer of the product with adequate warnings as to its proper use, or that the intermediate buyer was already knowledgeable of the product's hazards and uses. If this is established, the bulk seller will not be liable to the ultimate consumer for harm caused by the product because it did not bear the proper warnings and instructions. The injured consumer must then seek compensation from the retail seller of the product or from whichever intermediate seller failed to pass on the proper information about the product's use.

CAVEAT EMPTOR   Latin phrase meaning "let the buyer be-ware." This saying reflects the rule that the buyer of goods bears the risk of defects in them.

The origin of the *caveat emptor* maxim is lost in the mists of time. The concept was virtually unknown in the Middle Ages. At that time, the influ-ence of the church clearly put the onus on the **seller** of goods to account for any deficiencies in them, both in this world and the next. The first refer-ence in print to *caveat emptor* came in a horse trading case in England in 1534. By the beginning of the seventeenth century the saying was well known in England, although not universally applied.

Caveat emptor as a doctrine of the **common law** gained its greatest ascen-dancy in the nineteenth century in the United States. At that time it was widely held that the parties to a sale of goods were roughly equal in their expertise and bargaining power. A buyer was expected to know his or her business and to have the good sense to thoroughly examine products for sale before making a purchase. If the goods turned out to have defects, the buyer was out of luck.

A rule of **sales law** then developing in other countries that held that "a sound price requires a sound commodity" was considered by American jurists to be paternalistic and stifling to a robust market economy. Never-theless, in compelling cases where a gullible buyer had been fleeced by an unscrupulous seller, American courts were willing to construe the seller's words to the buyer about the goods as an **express warranty** and allow the buyer to recover on the grounds that the **warranty** had been breached.

Gradually, the sanctity of the *caveat emptor* doctrine began to erode in the twentieth century as the **consumer**-driven economy developed. Gone were the days when merchants savvy in the customs of trade did the buy-ing and selling for society. Now giant, distant manufacturers sold mass-produced goods through complex chains of distribution to ultimate consumers. The consumer generally had little expertise and less bargain-ing power against his or her giant trading partner. The law recognized this inequality by beginning to imply warranties for the quality of goods even where the seller had not made any express statements about them. The consumer no longer had to "beware" to the same degree as in the past. He or she now had a champion in the form of warranty obligations that would be imposed automatically on the seller of goods under certain circumstances. See *caveat venditor;* **implied warranty of fitness for a particular purpose; implied warranty of merchantability.**

Today the old *caveat emptor* rule survives intact only in the context of estate, judicial, or execution sales, where previously owned property is put up for bids to satisfy the owner's debts. In such sales it is understood that there are no warranties.

In addition, the parties to any sale may agree to shift the risk of defects in the goods to the buyer by the use of **disclaimers of warranty** and **limitations of warranty remedies.** In this case, though, *caveat emptor* is part of the bargain between the parties and not imposed automatically as a strict rule of law.

Caveat Venditor   A Latin phrase meaning "let the seller beware." The expression is used to refer to the situation in which the **seller** bears the risk of defects in his or her products and must make good to the buyer for injuries or losses caused by them. *Caveat venditor* is, therefore, the opposite of *caveat emptor,* the ancient doctrine under which the buyer bears the risk of losses caused by product defects.

Up until the early twentieth century, *caveat emptor* had been the dominant rule in the United States with regard to **consumer** products. However, the expansion of **warranty** liability for sellers, including the recognition of implied warranties that exist without regard to the seller's intent, have shifted the balance of risk greatly towards the seller. The development of **strict tort liability** has accelerated this trend considerably, so that today it is probably more accurate to describe the rule of law in America as *caveat venditor,* at least with regard to commercial sellers.

The rule of *caveat venditor* has always been dominant in other countries, which operate under the **civil law** system. See also **common law.**

Center for Science in the Public Interest   A con-sumer advocacy and educational organization primarily devoted to issues of food safety and nutrition. The Center for Science in the Public

Interest (CSPI) was founded in 1971 by scientists concerned with keeping science a force for the public good, rather than allowing it to be perverted to the detriment of the nation's health. The major founders, Albert J. Fritsch, Michael F. Jacobson, and James B. Sullivan, were also intent on setting an example for other scientists to dedicate themselves to the same cause.

Initially, the CSPI involved itself in all areas of concern to the modern consumer: air pollution, toxic wastes, and nuclear power, in addition to food safety and nutrition. However, the departure of the group's major chemist and meteorologist in 1977 left Michael Jacobson, a microbiologist, in charge as executive director. As a result, the group's efforts have focused increasingly on food issues since that time.

The center's activities focus on research and advocacy. Initially, it will research an issue: for example, by conducting careful scientific tests of chemicals added to food products or assessing the true nutritional values of a variety of foods. Results are then widely publicized, usually appearing initially in the CSPI's own newsletter, *Nutrition Action Healthletter*. Then, with the support of consumers who have been alerted to particular problems with the nation's food supply, the CSPI engages in direct advocacy by pressuring lawmakers and industry representatives to change unhealthy practices and conditions.

One of the CSPI's major accomplishments was to win passage of the **Nutrition Labeling and Education Act** of 1990, which has been called the most important piece of legislation concerning food since the **Food, Drug & Cosmetic Act** became law in 1938. The act mandates the use of standard, easy-to-understand nutrition labels on most food products. In addition, widely publicized CSPI research about the unhealthy contents of various types of restaurant and fast food fare has led directly to menu changes in thousands of national chain and locally owned restaurants.

The CSPI also serves as a watchdog organization to expose, and demand correction of, deceptive advertising concerning food products. The center has also successfully lobbied the **Food and Drug Administration** for restrictions on the use of a number of dangerous or carcinogenic food additives, such as sulfites on fresh vegetables or sodium nitrite in preserved meats. In the 1990s, the CSPI has been increasingly involved in informing citizens about the dangers of alcohol consumption. It has stepped up its lobbying efforts to have warning labels affixed to alcoholic products in the same way as cigarettes are required to carry such warnings [see **Federal Cigarette Labeling and Advertising Act**]. The CSPI publishes numerous books, pamphlets, and posters on issues concerning food additives, safety, and nutrition. Many of them are specifically designed for children, reflecting the center's concern that the nation's youngest citizens acquire healthy eating habits early.

With headquarters in Washington, D.C., the CSPI relies primarily on funding from subscriptions and donations. In 1994, subscription revenue from its newsletter provided roughly 75 percent of the CSPI's funding of $11.1 million for fiscal year 1994–1995. The group had a staff of 50 in 1994 and approximately 800,000 subscribers. Additional sources of revenue include donations, sales of products and other publications, royalties, and foundation grants. The CSPI does not accept any corporate or government funding.

CHASE, STUART (1888–1985) Economist, author, and **consumer** advocate whose most influential book, *Your Money's Worth* (1927), written with coauthor **Frederick Schlink** [see **Schlink, Frederick John,** opened the eyes of a complacent public to a variety of deceptive marketing practices.

Born in Somersworth, New Hampshire, in 1888, Chase attended Harvard University, from which he graduated with a degree in economics and statistics in 1910. Although he dreamt of being an architect, he eventually settled for a position as an accountant with his father's firm. In the 1920s, he became an investigator for the **Federal Trade Commission,** specializing in the accounting practices of the meat and dairy industries. His investigations, combined with his frugal New England Yankee mentality, nourished in him an obsession he would pursue all his life: exposing waste in the American economic system.

In Frederick Schlink, Chase found an ideal partner for his mission. Schlink was a mechanical engineer with experience in the objective testing of product performance. In 1927 the two published *Your Money's Worth,* the instant best-seller that described for the average consumer the practices of American manufacturers that resulted in high prices and low quality. The book exposed a host of fraudulent marketing schemes and high-pressure selling tactics. It explained how planned obsolescence and minor stylistic differences in products wasted the consumer's dollar. In particular, the book targeted competitive advertising that snowed the consumer with a blizzard of promises, conflicting claims, and showy packaging, all of which were designed to conceal the basic similarity of the products involved. The book explained how the enormous budgets for advertising these virtually nonexistent differences resulted in higher prices across the board for consumers. At the same time, the needless small differences that did exist between products meant higher prices for repair, since there were no standard replacement parts for the goods.

Your Money's Worth gave consumers advice on how to reduce the cost of living by carefully examining product claims, making some products at home, and supporting objective testing and reporting on product performance. The book described a small product testing organization run by Schlink in White Plains, New York, in conjunction with a church. It explained how members exchanged results of product tests and observations of products. The test results were compiled in two confidential lists: one recommending products and the other listing products to avoid. The authors were inundated with letters from consumers inquiring how they might obtain the product information as well as requesting help with the selection of products. Demand for the White Plains organization's small newsletter soared. The authors of *Your Money's Worth* realized the potential for a national organization to provide consumers with comparative information about products resulting from independent, objective testing. **Consumers' Research** was the organization they founded to fill that need.

Following his success with *Your Money's Worth* and Consumers' Research, Chase wrote several other books on public affairs, primarily concerned with wasteful practices, the ambiguity of language, and the difficulties of communication. Chase also served as an economic adviser to President Franklin D. Roosevelt, who adopted Chase's slogan "a New Deal" for his first administration. Chase died in Redding, Connecticut, in 1985.

Cipollone v. Liggett Group, Inc.   The case in which the Supreme Court of the United States [112 S. Ct. 2608 (1992)] determined that the **Federal Cigarette Labeling and Advertising Act** does not preempt [see **preemption**] claims for compensation for injuries resulting from the use of tobacco products brought under state **common law.**

Rose Cipollone and her husband filed suit against several manufacturers of cigarettes to recover for Rose's cancer, allegedly caused by lifelong smoking. Among other things, they claimed that the manufacturers failed to provide **consumers** with adequate warnings about the health risks associated with smoking and breached an **express warranty** as to the safety of their products. Some of these claims were based on state common law.

In defense, the manufacturers argued that the Federal Cigarette Labeling and Advertising Act preempted any **products liability** claims brought under state law. The labeling act requires cigarette manufacturers to place a warning on each package of cigarettes that cigarette smoking is dangerous to health. Normally, federal legislation will preempt, or override, not only any state laws that conflict with it but also any state laws within the same sphere of regulatory activity. The defendants claimed that so long as they complied with the federal act's requirements, they could not be held to any higher standards of conduct imposed by state laws. By corollary, they argued that neither could they be held accountable for damages in lawsuits brought under state common law.

The Supreme Court disagreed. It noted that the labeling act specifically mentioned the preemption of state laws that imposed different labeling standards on cigarettes, but it was silent as to the preemption of state common-law **tort** claims. In addition, the labeling act did not provide any scheme to compensate individuals injured by smoking. The Supreme Court followed the general rule that claims of preemption should be interpreted very conservatively in order to preserve avenues of redress for injured persons. Because the labeling act failed expressly to preempt state common-law tort actions while it did expressly preempt state labeling laws, it could be assumed that Congress did not intend to preempt the former. Moreover, preemption in this case was not favored because it would leave an injured party without any remedy, since the federal labeling act did not provide one. Therefore, the Court held that the act did not preclude lawsuits brought against cigarette manufacturers that were based on state law.

Importance to Consumers

The *Cipollone* decision is important because it removes a powerful defense against products liability lawsuits from the arsenal of cigarette manufacturers. Consumers may now confidently bring suit against tobacco companies based upon state common-law claims. The *Cipollone* litigation is also noteworthy for the fact that it was the first time a jury verdict was returned in favor of a plaintiff in a suit claiming injury as a result of smoking cigarettes. At the trial court level, the plaintiffs were awarded $400,000 in damages based on the plaintiffs' claim that the defendants breached an express warranty regarding the safety of their products prior to 1966 (the year the Federal Cigarette Labeling and Advertising Act of 1965 went into effect). This was the first time that a plaintiff in a cigarette case had been able to convince a jury that her injuries were actually caused by the use of tobacco products [see **proximate cause**]. This verdict was overturned on technical grounds, however, before the case reached the Supreme Court.

CIVIL LAW   In American jurisprudence, that branch of law that deals with the relationships of private citizens (individuals and legal entities, such as corporations) amongst each other. This branch of the law is concerned with the enforcement of promises between private parties for which something of value has been exchanged [see **contract**] and of standards of consideration among citizens for the well-being of others [see **tort**].

The main purpose of the civil law is to provide compensation to individuals harmed by the breach of these societal imperatives. Typically, the injured individual initiates a lawsuit against the alleged wrongdoer, which is conducted in a public court of law but prosecuted privately at the expense of the parties. If the injured party proves his or her case against the alleged wrongdoer, the wrongdoer will be required to make the injured party whole. The power of the state, or public authorities, may be enlisted at this point in order to enforce the judgment of the court. These types of lawsuits are known as private civil actions. They are simply disputes between two private parties that the courts will resolve and enforce.

Civil law differs from **criminal law** in the private nature of the prosecution and remedy. If the injured party does not bring the lawsuit, the wrong will go unredressed. By contrast, criminal offenses are considered wrongs against the public as a whole and are prosecuted at public expense in the name of the people in the society.

Importance to Consumers

The civil law provides the primary legal avenue for **consumer**s in the United States who have been disappointed or injured by defective [see **defectiveness**] products to obtain compensation or satisfaction for their losses. The most important civil lawsuits for consumers are those based on **warranty,** or tort—particularly the lawsuits known as **negligence** and **strict tort liability.** Civil lawsuits for **fraud, deceit,** and **misrepresentation** are also significant in protecting consumer interests. Most civil lawsuits are based on theories developed by the **common law.** However, a number of statutes dealing with consumer interests provide a **private right of action,** allowing a private individual to sue for damages if the statute is violated.

CIVIL LAW SYSTEM   The term *civil law* is also used to designate a system of law prevalent in a large number of foreign countries, particularly those of Western Europe and former European colonies. The state of Louisiana, by virtue of its heritage as a French colony, also operates under the civil law system, at least nominally. The civil law system was derived from ancient Roman law and is characterized by codes of conduct written for prospective application and imposed by public authorities from above. See also **common law.**

The civil law system differs from the common-law system mostly in its philosophy of the origins of legal principles. Under the civil law system, the government attempts to come up with a set of rules to govern conduct and the resolution of disputes before they happen. This set of rules is written down and imposed in advance and all at once from above, rather than built up brick by brick through the resolution of many specific disputes as they happen.

When disputes happen in a civil law jurisdiction, judges look to see what the written code of laws says about the situation and decide the dispute accordingly. In theory, the code will contain the answer to any dispute. In practice, however, this is rarely the case. First, the drafters of these civil codes, being only human, could not foresee all of the many circumstances that might arise in the course of human dealings. Second, even if a code provision pertinent to the dispute at hand exists, the exact meaning of the words in the provision may not be clear. The upshot is that judges in civil law jurisdictions act much the same way as judges in common-law jurisdictions: They rely on decisions in similar cases that have been made in the past. The difference is that civil law judges do not acknowledge past decisions as the basis for their holdings. Rather, they maintain the polite fiction that all authority for their decisions comes from the code alone.

CLASS ACTION   A lawsuit brought by one or more plaintiffs as representatives of a large number of people with similar complaints against the same defendant. Class actions are important because they allow a large number of **consumer**s to pool their claims against a particular **seller** so that the amount of money at stake is enough to justify the cost of litigation. Frequently, the amount of **damages** to which each individual consumer might be entitled is too small to justify the cost of a separate, individual lawsuit. Moreover, the availability of class actions theoretically deters unscrupulous sellers from engaging in unfair or deceptive practices because they cannot count on their victims to feel that it is not worth their trouble to sue. However, the usefulness of a class action to consumers may be limited because of the difficulty of meeting requirements necessary to bring one.

The right to bring a class action is not automatic. A court must give permission for a class action before it will be heard, and certain requirements must be met. First, there must be a definable class of consumers that is too large to list each separately as a plaintiff. To qualify as "definable," the class should consist of consumers who have suffered the same type of harm or loss—generally because they all purchased the same defective [see **defectiveness**] product or service from the defendant in the case.

Second, the legal or factual questions that the court will be asked to decide in the case must be common to all the members of the class. For example, a class action would not be allowed if some members of the class alleged that a **warranty** for the product was breached, while others complained of **deceit** by the seller regarding the price of the item. These two legal issues are separate and require entirely different types of evidence to prove. Therefore, it is not practical to lump them together in one lawsuit.

Third, the representatives who are bringing the lawsuit on behalf of the class must be competent to represent vigorously the interests of all of the members of the class. If the representatives who will actually take the case to court do not share the interests of all the other members of the class or if they actually have conflicting interests with some of the members of the class, the lawsuit will not be allowed. In some cases, the representatives must prove that their share of the claimed damages is sufficient to be a real incentive to prosecute the case very vigorously. This rule is necessary because the decision of the court will apply to all the members of the class and it is important to be sure that all have the best representation.

Finally, before a class action can be brought, notice must be given to all potential members of the class so that they may choose whether to be a part of it. Generally, "reasonable efforts" are all that is required to give notice. However, in some circumstances this may mean that a personal letter or other contact with potential members is necessary. In other circumstances, it may be sufficient to put a notice in the newspaper or other medium of mass communications.

CLAYTON ANTITRUST ACT   Federal legislation passed in 1914 for the purpose of strengthening and supplementing the **Sherman Antitrust Act.** The Clayton Act [15 U.S.C. §§12–27] specifically outlaws a number of practices when they detrimentally affect competition between **seller**s. A lack of competition can lead to higher prices for products and services, as well as to less innovation. **Consumer** interests are harmed when competition decreases.

The following practices are forbidden by the Clayton Act under certain circumstances: **price discrimination, tying agreement**s, **exclusive dealing** contracts, and corporate **merger**s. The key to determining whether a particular arrangement violates the act is whether it would be likely to harm competition. This is in contrast to the Sherman Act, in which the intention of the involved sellers is crucial to determining a violation. Under the Clayton Act, an intent to harm competition is not necessary for a practice to be illegal. The effect on competition is the only consideration.

The Clayton Act also forbids interlocking corporate directorates. This situation occurs when one individual sits on the corporate boards of several different companies. Generally, the rule is that an individual may not occupy a position on more than one board if an agreement between the companies involved would violate any **antitrust law**s. Moreover, under the Clayton Act, corporate officials can be found personally liable for corporate actions that violate the law.

The Clayton Act also exempted labor unions from antitrust laws. Under the Sherman Act, unions were considered to be illegal organizations that restrained trade [see **restraint of trade**].

The Clayton Act is enforced by both the United States Department of Justice and the **Federal Trade Commission.**

CLOSE-CONNECTEDNESS DOCTRINE   A common-law rule [see **common law**] developed by courts to mitigate the harsh consequences to **consumer**s of the **holder-in-due-course doctrine.** Basically, the rule abolishes the holder-in-due-course doctrine in cases in which **seller**s assign consumers' promissory notes to a party with whom the seller is affiliated.

Normally, when a seller sells a consumer goods or services, the consumer's duty to pay for them depends on the adequacy of the delivered products or services. However, frequently a seller sells or assigns the consumer's promise to pay for goods or services (the promissory note) to an unrelated third party. If the third party is unaware of any reason why the consumer should not pay (for example, because the goods he or she received were defective), the third party has an absolute right to collect payment from the consumer. This is true even if the goods or services later do turn out to be defective or nonexistent. This third party is known as a holder in due course of the consumer's promissory note.

However, in some cases the supposed "third party" to whom a seller sells or assigns the consumer's obligation to pay for goods or services is actually so closely connected to the seller as to be virtually the same entity. Courts considered this situation to be manifestly unfair because it amounted to a way in which a seller could place the entire risk of defects in the products or services he or she sold on the consumer. The seller was virtually insulated from claims brought by the consumer. Even if the consumer sued the seller for **fraud** or breach of **warranty,** such a lawsuit would be time-consuming and expensive.

Therefore, courts began to scrutinize the relationship between sellers and the parties to whom they sold consumers' promissory notes. If the two appeared to be merely divisions of the same company or in some other way closely related, the court would strike down the application of the holder-in-due-course doctrine. When such close-connectedness was proved, the court basically found that the seller and the third party were the same entity. This meant that the consumer's defenses to payment of the promissory note applied to the third party who held the note just as they would have applied to the seller.

The importance of the close-connectedness doctrine to consumer protection has waned somewhat because many states' statutes and federal rules have further restricted the use of the holder-in-due-course doctrine in consumer transactions. However, the development of the doctrine marked an important milestone in the fight for consumer protection. See also *Commercial Credit Company v. Childs.*

COLLATERAL SOURCE RULE   A rule in **tort** cases that evidence of payments made to the plaintiff, other than from the defendant, in order to compensate the plaintiff for the injury or loss involved in the case cannot be admitted in the trial. For example, the fact that an injured **consumer** suing to recover **damages** from the maker of a defective [see **defectiveness**] product had an insurance policy that also paid him or her for injuries caused by the product will not be allowed into evidence. The insurance payment in this example is a collateral source, because it does not come from the defendant in the case. The purpose of the collateral source rule is to ensure that any recovery of damages to the injured plaintiff from the defendant is not diminished because the jury finds out that he or she had already been compensated by someone else.

Critics of the collateral source rule argue that it is unfair because it allows plaintiffs to get a double recovery. Supporters of the rule point out that it is better for the injured party to get "too much" money than for the one who caused the harm to get off scot-free just because the injured party had the foresight to buy insurance or provide for protection from some other source.

COMMERCIAL CREDIT COMPANY V. CHILDS   The landmark case *Commercial Credit Company v. Childs* [199 Ark. 1073, 137 S.W.2d 260 (1940)] began the gradual dismantlement of the **holder-in-due-course doctrine** in **consumer** transactions. The holder-in-due-course doctrine normally allows one who has purchased a promissory note (an IOU note) to collect the debt in spite of defenses the note's signer might have against having to make payment. The circumstances in the *Childs* case, decided in 1940, were typical:

Mr. Childs purchased an automobile from the Arkansas Motors company. In payment, he traded in his old automobile and signed a promissory note in which he promised unconditionally to pay the remaining purchase price of the new automobile. That same day, Arkansas Motors sold Mr. Childs's promissory note to the Commercial Credit Company. Later, Mr. Childs discovered that the car he had purchased was so defective as to be nearly worthless. He claimed that he had been convinced to buy it through **fraud** and **misrepresentation** by Arkansas Motors. Therefore, he stopped paying installments on the remaining amount due on the promissory note. The Commercial Credit Company, which now owned Mr. Childs's promissory note, sued him to recover payment or repossess the automobile.

The Commercial Credit Company contended that it had purchased Mr. Childs's promissory note with no knowledge that there might be some valid reason for Mr. Childs not to pay. The company alleged that it was a holder in due course of the promissory note and, under the law, was entitled to payment or to repossess the car. The supreme court of Arkansas disagreed. It noted the extremely close relationship Commercial Credit

Company had with Arkansas Motors. Not only did Commercial Credit Company finance the sale by extending Mr. Childs credit to begin with, but it also prepared the promissory note that Mr. Childs signed, as well as the document through which Arkansas Motors assigned the note to Commercial Credit. The court found that the connections between Commercial Credit and the seller, Arkansas Motors, were so close that Commercial could not honestly say that it was an "innocent" purchaser of Mr. Childs's promissory note.

This was the first espousal of the so-called **close-connectedness doctrine,** which courts used with some effect throughout the next decades to invalidate sellers' attempts to defeat consumers' rights to withhold payment for defective or undelivered goods.

COMMON LAW   The system of law in which the rights and duties of citizens are derived from traditional notions of fairness within a culture and community as interpreted by judges in resolving disputes through time. The common-law system in the United States is derived from the system that developed in England beginning in feudal times. It was brought by colonists to America, where it underwent transformations consistent with the changing culture of its host country. Today the common-law system is prevalent in Great Britain and in most nations of English colonial heritage, including the United States. Within the United States, the state of Louisiana is an exception. It adheres to a **civil law system** stemming from its heritage as a French colony.

Features

The salient feature of the common-law system is that rules of conduct are not written down in a code that purports to resolve every possible contingency before it occurs. Rather, principles of common law build up slowly over time as actual disputes are resolved. Common principles of fairness may then be deduced from a study of these cases.

For example, suppose B agrees to sell A his house. A gives B a down payment for the house on Monday, but B sells the house to C on Tuesday. A sues B for breaking the agreement. A judge hearing the case decides that B did in fact breach a **contract** with A to sell the house to her. However, since C did not know about B's contract with A, C gets to keep the house. But, B must pay A some money to compensate her for the loss of the bargain she expected. A general principle may be derived from this decision: namely, that a purchaser who does not know that the purchased property was already promised to another party will get to keep it.

The *A v. B* decision will be written down, including a description of the facts of the case and the judge's reasons for deciding as he or she did. Judges may refer to the *A v. B* case when similar cases come before them. Unless there is some significant difference in the facts of the new cases, these judges will probably decide the same way as the judge in the *A v. B* case. This is known as the *rule of precedent:* Cases based on similar facts will be decided similarly. Legal scholars and professionals may also read the *A v. B* case and write articles about the principles to be derived from it. However, the actual principle of law that formed the foundation for the decision in the case will not be written down as a law. This is the basis of the often-heard statement that the common law is "unwritten" law.

There are many misconceptions about the common law. First, the rule of precedent is not ironclad and does not make the common law hidebound and unchanging. Judges at courts at the same or higher levels than the court where the precedent was made are always allowed to overrule the prior case holding if they do not think that it is correct. Judges at any level of court may decline to follow the precedent by distinguishing the facts of the case before them. They say, in effect, that something about the case they are considering is different from the prior case and that the difference is significant and requires a different decision. Because of this flexibility, the common law is constantly changing and adapting to new circumstances.

Second, the belief that the common law is "unwritten" is somewhat mistaken. The decisions in common-law cases are published in books called *reporters,* where they are available to lawyers and judges throughout the country. Legal scholars and commentators may study these case decisions and write articles and treatises about them with suggestions as to their meaning for similar disputes in the future. In addition, common-law principles are frequently codified, despite widespread belief that common law does not rely on codes. In many areas of the law, legislatures have extracted the principles from cases decided over time and written them into codes of law. These compilations of common-law principles, though written down, are still common law because they originated from decisions in actual controversies decided in the past. Furthermore, the codes that represent written principles of common law are themselves subject to interpretation by use of common-law methods. Disputes regarding the meaning of provisions in these types of codes are resolved by judges hearing actual cases in which the meanings of the codes are in dispute.

Place in U.S. Jurisprudence

Of course, common law is not the only type of law in operation in the United States. Many laws are written down right from the start, forming a large body of **statutory law.** The U.S. Congress, the legislatures of all 50 states, as well as the innumerable city councils and other local authorities all over the nation are constantly promulgating written laws on matters as diverse as alimony and zoning restrictions. In particular, **criminal law** is written down because a basic tenet of fairness in the common-law system holds that citizens should have advance notice of exactly what type of behavior is prohibited by the state and what punishment awaits those who engage in it. It would be unfair to expect every citizen to read judges' decisions in numerous lawsuits in order to find out what behavior constitutes a crime.

Other types of law must naturally start out as specific, written rules as well. After all, one cannot expect to "derive" the proper speed limits for city streets or the registration requirements for social security from the slow plodding of judge-made common law. In addition, written laws are occasionally passed specifically to change aspects of the common law. Generally, if a statutory law conflicts with a common-law principle, the statute will prevail.

Despite these many statutory laws, common law in the United States establishes the basic rules of fairness by which citizens relate to each other. It also establishes many of the basic rules of how government relates to the citizens and how citizens relate to the government. The many specific written rules and regulations imposed by legislatures and administrative bodies may be seen as intended to fill in the details only roughly sketched out by broad common-law principles. Even the Constitution of the United States may be seen as an embodiment of ancient principles of fairness that emerged from the old English common law after it had taken root in America. Significantly, the common law predates the Constitution.

Also indicative of the primacy of the common law in our system is the relative power of judges in our society. Common law is frequently said to be "judge-made" law. Judges make law in two ways: first, through the process of deciding cases that will be used as precedent by other judges; and second, by striking down legislation promulgated by legislatures and administrative agencies because it conflicts with the Constitution.

Importance to Consumers

The common law is important to **consumers** because it is the root of our concept of fairness in commercial transactions and the procedures by which goods or services are purchased and sold. The common law provides remedies for consumers who have been wronged in the form of ancient yet vital types of lawsuits that are recognized in all 50 states. These *causes of action* represent the most basic remedies available for unfair dealing in the marketplace. They include suits for breach of **contract,** including breach of **warranty.** They also include actions in **tort,** such as **fraud, deceit, misrepresentation,** personal injury or property damage caused by **negligence,** and many others.

Generally, common-law causes of action provide consumers with compensation for injury or loss resulting from unfair sales practices or defective goods in the form of monetary **damages.** However, the common law of the United States also recognizes certain extraordinary remedies, known as *equitable remedies,* that may be ordered by a court to bring relief to consumers in certain cases. An example of an equitable remedy is the court-ordered **rescission** of a contract in a case in which its terms are found to be unconscionable for one party.

COMPARATIVE FAULT   A system of apportioning legal responsibility between the plaintiff and the defendant in a case in which the conduct of both is found jointly to have caused the plaintiff harm. The apportionment is based on an assessment of the percentage of responsibility each party bears in causing the harm.

Comparative fault (sometimes called *comparative negligence*) evolved largely in response to criticism that prevailing **tort** law made it too difficult for injured persons to recover compensation from those whose **negligence** had been the major cause of the harm. Critics charged that there were too many absolute defenses available to parties charged with behavior that resulted in harm. An absolute defense is one that totally relieves a party from any legal responsibility. The major defense of this type is **contributory negligence.** Under this defense, if the victim of harm that was caused by negligence is even slightly at fault, he or she may not recover any compensation for the harm. This result was thought to be unfair, particularly where the victim had only been very slightly negligent, while the other party's conduct had been grossly negligent. Therefore, in the 1960s and 1970s, a movement to change the law resulted in a majority of states adopting the comparative fault system.

Under the comparative fault system, a court first determines whether the defendant (or defendants) in a case is responsible in any degree for the injury at issue. If so, it will then examine the conduct of the plaintiff, or injured party. If the injured party helped contribute to the cause of the injury, the court will determine the percentage to which his or her fault is responsible. The plaintiff's award of compensation will then be decreased by an amount corresponding to the percentage to which he or she was at fault. For example, if the plaintiff is 10 percent responsible for his or her own injuries, while the defendant is 90 percent responsible, the plaintiff will have his or her compensation reduced by 10 percent, representing his or her share of the fault.

There are two types of comparative fault systems. Under the so-called *pure* system, an injured party will recover compensation reduced by the percentage to which he or she was responsible for causing the injuries. This will be true even in cases in which the injured party caused most of the injury himself or herself. Thus, if the plaintiff in such a case was 90 percent responsible for the injuries while the defendant was only 10 perpect responsible, the plaintiff will still collect 10 percent of the sum necessary to compensate him or her for the injuries.

Under the so-called *modified* version of comparative fault, an injured party will collect compensation in an amount reduced by his or her percentage of fault in causing the injuries, provided he or she was not more than 50 percent at fault. If the injured party was 50 percent or more responsible for his or her own injuries, he or she will recover nothing.

Importance to Consumers

Comparative fault is important to **consumers** in states recognizing it as the rule in **products liability** cases in which a defective [see **defectiveness**] product causes harm. For example, if the consumer in such a case was responsible for his or her own injuries to some degree by misusing (see **misuse**) the product or using it carelessly, he or she will forfeit all or some compensation for those injuries.

Depending on the state's law, comparative fault may apply to lawsuits based on **strict tort liability** as well as those based on negligence.

CONFLICT OF WARRANTIES Frequently products are sold with more than one **warranty.** Sometimes these warranties may be in consistent with each other. For this reason, the **Uniform Commercial Code**

[§2-317] provides some rules for interpreting multiple warranties and resolving conflicts between them.

In general, warranties will be interpreted to be consistent with each other whenever possible. Thus, warranty protection will be cumulative, with every warranty given its full effect. However, if it is not possible to interpret the warranties in a consistent manner, certain types of warranties will be given preference over others.

Specifically, the **implied warranty of fitness for a particular purpose** will be paramount over other types of warranties. If the other warranties conflict in meaning with this one, they will be considered void. Next, express warranties [see **express warranty**] of all types will be given effect before the **implied warranty of merchantability**.

Within the category of express warranties, exact or technical specifications have priority over inconsistent general warranty language or any **express warranty by description.** Technical specifications will also displace an inconsistent **express warranty by sample** or an **express warranty by model.** An express warranty by sample will have greater priority over an express warranty in general language or an express warranty by description.

CONSUMER   Basically, a consumer is anyone who buys or uses a product or service. The word does not usually refer to buyers of real estate, or land, because technically such property cannot be "consumed" or used up.

For the purposes of many laws affecting users of goods and services this broad definition may be modified. For example, some consumer protection laws define *consumer* narrowly, restricting protection to the actual purchaser of a product or service. Traditionally, **warranty** laws fall into this category. Other laws define a *consumer* as anyone who uses the product or service. The laws of **tort** generally follow this definition. The broadest laws may even consider persons to be *consumers* who do not actually use a product or service but who are mere bystanders or observers of its use. The doctrine of **strict tort liability** recognizes this definition.

Some laws exclude commercial users of products or services from the definition of *consumer.* Under such laws, a person who buys a product in order to resell it is not a *consumer* entitled to the law's protection. Where this distinction is made, the user of a product must be the *terminal* or *ultimate* user of the product: That is, he or she must represent the last link in the chain of distribution of the product.

Under some consumer protection laws, the user of a product or service must be a natural, living person to qualify as a *consumer*. Under such laws, businesses, corporations, or other merely legal entities are not protected.

In addition, some laws intended to benefit consumers only apply to users of certain types of products or services. Most frequently, these are personal or household items, automobiles, credit or financial services, and insurance.

In determining rights under the many different types of consumer protection laws, one should keep in mind that laws will differ in their coverage, depending on how broadly *consumer* is defined.

CONSUMER BOYCOTT   An agreement among a group of **consumers** to cease buying goods or services from a targeted **seller** in order to induce him or her to take some desired action or refrain from some particular behavior.

While most consumer law is directed at ensuring that sellers treat consumers fairly, it also addresses some consumer practices that may be unfair to sellers. The law concerning boycotts of businesses by other businesses is well regulated by federal **antitrust laws** [see **refusal to deal**]. Similarly, the activities of labor unions in encouraging boycotts are also well regulated by federal labor laws. Less regulated are boycotts of businesses by groups of consumers.

The word "boycott" was coined in Ireland in 1880, when tenant farmers on British-owned estates in County Mayo refused to work for the British land agent in charge, Captain Charles Boycott (1832–1897). The tenants refused to sell Boycott or his family food or deal with him in any way in an effort to force him to lower rents on their plots. Since that time, "boycotting" has become a common tactic for historically disadvantaged groups to put pressure on those in power.

Generally, any individual consumer is privileged to deal or not to deal with any seller for any reason whatsoever. However, groups of consumers occasionally organize in order to persuade others not to do business with a particular seller. This is a valid form of consumer self-help against illegal or unfair activities by sellers. Sellers may be induced to stop fraudulent practices or repair defective goods under the pressure of reduced sales caused by a boycott.

However, some rules apply to such boycotts. Since no boycott can be successful without widespread participation by many consumers, most of the regulations concern the methods of advertising the boycott—particularly when this is done through picketing. Generally, picketing is a form of expression protected by the First Amendment of the U.S. Constitution. However, it generally must be done peacefully in areas open to the general public. It must involve truthful assertions of grievances and it must not be coercive. In other words, picketers must not use violence or intimidation to try to convince others to join their cause.

In addition, the law distinguishes between *primary* boycotts and *secondary* boycotts. A primary boycott is a boycott of the seller whose practices are the target of the consumer action. Generally, these boycotts are legal. But a secondary boycott—a boycott of a retail seller who merely resells the goods of the entity with whom the consumers have the dispute—may be illegal. For example, a boycott of a convenience store because it sells cigarettes may well be a secondary boycott. The boycotting consumers' real dispute in this case is with the manufacturers of the cigarettes, which they consider too unsafe to be sold. However, a boycott of the same convenience store because it sells cigarettes to minors would probably be a legal primary boycott. The consumers here are trying to alter the practices of this specific store. In addition, the store's practice of selling cigarettes to minors is, in itself, illegal.

The courts have not yet resolved whether the goal of a consumer boycott is relevant to determining its constitutionality. Clearly, a boycott formed to force a seller to stop engaging in illegal conduct would be constitutionally protected. Similarly, it is clear that a boycott intended to force a seller to engage in illegal conduct would not be protected. However, what if the boycott were aimed at stopping the seller from engaging in conduct that was perfectly legal? This, of course, is the question posed by the protests over abortion in the late twentieth century. The Supreme Court has ruled that abortion protesters may try to persuade potential consumers of abortion clinics' services to boycott them. This is part of the protesters' right to free exercise of speech, even though abortion itself is legal. However, it is not at all clear that all goals of a consumer boycott may be protected.

A seller subjected to a boycott that is not protected by the Constitution may simply decide that it is easier and more in his or her self-interest to give in to the consumers' demands. After all, "the customer is always right" is the maxim by which most successful sellers operate. However, if the boycotted seller decides to fight the boycott, there are several legal roads open to him or her. The seller may sue the boycott participants for the **tort** known as interference with business relationships or the tort of interference with prospective advantage. Both of these are ancient **actions** recognized by the **common law** in all states. Alternatively, the seller may sue the boycott participants for the tort of conspiracy. Generally, a conspiracy is an agreement between two or more individuals to accomplish an illegal goal through legal means or a legal goal through illegal means. A seller might also argue that a consumer boycott is a restraint of trade in violation of the **Sherman Antitrust Act** and other antitrust laws.

Generally, however, the law looks leniently on consumer boycotts, recognizing that the individual consumer has little power against the large economic enterprises that sell most of our goods and services in the late twentieth century. In order to level the playing field, most courts have favored consumers in the few cases brought by sellers trying to stop consumer boycotts.

CONSUMER CREDIT PROTECTION ACT   The name given to an overarching scheme of federal legislation governing **consumer credit transaction**s. The Consumer Credit Protection Act (CCPA) [15 U.S.C. §1601 et seq.] is actually a collection of laws dealing with different issues in the area of **consumer** lending and credit. Among them are the **Truth in Lending Act,** the **Consumer Leasing Act,** the **Equal Credit Opportunity Act,** the **Fair Credit Reporting Act,** the **Truth in Savings Act,** the **Fair Debt Collection Practices Act,** and the **Electronic Fund Transfer Act.** The CCPA also has rules regarding the **garnishment** of consumers' wages in order to repay debts. Most of the laws comprising the CCPA were initially passed in the 1970s to counteract abuses in the burgeoning consumer credit market.

CONSUMER CREDIT TRANSACTION   Any transaction in which a **creditor** grants a **consumer** the right to incur a debt and defer its payment, especially for the purchase of goods or services.

Consumer credit transactions typically involve either *open-end credit* or *closed-end credit.* An open-end credit transaction arises when a creditor grants a consumer a renewing line of credit to be used for repeated transactions. A finance charge is imposed periodically on the unpaid balance of the account. Provided the consumer makes regular payments, the extension of credit can go on indefinitely. For example, the creditor may give a consumer a line of credit in the amount of $2,000. The consumer may make purchases up to that amount at any time. Each time the consumer makes a payment on the outstanding balance, his or her credit is replenished by the same amount. A $50 payment means that $50 is available again as credit. **Credit card** charge accounts are the most common form of open-end credit.

Closed-end credit generally is the extension of credit for a limited period of time. The total amount of the credit and the date it is due to be repaid are negotiated in advance. Generally, closed-end credit is the same as a loan extended to a consumer for the purchase of a single, large item, such as an automobile or a house.

Consumer credit transactions are also classified as either *credit sales* or *consumer loans.* A credit sale occurs when the **seller** of a product or service is also the creditor—that is, the one who extends the credit for the purchase. For example, purchases made at a department store with a credit card issued by that department store are credit sales, because the store itself is granting the consumer the right to defer payment. A consumer loan occurs when the party extending the credit is not the same party who is selling the goods or services that the consumer buys with the credit.

Laws governing consumer credit may differ in what they consider to qualify as a consumer credit transaction. Therefore, consumers hoping to invoke the protection of such laws should be familiar with their applicability requirements. See also **Equal Credit Opportunity Act; Truth in Lending Act.**

CONSUMER EXPECTATION TEST   A test used by courts to determine whether a product is defective [see **defectiveness**] and, therefore, whether compensation must be paid to **consumer**s who suffer injury or loss as a result of the product's use.

Under the test, a product is defective if it is dangerous or ineffective beyond the expectations of reasonable consumers who might normally use it. For example, a reasonable consumer would not ordinarily expect the wheel assembly to break on a bicycle and allow the wheel to come off at ordinary speeds on a flat, paved road. A reasonable consumer would not expect a door handle to have a sharp metallic projection capable of cutting hands. Nor would a reasonable consumer expect that a face cream would contain corrosive lye. In each of these hypothetical cases, a court would probably find the products defective based on the results of the consumer expectation test.

The consumer expectation test uses an objective standard to determine what normal, reasonable persons might expect when using a product. The subjective expectations of any specific consumer are irrelevant. Thus, the fact that a portly consumer really expected a delicate Queen Anne chair to support his weight would not mean that the chair was defective because it collapsed when he sat on it. The important factor would be whether normal, reasonable consumers—when sizing up the chair and the weight to be settled into it—would believe that the chair was up to the strain.

Because of the objective nature of the test, some conjecture is required to imagine what a hypothetical class of reasonable consumers would expect from a particular product. Sometimes, jurors who are hearing such a case are allowed to use their own common sense and personal expectations of the safety or efficacy of a particular product. The law simply assumes that they embody a typical cross section of reasonable consumers upon whose judgment the test is based.

One aspect that must be considered in consumer expectations of product safety is the age of the particular product at issue. No product can be expected to last forever. If the product is relatively old and has had much use, it will be less reasonable to expect it to function perfectly and without hazard to users. On the other hand, a fairly new product could reasonably be expected to operate better and more safely.

If the product at issue is at all complex, experts will be asked to explain how it works to jurors hearing the case. This is important because a typical consumer frequently does not have sufficient knowledge about a product to have an opinion as to how it should perform. For example, most consumers have little knowledge of how an automobile transmission operates. However, with explanations, a normal consumer could decide whether it is reasonable to expect that an automobile's transmission might occasionally slip into gear from a neutral position and crash through its owner's garage door as she was placing something in the trunk.

Other evidence that a jury will be asked to consider when applying the consumer expectation test is whether the product conformed to government or industry safety or performance standards. These standards are important because they also reflect society's reasonable expectations. The fact that a product does not conform to these standards is powerful evidence that it is not reasonably safe or effective. On the other hand, the fact that a product does conform to government and industry standards does not end the inquiry. Such standards are considered minimal. It may be that society has reasonably come to expect more from the type of product at issue.

The consumer expectations test may be used in both **tort** and implied **warranty** cases. Its most frequent application, however, is in tort cases in which the safety of a product is at issue.

The test is most effective when used in cases involving unsafe **manufacturing defect**s in a product. It is reasonable to expect that one unit of a manufactured item will not differ from another. If a unit does differ and is dangerous because of the difference, it is likely that the product will be found defective under the consumer expectation test.

On the other hand, there may be products that consumers expect to be dangerous, but that might easily be made safer. For example, a reasonable consumer might expect that the wheel assembly on a bicycle would break and allow the wheel to pop off on a steep, mountainous, unpaved incline at high rates of speed. Under a consumer expectation test, such a bicycle would probably not be found defective. Yet suppose that there had been developed a new wheel assembly that was ten times stronger than the old model and cost about the same to make. New bicycles that still used the old-fashioned wheel assemblies might now be unreasonably dangerous by comparison. The consumer expectation test frequently is not adequate to determine these types of **design defect**s. For this reason, another test for defectiveness, the **risk-utility test,** is more often employed by courts in design defect cases.

CONSUMER FEDERATION OF AMERICA　A lobbying organization dedicated to advocating the interests of **consumer**s before the nation's Congress, regulatory agencies, and courts. The Consumer Federation of America (CFA) is also an educational enterprise, publishing a large number of regular periodicals and specialized books and reports regarding issues of interest to consumers.

Founded in 1967, the CFA purports to be the largest consumer advocacy organization in the United States. It represents a federation of over 240 nonprofit organizations nationwide, with a combined membership of over 50 million people. These member organizations are a diverse patchwork of grassroots consumer groups, each with a unique focus. The CFA is governed by a board of directors elected by the members to address specific areas of consumer interest as determined by the members at annual policy meetings. Presently, these areas of interest include product safety, energy costs, health concerns, antitrust issues, environmental protection, transportation safety, insurance regulation, and the rights of disabled, elderly, and low-income citizens. An executive director and a small permanent staff based in Washington, D.C., implement the federation's policy directives.

A major task of the CFA is to research consumer issues and disseminate the results of such studies. The organization's permanent staff conducts original research into issues identified by the organization's members as areas of focus. A primary recipient of the information thus gathered is the United States government. Federation representatives ensure that legislators and government regulators are kept informed of CFA's findings and positions on various consumer issues. Frequently, CFA research becomes the basis for new consumer legislation or regulations. Reports and information gathered by the CFA's research staff is also available to the general public upon request for a small fee.

In pursuing its advocacy function, the CFA forms alliances with other consumer organizations so that a united front may be presented when lobbying for consumer legislation. To this end, the federation maintains a network of contacts among other consumer organizations. It also sponsors an annual consumer assembly, at which leading consumer advocates meet and exchange information with the representatives of government, industry, and academia.

CONSUMER INFORMATION CENTER   A department of the federal government within the General Services Administration that is devoted to developing, promoting, and distributing **consumer** information to the public. Established in 1970, the Consumer Information Center (CIC) is primarily engaged in reporting and publishing the activities of various government organizations that affect consumers. When new federal legislation on consumer issues is passed or when old rules are updated, the center works with the appropriate federal agency to develop publications explaining the changes in a way that will be accessible to the general public. The center also prepares materials with general advice to consumers on subjects such as how to choose products and services for value and quality, and how and where to complain if products prove unsafe or unsatisfactory.

The CIC's flagship publication is the *Consumer Information Catalog*, containing descriptive listings of more than 200 booklets on consumer issues that are available at no cost or for a small fee from various government agencies. The catalog itself is free upon request. Highlights from these booklets are presented in the center's press releases to periodical publications as well as in live copy scripts of its "Federal Consumer Focus" programs, which are distributed to radio and television broadcasters. These programs are available in Spanish as well as English. The center also sponsors an electronic bulletin board from which the complete text of all the booklets listed in the catalog may be downloaded. The center sponsors a media hotline to help reporters research consumer stories by providing the latest information from the federal agencies involved in developing consumer legislation. A small staff of consumer specialists from the center is available to speak or participate in conferences on consumer affairs.

CONSUMER LEASING ACT   An amendment [15 U.S.C. §1667(a)–(e)] to the federal **Truth in Lending Act** in 1968 that requires rental dealers to make certain disclosures to **consumer**s who rent personal property. The law applies only to lease contracts of more than four months. Since the individual terms of most **rent-to-own contract**s are shorter than this period, the law usually does not apply to them. Moreover, the Consumer Leasing Act applies only to leases of property for personal, family, or household purposes. Leases for business purposes are excluded. The total amount of the lease contract must not exceed $25,000.

The Consumer Leasing Act requires that certain information be disclosed in all phases of the leasing process. This includes any advertising before the lease is consummated. The information that must be disclosed includes:

- a description of the leased property;
- the total amount of any security deposit or other payment that must be made at the beginning of the lease;
- the number of payments in the lease period, their amounts, and due dates;
- the total amount payable on the lease;
- the total amount of any other fees, such as registration, title, and license fees, and/or any taxes on the leased property;
- a description of any warranties [see **warranty**] on the leased property;
- a description of any insurance on the leased property and whether it is to be paid by the rental dealer or the renting consumer;
- identification of the party responsible for repairing or servicing the leased property;

- a description of any consumer property to be retained by the rental dealer to secure payment of the lease terms;

- the amount, and the method used to determine the amount, of any charges for late payments or failure to pay;

- how the parties may terminate the lease prior to the end of the lease term, including a statement explaining any penalty charges for doing so; and

- conditions under which the consumer may purchase the property at the end of the lease term.

All of this information must be stated clearly and in language an average adult can understand. All numerical amounts and percentages must be given in figures and printed in conspicuous type.

Remedies for a rental dealer's failure to comply with these requirements are the same as those provided in the body of the Truth in Lending Act. See also **rent-to-own contract.**

CONSUMER PRODUCT   A product that can be consumed or used up. This includes almost every type of tangible thing for sale except real estate and financial property, such as stocks and bonds. Thus, everything from paper clips to refrigerators may qualify as a **consumer** product. Real estate, or land, is not considered to be a consumer product because it cannot be used up or worn out—at least not in the same way as manufactured articles. The same is true of financial securities.

Many consumer protection laws specify that they apply only to consumer products. Services that are directed at consumers also may come within the definition of a consumer "product" that is subject to regulation by consumer protection laws. Some laws specify that only products or services purchased for normal "household or family" use are within their protective scope. For example, a refrigerator purchased for a business may not be covered by such a consumer protection law. Similarly, a loan taken out for business purposes may not be regulated by certain consumer protection statutes.

CONSUMER PRODUCT SAFETY ACT   A federal law [15 U.S.C. §§1693–1693r] passed in 1972 to protect the public from unreasonable risks of harm presented by **consumer products**. To this end, the **Consumer Product Safety Commission** was created to administer its provisions.

The act promotes **consumer** safety in two ways. First, it mandates investigations into the safety records of consumer products. **Sellers** of consumer products are required to report to the Consumer Product Safety Commission about the hazards presented by their products. This includes reporting about the details of any personal injury litigation in which the seller's product has been involved. Informal reporting to the commission by consumers as to their opinions on the safety of products is also encouraged.

Using this data and its own independent investigations, the commission assists in the development of voluntary industry safety standards for various products. The act also gives the commission the power to set standards for products on its own initiative. Moreover, the act empowers the commission to declare products unreasonably unsafe and have their sale banned. Rules regarding product safety that are promulgated by the commission have the force of law.

The Consumer Product Safety Act also advances public safety by promoting consumer education and aiding consumers in evaluating the relative safety of products on the market. The act empowers the Consumer Product Safety Commission to make its data on the safety of specific products available to consumers who request it. However, information that constitutes a trade secret of the product's manufacturer need not be disclosed.

The commission also administers outreach programs to inform consumers, industries, and state and local governments as to its activities pursuant to the act.

The Consumer Product Safety Act is unusual among federal laws in that it grants consumers a **private right of action.** This means that a consumer may sue violators directly to enforce the rules promulgated by the Consumer Product Safety Commission. The consumer may seek an **injunction** to force the manufacturer of a consumer product to stop violating rules issued pursuant to the act. Or, if the consumer was injured by a product that did not conform to safety standards issued under the act, the consumer may sue for **damages.** Moreover, these remedies are in addition to other remedies the consumer may have under other federal or state laws.

CONSUMER PRODUCT SAFETY COMMISSION   An independent federal regulatory agency established in 1972 by the **Consumer Product Safety Act** to protect the public against unreasonable risks of injury from **consumer products.**

Activities

The Consumer Product Safety Commission conducts investigations into the safety of various consumer products. To this end, the commission collects data from **sellers**, **consumers**, and other agencies and organizations regarding product dangers. Based on the results of its investigations, the commission encourages sellers to set voluntarily safety standards for their products in order to eliminate the reported hazards. The commission may also set mandatory safety standards for products on its own initiative. When necessary to protect the public, the commission is also empowered to prohibit the sale of consumer products found to be especially hazardous.

Many the commission's activities are directed at educating the consuming public about the relative hazards of various consumer products. The commission maintains a large database on a wide variety of products and the types of injuries that have been caused by them. This information is made available to consumers upon request. In order to facilitate the flow of information about product safety hazards to and from the public, the commission maintains a toll-free telephone hotline and a public reading room, which consumers are encouraged to use.

The Consumer Product Safety Commission has its headquarters in Washington, D.C. It also maintains branch offices throughout the country.

Procedure and Enforcement

Product safety standards under the Consumer Product Safety Commission may be initiated when any interested party, including consumers, files a petition explaining the need for action with regard to a particular product. Public notice is given and a period of time is set aside for interested parties to submit arguments, facts, and data for and against proposed safety standards. Upon consideration of all the information submitted, the commission will either promulgate a rule imposing the suggested safety standards on the product or will determine that mandatory standards are unnecessary. Rules issued are subject to challenge by any interested party in federal district court.

The commission is empowered to seek **injunction**s to stop the sale of products that do not conform to its regulations or that have been found to be so hazardous that no standards can make them reasonably safe. The commission can also impose money fines on sellers of products that violate the agency's rules. In addition, it may seek criminal penalties against the directors, officers, or other employees of companies that violate its standards.

Other federal laws the Consumer Product Safety Commission is charged with enforcing include the **Flammable Fabrics Act,** the **Poison Prevention Packaging Act,** and the **Hazardous Substances Act.**

CONSUMER REPORT   Any communication of information by a **credit reporting agency** about a **consumer**'s creditworthiness, character, general reputation, personal characteristics, or mode of living that is expected to be used for the purpose of establishing the consumer's eligibility for credit, insurance, employment, or for another legitimate business purpose. Information that meets this definition is subject to regulation by the federal **Fair Credit Reporting Act.**

Controversy about the definition of this term is not surprising, considering the importance of consumer reports to consumers' privacy and ability to secure credit and employment. Previously, it was held that if information about a consumer was not used for one of several enumerated legitimate reasons, it did not qualify as a consumer report and the federal law could not be used to regulate it. Later, courts realized that this interpretation defeated one of the primary purposes of the Fair Credit Reporting Act: to protect the consumer's privacy. Today, the emphasis is on the consumer reporting agency's expectations about how information it supplies will be used. If the agency expects that a recipient of the information will use it in one of the listed ways, the information qualifies as a consumer report even if the recipient uses it differently.

Another area of contention has been what qualifies as other legitimate business purposes to which the information might be put. Generally, this means consumer purposes related to the buying and selling of goods and services.

Some types of information that have specifically been held to be consumer reports are:

- information consisting only of names and addresses
- information from the public records of state and local agencies
- listings that rate how well consumers pay their bills
- motor vehicle reports
- bad check lists
- tenant screening reports

Some types of reports that are specifically excluded from the definition are law enforcement bulletins and directories such as telephone books. In addition, reports about consumer transactions prepared by one of the parties to the transaction are not consumer reports. For example, a bank's report to a credit reporting agency about a particular customer's habits in repaying a loan is not a consumer report. See also **consumer credit transaction.**

CONSUMERS' RESEARCH   The first organization dedicated to impartial testing of products for the benefit of **consumer**s. Founded in 1928, Consumers' Research was formed by **Frederick Schlink** [see **Schlink, Frederick John**] and **Stuart Chase** [see **Chase, Stuart**] in response to interest aroused by the publication of their book, *Your Money's Worth.*

Your Money's Worth was a frank exposé of how modern marketing methods and slick advertising deceived consumers and resulted in high prices for goods and services. The book also described a small product-testing station run by Frederick Schlink and a community church in White Plains, New York, that provided information to its members about reasonably priced, high-quality products. It also recommended products to avoid because of inferior quality, unreasonable prices, or false advertisements. Following publication of the book, the authors were inundated by letters from consumers all over the country seeking unbiased assessments of products they were considering. Schlink and Chase realized the potential for a national service devoted entirely to reporting the results of impartial product testing. Consumers' Research was incorporated for that purpose. Its publication, *Consumers' Research Bulletin* (later renamed *Consumers' Research Magazine*) started with a circulation of 565 and rose to 45,000 by 1933.

Success was short-lived, however. Labor troubles broke out at Consumers' Research in the mid-1930s, when a union formed by the employees sought recognition from management. Frederick Schlink, believing the movement to be inspired by Communists, fired the union organizers. A strike broke out that was settled only when some 70 employees, headed by Arthur Kallet, left to form a rival organization, **Consumers Union.**

Schlink went on to head Consumers' Research until 1983. Unlike Consumers Union, Consumers' Research never engaged in political activism. In Schlink's view, the government had already shown its favoritism to the **seller**s of consumer products. Government intervention in consumer affairs—if not exactly harmful—was unlikely to achieve lasting benefits. Rather, Schlink maintained that "the alert and informed consumer is his own best friend." [*Consumers' Research Magazine* (August 1974, page 3)] Perhaps as a direct result of Schlink's reluctance to engage in the political process, Consumers' Research was gradually eclipsed by its old rival, Consumers Union.

Today, Consumers' Research is a nonmember, nonprofit organization. After Schlink retired in 1983, the organization ceased independent product testing. Its newsletter is still published, but concentrates on general information about wise purchasing, consumer trends, nutrition, safety, health, and government regulation of consumer products. Consumers' Research is funded by subscriptions. It accepts no funds from manufacturers, sellers, or government agencies. It does not accept advertisements.

CONSUMERS UNION   A nonprofit organization devoted to aiding **consumers** in choosing quality products at fair prices. Consumers Union performs impartial, scientific testing on products to determine their relative merits. Results are published in its monthly magazine, *Consumer Reports.* The organization also reports on the labor conditions under which the products reviewed are produced and is active in the areas of health care services, consumer credit, packaging, fair trade laws, **drug** pricing, warranties [see **warranty**], insurance, **food** and drug inspection, the government release of scientific data, unit pricing, misleading advertising, and quality control. The organization also publishes numerous periodicals devoted to specific consumer services.

Consumers Union was founded in 1936 by **Colston Warne** [see **Warne, Colston E.**] and others who left **Consumers' Research** over a labor dispute. The new organization was initially greeted with hostility from **sellers** and the mainstream media alike. Most newspapers and magazines of the time refused to sell space to Consumers Union, claiming that consumer testing was an unfair attack on legitimate advertising. Some went so far as to brand Consumers Union "subversive." Direct mail promotion and advertisements in liberal journals kept the organization alive. Ironically, the virulent opposition from large corporations actually served to rally support for the fledgling consumer group. By 1946, Consumers Union was on firm ground.

Consumers Union's emphasis on product testing arose in response to the emergence of competitive advertising for nationally marketed brand-named goods that occurred in the 1920s and 1930s. Consumers Union perceived a need to provide for the ultimate consumer what corporate research and development was already doing for the sellers of products: that is, assessing the actual performance of products through standard testing techniques and rating systems. Today, consumer product testing is generally praised as a way to level the playing field for consumers against the giant corporations that provide most **consumer product**s. It has also been suggested that the product testing conducted by Consumers Union and other groups helps maintain viable competition among sellers. Presently, the enormous expenditures made by large corporations for competitive advertising may impede small, start-up companies from entering the market. The small companies are unable to make their own claims heard amid the din. Some commentators have gone so far as to suggest government subsidies for consumer product testing organizations such as Consumers Union as a method of antitrust enforcement [see **antitrust law**]. Presently, however, Consumers Union is completely privately funded.

Despite the positive response, some problems with product testing have also been suggested. For example, there is some concern that companies whose products have been tested may tend to raise their prices and/or lower their quality after receiving a positive rating. Conversely, those who have received less than positive ratings may take steps to improve that go unnoticed.

In choosing products to test, Consumers Union's testing committee is guided by members' interests. Typical choices are clothing, furnishings, appliances, automobiles, and leisure products. The chosen products are purchased on the open market for market prices. They usually represent brands that have a significant national market share.

Techniques used for testing by Consumers Union are largely adapted from those used by the industry that made the product. A special rating system balances the importance of various attributes of the products to consumers. Then, the testing committee uses its composite judgment to rank the brands in order of overall quality. While the ranking of products is useful to consumers, perhaps even more important is the education it provides to consumers as to what attributes in a particular type of product are important to look for. The discussion of the tests gives consumers a degree of knowledge to enable them to rate the products they try themselves. Consumers Union attempts to be completely impartial in its testing. It does not accept advertising and does not permit the companies whose products have been tested to use the test results in their advertising.

In addition to helping consumers make informed choices, the publication of test results by Consumers Union has played an important role in revealing safety problems in products and mobilizing consumers to pressure sellers and lawmakers involved in regulating them to increase safety and quality standards. Consumers Union itself is active in lobbying for reform at every level of government. Its representatives' testimony is frequently part of the basis for regulatory decisions involving the products it tests. Consumers Union's political activism has increased since the 1970s, when **Ralph Nader** [see **Nader, Ralph**] resigned from its board of directors after criticizing the organization for timidity in public affairs.

Today, the organization has approximately 4 million subscribers to its publications, each of whom has the right to join. This arguably makes Consumers Union the largest consumer organization in the nation. Its budget of approximately $100 million also makes it a powerful political force for consumers. Control of the organization is exercised by a 21-member board of directors, who are elected for three-year terms. The members comprise representatives from industry and finance. Consumers Union has its headquarters in Yonkers, New York. It is a member of the **Consumer Federation of America.**

CONTEST   The use of contests and games to promote the sale of goods has become a popular marketing technique in the United States. Basically, these techniques involve the offering of a prize in exchange for some action by a participating **consumer. Seller**s of goods have found them remarkably effective in stimulating sales by appealing to the universal hope of "getting something for nothing."

Most contests are one of four basic types:

1. "Pay to play" games in which participants pay money directly for the chance to receive a prize;
2. Competitions in which the winner is chosen on the basis of his or her skill in performing some action;
3. "Purchase to play" games, which require the purchase of a product that includes a chance to win a prize; and
4. "Entry only" games that require only that the participant enter by performing some minimal action that does not involve any skill.

Legality

Contests and games present a number of issues concerned with fairness to consumers. Since many states have laws prohibiting private lotteries, it is first important to determine whether a contest or game is really a lottery.

Traditionally, three elements must be present to make a contest into a lottery: (1) winning must be based on chance; (2) a prize must be offered; and (3) something of value, or *consideration,* must be given in order to participate. Under this definition, the "pay to play" game described above is most likely to be considered a lottery. In this type of game, money is exchanged directly for the chance to win a prize. Frequently, the sponsor of such a contest makes money solely off the revenue generated by the game. It has no other business or product. Therefore, this type of game will usually be illegal in states that ban private lotteries.

On the other hand, contests in which winning is based on skill, and not on chance, are least likely to be considered lotteries. However, the inquiry into the legality of such contests does not end there. In some cases, the skill required to enter the contest may be very minimal. It may be so minimal that virtually anyone could come up with the correct answers or perform some other required action. In such cases, there almost inevitably is a second step to the contest in which the winner is selected by chance from a pool of all of the contestants who gave correct answers or performed the requested action. If participants are required to pay money in order to compete in such a contest, it may well be found to be an illegal lottery under state law.

The legality of the "purchase to play" type of game depends on how a particular state's law defines *consideration.* In this type of game, a participant buys a product that also includes a "free" chance to win a prize. Some state courts have held that something of value has been exchanged for the supposedly "free" chance to win the prize. First, the consumer is required to buy something in order to participate. Some consumers may buy the product solely to get a chance to participate in the contest. Therefore, the consumer has exchanged money for a chance to win a prize—the classic definition of a lottery. Second, it has been pointed out that consumers who participate in a "purchase to play" contest end up paying for the chance to win the prize, even though the chance appears to be "free." Because the sponsor of the contest inevitably buys the prize it offers from the proceeds of the sale of its products, each consumer who purchases the product is helping to pay for the prize and the chance to win it. This latter analysis is tenuous, but it has been sufficient to convince some courts that an illegal lottery is involved.

The "entry only" type of game may also be found to be an illegal lottery under some states' laws. In this type of game, no money is exchanged, but the participant must perform some action, usually very minimal, in order to participate. Typically, this may involve stopping by the sponsor's store to register for a drawing or sending away for a free game piece. Some state courts have decided that even these minimal actions constitute *consideration,* that is, the exchange of something of value for the chance to win a prize. In these very strict jurisdictions, these types of games may also be found to be illegal lotteries.

However, in most circumstances, contests in which participation depends only on performing some minimal action to enter and where no money is exchanged for a chance to win are legal. Of course, the offer of free entry to participate must be genuine. A game sponsor may not merely state that free game pieces are available when there is no way for a consumer to get them without buying a product or paying money.

Federal Trade Commission Rules

Assuming that a game or contest is legal under state laws banning private lotteries, another issue bearing on the legality of the promotion is whether it is fairly conducted. The **Federal Trade Commission** (FTC) has promulgated rules to which promotional games and contests must conform in order to be considered fair.

Under these rules a game or contest must actually be what it represents itself to be. If it is a competition involving the skill of participants, there must be objective standards by which the contest will be judged. If the skill involved is so minimal that nearly all participants can qualify, the game may not be advertised as a contest.

If the promotion is a game of chance, winning must be truly random. The FTC has closed down games in which corporate sponsors gave more winning tickets to retail outlets that they considered most in need of promotion. Other illegal practices have included programming winnings for the early stages of the contest, continuing to provide entry forms and promoting the game even after all the prizes had been given out, terminating a contest before all the prizes are awarded, and allowing retailers to give winning pieces to favored customers.

FTC rules require that the sponsor of a game of chance provide tight security to prevent anyone from "cracking" the winning combinations or finding the winning game pieces, except in accordance with the game's rules.

The prize for the game or contest must not be misrepresented. Generally, a contest prize must be of the same type and quality as it is advertised to be. In one notorious instance, promotional advertising for a game stated that the winner would receive a "Chevy Blazer." The actual prize turned out to be a sports jacket—a "blazer"—with the word "Chevy" silk-screened on it! The furnishing of prizes that are of inferior quality or involve undisclosed restrictions on their availability is perhaps the most serious problem involving promotional contests and games.

The FTC requires full disclosure to the public of all aspects of the game. The actual odds of winning must be disclosed. In the past, aggressive advertising of extravagant prizes without the sobering details of the remoteness of winning them has been found to unfairly induce consumers to participate. In addition, the number of prizes to be awarded must be disclosed, as well as the time period during which the game or contest will be run.

All of the rules of a game or contest must be publicized. There must not be any undisclosed requirements for winning. However, the sponsor is entitled to require strict adherence to the contest rules before awarding any prizes. The FTC encourages game sponsors to make all of the necessary information available to the public whenever the game is advertised.

Consumer's Rights

Generally, the law considers that a unilateral **contract** is formed between the sponsor of a game or contest and the participant who wins. Therefore, the sponsor is contractually obligated to award the prize to that person or persons. If the sponsor fails to do so, the disappointed winner may have grounds to sue for breach of contract.

However, if the contest or game turns out to be an illegal lottery, the winner may not be entitled to the prize. In such a case, the law considers that any contract that was formed was an illegal contract and it may decide not to enforce it. However, depending on the facts of the case, consumers who have suffered injury as a result of innocent participation in an illegal lottery may sue the game's sponsor for the **tort** of **fraud.**

Participants in a game or contest who have suffered harm as a result of **misrepresentation**s about the prize or contest rules may also be able to recover from the contest's sponsor in an **action** for fraud. This includes participants who were denied an opportunity to win because of unfairness in the way the game was run.

Occasionally, something may go awry in the way a game is conducted that is not the fault of the sponsor. For example, a mistake may be made in the number of winning game pieces that are circulated, resulting in a number of "winners" far in excess of the sponsor's intentions. In such a case, courts may decline to force the sponsor to award the claimed prizes. The legal justification for this varies. However, it usually boils down to a question of equity. Since the sponsor did not intend to obligate itself to the extent that the mistake occasioned and the resulting excess of "winning" claims was not the sponsor's fault, it would simply be unfair to require it to honor all of the claims.

CONTRACT An agreement between two or more parties that the law will enforce. Not all agreements are contracts. In order to be enforceable under the law, an agreement must have certain characteristics.

First, the parties to the agreement must understand its terms and intend to be bound by them. This is what is known as the *meeting of the minds*. An agreement is not enforceable if there is no mutual understanding of the terms of the bargain and a mutual intent to carry them out. The process by which parties come to a meeting of the minds is known as *offer and acceptance.*

Second, each party to the agreement must have given up something of value under the terms of the agreement in order to make the agreement enforceable. This is known as *consideration.* Money, or something that can be exchanged for money, is frequently given as consideration for a contract. However, consideration need not be money or even a tangible thing. The mere promise to act in a certain way, or to refrain from acting, can be sufficient consideration to make a reciprocal promise enforceable.

The law considers that a promise to behave in a certain way confers a benefit on the other party to the agreement. At the same time, it results in a detriment to the party making the promise because his or her freedom of action is thereby restricted. Something of value has been exchanged. Of course, in order to be consideration for a contract, a promise to restrict one's freedom to act must be real. A promise to do something if one "feels like it" is not an enforceable promise because the promisor's freedom to act is not really restricted at all. However, a promise to do something "if it rains tomorrow" may be an enforceable promise. Since people have no control over the weather, the promisor has, in fact, restricted his or her freedom to act.

Generally, the actual monetary value of the promised exchange will not affect the validity of a contract. For example, one may agree to sell a mansion in Beverly Hills for $1, if one wishes. The law usually will not inquire into the "fairness" of a contract, provided there is no gross disparity in bargaining power between the parties.

There are many different types of contracts. Contracts may be *unilateral* or *bilateral*. A *unilateral* contract is one in which one party makes a promise and the other party performs an action. For example, A may promise to pay B to fix her roof and B goes ahead and fixes it. A *bilateral* contract is one in which both parties make promises. C promises to pay D to fix his roof and D promises to fix it if she is paid.

A contract may be *express* or *implied*. An *express* contract is one in which the parties actually articulate their agreement. An *implied* contract is one in which the parties' actions show their intentions. If I give a dollar to a balloon **seller** standing by a sign advertising balloons for sale for a dollar apiece, we have an implied contract for the sale of a balloon.

A contract may be written, oral, or implied by the actions of the parties. However, some contracts must be in writing to be enforceable. These are generally contracts to sell real estate or contracts that cannot be performed in one year's time.

Except where illegal acts are involved, the law will not generally be concerned with the terms of an agreement between competent parties. In other words, provided the requirements for making a contract have been met, the law will enforce the agreement regardless of the terms. Thus, if one of the parties fails to perform his or her promises under the contract, the law will provide a remedy. Generally, this remedy will be in the form of money **damages.** However, sometimes a court will order some other action to be taken in order to compensate the party who was disappointed by the other party's breach of the contract.

Disputes about contracts are settled in lawsuits known as *civil actions.* Generally, these lawsuits are initiated by private parties, usually one of the parties to the contract.

Importance to Consumers

To be a **consumer** is to be a party to contracts. Not only will most consumers eventually enter express contracts to buy automobiles, houses, or other substantial goods, but they are parties to implied contracts every time they make a purchase.

Generally, every time a sale is made, the parties to the sale have executed a contract. The seller presenting an item for sale is making an offer. The buyer who presents money to meet the seller's price is accepting that offer. A contract is formed. Thus, if the seller does not deliver the item after receiving the buyer's money, the contract has been breached and the buyer will have a legal remedy for that breach.

In addition, sellers frequently make promises about the quality or usefulness of the goods they are selling in order to induce consumers to buy them. These promises are known as *warranties* [see **warranty**]. Under certain circumstances these warranties will be considered part of the terms of the contract. This means that a consumer will have a legal remedy if the product does not measure up to the promises made in its warranty.

Moreover, the law implies some promises regarding the quality or usefulness of goods in sales contracts whether or not the seller explicitly makes these promises or not. These are known as *implied warranties*. These promises also may be considered terms in a contract of sale. Therefore, a buyer will also have a legal remedy if these implied promises are broken.

Along with the law of **tort,** contract law is one of the great pillars of the **common law** upon which the rights of consumers rest.

CONTRIBUTORY NEGLIGENCE Negligent or careless conduct by the victim of the negligent conduct of another that contributes to the cause of the victim's own injury. A claim of contributory negligence is usually raised as a defense in a **tort** case involving **negligence.** The basic rule is that if the victim of negligent conduct by another contributed to bringing the harm about by his or her own carelessness, he or she may not recover any compensation for the harm.

History and Relevance to Consumers

The doctrine of contributory negligence first appeared in America in 1850. In the early days the rule was harsh in its effect: If the victim of negligently caused harm contributed in any way to causing the harm, he or she was denied any relief. Thus, contributory negligence was what is known as an *absolute defense* to a charge of negligence. Some have speculated that this strict rule was designed to protect the infant enterprises of the Industrial Revolution from ruin that might have resulted from having to pay for injuries caused by their new products and machines.

The strict rule of contributory negligence began to erode in the twentieth century. By midcentury, the rule was considered especially unfair in cases involving defective [see **defectiveness**] products that cause physical injuries. Courts recognized that the modern **consumer** has little hope of protecting himself or herself from dangerous products, even when exercising the most extreme care. Most product defects are latent, or hidden, and only the manufacturer would have reason to know the ways in which they might injure an unsuspecting user.

Accordingly, some courts abolished the rule of contributory negligence in **products liability** cases altogether. However, by the mid-1970s, a majority of states had adopted a new rule, that of **comparative fault,** which allows juries to decide the degree of fault each of the parties bore in causing an injury and apportion compensation to the injured party accordingly. At about the same time, a new type of lawsuit, **strict tort liability,** in which the fault of any party is irrelevant to recovery of compensation, was gaining prominence.

Today, consumers who are injured by a defective product generally need not fear that some inadvertent behavior on their part that contributed to the harm will deprive them of all compensation. Conduct on the part of a consumer injured by a defective product that contributes to the harm must be relatively reckless before compensation will be denied in negligence cases [see **assumption of the risk**]. In strict tort liability cases, contributory negligence is not a defense. However, **misuse** of a product or the use of a product that poses an **open and obvious danger** may result in diminished or denied compensation.

Application

In order for contributory negligence to exist, there must first be primary negligence that sets into motion a chain of events resulting in harm. For example, the maker of an ocelot enclosure negligently installs the latch, allowing the animal to escape and attack a passerby.

Second, the victim of the initial negligence must himself or herself act in a negligent way with respect to the risk posed by the first person's negligent acts. A person is contributorily negligent if his or her behavior is unreasonable under the circumstances [see **reasonable person test**]. For example, approaching a stray ocelot on the street might be unreasonable because most people would recognize that a very large, unfamiliar cat may be inclined to bite.

Third, the victim's own negligent conduct must be a **proximate cause** of the injury. This means (1) that the accident would not have happened but for the victim's carelessness, and (2) that the victim's carelessness was a significant factor in bringing about the harm. For example, the victim in the above example would not have been bitten by the ocelot if she had not approached it. Clearly, therefore, the victim's action was also a cause in fact of the accident. In addition, the action of approaching the ocelot was clearly a major, or significant, factor in the attack. On the other hand, the significance of the victim's action is not so great if, instead of approaching the ocelot, she thoughtlessly turned her back on it, emboldening it to strike. Although the accident would not have happened if the victim had not turned her back, the action of doing so was not nearly so major a factor in causing the bite as the negligent installation of the ocelot enclosure latch.

Thus, in the escaped ocelot example, a victim who was bitten when she approached the animal would probably be found to be contributorily negligent, while a victim who merely turned his back would not.

COSMETIC   Under the **Food, Drug & Cosmetic Act,** a cosmetic is any substance intended to be used on the human body for cleansing, beautifying, promoting attractiveness, or altering the appearance of the user. With the exception of soaps and hair dye, products that come within this definition are subject to regulation by the **Food and Drug Administration.** Generally, only products that have superficial effects are included in the definition. If a product has chemical effects that alter body structures or functions, or merely claims to have such effects, it will be considered a **drug** and be subject to the much stricter regulations pertaining to drugs provided by the Food, Drug & Cosmetic Act.

Compared with the regulation of other products that come into intimate contact with the human body, regulation of cosmetics is relatively loose. The Food and Drug Administration has the power to prevent the sale of cosmetics if they are adulterated [see **adulteration**], if they contain color additives that have not been approved by the agency, or if they are misbranded [see **misbranding**]. The Food and Drug Administration may also set labeling requirements for cosmetics. Any false or misleading statements or the use of deceptive containers is forbidden. For example, a cosmetic product that claimed to "nourish" skin was found to be misbranded because the vitamins it contained could not actually be absorbed into the skin. The Food and Drug Administration may also require specific warnings on cosmetic products. These warnings may concern particular ingredients in cosmetic products; for example, those found to cause allergic reactions in some individuals. Or the warnings may apply to certain products as a class, such as warnings about the hazards of getting shampoo in the eyes. In addition, the Food and Drug Administration may require a warning that the safety of a particular product has not been determined.

The Food and Drug Administration does not have the power to require safety testing for cosmetic products. Moreover, the burden is on the federal government to show that a cosmetic product is harmful before it may be taken off the market. The opposite is true of products such as drugs and **medical device**s, where the burden is on the manufacturer to show that the product is safe. Premarketing approval is not necessary for cosmetic products, as it is for drugs and some medical devices. This weak system for regulating cosmetic products reflects the perception that cosmetics are relatively safe and do not require government oversight to protect **consumer**s.

However, the line between cosmetic and drug products is likely to be blurred as more cosmetics claim to cause actual changes in the structure of the body instead of just the appearance of change. For example, cosmetic companies are working to find ingredients that actually will alter the structure of aging skin. Self-tanning products that work by chemical means are also on the edge of the cosmetic definition. As cosmetic science progresses, it is possible that greater government regulation into this area will be justified to protect the consumer.

Since government regulation of cosmetics is not very extensive, a consumer generally must fall back on common-law [see **common law**] remedies to compensate for disappointment or injury in using these products. Cosmetic manufacturers generally do not make express warranties [see **express warranty**] about the effectiveness of their products, and reasonable consumers generally do not expect miracles. Therefore, it makes little sense for a consumer to sue to recover for the disappointment of not achieving desired beauty effects from using a cosmetic product.

However, if a cosmetic advertised as "safe" causes harm, a consumer may have grounds to sue for the breach of an express warranty. Words such as "gentle" or "mild" also may give the impression that the product is harmless to use, and may create a warranty to that effect. Even if the product makes no claims about safety at all, a court of law may find that an implied warranty was breached if the product causes harm.

Moreover, the **seller** of a cosmetic that causes injury may be liable for the **tort** of **negligence** in making or marketing it. If the cosmetic is defective [see **defectiveness**], the doctrine of **strict tort liability** may also be an avenue for the injured consumer to collect compensation.

Generally, the seller of cosmetics has a duty to warn consumers about any dangers associated with using the product. The failure to provide warnings and instructions with cosmetic products that are easily understandable by persons of ordinary intelligence may provide grounds for a lawsuit [see **warning defect**]. The required warnings extend to all hazards associated with using the product, even those that affect only a very small number of people. In addition, it may be necessary to instruct consumers to conduct "patch tests" or other limited exposure to cosmetics prior to use in order to avoid unanticipated allergic reactions.

A seller of cosmetics must also anticipate possible **misuses** of the products that might cause harm to consumers and warn against them. Only misuses that are foreseeable [see **foreseeability**] require a warning. For example, some users of hair dyes will doubtless attempt to dye their eyebrows with the same product. A warning against this misuse will probably be necessary. On the other hand, it is difficult to imagine that a consumer would use hair spray to hold decorations on cookies. It is probably not necessary to warn against such a preposterous misuse.

CREDIT CARD   A card that identifies a **consumer** as having credit to purchase goods and services. Today's credit cards are descendants of *credit coins* that first appeared in large retail establishments in the 1920s. Issued by the **seller** itself, the coin displayed the seller's name along with the account number to which purchases would be billed upon presentation by the customer. Large retailers have retained this system in so-called *merchant credit cards,* which are issued and accepted only by the retailer itself. A merchant credit card, therefore, is nothing more than an abbreviated memorandum of an ongoing credit agreement between the seller and the consumer.

Beginning in the 1950s, a new type of credit card appeared. These cards are known as *bank credit cards* or *lender credit cards* and today account for by far the largest percentage of all credit card sales. They differ from merchant credit cards in that, instead of involving only one agreement (between the merchant and the consumer), they involve three separate agreements between three separate parties.

Basically, bank credit cards work in this fashion: An issuer (typically a bank) agrees to provide credit to a consumer on certain conditions. For example, the consumer may make purchases up to a certain monetary amount at a stipulated percentage of interest on a certain schedule of payments.

At the same time, the issuer has a second agreement with various sellers who agree to accept the card in lieu of payment from the consumer. Upon the performance by the seller of certain agreed procedures, such as presenting a sales slip signed by the card-holding consumer, the issuer agrees to pay the seller for the bill run up by the consumer.

The third agreement exists between the seller and the consumer. It is basically a contract of sale, in which certain warranties [see **warranty**], both express and implied, may be given concerning the goods or services sold. The consumer in turn authorizes the seller to apply for payment from the issuer of the consumer's credit card.

Historically, this three-part arrangement had different consequences for consumers, depending on how the law chose to characterize it. Under one view, the issuer is seen as a lender of money directly to the consumer for the purpose of making purchases from a third party, the seller. The consumer's duty to pay the issuer when the bill arrives and the issuer's duty to pay the seller are entirely independent. This means that the consumer must pay the issuer even if he or she has a disagreement with the seller about the cost or the quality of the goods received.

Under another view, the consumer's duty to pay is seen as owed directly to the seller. The seller is seen as merely assigning his or her right to collect payment from the consumer to the issuer. Consumer groups prefer this view, because, as an assignee of the seller's rights to collect from the consumer, the issuer would also be subject to any counterclaims and defenses against payment that the consumer might have against the seller.

Echoes of this debate are still heard. However, federal legislation governing credit card transactions has resolved it in favor of preserving the consumer's rights in a dispute with a seller over payment even against the issuer. This means that if the consumer has a valid reason for withholding payment from the seller—for example, because of the poor quality of the goods received—the issuer has no absolute right to payment either. See **Fair Credit Billing Act.**

Federal laws also govern other aspects of credit card use. The **Truth in Lending Act** mandates that certain disclosures be made to consumers regarding interest rates, finance charges, and periodic account status reports. It also deals with a cardholder's liability for unauthorized use of a credit card. Generally, a consumer's duty to pay for unauthorized charges made on his or her credit card may not exceed $50. If the consumer notifies the issuer of the lost or stolen card before any unauthorized use of the card is made, the consumer will not be liable at all.

Sometimes it is disputed as to whether the use of a credit card was authorized. Generally, a consumer will be liable for charges run up by a friend or acquaintance using the card with his or her permission, even if the charges exceed the limit for which the consumer gave permission. More difficult to decide are cases involving consumers who have allowed family members to use their cards in the past, but for some reason (such as divorce) have decided to revoke permission. Courts have decided both ways. Some have held that the cardholder's liability to pay for the family member's charges continues until the card is returned to the issuer, regardless of whether the cardholder notified the issuer that permission had been revoked. Others courts have decided the issue oppositely.

A consumer will never be liable for charges made on a card that he or she did not request or accept once it was received. A card is only considered to be accepted if the consumer has signed or used it, or authorized another to use it. The issuance of unsolicited credit cards is prohibited. The issuer of a credit card must notify the cardholder of the circumstances under which he or she will be held liable for unauthorized use of the card. A statement must be included that liability will not exceed $50, along with procedures for notifying the issuer of lost or stolen cards. In addition, the card issuer must make reasonable efforts to ensure that any credit card adequately identifies its holder as authorized to use it. This may include a required signature, a photograph of the holder, a fingerprint, or some other means of determining whether the person presenting the card is the person authorized to use it.

CREDIT INSURANCE   Insurance sold to a **consumer** in connection with a **consumer credit transaction.** Credit insurance is designed to pay off the **creditor** in the event that the consumer is unable to repay the loan because of death, disability, or illness. The creditor, not the consumer (or the consumer's family), is the ultimate beneficiary of the insurance policy.

Some states' laws prohibit creditors from requiring credit insurance as a prerequisite to extending a loan. However, in most cases it is up to the creditor as to whether credit insurance will be mandatory or optional. If the credit insurance is required by the creditor, the federal **Truth in Lending Act** requires that the insurance premium be included as part of the finance charge on the loan and be subject to full disclosure. This is to prevent lenders from deceptively advertising low interest rates while inflating premiums with required, but undisclosed, credit insurance.

Whether or not credit insurance is necessary to get a loan, creditors usually may require the consumer to buy the insurance through them. These creditors typically have an arrangement with a particular insurance company to provide group rates for consumers to whom the creditor intends to extend a loan. Although creditors are forbidden from charging a consumer more for the premiums for this insurance than the insurance company charges them, creditors frequently benefit from the arrangement because the insurance company pays them dividends based on the insurance company's profits. This can lead to a conflict of interest between the consumer and the creditor because the creditor naturally wishes to contract with an insurance company that charges high premiums leading to large profits. Since the consumer is required to buy insurance through the creditor, there is no competitive pressure to keep insurance premiums low.

Some states have addressed this problem by allowing a consumer to purchase required insurance through a company of his or her choice. Unfortunately, this does little to cure the problem because the individual consumer will not be able to purchase the insurance at a low group rate. He or she will have to pay higher individual rates. Hence, the rate offered by the creditor's insurer will look attractive even though it may be higher than it would be if competitive pressures were present.

Even though credit insurance may not be required by a creditor in order to get a loan, consumers often are under the impression that it is, and creditors do nothing to correct this misimpression. Because the typical consumer is not in a position to bargain with the creditor, he or she frequently will be happy just to be getting a needed loan and will sign documents for credit insurance without question. The premiums for the insurance may then be added to the amount the consumer is borrowing, making the debt higher than the consumer expected. Some lenders engage in hard-sell tactics to persuade the consumer to buy not only a single policy but many different types of insurance. This is known as *packing*.

With all the different options being presented to them, consumers—often thinking the insurance is required—may end up with much more coverage than is needed to pay back the debt if the insured-against event occurs. Sometimes the lender persuades the consumer to buy more insurance even though the consumer's current policies are enough to pay back the debt. One subtle practice involves charging the same premium for insurance throughout the life of the loan, even though the amount owed on the debt is continually getting smaller. Another practice is *pyramiding,* in which insurance charges are not refunded to a consumer when a loan is refinanced, but instead are kept by the new creditor who adds the old premiums to the amount of the new loan. A number of states' laws prohibit these practices.

To make matters worse, insurance companies sometimes refuse to pay claims because the creditor misrepresented their policies to the consumer.

For example, creditors have been known to sell consumers insurance for which the consumer is ineligible. The insurance company refuses to pay a subsequent claim, arguing that the consumer was ineligible all along. Consumers in this situation may only collect from the insurance company if they can show that the creditor was an agent of the insurance company with authority to change eligibility requirements. The way the relationship between insurance companies and creditors is structured makes this difficult to do. A lawsuit against the creditor for **fraud** may be possible if the consumer can show that the creditor knew the consumer was ineligible for the insurance but sold it to the consumer anyway.

In addition to insurance on the consumer's ability to repay the loan, creditors often require property insurance on any property used as collateral for the loan. This may be the very property that the creditor sold to the consumer on credit. This practice is legal because a lender has a legitimate interest in protecting property that has not yet been paid for from damage or ruin. However, consumers should be aware that such policies often pay only the lesser of the amount remaining on the consumer's loan or the actual value of the property at the time of the loss. For example, if a consumer has paid all but $100 to buy a $500 television set on credit and the set is destroyed in a fire, the insurer may pay only the $100 left on the loan to the creditor. The consumer would get nothing. Even worse, if the set at that time was worth $50, the insurance company will pay only $50 and the consumer still must pay the remaining $50 to buy a television set that no longer exists!

See also **unfair or deceptive acts or practices statute.**

CREDIT PRACTICES RULE A rule promulgated by the **Federal Trade Commission** (FTC) to curb unfair conditions for obtaining credit imposed on **consumer**s by **creditor**s. The rule was intended to extend to creditors engaged in collecting their own debts many of the same rules the **Fair Debt Collection Practices Act** imposed on debt collectors specializing in collecting debts owed to others.

The FTC Credit Practices Rule applies to direct creditors and anyone to whom they may sell or assign the right to collect a debt. It applies only to financing of traditional consumer goods and services: that is, those for personal, family, or household purposes.

The main effect of the Credit Practices Rule is to prohibit creditors from forcing consumers to agree to waive certain rights as a condition for receiving credit. Among the forbidden clauses in consumer credit contracts are:

- *Confession of judgment clauses.* Also called *cognovit* clauses, these provisions require the consumer to agree in advance not to contest the creditor's lawsuit to seek a court judgment declaring the consumer in default and authorizing seizure of his or her property in satisfaction of the debt. Under these clauses, the consumer waives the right to be notified of the process against him or her and agrees to whatever forum the lender selects to hear the case.

- *Limitation of exemptions from attachment and nonpossessory security interest clauses.* These provisions allow a creditor to treat all of the consumer's property as collateral for the credit extended, not just the goods the consumer is buying with the credit. If the consumer fails to pay, the lender has the right to take possession of anything owned by the consumer in order to satisfy the debt.

- *Assignment of wages clauses.* These clauses force the consumer to agree in advance to allow the creditor to take part of the consumer's future wages to pay off the loan received from the creditor. However, such clauses are legal if the consumer retains the right to revoke the assignment of wages at any time.

State laws that provide at least the same degree of protection to consumers as the FTC Credit Practices Rule may take precedence over the rule.

CREDIT REPORTING AGENCY   An organization that compiles information relevant to **consumer**s' potential for paying back consumer credit loans. The information is then provided to others in order for them to make reasonable decisions regarding whether to grant credit to particular consumers.

There are four major types of credit reporting agencies: (1) investigative reporting agencies; (2) credit bureaus; (3) credit card authorization services; and (4) bad check list services. Each is designed to gather particular types of information about individuals that may have a bearing on how likely they are to repay a loan.

- *Investigative reporting agencies* are the most invasive of consumer privacy. Information for these reports is gathered by investigators through questioning a target consumer's friends, acquaintances, and coworkers. The questions need not be directly related to financial matters, but may include such intimate matters as substance abuse and sexual behavior. The resulting reports are made available to lenders who commission them.

- *Credit bureaus* are the most popular type of consumer reporting agency, gathering and maintaining information on nearly every adult citizen. Credit bureau reports contain information on individual consumers' employment histories, sources and amounts of income, lines of credit (including amounts and due dates), payment habits, billing disputes, and other information of a financial nature. Typically, the information contained in the reports comes from **creditor**s who have dealt with the individual consumer in the past. They feed information into a central computing source, from which credit bureaus can extract the data, or directly to local credit bureaus. Credit bureaus use this data in order to rate consumers on a scale designed to predict their reliability in paying back loans. The most crucial information necessary to such a determination will usually concern an individual's past payment habits (did he or she pay on time without dispute?) and the total amount the individual owes.

- *Credit card authorization services* keep information on the status of credit card accounts, including expired cards, stolen cards, and cardholders who have exceeded their credit limits. The individual card issuer often maintains these records on an in-house system. However, larger organizations also gather and provide credit card information worldwide, usually for such giant issuers as MasterCard and Visa. Typically, when a **seller** accepts a credit card from a consumer for payment, he or she will verify the account's status with a credit card authorization service before concluding the transaction.

- *Bad check list services* provide subscribing sellers with information about consumers who have previously passed bad checks. Information typically comes from the subscribers themselves, who report bad checks to a central location. Other subscribers may then pick up that information.

In addition to these four major agency types listed above, the Lenders' Exchange is a nonprofit cooperative organization maintained by finance companies to keep track of consumers with existing debt obligations. Members of the exchange can check the list before granting credit to a consumer who may already be overextended.

Importance to Consumers

Considering the pervasive and invasive nature of credit reporting agencies' activities, there is real danger that information gathered concerning individual consumers will be abused. Consumers must always be concerned that information kept about them is accurate and that it will only be used for the proper purpose of assessing creditworthiness. The consequences of improper use can be devastating, from unjustified denial of credit to damaged personal reputations. The federal **Fair Credit Reporting Act** is the major piece of legislation in the United States designed to ensure the accuracy and proper use of information gathered by these agencies.

CREDITOR   Any person or institution that grants **consumers** the right to incur a debt and defer payment. A creditor may also be one who is entitled to be repaid for a debt initially payable to another. For example, the right to collect a debt may be assigned or sold to someone other than the person or institution that initially extended the credit.

In the United States there are basically three types of creditors: depository institutions, nondepository institutions, and **sellers**. Depository institutions are banks that are chartered under federal or state law to accept deposits of money, make loans, and buy the rights to collect on debt obligations originally made to others. The most common of these are commercial banks, savings and loans, and credit unions. Nondepository institutions are similar to banks, but they do not take deposits, issue checks, or conduct other banking operations. These institutions are in the business of lending money only. They include finance companies, small loan companies, and pawn shops. The money to make the loans is obtained from investors. Many state laws allow these institutions to charge higher interest than others in order to open up the supply of consumer credit.

Sellers also may be creditors when they extend credit directly to consumers in order for them to buy the seller's goods. Usually, the seller does not keep the right to collect the debt but instead sells it to another type of financial institution, such as a bank or even a nondepository institution.

Importance to Consumers

Without those willing to extend credit, the consumer economy in the United States would probably collapse. Who could afford to pay cash for everything all the time? Therefore, creditors are extremely important to consumers. Because consumers depend on credit not only for luxuries and incidentals but for necessities as well, both federal and state laws impose many regulations and restrictions on credit holders. These laws generally govern how credit will be advertised, what disclosures about loan obligations are necessary, how much credit costs, and how creditors may exercise their rights to repayment.

CRIMINAL LAW   The branch of law that deals with the relationship of individuals with society at large, as embodied in the state. Criminal laws represent duties that each member of a community owes to the community as a whole. In the United States, these laws are always statutory [see **statutory law**], so that those subject to them are informed as to exactly what behavior is required or forbidden. This is in contrast to **common law,** which is not typically written into codes of conduct.

Criminal laws may forbid certain behaviors or require certain actions. Infractions of criminal laws may be punished by deprivation of life or liberty or by monetary fines. Because violation of criminal laws is considered an offense against society as a whole, it is the state, as representative of the society, that is responsible for prosecuting crimes. An individual who is the victim of a crime may complain to the public authorities to request that the criminal be prosecuted. However, it is the decision of the public prosecutor as to whether prosecution will be pursued. The role of the victim of the crime in a criminal prosecution will be no more than that of a complaining witness.

Basically, the purpose of criminal prosecutions is to punish a wrongdoer in order to prevent him or her from repeating the infraction and to deter others from similar conduct. It is not the purpose of the criminal law to compensate the individual victims of crimes for their injuries or losses. In order to achieve compensation for injuries, the victim of a crime must generally turn to the **civil law** and bring a private lawsuit against the perpetrator of the crime based on **tort,** or a private wrong. Not surprisingly many actions that violate criminal laws are also torts and may be prosecuted both publicly as a crime or privately as a tort.

Criminal law also differs from civil law in that violation of criminal laws always involves some blameworthy mental state on the part of the criminal: usually the intent to engage in the forbidden action. By contrast, harms compensable by the civil law may be unintended by the perpetrator [see **negligence**].

Importance to Consumers

Most states have criminal laws against **fraud** that protect **consumers** against intentional **deceit** by the sellers of goods. Most also have **unfair or deceptive acts or practices statutes** directed at sellers of goods and services that may provide both criminal and civil penalties. The regulatory statutes of the federal government, such as the **Food, Drug & Cosmetic Act,** may also entail criminal penalties for violators. The existence of these criminal statutes and penalties benefits consumers as a whole by deterring deceitful practices in the sale of goods and encouraging compliance with safety standards that improve products available on the market.

However, criminal law is not of much use to an individual consumer who has suffered injury or loss as a result of a seller's deceptive practices or a product's **defectiveness.** Such a consumer must usually turn to the civil law for redress. The fact that a seller has been convicted of a criminal offense stemming from the same transaction in which the consumer was harmed may, under some circumstances, be introduced as evidence in the civil case to prove the seller's civil liability.

CUSTOM SPECIFICATIONS DEFENSE   A defense in a **products liability** lawsuit holding that the **seller** of a product built to a **consumer**'s specifications will not be liable for injuries caused by **design defect**s in the product. An exception to this rule arises if the seller has special knowledge concerning obvious defects in the specifications given to him or her. If so, the seller has a duty [see **duty of care**] to tell the consumer of the danger and, perhaps, even to refuse to manufacture the dangerous product.

The custom specifications defense is of most use to sellers of products to commercial buyers who can afford to order mass-produced goods to specification. However, the defense may also apply in cases in which the rare individual consumer orders a custom-made product to be built to specifications he or she provides.

DAMAGES A sum of money intended to compensate the winning plaintiff in a lawsuit for harm or loss caused by the defendant. In **consumer** protection litigation, this usually means money to compensate for personal injuries or property damage caused by a defective [see **defectiveness**] product, or to compensate for the failure of a product or service to perform as promised. The person responsible for causing the harm, the defendant, is liable to pay the sum assessed.

Under American law, the purpose of an award of damages is to place the injured party as nearly as possible in the position he or she would have been in if the wrong had not occurred. Thus, the injured party is not normally entitled to any more compensation than will make him or her whole. Generally, the purpose of damages is not to punish the defendant or exact retribution. However, there are exceptions to this rule, as for example, when *punitive damages* are assessed. Application of the **collateral source rule** may also result in a double recovery for the plaintiff.

Another general rule is that the party seeking damages in a lawsuit may not just sit back and allow damages to accumulate once the harm has occurred. The injured party has a duty to take reasonable steps to mitigate the damages, or make them less, if possible. For example, if A loses profits in his venture to take tourists on an excursion of the Norwegian fjords because B failed to deliver a boat she promised on time, A has a duty to try to find another boat. He cannot merely do nothing and then expect B to make up for the amount the tourists who could not take the tour would have paid.

The determination of an appropriate sum of damages is a complicated issue. Most difficult, of course, is the fact that money alone simply cannot make up for many types of injury or loss. Then also there are different legitimate viewpoints regarding a formula for compensation. In cases involving breaches of **contract,** for example, there are at least three reasonable goals for a damages award. The first is to get back from the defendant anything of value that the plaintiff gave him or her in exchange for the contract. For example, if A gives B a down payment on a house B has agreed to build, but B uses the money to go to Fiji instead of building the house, A should be entitled to get the down payment back. Interest on that sum should also be included since, by giving the money to B, A gave up the interest she could have earned in a bank.

The second goal of contract damages is to restore the plaintiff to the position he or she was in before the contract was signed. For example, if A sold her old house in **reliance** on B's promise to build the new house, A may wish her measure of damages to be the amount necessary to buy another house of the same value as the one she gave up.

The third goal of contract damages is to put the plaintiff in the position he or she would have been in if the contract had been fulfilled as planned. In A's case, a sum equal to any extra amount necessary to have the planned new house built by someone else, with a bonus to compensate for the delay caused by B's breach of contract, may fulfill this purpose. Sometimes these approaches may all be tried in the same case. More often, however, they lead to contradictory results and only one approach will prevail.

In **tort** cases, the biggest problem is usually how to put a monetary price on things that no sum of money can replace, such as good health. If the case involves mere property damage, a sum adequate to replace the damaged property is usually easy enough to determine. However, if personal, physical injury is involved, the issue of damages is very thorny. Of course, medical expenses are a usual component of such damages, both for past expenses and those expected in the future. In addition, a monetary award may be given to compensate for the plaintiff's pain and suffering, mental anguish, and emotional distress. Future wages that the injured party lost because of the accident are also a common component of tort damages. Fixing a sum on these intangible losses involves a great deal of speculation in many cases.

There are many different types of damages. Some of the most common are described below.

Compensatory damages. Sometimes called *actual damages,* compensatory damages are designed to make the injured party as nearly whole as possible.

Consequential damages. This usually refers to compensation for injuries or losses that, while definitely caused by the wrong in question, are removed by one or more links in a causal chain. For example, if a trick cigar explodes and singes A's eyebrows as well as soils his shirt, payment for medical expenses and cosmetics to treat A's eyebrows are compensatory damages. Payment for the dry cleaner to clean his shirt is probably also compensatory damages, because these effects were the natural result of the accident. However, suppose A was not offered a job as a television newscaster because the network thought that a man without eyebrows was not telegenic. This loss to A was definitely caused by the exploding cigar. However, it is arguably not an expected result of an exploding cigar. Damages to compensate A for the loss of this job opportunity would be considered consequential. Whether consequential damages will be awarded by a court frequently depends on what type of injury occurred. Causally remote injuries that are only financial in nature are more likely to be considered consequential and are not subject to payment. On the other hand, physical injuries to a person are likely to be payable, even if they are causally remote.

Liquidated damages. Sometimes called *stipulated damages,* this is a sum of money that the parties to a contract have agreed in advance will be sufficient to compensate either of them if the other party breaches the contract. If one party does breach the contract, the sum of money agreed upon must be paid to the other.

Punitive damages. An exception to the rule that damages are only intended to compensate the injured person for the injury or loss, these damages are specifically designed to punish the wrongdoer who caused the harm. Generally, punitive damages are only awarded if the wrongdoer exhibited particularly blameworthy conduct. For example, intentional, malicious, or even extremely reckless actions that bring harm to another may justify exacting punitive damages. Punitive damages are sometimes called *exemplary damages,* because they are designed to serve as an example for others to encourage them to act with care and integrity.

Generally, there is no cap on the amount of punitive damages that may be awarded. This has generated calls for reform by many who believe that overly sympathetic juries award punitive damages that are not only out of proportion to the harm done, but may put smaller companies that are defendants in such cases out of business entirely. At the very least, large punitive damage awards in **products liability** cases can result in higher prices for consumers, because all businesses are forced to buy more expensive insurance to cover the possibility of such a judgment against them. They then pass that cost on to consumers. Another issue regarding punitive damages concerns whether they should be given to the injured party. Some critics believe that it is unfair for the injured party to receive a huge windfall as a result of the injury. They argue that punitive damages should be paid into a special government fund to be used to compensate other victims of defective products, to educate consumers, or for other public uses.

Special damages. Similar to *consequential damages,* special damages represent compensation for losses that are not normally to be expected from the type of wrong that has occurred. However, these damages may be recovered if the injured party can show that the special circumstances that led to the unusual injury were known to the wrongdoer at the time of his or her wrongful conduct. These type of damages are usually claimed in breach of contract cases. For example, if B has a contract to deliver a boat to A, and B knows that A intends to use the boat to take tourists on an excursion of the Norwegian fjords, B may be liable to pay for A's lost profits from this venture if she fails to deliver the boat on time for the excursion. These lost profits are special damages.

DECEIT   The deliberate use of falsehood to influence another's behavior with the purpose of achieving an unfair advantage.

In technical legal terms, deceit is a **tort,** or private wrong, that is very ancient in origin. It was recognized in English **common law** as early as 1201. For centuries, it was one of the very few avenues that a **consumer** could use to undo a bad bargain he or she had entered into because of a **seller**'s dishonesty. Unfortunately for consumers, the rules about the proof necessary to win were very strict and dealt with the trickiest of issues: the seller's state of mind.

In order to win an **action** for deceit, an injured consumer must prove that the seller made a false representation. A representation may be a direct statement, but it may also be an indirect or ambiguous statement that leads a reasonable person to conclude that something in particular was meant. A representation may also be conveyed by conduct. For example, a seller's mere act of showing goods for sale may be a representation that he or she owns the goods or has authority from the owner to sell them.

A representation must be about a fact. A fact is something that could be verified if enough information were available. An action for deceit cannot generally be based on a representation of opinion, because an opinion cannot ever be really true or false. For example, if a seller says that a product is the "best" of its kind, the consumer may not usually complain of having been deceived when he or she does not share the same opinion. The expression "best" clearly represents only the opinion of the seller. It is not a fact, but mere **puffery,** or exaggerated opinion. On the other hand, it is possible to charge a seller with deceit for the statement: "In my opinion this product is the best of its kind" if it turns out that this was not the seller's true opinion after all. Whether or not one holds a certain opinion is a statement of fact.

In order to win a lawsuit based on deceit, the consumer must also prove that the seller knew at the time the representation was made that it was false. Or, at the very least, the consumer must prove that the seller knew at the time of making the representation that he or she did not know whether it was true or not.

The consumer must prove that the seller intended for the consumer to rely on the false representation when deciding how to act or to refrain from acting. It is not enough for the seller merely to make false statements into the air without any intention to influence anyone's behavior with them.

The consumer must also prove that **reliance** on the false representation was reasonable. If the false representation was so preposterous that no reasonable person would believe it, the consumer will not win the lawsuit for deceit. For example, a seller's statement that a carpet will fly is so at variance with normal experience that it is simply not deceitful.

Finally, the consumer must show that he or she suffered losses as a result of reasonably relying on the seller's false representation. For example, assuming it was reasonable to believe the seller's statement about the flying rug, the deceived consumer would have to prove that he or she already sold tickets around the neighborhood for rides on the flying carpet and will now have to refund money that has already been spent.

These requirements of proof for a deceit action are generally very hard to establish. This is particularly true of proving the seller's knowledge that a representation was false and his or her intention to influence the consumer's behavior with it. For these reasons, private lawsuits based on a seller's alleged deceit are not often successful.

Fortunately for consumers, the legal trend for the past 100 years has been to make things easier for them. An action for deceit for harm caused by false statements made by sellers about their products or services is not the only, and far from the best, avenue for an aggrieved consumer to take. The consumer would be far better off suing for breach of a **warranty,** or even a negligent **misrepresentation,** because the requirements for proof are not nearly so onerous in those types of lawsuits.

Today, consumers are protected in yet another way against deceitful representations made by sellers. The **Federal Trade Commission** has the power to investigate the truth of claims made by sellers for their products and to stop sellers from making any statements found to be false or misleading. Numerous state laws also forbid **false advertising** of all sorts.

See also **nondisclosure.**

DECEPTIVE PRICING   Deceptive tactics designed to mislead **consumer**s into the belief that they will achieve price savings when they buy certain products. There is no way to enumerate all the ways that **seller**s have touted illusory savings in order to induce sales. However, there are a number of common commercial practices that fall into specific categories of deceptive pricing. These tactics are generally forbidden by the **Federal Trade Commission Act** as well as many state **unfair or deceptive acts or practices statute**s. They may also be grounds for a lawsuit based on principles of the **common law.**

Former Price Comparisons

Falsely suggesting that current prices are lower than former prices is deceptive and illegal. Common tactics of this sort include inflating the price of an item for a short period of time and then lowering its price and declaring a "sale," a "reduction," or "savings" without specifying the actual amount of savings. Even simply marking goods with two prices and then scratching out the higher one—leaving the impression that the item once sold for the higher amount—may be considered deceptive.

In order to comply with the law, a seller must have an established regular price for an item and have sold it for a reasonably substantial period of time to the general public before the seller may declare a sale on the item. The regular price of a sale item must be disclosed to the consumer or be easily ascertained from the sale advertisements. In general, the law discourages sellers from advertising sales or temporary reductions in price without also stating the period during which the advertised prices are effective. If the "sale" price is offered indefinitely, the practice is deceptive. Moreover, if the offer is only good in particular locations or stores, the seller must clearly disclose this fact.

Comparisons with Competitors' Prices

False or misleading comparisons with other sellers' prices is forbidden. To conform to the law, comparisons made with competitors' prices on a particular item must refer to the identical product. A product that is merely similar, is a different model, or is secondhand does not qualify as an object for price comparison. Moreover, a significant number of the seller's competitors must be selling the product at the alleged higher price for this type of advertising to be permissible. The area of reference must include the retail area in the vicinity in which the seller is located.

It is not necessary for a seller to be absolutely accurate in stating the prices of competitors when making price comparisons. However, it is necessary that the seller's information about competitors' prices be based on the seller's reasonable efforts to find out such prices through market surveys or some similar investigation. A seller may not just make up fictitious prices that it claims are being charged for a product elsewhere. Marketing surveys used to substantiate claims that a seller's prices are better "overall" than a competitor's prices must be based on comparisons of all of the target competitor's prices, not just prices on a few items.

Comparisons with Similar Products

To be permissible, claims that the price of an item is lower than prices found on "similar" or "comparable" products elsewhere must be with reference to products that are truly of like grade and quality. While definitions of similarity may legitimately vary, a difference in the sizes of the products being compared generally indicates that they are not similar enough to qualify for price comparisons of this type. Price advertising based on "similar" products must refer to the seller's general trade area and must be based on at least good faith efforts to determine the prices charged by a significant number of the seller's competitors in that area.

Comparisons Based on "List" or "Suggested Retail" Prices

Sellers frequently offer goods for sale at prices that are lower than the manufacturer's "list" or "suggested retail price" for the goods. Since these list or suggested prices are usually printed directly on the product container it is simple enough for a consumer to determine the truth of the seller's claim. However, consumers frequently believe that a manufacturer's "list" or "suggested retail" price actually represents the price at which the product is generally sold. This is not necessarily the case. Instead, the price of any item, including those with suggested retail prices, will fluctuate with supply and demand. Many times, due to one of these fluctuations, the price at which a product is sold within a wide geographic area will generally be lower than the manufacturer's list price. Therefore, a seller's claim that the consumer is getting a bargain because the seller is offering the item for below "list" price is deceptive, even though it is technically true.

In some cases, a manufacturer may deliberately inflate its suggested retail or list price so that retailers may pretend to be offering great discounts to consumers, thereby increasing sales of the item. In order to be legal, therefore, "list" and "suggested retail" prices must reflect a genuine effort on the part of the manufacturer to determine a fair price for the product based on normal market fluctuations. A manufacturer may usually prove that a list or suggested retail price was determined in good faith by showing that the suggested prices were communicated only to retail dealers and not advertised to the public.

"Free" Offers

Many deceptive pricing practices involve the use of words such as "free," "gift," "bonus," and "without charge" in advertising campaigns. The law requires that a product advertised as any of these things in a promotional campaign is actually provided to the consumer without charge. Of course, the seller may set conditions for the receipt of the free item, such as the required purchase of another item. However, the seller may not inflate the price of the purchased item so that, in effect, the consumer ends up paying for the supposedly "free" item. Nor may a seller substitute merchandise of inferior size or quality for the product that the consumer is required to purchase.

Sellers must disclose the terms of any free offer at the outset. If the free merchandise is only available upon purchase of another item, the seller must disclose this fact at the time the offer is advertised and not after the consumer appears to claim what he or she believes is a no-strings-attached gift.

In order for offers of "two-for-one" and "half-price" sales to be legal, a seller must actually have a "regular" price for a single unit of the item that is the subject of the giveaway. In one case, a paint company was forbidden to continue a "two-for-one" promotional offer on cans of paint because it had never established a price for a single can. Since there was no single-can price, it was necessary to assume that the price stated by the company in the "two-for-one" offer was actually the price for two cans of paint and that there was really no free bonus as promised.

Use of Other Vague Terms in Reference to Price

A number of words and expressions frequently used in reference to prices are suspect and may be found deceptive in certain circumstances.

Some of these expressions are objectionable merely because they are vague. Prime among deceptive expressions of this type are the words "value" and "worth." These terms are misleading because they imply that the value or worth of an item and the price at which it may be purchased are necessarily different. For example, a seller may advertise a "$10 value for $5." The consumer might believe that this represents a bargain because there is some immutable yardstick somewhere against which the product has been measured and found to equal $10. In truth, there is no such thing. The definition of a product's real "value" has been the subject of intense debate among both economists and philosophers for at least several centuries. Some believe that value is measured by the cost to produce the item, others that value represents the price the item will fetch in the market, among other theories. In order for advertisements that use the words "value" or "worth" to be truthful, they must define these words or make clear reference to some other price with which the product is being compared. For example, the seller of the "$10 value for $5" must add that the ten dollar figure is based on the price other sellers have set for the item or that it represents the wholesale price of the item or some other clearly established reference point.

The legality of many expressions used in price advertising is solely dependent on their accuracy. For example, common announcements such as "clearance sale," "manufacturer's closeout," "special purchase," "introductory sale" or "limited offer" that accompany products automatically imply that a reduced price is offered. In order to be legal, not only must the prices on merchandise advertised in this way be below the seller's established "regular" price, but the description must be accurate. A "manufacturer's closeout" must actually be due to the manufacturer's planned discontinuance of the item. A "limited offer" must actually terminate at some point. Likewise, statements that "prices cannot last" or that the price of goods will soon go up are deceptive if, in fact, no price rise is contemplated.

DECEPTIVENESS   A tendency of advertising to mislead **consumers** that is sufficiently serious to justify government prohibition.

Advertising and its relationship to consumer protection is one of the most difficult of all legal topics. One reason is the importance of the competing interests involved. Advertising is a form of expression that is protected by the First Amendment to the United States Constitution, although to a lesser extent than other types of speech. At the same time, consumers have a universally recognized claim to be protected from deceitful selling tactics.

Balancing these two important and legitimate interests has been, for the most part, delegated to the **Federal Trade Commission** (FTC). Under the **Federal Trade Commission Act,** the FTC has the power to define and prohibit "deceptive acts and practices" that affect commerce. Federal and state courts frequently use the FTC's guidelines for deceptiveness when reviewing the FTC's actions or determining whether **seller**s have broken any state laws prohibiting **false advertising.**

Another reason the area of advertising and consumer protection is so difficult involves the complexities of language itself. While the meaning of some expressions is clear, other expressions may be ambiguous—conveying many different or even contradictory thoughts. Moreover, the blending of media—pictures, music, and spoken and written words—that makes up today's advertising complicates the interpretation of commercial messages.

In general, advertising messages will be regulated only if they are deceptive. In order to qualify as advertising, a message must have a commercial purpose: That is, it must refer to a product or service to be provided in exchange for money or something else of value. The message must also be disseminated to a significant number of people. A commercial message conveyed only to one person or a very small number of people may not qualify as advertising.

An advertising message will be considered deceptive only if it makes a factual claim. In other words, it must be the type of statement that could be verified if enough information were available. By contrast, a statement that is merely an expression of opinion is not a factual claim. Statements of opinion are usually considered mere **puffery** and are not regulated.

Claims that qualify as factual are deceptive under the law if they are false or unsubstantiated. A claim is unsubstantiated if there is not sufficient information available to determine whether it is true or false. However, even a claim that is false or unsubstantiated will not be against the law if it does not concern an aspect of the product or service that is important to an average consumer when making a decision to buy. Only these so-called *material*, or important, advertising claims are regulated by the law.

It is not important under the law that the seller have an intent to deceive consumers with a commercial message. Even innocent misstatements may qualify as deceptive. Moreover, it is not even important that any consumers are actually deceived by the message. If an advertisement *might* deceive consumers because it is false or unsubstantiated, and material, it is unlawful.

In determining whether an advertisement is deceptive, the FTC looks at the entire message, and not just individual statements within the message. Occasionally, all the individual statements in an advertisement may be technically true, and yet the whole message conveys a false impression. On the other hand, the basic claim in the advertisement may be true, but underlying implications that are not true may result in the entire message being deceptive. Thus, unspoken implications in an advertisement are important in determining whether it is within the law. This area is particularly difficult, as might be imagined.

Some of the more common implications in advertising that the FTC has determined are deceptive include the following:

- The false implication that scientific proof exists for a claim. Such an advertisement typically makes a claim in technical or scientific jargon. Frequently, the statement will use figures or percentages to express a specific quantity such as "25 percent faster." The claim may make express reference to a test or experiment. It may show pictures of charts or graphs, people in white laboratory coats, or laboratory settings. The message to the average consumer is that scientific tests were performed that resulted in competent data to support the advertiser's basic claim. An advertisement such as this may be deceptive even if the basic claim is true. For example, a product may, in fact, be "25 percent faster," but if the advertisement implies that a scientific test was done that proved this, when in fact it was not, the ad will be deceptive. Moreover, even if a test was done, the ad may still be deceptive if the test was not, in fact, competently scientific. Bare statements that a product is safe or effective may also be deceptive, because they imply that tests were done that prove this. The FTC is particularly sensitive about such claims when they refer to **food** or **drugs** because federal law requires such tests before any claims can be made about these type of products.

- The false implication that an attribute of a product is important in contributing to its expected performance. For example, a dog food was advertised as having "all the milk protein your dog needs." This was deceptive because dogs do not, in fact, have any particular need for milk protein at all. Yet the advertisement implied that the presence of milk protein was somehow important in providing proper nutrition for dogs. Similarly, an ad that stated that a certain breakfast drink had the same mineral content as two strips of bacon was found to be deceptive, even though the claim was true. In fact, bacon is not a good source of minerals so the implication that the breakfast drink was nutritious because it had the same amount of minerals as bacon was deceptive.

- The false implication that there are no qualifications to a claim. Typically, the advertisement will make a true claim about the performance of a product but fail to inform the consumer that the claim is true only under certain circumstances. The most notorious example of this false implication is the claim that an automobile will achieve certain gas mileage, when, in fact, it will achieve the stated mileage only under certain conditions—such as level, highway driving at moderate speeds. Even when qualifications to a claim are stated, they must be prominent enough to attract attention or the advertisement may be found deceptive.

- The false implication that a product is unique in possessing a characteristic that, in fact, is common to many products of the same type. The claim that an olive oil has "no cholesterol" may be deceptive if made in such a way as to imply that other vegetable oils do have cholesterol. In fact, no vegetable product contains cholesterol.

- The false implication that a product possesses an attribute because its name is confusingly similar to the name of the attribute. The name "cashmora" for a fabric was found deceptive, for example, because consumers might reasonably think that the product contained cashmere, which it didn't. A topical ointment called "Aspercreme" was the subject of deceptive advertisements because consumers could believe from the name alone that it contained aspirin, which it did not.

- The false implication that a product possesses positive characteristics because technically neutral words used to describe it are normally interpreted in a positive way. For example, a product's claim to have "more food energy" was found to be deceptive because reasonable consumers might interpret this to mean that the product provided more nutrition, when in fact the words "more food energy" merely meant more calories.

- The false implication that a product possesses an attribute because it is pictured next to something possessing that attribute. For example, a breakfast drink pictured next to a plate of bacon, toast, and eggs with a voice-over saying that the drink provides 100 percent of daily nutrition requirements was found to be deceptive because it implied that the drink contained an equivalent amount of nutrition as the breakfast shown. The depiction of an automobile frame next to steel girders was deceptive because it implied that the frame was as strong as the girders.

- The false implication that an experiment showing a product doing one thing also shows it is capable of doing another thing. For example, a claim that a mouthwash kills germs in a petri dish may be deceptive if made in such a way as to imply that it will also cure an actual infection caused by the germs. An advertisement in which a plastic sandwich bag was shown keeping a sandwich dry while immersed in water was found to be deceptive, because the implication the seller wanted to convey was that the bag would keep food fresh in the refrigerator. The fact that it kept food dry underwater did not in any way prove this.

The ways in which advertising may be deceptive through false implications are virtually endless. The FTC must generally make a case-by-case assessment based on the unique features of each advertisement. This task is arduous because the truth of the claim must first be assessed. Then it must be determined whether any tests or experiments referred to in the advertisement actually supply the scientific proof to the claim. In addition, it is necessary to assess all the features of the advertisement, including visual and aural features, to determine what, in fact, is being implied. This generally means analyzing the particular advertisement for the reaction of the average consumer. Then it is necessary to determine whether the implication understood by the average consumer is truthful.

In the meantime, sellers have become more sophisticated in advertising their goods. Because the possibility of misleading consumers and subjecting themselves to the FTC's penalties is great, many advertisers have stopped making overt factual claims for their products and services. Instead, they resort to invoking vague sensations of well-being conveyed in nonverbal imagery that is difficult to interpret, let alone find deceptive. For example, scenes showing attractive young men and women together in a soft drink advertisement may imply that the drink will bring the satisfaction of youth, popularity, and sexual attractiveness. Yet these implications are so vague, so understated, so subjective, and so preposterous that it is difficult to believe they could mislead anyone. These developments in advertising, combined with ever-changing media configurations for delivering commercial messages, make the FTC's regulatory task monumental.

Another recent advertising development concerns the so-called "infomercial," typically a program-length television pitch for a particular product or system. Some critics argue that these commercial messages are intrinsically deceptive since they mimic an objective television show format. Frequently, they even feature "commercials" for the product being pitched in the middle of the main "commercial." All of this is calculated to make the viewer believe that he or she is watching an ordinary television show. A viewer may not realize the commercial nature of the program unless he or she has seen the beginning or watches until the end. The FTC's position on infomercials is not fully developed. It seems likely that infomercials will not be banned altogether, but a requirement that they disclose their advertising purpose at all times may be forthcoming.

Even assuming the FTC determines that an advertisement is deceptive and stops its further dissemination, consumers who have actually been deceived by the advertising must turn elsewhere than the federal government for recompense. The FTC's power to regulate includes enjoining the offending advertising and assessing fines and penalties. It does not normally extend to reimbursing consumers for their losses or disappointment. However, many states have laws banning various types of false advertising that allow consumers a **private right of action** to recover damages for harm caused by advertising deceptions. In addition, the **common law** may provide a remedy in the form of a lawsuit for **deceit, misrepresentation,** or breach of an express or implied **warranty.**

See also **demonstration.**

DEFECTIVENESS   In order to be compensated for injury or loss caused by a product, a **consumer** must prove that the product was defective. The mere fact that the consumer was not satisfied with the product, or even that the product caused harm, is not sufficient to show that it was defective in the sight of the law. The law recognizes that products cannot be made perfect and that the **seller** is not required to be an insurer of a product's safety or adequacy. Therefore, there must be some standard by which to judge if a product has crossed the line from expectedly imperfect to intolerably flawed, or *defective.*

The issue of defectiveness has preoccupied jurists from the earliest days of the consumer era—roughly from the start of the twentieth century. Unfortunately, the answer is not always easy or consistent. Generally, the definition of defectiveness depends on society's expectations in light of the feasibility of creating better products. The determination is made on a case-by-case basis as courts decide controversies involving products under the **common law.** Often the standard is vague and shifts from case to case. To aid in their decisions, courts frequently apply one or more "tests" for defectiveness that have evolved over time in legal cases concerning products.

The **consumer expectation test** involves determining what a reasonable consumer would expect from a particular type of product in terms of its effectiveness and safety and then comparing the product at issue with that standard. If the product falls short, it is defective and the consumer who was injured by it may be compensated.

The **risk-utility test** involves a balancing of the utility of the particular product at issue with its inherent risks. If the risks outweigh the product's benefits, it may be found defective. See also **prudent manufacturer test.**

Courts may use either one of these tests, or some unique combination of elements from each, in determining whether a product is defective under the law.

Defectiveness is an issue in any **products liability** case. However, the terms *defective* or *defectiveness* are not generally used in **warranty** cases. Usually the discussion in those cases will center on whether or not the warranty was breached. However, except in the case of an **express warranty,** deciding whether a breach occurred will depend on exactly the same analysis of consumer expectations and risk–utility comparison as any other case. Products covered by express warranties are an exception, because in that situation the consumer and the seller are deemed to have negotiated the definition of *defectiveness* among themselves. They then included it in the contract of sale as a warranty or promise that the product would have certain characteristics. A product will be defective if it does not conform to the express warranty.

The terms *defective* or *defectiveness* are most often used in the context of **tort** cases involving products that have caused injuries. This is especially true for **negligence** cases or those based on **strict tort liability.** In tort cases, product defects are usually classified as one of three types: a **design defect,** a **manufacturing defect,** or defective product warnings [see **warning defect**].

DEFERRAL CHARGE   Fee charged to a **consumer** for the privilege of deferring a payment due on an installment loan. Basically, the consumer is allowed to delay a payment already due in exchange for the deferral charge. The consumer may then resume payments at the original amount at the next billing period.

Deferral charges are considered to be interest and are subject to **usury** laws regulating the rate of interest that may be charged on loans. The fee must reflect the amount of principal due at the time the deferral occurs and the length of time the regular payment is postponed. The ratio the deferral charge bears to the unpaid principal may not exceed the original percentage of interest disclosed to the consumer when the loan was made. The parties to the loan must agree to any deferral.

DELANEY CLAUSE　A provision in the federal **Food, Drug & Cosmetic Act** that forbids the introduction into **food** products of any food additive that has been shown to cause cancer in man or animals. A food additive is a substance added to a finished food product that affects its characteristics, but does not significantly add to its nutritional value. This includes chemicals needed for processing, stabilizing, preserving, or coloring the food, as well as chemicals that leach out of packaging materials. Certain chemicals are specifically excluded from the definition, such as pesticide residues on raw agricultural goods. A food additive need not be intentionally put in the food to be classified as an "additive." Chemicals that are present accidentally may also be considered additives and banned if they have been shown to cause cancer.

The Delaney Clause was named after Congressman James Delaney who introduced it in an amendment to the Food, Drug & Cosmetic Act in 1958. It has been the subject of controversy since then. Critics argue that the absolute ban on any chemicals shown to cause cancer in any amount is too strict. Many substances cause cancer only at high dosages, but are perfectly safe in small amounts. These critics contend that the tests that are conducted on animals to determine the carcinogenic qualities of substances often involve the introduction of unrealistically large amounts of the substances that are far beyond what anyone would normally ingest. According to these opponents, banning such chemicals from food products deprives the public of useful chemicals that are perfectly safe and even beneficial when used in small quantities. Recently, there has been some support for relaxing the Delaney Clause provisions. This might be done by a special act of Congress, or simply by a redefinition of "carcinogenic" or "cancer-causing" to include only those chemicals that have been shown to cause cancer in quantities that might realistically be ingested by **consumers**.

DELINQUENCY   Occurs when a **consumer** misses or delays making a scheduled payment on an installment loan. Generally, when a consumer is delinquent in making payments on a loan, he or she may cure the delinquency by making up the late payments plus a delinquency charge. Delinquency is, therefore, different than *default*. Technically, *default* means that the consumer has failed to conform to the loan agreement in such a major way that the loan agreement is terminated and the **creditor** may demand full payment at once. He or she may then repossess any goods serving as collateral for the loan or take other action against the debtor to force immediate repayment.

In some cases, the loan agreement may provide that if the consumer is delinquent on a certain number of payments the loan will be considered in default. Occasionally, the creditor may treat the consumer in default even after the first delinquency if the creditor honestly believes that the chances of having the loan repaid are in jeopardy. Laws in some states have attempted to soften the consequences for a delinquent consumer by allowing him or her an absolute right to make up missed payments within a certain period of time and thus avoid having the contract terminated.

Generally, it is legitimate for a creditor to charge a consumer a fee as a penalty for delinquency in making payments. This is in order to recoup losses resulting from tardy repayment of loaned funds, and generally represents interest on the outstanding balance for the period of time in which the loan is in default. However, many states' **usury** laws regulate the amount and manner of assessing such charges. Usually, these laws place a cap on the amount of any delinquency charge. Some consumer advocates contend that any charge at all is unfair. However, states generally reject this view because it would result in delinquent consumers paying less interest than consumers who are diligent in making their payments.

State usury laws also prohibit practices in which creditors attempt to collect multiple delinquency charges stemming from a single late payment. For example, if a consumer misses a payment in January but makes February's payment on time, an unscrupulous creditor may apply February's payment first to the unpaid delinquency charge from January. This means that the consumer is again behind in payment in February, and another late payment is assessed. If this goes on month after month, a sizable penalty may build up, even though the consumer was delinquent only once. To prevent this abuse, some state laws require that periodic payments be applied first to current installments and any amount left over be applied to delinquent installments. In addition, many laws mandate a grace period during which a late installment payment may be made without any imposition of delinquency charges. See also **unfair or deceptive acts or practices statute.**

🏛 **DEMONSTRATION** Advertising consisting of showing how well a product works or, more commonly, how well the product works in comparison to competing products. Product demonstrations that are deceptive are proscribed under rules issued by the **Federal Trade Commission,** many state **unfair or deceptive acts and practices statute**s, and principles of the **common law.**

To be permissible, product demonstrations must be genuine. This means that (1) the claim they purport to be demonstrating must be true, and (2) the procedure shown to demonstrate the claim must be the actual test that it purports to be. For example, a demonstration claiming to illustrate that cats prefer Brand X cat food to Brand Y may show a number of cats running for a bowl labeled X while shunning a bowl labeled Y.

First, to be permissible, the claim that cats prefer Brand X must be true. At least, the makers of Brand X must have a good faith belief that cats prefer it—though it is difficult, of course, to tell what cats are thinking.

Second, the demonstration must be exactly what it purports to be. It would be deceptive to fill the cats' bowls with anything other than what the labels indicate. For example, the Brand Y bowl must not contain gravel painted to look like cat food, and the Brand X bowl may not contain tuna fish.

The latter part of this rule on demonstration advertising has been the subject of complaint by television advertisers. Because of the natural limits of televised images and time constraints, it is sometimes ineffective or impractical to show the actual demonstration in a commercial. So long as the underlying claim is true (e.g., cats really do prefer Brand X), what is wrong—these critics ask—with broadcasting a simulation of the test that will show the results of the real test much more dramatically than the real test itself?

This claim was the subject of the most famous case involving deceptive demonstration advertising, *FTC v. Colgate-Palmolive Company.* [380 U.S. 374 (1965)] In that case, a television advertisement purported to demonstrate the superior moisturizing properties of shaving cream by showing the announcer shaving a piece of sandpaper to which the product had been applied. In fact, what appeared to be sandpaper in the commercial was a mock-up made of Plexiglas sprinkled with sand. To charges that the ad was deceptive, the company explained that the claim was true: Sandpaper could, in fact, be shaved with its shaving cream—provided it had first been soaked in water for over an hour. Moreover, real sandpaper appeared to be a piece of plain brown paper in the televised image. In order for television viewers to see the truth of the claim that the product could shave sandpaper, it was necessary to use the mock-up.

Ultimately, the Supreme Court decided that the advertisement was deceptive for two reasons: first, because it did not disclose that the sandpaper had to be soaked for a long period of time in order for the product to work on it, and second, because the public is entitled to see the real test that forms the basis for an advertiser's claim.

In recent years, the furor over misleading product demonstration commercials has somewhat subsided. The reason may simply be that the viewing public, with many more decades of television advertising under its belt, is considerably less gullible with regard to claims it sees on that medium and regards them as mere **puffery.** Therefore, with the exception of advertising aimed at children, the rules with regard to truthfulness in product demonstration advertisement have been relaxed somewhat.

Today, demonstration advertising will be found deceptive only if it (1) purports to be actual proof of the claim made for the product, (2) is about an aspect of the product that the viewer will consider important in deciding whether to buy it, and (3) does not show a genuine test but rather an undisclosed mock-up.

Thus, if the advertiser discloses that a demonstration shown on television is a "simulation" or based on a "mock-up," the advertisement will not be deceptive. Moreover, if the mock-up is not used to support a "claim" about the product, it will not be illegal. For example, mashed potatoes may be substituted for ice cream in a television commercial even though they look better than the real ice cream if no "claim" is made about the look of the product. Likewise, some products may naturally look better on television than in real life. Provided no claim is made that the look of the product on television is the way it will look in the **consumer's** hands, there is no deception.

Finally, if a demonstration does not concern an aspect of the product that is of real importance in a consumer's decision to buy it, the law will generally consider it harmless. For example, most consumers probably do not care if their cats prefer Brand X over Brand Y. What is important to them is that the brand they buy is nutritious and that their cats will deign to eat it.

DESIGN DEFECT A defect in a product that results from a conscious decision by the manufacturer to make it a certain way. The design of a product encompasses everything from the materials used to make it and the configuration it will have to the color or even label that it will bear. Basically, every decision that must be made about a product prior to its manufacture is a part of its design.

Of course, a manufacturer never intends to make a defective product. However, a product that is made perfectly according to the manufacturer's intention may turn out to be defective if aspects of its intended design are not reasonably safe or effective.

Determining whether a design defect exists, therefore, presents a more perplexing problem than determining the presence of **manufacturing defect**s. In a manufacturing defect case, the product may be measured against the manufacturer's own specifications. If it differs from those, it is likely defective. In a design defect case, the product conforms exactly to the manufacturer's specifications. A court deciding a design defect case must, therefore, look elsewhere for a standard against which to measure the product for defects.

Design defects may be viewed as falling somewhere on a continuous spectrum ranging from those that are very obvious because they differ from established standards for the design of similar products to those that are latent because they inhabit unexplored design territory.

Consider three examples: First, the maker of the proverbial lead balloon has an obvious design defect on his or her hands. Years of experience in balloon manufacturing by many different manufacturers have already determined that lead is an ineffective material from which to make the product. Even a layperson can readily see this defect.

Then imagine a balloon made of a thin membrane of sodium salts derived from various fatty acids and held together by the surface tension of hydrogen dioxide. No manufacturer has ever made a balloon from this material before so there are no other products with which to compare it. However, applying basic scientific knowledge predicts that this balloon would not be very durable, because its formula is that of a common soap bubble. In this instance, the design is new, but existing scientific knowledge indicates that it is not a good one.

Finally, consider a balloon made from a previously unknown material, let us say kryptonite, which was found in a meteor that fell to Earth from a distant planet. Preliminary tests have indicated that its tensile strength and weight are superior for balloon purposes. However, it later turns out that the material is lethal to a certain small number of resident aliens.

The defective nature of the design of the first two balloons is easy to determine because it is foreseeable—both to ordinary citizens and to design engineers—that the designs will not be successful. It is the last example that would create the most problems. Not even scientists could have known at the time the product was developed that it carried a special risk. A case such as the last one is perfect for the application of the **risk-utility test** to determine if the product is defective.

Using that test of product **defectiveness,** a court would first balance all of the useful features of the kryptonite balloons against the risks they entail. On one side of the balance would be the superior features of the balloons as well as the desirability of having such balloons available to **consumer**s. On the other side of the balance would be the seriousness of the danger presented by the balloons (i.e., death), as well as the fact that the danger of death due to kryptonite exposure is one that affects only a very few citizens. The court may also take into account whether the product could be made safer by the application of a warning label directed at those citizens who are sensitive to kryptonite. See **warning defect.**

Importance to Consumers

Design defects figure into all types of **products liability** cases, including cases based both on **warranty** theories and **tort** theories. However, the question of design defects in products is of by far the greatest importance in personal injury cases, in which a product has caused physical injury. See also **negligence; state-of-the-art defense; strict tort liability.**

DISCLAIMER OF WARRANTY Sellers frequently attempt to avoid responsibility for defects in their products by denying, or *disclaiming,* that they have made any binding promises about the quality of the products. This is known as disclaimer of warranty.

Because warranties [see **warranty**] are viewed as part of the **contract** of sale for goods, it is normal practice for the parties to the sale to bargain over their terms. Thus, disclaimers of warranty are perfectly legitimate devices by which a seller may shift the risk of a product's failure to perform properly to the **consumer.** The only requirement is that the warranty, as limited by any disclaimers, becomes a part of the bargain, understood and approved in advance by both parties to the sale.

Unfortunately, consumers frequently have been drawn into sales in reliance on seemingly ironclad warranties, only to be disappointed by artfully drafted disclaimers that take away the protection the warranty has just given. For this reason, the **Uniform Commercial Code** [§2-316] and the federal **Magnuson-Moss Warranty Act** have specific provisions governing fair practices in the drafting of warranty disclaimers on the sale of goods.

Disclaimer of Express Warranties

The law views disclaimer of express warranties [see **express warranty**] with disfavor, because it involves the negation of expressly given promises about a product. The Uniform Commercial Code provides that where both an express warranty and a disclaimer exist, the disclaimer is valid only to the extent that it does not conflict with the express warranty. For example, if the express warranty is a promise to repair defects in the picture tube of a television, a disclaimer of any warranties to repair the speakers of the television would not be inconsistent and, hence, would be valid.

However, if the disclaimer directly contradicts an express warranty, the disclaimer will be considered void. In the above example, a disclaimer that stated flatly that the television was sold without any warranties "express or implied" would be a direct contradiction of the express warranty to repair the picture tube. Therefore, the disclaimer would be considered null and void, and the buyer of the television could count on the seller's promise to repair the picture tube.

Problems for consumers develop when an express warranty has been made orally—by one of the seller's employees, for example—but the written contract of sale explicitly denies that any express warranties have been made. The trouble concerns a long-established rule of evidence that courts use when interpreting contracts, known as the *parol* [pronounced pa-ROLE] *evidence rule.* Generally, the law presumes that if a written contract between parties exists, it contains all of the terms to which the parties have agreed. If the parties had made any oral agreements before making the written contract—so goes the reasoning—they would have included them in the written contract. Besides, chaos would result if parties to contracts could continually claim that one or the other made some oral promises in addition to the written ones, and the courts would have to sort out who was telling the truth. For this reason, courts frequently refuse to admit evidence of oral agreements made before, or at the same time as, the written agreement when deciding whether a written contract between a seller and a consumer has been broken. This includes oral express warranties.

Fortunately, this rule has been relaxed when consumers, who typically have little bargaining power or expertise regarding the product at issue, are involved. In such cases, a court will frequently admit evidence of an oral express warranty that is inconsistent with a written disclaimer. The reasoning is that the written contract did not, after all, include all of the parties' agreements, or that the oral promises are needed to explain the written contract of sale. Oral promises made after the contract of sale may be introduced into evidence to show that the parties modified their written agreement.

Disclaimer of Implied Warranties

Because implied warranties come into existence without any action on the part of the seller of goods, it seems fair that the seller should be able to negate them, provided proper notice is given to the consumer. This is, in fact, what the Uniform Commercial Code provides.

A seller may disclaim the **implied warranty of merchantability** for goods either orally or in writing. In either case, the word *merchantability* must specifically be used. The **implied warranty of fitness for a particular purpose** may be disclaimed only in writing. However, no particular words or phrases must be used.

A seller may disclaim both the implied warranties of merchantability and fitness for a particular purpose by language in the contract that the product is sold "as is," "with all faults," or "as it stands." This type of language in a disclaimer creates what is known as an "as is" sale. It puts the consumer on notice that the product does not come with any implied warranties and that the consumer accepts the full risk of the product's possible failure to perform. However, if the "as is" language in the disclaimer conflicts with an express warranty for the product, the express warranty will prevail.

A seller may also disclaim the **implied warranty of title.** However, specific language to that effect must be used, or the circumstances of the sale must make it plain to the consumer that the seller does not claim to have full ownership of the product and is selling only those ownership rights in the product that he or she may have. Clearly, a direct statement that the seller does not claim title to the goods being sold would be sufficient to disclaim the warranty. Some courts have found language that the seller "quits claim to all rights and title in the goods in favor of the consumer" to be sufficient as well.

Conspicuousness

The Uniform Commercial Code requires that any written disclaimer of warranty be conspicuous, so that the consumer's attention will be drawn to it. Although there is no hard and fast rule about what makes a disclaimer conspicuous, it is reasonable to assume that it must be printed in a way that distinguishes it from other text about the product. Generally, capital letters, bold-faced type, or type of a contrasting color is sufficient to make a written disclaimer conspicuous. The placement of the disclaimer is also important. If the disclaimer is printed on the back of a written contract of sale, there must be some device on the front of the document calling attention to the fact that there is a disclaimer on the back.

An unresolved issue concerns the validity of a written disclaimer that is not conspicuous, but which was actually pointed out to the consumer. Some courts have held that, because the consumer had actual knowledge of the disclaimer, it was not necessary for the disclaimer to be conspicuous in the written document in order to be valid. Other courts reject this view, holding that the consumer's actual knowledge of the disclaimer is irrelevant to the question of its validity.

Timeliness

In order to be valid, a disclaimer of warranty must be timely. This means that it must be presented to the consumer at the time of the sale. This rule is meant to remedy the situation in which the consumer signs a sale agreement with a warranty one day only to receive a written disclaimer with the product when it is delivered some days later. A disclaimer presented in such a fashion is invalid under the Uniform Commercial Code.

Parties to a sale may modify a product's warranties after the sale by including warranty disclaimers. However, such a modification is considered to be an entirely new and separate agreement. As such, it must be approved by both parties to the sale.

Disclaimer by Examination

A seller may disclaim any warranty by insisting that the consumer examine the goods prior to sale. This method of disclaimer will be effective to nullify any warranty claims concerning product defects that the consumer ought to discover during the examination. However, an examination of the goods by the consumer will not be effective to disclaim warranties for defects that are latent, or hidden, and that the consumer cannot be expected to discover.

Interestingly, the seller's demand that the consumer examine the goods will be an effective disclaimer of warranty even if the consumer refuses to examine them. If the consumer refuses to examine the goods under such circumstances, the law presumes that the consumer is ready to assume the risk of their possible failure to perform. It is important to note that this method of disclaiming warranties is only effective when the seller actually demands that the consumer examine the goods. Just having the goods on hand and presenting the consumer with the opportunity to examine them if he or she wishes does not suffice.

Other Limitations

Because of the importance of product warranties to consumers, many states have passed laws limiting the ability of sellers to disclaim warranties. In many states, for example, it is not possible for a seller to disclaim the implied warranty of merchantability. In others, disclaimers of any warranty must be accomplished by certain procedures.

In addition, the federal Magnuson-Moss Warranty Act places some restrictions on the ability of sellers to disclaim warranties on consumer goods.

Unresolved Issues

The law on product warranties and sellers' attempts to disclaim them is still evolving. One important issue is whether warranty disclaimers extend beyond the original purchaser of a product. For example, if a purchaser of a secondhand product is injured because the product does not conform to a warranty, is he or she barred from suing the seller for a breach of warranty because the seller disclaimed that warranty when it initially sold the product? The resolution of this issue may depend on whether the injured person suffered only monetary losses or whether he or she was physically hurt. See also **privity of contract.**

DIVISION OF MARKETS A practice whereby competing **sellers** divide the markets for their goods or services among themselves. Division of markets is illegal under the **Sherman Antitrust Act** and other **antitrust laws** of the United States because it reduces competition, resulting in higher prices for **consumers**.

Illegal division of markets may result from attempts to parcel out geographical areas among sellers or to allocate certain classes of customers among sellers. In either case, by agreeing to stay out of certain markets in exchange for exclusivity in others, a seller reduces his or her competition and the natural downward pressure on prices that competition entails.

Generally, it is not illegal for a single seller to allocate markets among its own subsidiaries or franchisees. Technically, the subsidiaries or franchisees are not separate, competing companies, but part of one single company that may choose to structure distribution of its products as it sees fit. Occasionally, however, separate, competing companies try to allocate markets by pretending to be part of a larger organization. In one such case, competing manufacturers formed a licensing company of which they were all members. The licensing company then proceeded to distribute licenses to the members for the privilege of using the company's trademark. The licenses were divided according to territory. This arrangement was found to be illegal because the so-called licensing company was really just a shell used by its members to allocate market territory.

DOOR-TO-DOOR SALE   A sale that occurs at a **consumer**'s home that was initiated by the **seller.** Laws that regulate door-to-door selling may also include sales that occur any place other than the seller's established place of business.

Door-to-door sales present risks for consumers for several reasons. The mere fact that a seller comes uninvited to the consumer's home can be an intimidating invasion of privacy. High-pressure selling tactics, combined with the awkwardness of trying to eject someone from one's home, may induce consumers to make a purchase just to get rid of the seller. In addition, the transient nature of door-to-door sales frequently means there is little accountability for defects in the products sold. The consumer may not even know to whom to turn with complaints. Moreover, persons most likely to be home when a door-to-door salesperson comes calling are often those least able to defend themselves against high-pressure sales techniques: the elderly, the handicapped, and children.

The **Federal Trade Commission** and many state **unfair or deceptive acts or practices statute**s provide for extensive regulation of door-to-door sales practices. Federal law and many state laws mandate a "cooling-off" period, during which a consumer who has purchased something from a door-to-door salesperson may cancel the transaction. Under the federal rule, a consumer may cancel a door-to-door purchase, lease, or rental of goods up to three days following the transaction. The federal rule requires the seller orally to notify the consumer at the time of the transaction that the consumer has the right to cancel and to provide the consumer with a written cancellation notice. The cancellation notice must be written in large type in capital letters, it must contain the seller's name and address, and it must provide a place for the consumer's signature. The consumer must be informed that by signing the notice and sending it to the seller, the transaction will be canceled. Upon receipt of the cancellation notice, the door-to-door seller must refund within ten days all payments made by the consumer.

State laws regulating door-to-door sales are usually very similar to the federal rule. Where state laws differ from the federal rule, the law that is most protective of consumer rights will apply.

Laws allowing for a cancellation period on door-to-door sales typically do not apply to certain types of transactions. First, the amount of the sale must be above a certain threshold before the laws will apply. Under the federal rule, the amount is $25. Thus, children selling candy, and similar low-cost, small-scale operations, are exempt from the rules. Restrictions on door-to-door sales generally do not apply to sales or rentals of real property or the sale of insurance or securities that are sold through a broker registered with the federal **Securities and Exchange Commission.**

Generally, a consumer does not have a right to cancel a door-to-door sale that was initiated by the consumer himself or herself to fill an immediate personal need, if the consumer signed a waiver of the right to cancel the transaction. This last rule was designed to protect sellers from consumers whose need for the product can be satisfied within the three-day cancellation period, thus allowing them to use the product and return it without having to pay for it.

DRUG   Any substance intended to be used in the diagnosis, prevention, treatment, or cure of disease that affects any structure or function of the body through chemical means is a *drug* under the **Food, Drug & Cosmetic Act.** The classification of a substance as a drug will directly affect the degree of safety and effectiveness a **consumer** may expect when using it, since substances that come within this definition are subject to very rigorous testing and marketing standards administered by the federal government through the **Food and Drug Administration** (FDA).

The protective stance taken by the regulatory system in regard to drugs relates both to the great risks entailed by ingesting chemical substances and the emotional vulnerability of people in need of a cure. Not by accident does the definition of drug include any substance "intended" to have an effect on the body, rather than just substances that actually do have an effect. The reason is to protect consumers from ineffective "cures" that merely raise hopes or divert the consumer's attention from other methods of treatment that might be effective.

Generally, only "substances" may be drugs. Moreover, a substance must be intended to act chemically on the body, rather than by mechanical manipulation. These specifications are to distinguish drugs from **medical devices**, which affect the body by mechanical means, or **cosmetics**, which merely appear to have an effect. **Foods** are excluded from the definition of drugs, because their effects on body structures and functions are only incidental. Foods, medical devices, and cosmetics are regulated by other provisions of the Food, Drug & Cosmetic Act.

Under regulations issued by the FDA, sellers of drugs must test their products rigorously both for efficacy and for unwanted side effects. All of the results must be presented to the FDA. If a drug meets the FDA's standards for safety and effectiveness, it may be marketed with proper warnings and instructions. Nonaddictive drugs safely taken without a physician's supervision may be sold "over the counter" without a prescription. Otherwise, drugs may only be sold upon prescription by a licensed physician. Generally, advertisements for prescription drugs, known as *ethical* drugs, may be made only to physicians. Over-the-counter remedies may be advertised in the mass media.

Usually, the duty to warn users of prescription drugs about dangers associated with their use is discharged by informing the physicians who will prescribe them. In other words, the drug seller has no duty to warn consumers directly about the dangers and recommended uses of prescription drugs. However, if a drug is to be used on a long-term, continual basis by a consumer without repeated consultations with a physician, as, for example, with oral contraceptives, the seller must warn the consumer directly about dangers associated with the product. Also, if the drug is to be dispensed in mass campaigns aimed at protecting the public from epidemic diseases, the seller may be required to warn the public directly about its product. An example of this situation would be mass immunizations held at schools or other public buildings where each consumer's individual physician is not expected to be present. The seller of over-the-counter drugs must also inform the consumer directly about risks posed by using the product.

Usually, a consumer has no legal claim if a properly prescribed drug is ineffective in treating a disease or condition. The law recognizes that medicine is an inexact science and that individuals will react differently to different chemical substances. Drug companies are, therefore, not required to ensure that their products are effective in all cases. So long as a drug has passed the efficacy tests required by the FDA prior to marketing, the only way a consumer may recover compensation for its failure to have an effect is to show that the seller made an **express warranty** that it would work. Needless to say, drug sellers rarely make such promises.

A consumer may have a legal claim for compensation if a drug causes personal injury. However, it is rare that a court will find that a drug that cleared the FDA's rigorous tests is defective [see **defectiveness**]. Proposed **tort** reforms in the 1990s would make it impossible for consumers to recover compensation for injuries caused by drugs that meet the FDA's requirements for safety, effectiveness, and marketing. Moreover, drugs are frequently considered **unavoidably unsafe products**, which means that society will tolerate a certain degree of risk from them because of their great utility.

However, occasionally a consumer may be able to show that a seller fraudulently [see **fraud**] withheld important information about dangerous side effects from the FDA, or that the seller was negligent [see **negligence**] in conducting the required tests and failed to discover a dangerous aspect of the drug that later caused harm. Or, it may be possible to show that the seller of a drug failed to provide sufficient warnings and instructions to physicians responsible for prescribing it [see **warning defect**]. A seller of drugs has a continuing duty to warn of new dangers associated with a drug that come to light after it is marketed. A consumer may be able to show that the seller failed to investigate reports of injuries or failed to provide the results of investigations taken in response to such reports. Occasionally, a drug may cause injury because it deviates from the proper formula or is contaminated or adulterated with harmful substances [see **manufacturing defect**]. A consumer who has been injured by the drug may then have a legal claim against the drug company based on negligence in manufacturing or **strict tort liability.**

Frequently, the real fault for an injury caused by a drug will lie with the physician who prescribed it. If the physician was negligent in diagnosing the consumer's condition and determining that the drug should be prescribed, the consumer may receive compensation for the injury by bringing suit against the physician. Occasionally, a pharmacist is to blame for an inappropriate or contaminated drug reaching the consumer. A lawsuit may properly be instituted against the pharmacist in that situation.

DUTY OF CARE   The legally recognized obligation of one to act with due regard for the safety of others. The existence of a duty of care is an element that must be proved in any **tort** case based on the alleged **negligence** of one party that results in harm to another.

Until the twentieth century, the existence of a duty of care imposed on one individual to act with regard for the safety of another depended almost entirely on special relationships between the two. For example, an innkeeper had a duty of care to act with regard for the safety of a guest, a landowner had a duty of care to act with regard for the safety of visitors on his property, and the seller of goods had a duty to act with due regard for the safety of buyers of the goods. There were many more such special relationships. Basically, the law held that if a person did not stand in one of these special positions relative to another, no duty to take care for the other's safety was owed or expected. For example, the **seller** of a product had no duty to take care that the product did not present a danger to anyone other than to the immediate buyer [see **privity of contract**].

Gradually, these distinctions have eroded, until they are all but irrelevant in most U.S. jurisdictions. Instead, the much more practical rule has developed that every individual has a legally recognized duty of care to act reasonably with regard for the safety of every other individual [see **reasonable person test**]. This includes the maintaining of one's property in a condition so that it does not present an unreasonable risk to persons who are likely to be present. The exact requirements of the duty will vary depending on the particular circumstances of each situation [see **standard of care**].

Generally, the duty of care applies only to actions. It does not apply to omissions to act. The **common law** of the United States does not impose a duty on any individual to take affirmative steps to extricate another from a dangerous situation that the first individual had no part in creating. The exception to this rule is when the two individuals have a legally recognized special relationship with each other. For example, a parent may be under a duty of care to take action to save his or her child from a dangerous situation, even if the parent did not create the situation. Of course, if one creates a dangerous situation or allows it to develop on property owned by him or her, the creator of the situation may have a legal duty to act to aid an unfortunate individual who encounters harm on the property.

Importance to Consumers

Any **consumer** who has been injured by a defective [see **defectiveness**] product as a result of the seller's negligence will be concerned with the seller's duty of care. Under the law today, the consumer can count on the existence of the seller's duty of care to ensure that the product does not present an unreasonable danger to consumers. However, the exact requirements of this duty, which are known as the standard of care, will also be crucial in proving that the seller was negligent and must compensate the consumer for his or her injuries [see **negligence**].

ELECTRONIC FUND TRANSFER ACT   Federal law [15 U.S.C. §§1693–1693r] governing the use of electronic fund transfer systems. Since the 1970s, technological advances have facilitated the increase of "cashless" transactions in which funds can be withdrawn from or deposited into **consumer**s' bank accounts entirely through electronic means. These advances bring ease and convenience to consumer transactions. However, they also raise risks to consumers' privacy and freedom, as well as difficulties in ensuring the accuracy of accounting. The Electronic Fund Transfer Act (EFTA) was designed to minimize these problems by spelling out the rights and responsibilities both of consumers and of the financial institutions who are parties to electronic fund transfers.

Generally, EFTA applies to any transfer of funds that is not initiated by means of a paper document, such as a check or bank draft. Therefore, it does not apply to electronic transfers within or between banking institutions that occur after presentation of such paper documents. EFTA covers transfers that are initiated by a telephone conversation if they are recurring or regular and occur pursuant to a prearranged plan, but not those that are unexpected and isolated.

For covered transactions, EFTA requires that certain disclosures be made to consumers. These disclosures include the type of transfers that may be made, any fees charged for making the transfers, and whether or not transfers are limited in amount or frequency. However, the bank need not disclose the actual amount or frequency to which transfers are limited if this disclosure would compromise the bank's security. The consumer must also be informed of the conditions under which he or she will be held responsible for unauthorized transfers. A contact address for the bank offering the transfer service must be provided, along with a detailed written statement explaining the procedures the consumer must follow to report errors, discuss disputes, or raise questions.

Unlike credit cards, access devices to initiate electronic fund transfers (such as ATM cards) may be sent to consumers unsolicited. However, such devices must be inoperative until the consumer activates them by contacting the issuing bank. The bank must inform the consumer that an unsolicited access card is not valid and tell the consumer how he or she may activate it or dispose of it if activation is not desired. Sending the consumer a card and PIN (personal identification number) and telling the consumer not to use it unless he or she first contacts the bank is not in compliance with the act because it does not ensure that the device will be used only by the consumer to whom it was sent.

EFTA ensures that consumers retain freedom to decide whether or not to use electronic fund transfers. The act forbids **creditor**s from making repayment by periodic preauthorized electronic transfers a condition of extending credit. However, creditors may require repayment by means of electronic fund transfers so long as automatic debits from the consumer's account are not required. In addition, employers and government agencies may require consumers to receive paychecks and government entitlements by means of electronic fund transfer. However, the consumer must be free to choose the financial institution to which these transfers will be made.

Because electronic transfers leave no "paper trail," it is imperative that consumers have a means of documenting them. Therefore, EFTA requires that receipts be available at all electronic transfer terminals. If the machine is out of order, a written receipt must be mailed by the bank to the consumer on the next business day. If the terminal is a point-of-sale debit machine, the **seller** who operates the terminal must provide a receipt. In addition to receipts, EFTA requires that periodic statements be mailed to the consumer showing the date upon which each electronic transfer was made, the type of transfer, and the location at which it was made. A receipt or periodic statement is considered presumptive evidence that the transaction recorded on it actually took place.

Preauthorized transfers occur when the consumer has initially instructed the bank in writing to have his or her account credited or debited regularly—for example, to receive a paycheck or to pay recurring bills. The bank must document each such transfer within two business days. This may be done by sending the consumer a receipt showing that the transfer occurred or a statement that an expected transfer did not occur. The consumer has the right to stop payment on a preauthorized transfer by notifying the bank in advance of the scheduled payment. The bank may require written notice up to 14 days prior to the scheduled transfer.

Generally, a consumer will be responsible for any authorized transfers from or to his or her account. This includes transfers made by third parties to whom the consumer has furnished his or her access device and code, even if such transfers exceed the amount the consumer permitted the third party to make. However, this excludes situations in which the third party procured the consumer's access device and code through **fraud** or duress.

Under certain conditions, a consumer may also be held responsible for unauthorized transfers. Generally, a consumer's liability for an unauthorized transfer will be limited to $50 if the consumer notifies the bank within 2 business days of learning that his or her access card was lost or stolen, or that an unauthorized transfer occurred. However, if the consumer fails to notify the bank within 2 business days, the liability limit jumps to $500. If the consumer still fails to notify the bank within 60 days of transmittal of the periodic statement upon which the unauthorized fund transfers are recorded, the consumer's liability will be unlimited until the bank is notified. These time periods may be extended if circumstances warrant, such as when the consumer is abroad. A consumer will not be liable at all for unauthorized transfers made by the bank itself or by its employees.

EFTA prescribes very strict procedures to identify and correct errors in electronic transfers. A consumer has 60 days from the time a periodic statement is transmitted to question or dispute documented electronic transfers. The consumer must identify the alleged error and explain to the bank his or her reasons for believing that it is incorrect. The bank then has 10 days to investigate. However, the bank may take up to 45 days to investigate if it recredits the consumer's account on a provisional basis with the amount of the disputed debit. During the time of the investigation, the consumer may use the provisionally recredited funds to pay third parties. However, the bank may prohibit the consumer from withdrawing the provisional funds as cash. If the bank determines that an error was made, it must notify the consumer within 1 business day and permanently recredit the consumer's account with the disputed amount plus any applicable interest. However, if the bank determines that an error was not made, it has 3 business days in which to notify the consumer in writing of the reasons for its decision. The consumer has the right to request a copy of all documents upon which the bank based its decision. In addition, the bank must continue to honor requests for payment from provisionally recredited funds for up to 5 business days before it debits the account again.

Occasionally, a bank may fail to make an electronic transfer authorized by the consumer or stop payment on one at the consumer's request. Under EFTA, the bank will be liable for any compensatory **damages** suffered by the consumer as a result. These may include mental distress and humiliation as well as actual damages. However, the bank need not make a requested transfer if the consumer's account contains insufficient funds, nor must it honor a stop payment order if the order was not received within a reasonable time up to 14 days before the scheduled transfer.

Financial institutions that intentionally violate provisions of EFTA may be subject to criminal liability as well as civil liability. Many states have their own laws regulating electronic fund transfers. Such state laws may be preempted by EFTA if they are inconsistent with it. However, a state law is not considered to be "inconsistent" if it provides more protection for consumers than EFTA. See also **preemption.**

ENDORSEMENT   A statement by a person unrelated to the **seller** of a product or service that attests to the merits of that product or service. Because of the effectiveness of endorsements and testimonials as a marketing tool, it is not surprising that deceptive practices concerning them have been a recurring theme in efforts to protect **consumer**s. The **Federal Trade Commission** (FTC) has been active in setting guidelines for sellers who advertise their products by means of endorsements or testimonials.

Generally, it is illegal to make claims that a third party has endorsed a product or service when no such endorsement was made. It is also illegal to use the testimonial of a person claiming to use a product or service if that person does not use the product or service. Moreover, it is illegal to distort or alter the text of any endorsing statement that has been made so that it does not accurately reflect the endorser's opinion. In other words, an endorser must actually hold the opinion expressed in the endorsement.

Thus, the use of the mark of **Underwriters Laboratories Inc.** on a product would not be permissible unless the product was, in fact, endorsed by that organization. Likewise, a testimonial about the benefits of eating beef would be deceptive if made by a fashion model who was, in fact, a vegetarian. And a statement that a product was given the "highest rating" by an organization that investigates the safety of consumer products would be misleading if the organization only rates products on a "pass/fail" basis.

In addition to the requirement that an endorser actually believe what he or she says in the endorsement, there must be some independent basis for the statement. Unless the endorser's statement is clearly only an expression of personal taste, there must be some way to verify the statement objectively. If, for example, an endorser states that a certain diet drink will help one lose weight, there must be some scientific proof that the product does have the desirable weight loss effect. It is not enough that the endorser genuinely believes that this is true.

If an expert is used to endorse a product, the expert's opinion must be based on his or her own evaluation of the product using his or her expertise. Reliance on test results or data supplied by the seller of the product is not allowed. Needless to say, the proffered expert must actually possess expertise in the area in which he or she expresses an opinion. An astronaut may not offer an expert opinion about the engineering of an automobile, for example, if he does not, in fact, have any training in that area. Of course, the astronaut may state that he finds an automobile exciting to drive, because this judgment is not dependent on his having any engineering expertise and merely reflects his personal taste in driving.

If a seller claims that "ordinary consumers" endorse a product, the actual consumers must be depicted in any advertising. If actors are used to portray an "ordinary consumer" giving a testimonial, this fact must be disclosed. However, statements made by character actors who are paid to dramatize a fictional situation in a television commercial are not endorsers and no disclosure need be made. In this situation, the public understands that the seller is merely speaking about his or her own product through the dramatic medium.

Generally, it is not necessary for a seller to reveal that an endorser has been paid. The public expects that this is the case. However, if the payment is something more than a straight fee for making the endorsement, the endorser's relationship with the seller must be disclosed. For example, if the endorser owns a partial interest in the seller's company, is receiving payment in the form of stock in the company, or is receiving commissions based on the number of units of the product sold, this must be revealed. The fact that a purportedly "independent" organization that makes an endorsement is actually associated with, or funded by, the seller must also be disclosed.

Celebrity endorsements are the subject of special scrutiny by the FTC because of the disproportionate importance consumers may ascribe to their views on any subject. The FTC is also particularly sensitive about endorsements or testimonials made for medical products or devices. Generally, an advertiser may not use medical symbols or insignias that suggest that a product has been made under the supervision of physicians or according to a medical prescription. Thus, the use of the letters *M.D.* or the word *doctor* is proscribed if the product does not, in fact, have the endorsement of real physicians. Moreover, it is forbidden to use the endorsements of either doctors or ordinary consumers for medical products unless (1) the claims made are consistent with the judgment of the **Food and Drug Administration** regarding the product's capabilities, and (2) the seller of the product has scientific substantiation for the claims made in the endorsement.

If the FTC finds that an endorsement or testimonial violates one of its rules, it may take legal action to put an end to the deceptive practice.

A consumer who has been injured as a result of a deceptive endorsement or testimonial may have several alternatives for redress. For example, the consumer may bring a private lawsuit for the **tort** of **deceit** against the seller of the product who procured the false endorsement. Recently, consumers have been suing the endorsers of a product that caused injury as well. Their claims are based on allegations that the endorser either knew, or should have known, that claims made about the endorsed product were false. These types of lawsuits are most frequently brought where the seller of the product is bankrupt and the endorser is a celebrity expected to have "deep pockets," and thus the financial resources to satisfy the claim.

ENHANCED INJURY DOCTRINE   A doctrine under which the **seller** of a product may be liable for the aggravation of a **consumer**'s injuries caused by something other than the product. Thus, a product may be found to be defective [see **defectiveness**], and its seller negligent [see **negligence**], if some aspect of the product aggravates the injuries suffered by a consumer in an accident not directly caused by the product.

Sometimes called the *crashworthiness* or *second collision* doctrine, the enhanced injury doctrine is most relevant in accidents involving automobiles. Most automobile accidents are caused by something other than defects in the automobiles involved. However, in many cases injuries suffered by persons involved in automobile accidents may be made worse because of some internal feature of the automobile: for example, weakness in the frame, lack of interior restraints, placement of the gas tank, and so on. If the internal features of the automobile do not provide reasonable protection against such added injuries, consumers injured in accidents may be entitled to recover compensation for the extent to which their injuries were aggravated by them.

The application of the enhanced injury doctrine is complicated by several factors. First, it must be proved that the seller's failure to take into account hazards external to the product made the product defective. Generally, this involves determining the likelihood of accidents in which the product could cause aggravated injury if not designed for safety [see **foreseeability**]. In the case of automobiles, this is easy. Everyone expects that automobiles will be involved in collisions from time to time. The failure to make the internal features of the machine reasonably safe from causing aggravated injuries constitutes a defect. Other types of products do not present so clear a case. For example, if a consumer's jaw implant causes her aggravated injuries resulting from a punch in the face, it will be more difficult to show that the implant was defective because its manufacturer did not take into account the possibility of a blow to the face of the user when designing it. The question would be resolved by determining whether punches to the face are so common that the designer of the product should have taken them into consideration.

Second, it will be necessary to determine how much of the consumer's injury was caused by the initial accident and how much was caused by the defective feature of the product that aggravated the injuries. This determination is difficult because it invariably calls for some speculation as to how injured the consumer would have been if the product at issue had not been defective. To get around this difficulty some states hold that once the consumer proves that a defect in a product aggravated injuries suffered in an accident, both the seller of the product and the party that caused the initial accident are jointly and severally liable [see **joint and several liability**]. This means that either of them could be required to compensate the consumer for the full extent of his or her injuries, despite the fact that each was only responsible for a part of those injuries. Other states demand that the injured consumer present some evidence of the degree to which each party who caused harm contributed to it. The seller of the product will then be required to pay compensation only for the amount by which the initial injuries were aggravated by the defective product.

EQUAL CREDIT OPPORTUNITY ACT   Federal law [15 U.S.C. §1691 et seq.] that prohibits **creditors** from discriminating against **consumers** applying for credit based on race, gender, marital status, color, religion, or national origin. Age discrimination is also prohibited, except to ensure that an applicant is old enough legally to enter into a contract. In addition, a creditor may not discriminate on the grounds that an applicant's income derives from public assistance funds or because an applicant has exercised other rights under the **Consumer Credit Protection Act.**

The Equal Credit Opportunity Act (ECOA) prohibits discrimination in all aspects of the credit granting process, from taking applications to evaluating applicants for creditworthiness. However, the law recognizes that creditors have legitimate interests in determining whether a particular applicant is a good risk for paying back credit extended to him or her. Therefore, the rules governing the credit application process are designed to balance the interest of consumers to be free from discrimination with the legitimate needs of creditors to make credit decisions based on the degree of risk an applicant presents.

Thus, although a creditor may not decide whether or not to extend credit solely on a prohibited basis (e.g., gender, age, race, etc.), he or she may consider factors related to those bases if they legitimately affect the likelihood that a loan will be repaid. For example, the law prohibits creditors from determining creditworthiness on the basis of a consumer's marital status. Yet it permits a creditor to consider marital status if an applicant's spouse is to be allowed to use the credit account, if the applicant is relying on a spouse's income to meet credit obligations, or if the applicant lives in a state in which property accumulated during marriage is considered to be jointly owned by both spouses. The last factor affects the creditor's right to seize the consumer's property should the consumer default on the loan.

Similarly, the act prohibits making credit decisions based on an applicant's age. Yet a creditor may consider how many years an applicant has before retirement, whether his or her estimated retirement income will be sufficient to pay back the loan, and whether or not the loan period is likely to exceed the applicant's estimated life span. All of these factors genuinely affect an applicant's likelihood of paying back a credit loan.

On the other hand, ECOA prohibits a creditor from using criteria for determining creditworthiness that appear to be nondiscriminatory yet have a discriminatory effect when they are applied. For example, requiring a minimum income level from an applicant as a prerequisite to granting any credit may be illegal if its effect is to reject blacks in greater numbers than whites. However, minimum income levels may be implemented to determine the amount of credit that will be granted, since that factor genuinely affects the ability of an applicant to repay a loan.

Along with its prohibition of discrimination in credit transactions, ECOA's most important feature is its requirement that consumers be notified of the reasons why a creditor has made an unfavorable decision regarding their applications for credit. Not only does this allow the consumer to ensure that he or she was not the victim of discrimination, but it also enables consumers to cure whatever nondiscriminatory basis led to a denial or increased price of credit. For example, if credit was denied because of too many outstanding debts, the applicant can pay off the debts and reapply knowing that he or she is now creditworthy. Reasons given by a creditor for unfavorable decisions regarding credit applicants must be reasonably detailed. It is not sufficient, for example, for a creditor merely to say that an applicant "did not meet relevant criteria."

The act provides consumers with a **private right of action** to sue violators directly in order to recover compensation for monetary losses, damage to credit rating, or any humiliation and emotional distress. Punitive **damages** are also recoverable, whether or not actual losses are proved. The act also specifically allows **class action**s. Besides private lawsuits, most enforcement of the act and prosecution of violators is left to the **Federal Trade Commission.**

EXCLUSIVE DEALING   An arrangement whereby one independent **seller** agrees to buy goods, supplies, or services exclusively from another seller and to refuse to buy from that seller's competitors. Such agreements are illegal under the **Clayton Antitrust Act** if they have adverse effects on the competitors' ability to market their goods. See also **antitrust law.**

EXPRESS WARRANTY   A **warranty** that is created when a **seller** makes a statement or representation about the quality of goods for sale. This type of warranty is called *express* in order to distinguish it from an *implied* warranty. An implied warranty arises automatically when a product is sold, regardless of whether any statement about the product has been made. For more on implied warranties, see **implied warranty of fitness for a particular purpose; implied warranty of merchantability.**

Most express warranties of importance to **consumer**s are regulated by the **Uniform Commercial Code** (UCC), which applies to the sale of goods. In some states, the Uniform Commercial Code rules have been expanded to cover express warranties on leased goods and on the provision of services. Written warranties on consumer products are also subject to the provisions of the federal **Magnuson-Moss Warranty Act.** Warranties concerning the condition of real estate are generally subject to the rules of the **common law** as well as various state laws regulating the sale of real estate.

Definition under the Uniform Commercial Code

The UCC defines an express warranty as (1) an affirmation of fact or a promise, (2) made by the seller to the buyer, (3) which relates to the goods, and (4) becomes part of the basis of the bargain. Like many legal definitions, this one appears deceptively simple. Actually, it is rife with ambiguity and vagueness that has taken the courts years to sort out. Each of these factors will be considered separately below.

Affirmation of Fact or Promise

The requirement of an affirmation of fact or a promise embodies the essence of an express warranty and has been particularly thorny to interpret.

When is a statement a promise? Generally, a statement is a promise if it refers to future events that the maker of the statement is capable of realizing. For example, a seller's statement that the seller will repair a product for a period of one year free of charge is clearly a promise. A statement that the seller will attempt to secure financing for the buyer to purchase an automobile is also a promise. Although the outcome is not certain, the seller is capable of performing the promised act—*attempting* to secure financing. However, the statement that members of the opposite sex will be irresistibly drawn to the consumer of a love potion is not a promise. A promise refers to the maker's future behavior, not to the future behavior of others.

When is a statement an affirmation of fact? Generally, a statement that is capable of objective verification is an affirmation of fact. For example, the statement that an automobile has a certain type of engine is an affirmation of fact because it is readily verifiable. Verification does not have to be easy. A statement that an automobile was owned by a little old lady who only drove it to church on Sundays is also an affirmation of fact, even though verification would be more difficult. One could ask the old lady herself. One could question her neighbors, friends, or her pastor to corroborate that they never saw her drive it anywhere else. One could check the odometer on the vehicle and compare it to the product of the number of Sundays the old lady owned the car times the miles from her home to the church.

On the other hand, if a statement made by the seller is merely an opinion regarding an aspect of the product about which the buyer could also be expected to have a valid opinion, there is no affirmation of fact and no express warranty will be created. This is the exception for so-called **puffery.** Everyone knows that sellers are prone to exaggerate the virtues of their wares and buyers do not base their decisions to purchase them on this overblown praise.

When is a statement a mere opinion? There is no fast answer to this question. However, certain factors are more likely to indicate that a statement represents a subjective opinion and not a verifiable fact. For example, the use of superlatives such as "great," "best," "wonderful," and the like indicate that an opinion is being expressed. Vague relative adjectives such as "ample," "reliable," and "affordable" are also indicative of an opinion, unless there is some standard definition for them in the seller's trade. Likewise, statements about the value of goods are generally considered to be opinions only, because value is an inherently vague concept. In addition, words that express uncertainty, such as "maybe," "probably," or "possibly" indicate that the statement that follows is a mere opinion and not a statement of fact.

Statements about future events are also more likely to be considered expressions of opinion and not affirmations of fact. Everyone understands that the future cannot be predicted with certainty.

Nevertheless, products are purchased to perform in the future. If every statement regarding future performance of a product were merely an opinion, no express warranty could ever be created. How, then, is it possible to determine when statements relating to the future are affirmations of fact that could lead to the creation of an express warranty? The answer may simply depend on general notions of the possible. A statement like "this automobile will get you to Denver" can qualify as an affirmation of fact, even though it refers to the future, because the typical consumer knows that there are automobiles in existence that can take one to Denver. By contrast, the statement that a love potion will make the consumer irresistible to members of the opposite sex is clearly an opinion, because consumers generally understand that the claim is not in the realm of the possible. More problematic would be the statement that "this wrinkle cream will take years off your looks." Most consumers know that scientific progress has not progressed so far, yet the possibility is not out of the question. Probably, this statement would fall into the category of mere opinion—not just because it relates to the future, but because "years off your looks" is a vague description that depends on a viewer's subjective judgment.

In any case, in recent years there has been a trend to interpret sellers' statements regarding their products as warranties rather than harmless puffery—no matter what the subject or form of the expression. This is particularly true in cases in which there is a disparity in expertise between the parties regarding the product for sale. If the seller is knowledgeable about the type of product for sale and the buyer is not, statements made by the seller are much more likely to be found to be warranties.

Made by Seller to Buyer

The second prerequisite to the formation of an express warranty has its share of interpretive difficulties.

First, how must a representation regarding a product be made in order to qualify as an express warranty? Generally, there are no magic words that must be stated to form an express warranty. It is not necessary for the seller to use the words *warranty* or *guaranty* in order for a warranty to arise. In fact, the seller need not intend to create a warranty at all when making a statement or promise about a product. Even statements about a product made without any intention to induce a consumer to buy may become express warranties if the other requirements for creating an express warranty are met.

Statements made about a product in advertisements, catalogs, and brochures may be considered warranties. Moreover, a statement need not be written in order to constitute an express warranty. Oral statements made by the seller or the seller's representatives can also be express warranties.

Second, who is a seller and who is a buyer for purposes of determining whether a warranty exists? Under the traditional common-law rule, only parties with direct contractual relations with each other would qualify. That is to say, only the person who bought directly from a seller was a *buyer,* and only the person who sold directly to a buyer was a *seller* for warranty purposes. This rule served to relieve manufacturers from having to make good on statements about their products to remote buyers, who typically purchased the products from intermediate retail dealers. See **guaranty; privity of contract; warranty.**

Under the UCC, this rule has been relaxed. Generally, any party who purchases goods may hold any party selling the goods to account for statements about the goods, regardless of whether the selling party is removed from the buying party by one or more levels of distribution. Therefore, advertisements disseminated by the manufacturer of a product can serve to create a warranty in favor of anyone who buys the product, despite the fact that the statements in the advertisement are not directed to any specific buyer and despite the fact that the buyer purchases the goods from an intermediate retailer. See **Baxter v. Ford Motor Company.**

Moreover, there is a trend to allow persons who did not buy the product at all to take advantage of warranty statements made by manufacturers or other sellers of the product. For example, the family of the buyer or, in some cases, even chance bystanders may sue for breach of warranty if a product causes them injury because it does not conform to the seller's statements about it. See **Henningsen v. Bloomfield Motors, Inc.**

Under the UCC, anyone who sells a product may create an express warranty by his or her statements about the product. The seller need not be a merchant or be "in business" selling the type of product at issue. A private citizen who sells a used bicycle at a garage sale may be liable for breach of an express warranty if statements made about the bicycle to the purchaser turn out to be false. Even isolated or onetime sales of goods qualify for purposes of creating an express warranty. This is in contrast to the implied warranty of merchantability, which may only be created by sellers who qualify as merchants.

Relating to the Goods Being Sold

A seller's statements must relate to the goods being sold in order for an express warranty to be created. If the seller's statements concern something else there can be no warranty. For example, a seller's statement that replacement parts for a product were available was found not to create a warranty because it was not about the product itself but about something else: replacement parts. Similarly, a statement that no other store sells the same product for less would not be a warranty because it refers to something other than the product: the activity of other sellers. However, a statement that a seller would not be undersold may create an express warranty because it is a promise to sell a product for no more than other stores. See section above on Affirmation of Fact or Promise.

Forming Part of the "Basis of the Bargain"

Under the UCC, a seller's statement about a product must become part of the "basis of the bargain" in order to create a warranty.

There is some dispute about the meaning of this phrase. Under traditional common-law rules about warranty, a buyer must rely on the seller's statement when making the decision to buy the product before any warranty is created. If the buyer does not consider the subject matter of the statement important, or if he or she did not hear the statement, the buyer could not have relied on the statement when deciding to make the purchase. Under the common law, the statement would not create a warranty. See **reliance.**

The situation may be different under the Uniform Commercial Code, depending on the state in which the sale takes place. Presently, courts in different states interpret the "basis of the bargain" requirement differently. Some of them view it as the same as the old reliance requirement at common law. Others have gone to the opposite extreme and have held that any statement about a product is automatically part of the "basis of the bargain." Most states, however, have adopted a compromise view. Under this view all of a seller's statements are presumed to be part of the "basis of the bargain" unless proven otherwise. The seller who wants to defend against a breach of warranty claim by showing that no warranty was created must then prove that the buyer did not rely on the seller's statement about the product when making the decision to purchase it. The practical result of this interpretation is to make it easier for a consumer to prove a breach of express warranty by shifting the burden of proving the reliance issue to the seller.

Interestingly, under the UCC interpretation of the "basis of the bargain" a warranty can be created by statements made by the seller after the sale of the product takes place. This is true even though the buyer could not possibly have relied on the statements when making the decision to purchase the product, because the statements had not yet been made at that time.

The law gets around this difficulty by some clever interpretations. One view holds that a sales transaction is not an instantaneous event, but begins sometime before and continues sometime after the actual exchange of the product for money. Therefore, a seller's statement to a buyer as he or she is going out the door with a newly purchased can of paint that the paint is suitable for outdoor use as well as indoor use would create a warranty. At what point the "event" of the sale terminates is not exactly clear under this view. If the buyer hears the seller tell another customer that the paint is suitable for outdoor use years after the buyer himself or herself applied it, a warranty would probably not be created in favor of the first buyer, even though the new customer would have a warranty to that effect.

Another way in which the law interprets the "basis of the bargain" requirement to allow postsale express warranties to arise is simply to consider the statement at issue to be a modification of the original contract for the sale of the product. For example, if a buyer complains that his new refrigerator has stopped working and the seller promises to fix it, a warranty to fix the refrigerator has been created even though the sale of the refrigerator has already taken place. The promise to fix it is viewed as a modification to the original contract of sale that the parties are perfectly free to make.

Importance to Consumers

Express warranties are a major source of rights for consumers. The existence of an express warranty is frequently the deciding factor for a consumer in determining which product to buy, because it takes some of the risk out of the transaction. In a sense, an express warranty is a type of insurance policy for the consumer that the product will perform in a certain way.

Express warranties have certain benefits for buyers over other types of consumer safeguards. First, of course, is the fact that they are *express*: The parties know, more or less, what the terms of the warranty are. Second, express warranties are difficult to disclaim. In other words, the seller may not make an express warranty for the product and then state later that there are no warranties. See **disclaimer of warranty.**

Express Warranty by Description   The **Uniform Commercial Code** provides that a **seller**'s description of goods for sale may create an **express warranty** that the goods will conform to the description. A description includes any expression that portrays characteristics of the product. For example, statements that a product is a certain model, a certain color, or has a certain capacity are all descriptions that may create an express warranty.

Descriptions creating express warranties may be very detailed, such as those contained in blueprints or specification lists. They may also be expressed nonverbally. A picture of a product may create an express warranty that the product will have the depicted features. Specifications expressed mathematically may also create an express warranty by description.

As with any express warranty, the description must become a part of the "basis of the bargain" before a warranty is created. That is to say that the buyer must have considered the characteristics portrayed in the description when making the decision to purchase the product.

One difficulty presented by express warranties by description involves just how specific an expression must be before it becomes a *description.* For example, does the word "automobile" standing alone embody a description of the functions of the product upon which an express warranty can be based? Proponents of this idea argue that the word "automobile" means something more than just a metal body on four wheels. Under this theory the word "automobile" by itself describes a machine that will transport people at least a reasonable number of miles before needing major repairs. Anything that does not perform in this way does not meet the description of "automobile," according to these theorists.

Fortunately, it is not necessary for **consumer**s to press this type of metaphysical quandary on the courts in order to seek satisfaction from a product accompanied by a minimal description. Instead, they can turn to implied warranties, such as the **implied warranty of merchantability,** for relief.

EXPRESS WARRANTY BY MODEL   Because it is not always possible for **sellers** to keep an inventory of goods at the selling location, sales are often made on the basis of models of the product. A buyer's decision to purchase a product based on inspection of such a model can create an **express warranty** that the product actually delivered will conform to features illustrated by the model.

Unlike samples [see **express warranty by sample**], models of products for sale are not drawn out of a bulk supply of the product. They do not purport to "be" the product, or even to "represent" the product in the same literal way as a sample. Rather, models attempt only to "illustrate" or "suggest" the product for sale. Usually, models are not made of the same materials as the actual product or are not the same size as the actual product. Because of these obvious differences between the model and the actual product, the scope of the express warranty created is not so broad or solid as that created by an actual sample of the product.

Nevertheless, a model can create an express warranty about aspects of the product for sale that are readily illustrated by the model. For example, a small-scale model of a house can create a warranty as to the layout of the rooms, the relative sizes of the rooms, or the configuration of the windows. The model probably would not give rise to a warranty about the quality of the building materials to be used in the house, because the model would necessarily be made of some material quite different from an actual house. A prospective buyer inspecting the model would realize that the model was not intended to convey any promises about the materials used to build the actual house upon which it was based. Thus, no express warranty regarding those aspects of the house would be created by the model.

In order for a model of a product to create an express warranty, the attributes illustrated by the model must be part of the "basis of the bargain" upon which the buyer's decision to purchase the product rests. If, for example, the buyer makes changes in the plan for the product that are not present in the model, the buyer cannot claim a breach of warranty if the actual product does not look like the original model. The reason is that, by changing the model, the buyer showed that he or she did not rely on its features when deciding to purchase the actual product. See **express warranty; reliance.**

Like warranties created by samples of a product, express warranties created by a product model can be disclaimed by the seller [see **disclaimer of warranty**].

EXPRESS WARRANTY BY SAMPLE   A common technique for selling products in bulk involves the presentation of a sample of the product to the prospective buyer. The notorious practice of offering a "sample" of considerably better quality than the product actually delivered to the buyer prompted the rule that the presentation of product samples may create an **express warranty** that other units of the same product will be roughly the same in quality. Generally, a sample is a unit of the same product drawn from bulk on hand. It is supposed to actually "be" the product for sale or to represent that product so closely as to be almost identical.

In order for the sample to create an express warranty it must generally be presented to the buyer by the **seller** in connection with the proposed sale. This does not mean that the seller must literally state that the item is a "sample" of the subject goods. It is enough if the seller implies this by his or her conduct or by the circumstances surrounding the sale. For example, the fact that swatches of carpeting are available for inspection at a seller's store would be sufficient to create a warranty that the carpeting delivered will be the same as the swatch the buyer indicates he or she wants when in the store. No special statement that the swatches are samples is necessary. On the other hand, a seller may prevent a warranty from being created by specifically stating that samples on hand or presented to the buyer are not exactly representative of the product that the seller is offering for sale [see **disclaimer of warranty**].

As with any express warranty, the attributes of the product represented by the sample must become part of the "basis of the bargain" before an express warranty by sample will arise. Generally, it is assumed that the buyer is relying on the fact that the product he or she buys will be roughly the same as the sample offered for inspection when making a decision to purchase. However, this presumption may be rebutted by the seller with evidence that the sample was not important to the buyer, that the buyer never saw the sample, or that the seller disclaimed any notion that the sample represented the goods for sale [see **express warranty**].

Goods that are sold subject to an express warranty by sample do not have to be exactly the same as the sample in order to conform to the warranty. Everyone understands that no two items are exactly alike, particularly where bulk natural produce or resources are concerned. It is sufficient if the goods that are delivered to the buyer are of approximately the same type and quality as the sample.

Of course, it is rare that a sale takes place on the basis of a sample inspection alone. Usually there are other expressions about the product that are made as well. Other express warranties created by specific statements or descriptions about the product at issue will override any warranty created by sample. See also **conflict of warranties; express warranty by description; express warranty by model; implied warranty of merchantability.**

FAILING COMPANY DEFENSE   An argument in favor of a **merger** between companies that otherwise would violate the **antitrust laws**, based on the claim that the company targeted for acquisition is failing and likely to go out of business without help. Provided that the failing company is not in trouble because of illegal predatory behavior on the part of the acquiring company, a court may find it preferable to allow the merger and save the failing company. In order to prevail, the parties to the merger must prove that the targeted company is not only very likely to go out of business, but that it also tried and failed to find a merger candidate that was less objectionable. See also **Clayton Antitrust Act.**

FAIR CREDIT AND CHARGE CARD DISCLOSURE ACT   A federal law [Pub. L. No. 100-583, 102 Stat. 2960] designed to provide **consumers** with additional information about the comparative terms of **credit card** agreements.

In addition to the general disclosures that **creditors** must make about credit card charge accounts under the **Truth in Lending Act,** the Fair Credit and Charge Card Disclosure Act requires that the following information be given to a consumer to whom a credit application has been sent:

- the annual rate of interest charged on the outstanding balance of the credit card;
- any annual or periodic fees;
- the length of any "grace period" during which no interest will be charged on an outstanding balance after payment is due;
- the method used to calculate the balance on which interest will be charged;
- the date on which the credit card agreement will expire unless renewed; and
- the method by which the consumer may terminate the credit card agreement.

FAIR CREDIT BILLING ACT   A federal law [15 U.S.C. §1666] governing disputes between **credit card** holders, the credit card issuers, and the **sellers** from whom goods and services are purchased with credit cards. The main effect of the law is to make the issuer of a credit card subject to any claims and defenses that the cardholder has against the seller of goods or services purchased with the card. For example, if a **consumer** has a dispute with a seller because goods purchased with a credit card do not conform to a **warranty,** the consumer will not be required to pay the card issuer for those goods until the dispute is resolved with the seller. If the cardholder has other accounts with the issuer, the issuer may not use funds in the other accounts to satisfy the disputed debt. However, a consumer may refuse to pay the credit card issuer only after a good faith attempt at resolving the dispute with the seller. No particular procedure for dispute resolution is required.

The Fair Credit Billing Act applies only when the amount in dispute is over $50, and only where the disputed transaction occurred within 100 miles of the cardholder's address. When the transaction takes place over the telephone, the applicability of the act will depend on the laws of the states in which the parties to the sale reside. The act applies only to bank credit cards, not to credit cards issued directly by a seller.

The Fair Credit Billing Act can be used by a consumer as a shield to avoid paying a credit card bill for goods or services where there is a genuine dispute with the seller of the goods or services about whether payment is due. However, the consumer may not use the law as a sword to sue the issuer of the credit card for losses or damages caused by defective [see **defectiveness**] or undelivered goods or services purchased by the consumer from the seller.

FAIR CREDIT REPORTING ACT   A federal law [15 U.S.C. §1681 et seq.] intended to safeguard **consumers'** privacy rights by regulating the activities of credit reporting agencies [see **credit reporting agency**] and the users of the **consumer reports** that they generate.

The Fair Credit Reporting Act imposes an obligation on credit reporting agencies to maintain reasonable procedures to ensure the currency and accuracy of the information they compile about consumers. At a minimum, this means that some method of checking the accuracy of the data gathered must be instituted as standard operating procedure. It is not sufficient to wait until a consumer complains about inaccuracies before verifying the information. However, the mere fact that a credit reporting agency reports untrue information about a consumer is not a violation of the act. It must be shown not only that the information is false but that whatever verifying procedure the agency followed was not reasonable.

Under the Fair Credit Reporting Act, a credit reporting agency is obligated to disclose the contents of a consumer's file to the consumer upon request and proper identification. The disclosure need not be complete. It may be no more than a summary of the nature and substance of the information in the file. Medical information about the consumer is specifically excluded from the duty to disclose because of the concern that consumers would misunderstand technical medical terms used about them. The reporting agency must also disclose to the consumer the sources of the information in the file and the identities of any other parties that have requested the information.

If an investigative report about a consumer is requested from a credit reporting agency, the consumer who is the subject of the request must be informed within three days. An investigative report typically contains broad information about a consumer's habits and lifestyle, in addition to financial status. Such reports are gathered through personal interviews with persons who know the consumer. In addition, the party who requested the investigative report must inform the consumer as to the reason for the request. Investigative reports requested for purposes of determining a consumer's qualifications for a job for which he or she did not apply are specifically excluded.

Disclosures to consumers about their credit reports must be made during business hours. They may be made in person or on the telephone so long as the agency has received a written request first. Credit reporting agencies are obligated to have personnel on duty who are trained to explain the meaning of various features in a consumer's file.

Should a consumer dispute the accuracy of an item in his or her credit report, the credit reporting agency is obligated to investigate. If investigation reveals that the disputed information is inaccurate or can no longer be verified, the agency must delete it from the consumer's file. If, after investigation, the agency still believes that the information is accurate, it must allow the consumer to append a statement justifying his or her view of the disputed matter to the consumer's file. This statement must then be supplied along with the consumer's file to requesters of the information.

The Fair Credit Reporting Act also imposes duties upon the users of consumer credit reports. Under the law, users include anyone who obtains a consumer report. Generally, a user who takes action on the basis of unfavorable information in a consumer report must disclose to the consumer the nature of the information and the name and address of the credit reporting agency from which it came. If the user has requested an investigative report, the user must inform the consumer of this and that the consumer has a right to be informed of the nature of the investigation upon request. However, if the investigative report was requested for purposes of determining the consumer's qualifications for employment that he or she did not seek, no disclosure need be made.

The act provides a **private right of action** for consumers to sue directly any credit reporting agency or user of a consumer report that violates its provisions. A successful consumer is entitled to **damages,** including any monetary losses resulting from the violation, as well as compensation for emotional distress. Punitive damages may also be available if the violation was intentional.

Criminal penalties are also prescribed under the Fair Credit Reporting Act for any employee of a credit reporting agency who knowingly provides information about consumers to someone who is not authorized by the act to receive it. Anyone who uses false pretenses to obtain a consumer report is also subject to criminal prosecution. It is not clear whether the act allows a consumer to sue these parties directly in a civil action.

The Fair Credit Reporting Act is also subject to administrative enforcement by the **Federal Trade Commission.**

Fair Debt Collection Practices Act   A federal law [15 U.S.C. §§1692–1692m] designed to restrict abusive or deceptive practices by debt collectors. Passed in 1977, the law was an attempt to remedy debt collection methods that compromised **consumer**s' privacy and contributed to job losses and familial instability.

The Fair Debt Collection Practices Act applies only to obligations stemming from the purchase of traditional **consumer product**s and services: that is, those meant for personal, family, or household purposes. The act also applies only to those who routinely collect debts for others. It does not apply to a **creditor,** or a creditor's employees, who are attempting to collect a debt owed directly to the creditor. The drafters of the law believed that the greatest possibility for abuse came from companies collecting bills for others, since they had no incentive to maintain goodwill with the delinquent consumers they were approaching for payment.

One of the main purposes of the Fair Debt Collection Practices Act is to prevent embarrassment to the consumer or harm to his or her reputation because of overdue bills. To this end, the law restricts what bill collectors may say to third parties about the consumer. First, a bill collector is allowed to speak to third parties only in order to locate the delinquent consumer. The bill collector must identify himself or herself to such third parties, but may not state the name of his or her employer unless requested. When speaking to a third party, the bill collector may say that he or she is attempting to verify information concerning the whereabouts of the consumer but may not state that the consumer owes any debt. The bill collector may not communicate with a third party regarding a consumer's whereabouts more than once unless the collector honestly feels that the third party can correct erroneous information.

However, a bill collector may communicate with the consumer's attorney regarding the consumer's affairs. In fact, the consumer may insist that the bill collector communicate solely with the consumer's attorney. In addition, a bill collector may report on the consumer's financial affairs to a genuine **credit reporting agency.** The consumer's spouse is not considered to be a third party, so a bill collector may also speak with the consumer's spouse about the debt.

Once the delinquent consumer has been located, the Fair Debt Collection Practices Act strictly controls the bill collector's communication with him or her. The bill collector may not communicate with the consumer at any time or place that is "inconvenient." Generally, this means that the bill collector may not call the consumer before 8 A.M. or after 9 P.M., and may not call or visit the consumer at his or her place of employment. Bill collectors may not communicate with the delinquent consumer by means of postcards or any stationery that identifies the bill collector's company or purpose as being to collect debts. A consumer may waive the right not to be approached by bill collectors at odd times and inconvenient places. However, the waiver must be expressly made by the consumer directly to the bill collector. Creditors may not slip waivers of this type into credit agreements and force consumers to sign away their rights to be free of inconvenient and harassing bill collecting tactics as a condition of receiving credit.

If the consumer informs the bill collector that he or she does not intend to pay the debt or wishes no further communication on the subject, the collector must cease trying to communicate with the consumer. However, the bill collector may inform the consumer that the creditor to whom the money is owed will seek a court judgment to collect the debt, if this is the case.

The act prohibits communications that amount to harassment or abuse. These include violence, or any threat of violence, to the person or property of the delinquent consumer or his or her family. The use of obscene or profane language directed at the consumer or his or her family is also prohibited, as is calling the consumer on the telephone incessantly. Generally, calling more than six times in one hour is considered harassment. In addition, a bill collector may not publicize the name of a delinquent consumer, either as part of a list of alleged credit "deadbeats" or in connection with advertising a debt for sale.

The Fair Debt Collection Practices Act outlaws false, deceptive, or misleading statements by bill collectors. A collector may not pretend to be a government or law enforcement official or to be affiliated with, or authorized by, any government agency. It is also illegal for the debt collector to mislead the consumer into believing that he or she is an attorney or is communicating on behalf of an attorney.

A bill collector is forbidden to mislead the consumer as to the character, amount, or legal status of the debt. For example, a bill collector may not neglect to tell a consumer that a **statute of limitations** has run on collecting the debt in question. The collector may not tell the consumer that he or she will be charged debt collection fees or any charges that are, in fact, illegal. It is forbidden for a bill collector to lead the consumer to believe that non-payment of the debt will result in the consumer's arrest or imprisonment, the garnishment of his or her wages, or the seizure of his or her property, unless these measures are really intended. This rule is to prevent so-called *flat rating*, which is the automatic sending of threats of legal action (such as arrest or garnishment) against the delinquent consumer when the creditor does not really intend to take such action.

Many other types of communications by bill collectors are forbidden by the Fair Debt Collection Practices Act. Some of these include:

- Telling the consumer that the debt will be sold or reassigned to an innocent third party and that the consumer will thereby lose any valid defenses against paying it. This result has been abolished in consumer transactions. See **holder-in-due-course doctrine.**

- Threatening to report false information about the consumer to consumer reporting agencies, including failure to report that a debt is disputed.

- Falsely stating that the consumer has committed a crime by failing to pay the debt.

- Using documents to collect the debt that give the false impression that they are approved or generated by a government agency, including fake summonses, writs, or other court documents.

- Giving the false impression that documents sent to the consumer do not have legal effect and need not be given a response. This is to prevent bill collectors from lulling consumers who have received notice of court proceedings against them into ignoring their right to appear and defend themselves. Failure to appear could result in a default judgment that would give the creditor the right to seize the consumer's property.

- Failing to tell the consumer that the purpose of a communication is to try to collect a debt.

- Using false pretenses to try to collect the debt. This includes giving false names or false business names when communicating with the consumer about a debt, or falsely stating that the bill collector is representing a credit reporting agency. Tricking the consumer into incurring other charges, like accepting collect telephone calls from bill collectors using false names, is also illegal.

- Collecting sums that are not in the original credit agreement or are not allowed by law. This includes trying to collect interest that amounts to **usury** under state law.

- Soliciting a postdated check from the consumer in order to threaten the consumer with criminal prosecution for writing bad checks unless the consumer pays the debt immediately. However, accepting a postdated check and depositing it after the date stated has come is not in itself illegal.

- Repossessing or threatening to repossess property in ways that violate state or federal laws. Generally, state laws allow creditors to engage in self-help methods of repossessing property from debtors who have defaulted on their obligations to pay. This means that midnight forays onto the debtor's property to take back property that has not been paid for may be perfectly legal. However, this depends on the laws of the state involved. Some state laws regulate how and when such self-help may be taken. Also, some property is exempt from seizure.

One of the most significant provisions of the Fair Debt Collection Practices Act is the requirement that a bill collector validate any debt that he or she is attempting to collect. Within five days after initially contacting the consumer concerning the collection of a debt, the debt collector must send the consumer a written notice with the following information:

- the amount of the debt;
- the name of the creditor to whom the debt is owed, including an offer to send the name of the original creditor to whom the debt was owed if this is different from the present creditor;
- notice that the debt collector will assume the debt is valid unless the consumer notifies the bill collector in writing that he or she disputes the validity of the debt;
- a statement that the bill collector will obtain a verification of the debt or a copy of a judgment against the consumer and forward it to the consumer for any debt that the consumer disputes.

A consumer who opts to pay debts that a bill collector is collecting has the right to allocate any amounts paid to a particular debt. The bill collector may not apply payment to any debt that the debtor disputes.

Under the Fair Debt Collection Practices Act, a consumer is entitled to a convenient judicial forum in which to settle a disputed debt. A creditor may not insist on a forum that is far away or inconvenient to the consumer in hopes of getting a default judgment because the consumer did not appear to defend himself or herself. Generally, a convenient forum will be in the place where the property that is the subject of the debt is located, where the credit agreement that created the debt was signed, or where the consumer lives.

A **private right of action** is available to any consumer who has been the victim of bill collecting practices outlawed by the Fair Debt Collection Practices Act. The consumer may recover actual **damages,** including compensation for mental distress, and fines of not over $1,000 in any individual suit. Court costs and attorney's fees may also be awarded to the successful litigant.

The act is generally administered by the **Federal Trade Commission,** and any violation of it is automatically also a violation of the **Federal Trade Commission Act.** Therefore, the Federal Trade Commission may take any administrative or judicial action against violators permitted under that law.

Fair Packaging and Labeling Act　A federal law [15 U.S.C. §1451 (1976 of Supp. V, 1981)] designed to aid **consumers** in making value comparisons among competing products by requiring accurate information as to the quantity of the contents on the labels of packaged goods. Passed in 1966, the Fair Packaging and Labeling Act is ad-ministered by the **Federal Trade Commission** and the **Food and Drug Administration.**

The law applies only to consumer commodities, or goods sold packaged in bulk that are intended for consumer use [see **consumer product**]. This includes **food** products. The administering agencies decide on a case-by-case basis which types of products are subject to the law. For those products that are covered, the law requires that each package bear a label specifying the name of the product, the name and place of business of the manufacturer or distributor, the net quantity of the contents, and an estimate of the number of servings or applications contained in the package. Quantities are expected to be described in commonly used units of measure, such as ounces or inches. Numerous detailed rules regulate the placement and size of this information on the package. Other regulations require the explanation of any value advertising on the package, such as "economy size" and "special offer" features on the label [see **deceptive pricing**].

The Fair Packaging and Labeling Act has been criticized for not going far enough towards facilitating easy comparative shopping. The law does not require standard package sizes or the price per unit of the product contained in the package. However, to remedy these deficiencies, numerous state laws require retail sellers to provide the unit price of goods, either on labels for the goods or on store shelves where the goods are displayed. See also **Nutrition Labeling and Education Act.**

FALSE ADVERTISING A general term given to any deceptive, misleading, or untruthful promotion by which a **seller** attempts to induce sales. There is no single law, federal or state, that regulates the practices sellers may use when advertising their products. Remedies available to **consumers** who have suffered loss or disappointment as a result of such unfair advertising practices will depend on the type of practice involved, as well as the type of product or service. The following lists some of the avenues through which advertising practices are regulated.

Common Law

Traditionally, the **common law** did not regulate advertising. Instead, the rule of *caveat emptor,* or "let the buyer beware," prevailed. The best the disappointed consumer could do prior to the twentieth century was sue the seller for the **tort** of **deceit.** However, to recover under this theory, the consumer must prove that the seller intended to deceive him or her. This is usually very difficult. Moreover, a number of traditional defenses to charges of deceit often prevent consumers from winning such cases.

As the twentieth century progressed, courts began to use the law of **warranty** more freely in order to afford protection to disappointed consumers. In particular, the statements made by sellers in their advertising have more often been construed as express warranties [see **express warranty**] rather than mere **puffery.** If the goods do not turn out to be as represented, the consumer may sue for breach of warranty. In addition, the tort of negligent **misrepresentation** gained acceptance. In this **action,** it is not necessary for the consumer to prove the seller's intent to deceive.

Statutory Law

The growing imbalance of power between large corporate sellers and individual consumers in the late nineteenth and early twentieth centuries led many states to adopt laws designed to regulate truth in advertising. Some of these were directed at particular industries or sellers. Others were directed at particular practices, such as **bait-and-switch advertising.**

Others, such as the **Printer's Ink Model Statute,** were general injunctions against all deceptive or misleading statements by sellers. Today, all states have some form of **unfair or deceptive acts or practices statute,** which outlaws various unfair commercial activities, including false advertising.

On the federal level, the **Federal Trade Commission** has broad powers under the **Federal Trade Commission Act** to prohibit unfair and deceptive practices in commerce on a nationwide scope. In particular, the Federal Trade Commission has been active in determining what advertising practices qualify as deceptive [see **deceptiveness**] and enforcing rules against them. In addition, the **Lanham Trademark Act** forbids sellers to make false statements as to the "characteristics or qualities" of their own or others' goods and services.

The drawback of much statutory law regulating advertising is that it is not designed to provide a remedy to consumers who have been mislead by false claims, but merely to stop the offending practices. Some state laws do, however, provide consumers with a **private right of action** to sue for violation of the statute and recover **damages.**

Self-Regulation

Generally, sellers recognize that the deceitful acts of a few can hurt business for all of them by turning consumers sour on a whole industry. For this reason, sellers themselves are often the most effective regulators of their own advertising practices. Through trade associations and general organizations such as the **Better Business Bureau,** sellers set their own guidelines for honesty in advertising and provide forums for consumers to bring complaints and resolve conflicts. Consumers who believe they have been mislead by advertising frequently find the swiftest resolution of their problems through mediation by one of these groups.

FEDERAL CIGARETTE LABELING AND ADVERTISING ACT
A federal law [15 U.S.C. §§1331–1340] passed in 1965 for the purpose of informing the public regarding the dangers of cigarettes. The immediate impetus for the act was a 1964 report issued by the U.S. Surgeon General's Advisory Committee on Smoking and Health that explicitly spelled out the medical evidence on the health effects of smoking.

Under the provisions of the original Federal Cigarette Labeling and Advertising Act, every package of cigarettes was to contain the warning "Caution: Cigarette Smoking May Be Hazardous to Your Health." In 1969, the act was amended to strengthen the warning. Thus, the warning that smoking "May Be Hazardous" was replaced with the words "Is Dangerous." The 1969 amendment also banned advertising in any medium of electronic communication that was subject to oversight by the Federal Communications Commission. This effectively proscribed any television or radio promotion of cigarettes.

While the warning provisions of the act were clear and easy to understand, another provision was not. One of the stated purposes of the act was to eliminate confusion caused by a multiplicity of labeling provisions passed by the states or promulgated by the **Federal Trade Commission.** This provision suggested that any state or local attempts to pass regulations about cigarette labeling were preempted [see **preemption**] by the federal law and would not be valid. In a lawsuit brought in 1982 and finally decided by the U.S. Supreme Court in 1992 [see *Cipollone v. Liggett Group, Inc.*], a smoker sued various tobacco companies for her terminal lung cancer allegedly caused by cigarettes. In their defense, the cigarette manufacturers seized on the language in the Federal Cigarette Labeling and Advertising Act that seemed to preempt state attempts to regulate cigarettes. Since the plaintiff sued under state law, the cigarette companies contended that she had no case since state laws about cigarettes were invalid. The Supreme Court disagreed, holding that only labeling laws passed by the states were preempted. Other laws, including **warranty** laws and actions such as **tort**s under the **common law,** were not preempted.

FEDERAL TRADE COMMISSION   The most significant federal agency regulating business practices in the United States for the protection of **consumers** and promotion of fair competition among **sellers**.

History and Organization

The Federal Trade Commission (FTC) was established as an independent federal agency in 1914 pursuant to the **Federal Trade Commission Act.** In a political climate where abusive practices by monopolistic corporate conglomerates were finally wearing on the patience of the public, the agency's first mandate was to enforce the provisions of the **antitrust laws**. This included the power generally to investigate and proscribe "unfair methods of competition" among businesses.

In 1938, an amendment to the Federal Trade Commission Act gave the FTC the power to define and proscribe any "unfair or deceptive acts or practices." This language has been interpreted to allow the agency to proscribe business practices that hurt consumers directly.

Today, the FTC is organized into two major divisions, reflecting its dual tasks of fostering competition among businesses and protecting consumers from abusive business practices. These divisions are the Bureau of Competition and the Bureau of Consumer Protection. In addition to enforcing the Federal Trade Commission Act, the FTC enforces numerous other consumer protection laws as well.

Activities

The major activities of the Federal Trade Commission include the following:

- preventing the use of deceptive [see **deceptiveness**] and **false advertising** to sell **consumer products** generally, with special emphasis on advertisements relating to **food, drugs, cosmetics,** and **medical devices**;
- regulating the packaging and labeling of certain consumer commodities under the **Fair Packaging and Labeling Act** in order to prevent consumer deception and facilitate value comparisons;
- investigating and stopping fraudulent telemarketing schemes;
- promoting accurate disclosure of credit costs as provided for in the **Truth in Lending Act**;

- preventing the fraudulent use of credit cards by promulgating rules regarding their issuance and use;
- protecting consumers from the circulation of inaccurate credit reports pursuant to the **Fair Credit Reporting Act,** the **Fair Debt Collection Practices Act,** and other federal legislation;
- educating consumers about fraudulent business practices and about their rights under the various consumer protection laws administered by the FTC; and
- stopping anti-competitive business practices and other unfair methods of competition among companies.

Enforcement

Generally, the FTC seeks voluntary compliance by businesses with the laws it administers. In order to encourage businesses to comply, the FTC issues specific guidelines or rules as to particular practices, which it makes available to the business community. The FTC also issues advisory opinions to businesses in response to their inquiries about the legality of various business practices. If businesses do not voluntarily comply with its rules, the FTC may institute formal legal proceedings against them that may result in the issuance of **injunction**s to stop violations and the imposition of fines to punish violators.

Most laws enforced by the FTC do not give consumers a **private right of action** to sue violators directly. An exception to this is the **Magnuson-Moss Warranty Act.** However, even though consumers may not sue directly in most cases, the FTC solicits complaints from individual consumers regarding unfair or deceptive business practices that they have encountered. If an investigation reveals that a complaint has merit, the FTC will initiate a proceeding to have the practice stopped. The individual consumer who has been a victim of such an unfair business practice must, however, pursue other avenues for compensation.

Issues

Over the years, the FTC has been alternately criticized for ineffectiveness and overzealousness. After being the target of criticism from consumer organizations in the late 1960s for lax enforcement and failing to stop business frauds perpetrated on the poor, the FTC moved into a period of activism in favor of consumers under the leadership of **Michael Pertschuk** [see **Pertschuk, Michael**] in the late 1970s. However, the pendulum swung towards less regulation in 1980 when the Federal Trade Commission Improvements Act imposed severe limitations on the agency's power to issue and enforce new rules and Pertschuk was replaced. In the 1990s, it appears that conservatives will continue to keep the FTC on a short leash with regard to issuing and enforcing regulations in both the consumer protection and business competition areas.

FEDERAL TRADE COMMISSION ACT   The major piece of federal legislation authorizing the federal government to regulate trade for the benefit of free competition and fairness to the **consumer.** The Federal Trade Commission Act [15 U.S.C. §§41–58] prohibits "unfair methods of competition" and "unfair or deceptive acts or practices" in or affecting commerce.

Passed in 1914, the main purpose of the Federal Trade Commission Act was to create an administrative agency, the **Federal Trade Commission** (FTC), to enforce the provisions of the **Clayton Antitrust Act,** which was passed the same year. The Clayton Act was designed to remedy shortcomings in the 1890 **Sherman Antitrust Act,** which was considered vague and had proved singularly ineffective in curtailing the consolidation of business entities into ever larger monopolistic units. The Clayton Act attempted to clarify which specific types of anti-competitive behavior by businesses were forbidden. The Federal Trade Commission Act authorized the FTC to aid the Justice Department in prosecuting businesses engaged in these activities and to investigate and define other activities that might constitute "unfair methods of competition."

Despite the mandate for reform, the Federal Trade Commission Act was interpreted very strictly in the years following its passage. Essentially, the FTC could enjoin only those practices that fit traditional definitions of monopolistic practices enumerated in the Clayton Act. It was not until 1934 that the U.S. Supreme Court recognized the FTC's authority to proscribe and enjoin other behavior by businesses that fit the agency's own definition of "deceptive and unfair." Since that time, the act has been interpreted to allow the FTC broad discretion in defining and outlawing business practices that it determines are harmful to competition in a free enterprise system.

Consumer Protection Provisions

In 1938, the Federal Trade Commission Act was amended to permit the FTC to enter the field of direct consumer protection. Prior to this point, benefits to consumers deriving from the FTC's activities were indirect only, in the sense that consumers would be best served when competition between commercial enterprises is fostered. The Wheeler-Lea Act, as this amendment is known, added a prohibition on "unfair or deceptive acts or practices" by businesses. This provision has been interpreted by courts and state legislatures to outlaw practices that directly harm consumers, not just business competitors.

The substantive provisions (as opposed to merely administrative provisions) of the Federal Trade Commission Act are contained in its famous "Section 5." Within this section are the proscriptions on unfair and deceptive practices that have launched the federal government into the consumer protection business. Quite deliberately, these proscriptions have been left vague. It is up to the Federal Trade Commission to determine exactly what business conduct is unfair and/or deceptive. Moreover, a business activity need not be shown to deceive consumers or injure competition before the FTC can act to outlaw it. The mere likelihood that consumers will be harmed is enough to declare a business practice in violation of the Federal Trade Commission Act.

Until 1972, the FTC operated on the assumption that business activity had to be deceptive or anti-competitive in order also to be "unfair." The Supreme Court opinion in *FTC v. Sperry & Hutchinson Company* changed this by ruling that the FTC could also outlaw practices that were neither deceptive nor harmful to competition, but simply contrary to some notion of the public interest. For example, advertising aimed at children that contains no misrepresentations and does not hurt competitors might still be found "unfair" because it takes advantage of the suggestibility of the very young.

In the years since adoption of the Wheeler-Lea amendment, the Federal Trade Commission Act has been amended many more times to allow the FTC more authority over business practices in specific industries. Today, there is hardly a sector of the economy that is not subject to regulation by the FTC for the benefit of consumers. In addition, successive amendments have given the FTC more power to enforce its regulations, including the power to seek injunctions in federal court against unfair activities and to impose fines on violators.

Generally, the Federal Trade Commission Act and its amendments do not provide consumers with a **private right of action.** In other words, violations of the act may be enforced only by the FTC. An exception to this rule is the **Magnuson-Moss Warranty Act,** which was added as an amendment to the Federal Trade Commission Act in 1975. Under this amendment, consumers may sue directly for violations of federal rules regarding warranties for consumer goods [see **warranty**].

Since the 1980s, there has been a trend towards restricting the powers of the FTC as the political pendulum has swung from a belief in government regulation for the benefit of consumers towards a free market approach. Nevertheless, the role of the FTC as the major government player in the consumer protection arena has been too well established in American law to be too much diminished by the vicissitudes of politics. Moreover, the Federal Trade Commission Act has served as a model for many state **unfair or deceptive acts or practices statute**s that are vital to protecting consumer interests at the state level.

FLAMMABLE FABRICS ACT   Federal legislation [15 U.S.C. §§1191–1204] first adopted in 1953 that is designed to improve the safety of fabrics used by **consumer**s for clothing, bedding, and other intimate uses. As with many consumer safety laws, passage occurred only after several well publicized tragedies in which consumers—particularly children—were seriously or fatally burned when their clothing caught fire. Also, the development of new synthetic fibers with unknown properties after World War II underscored the need for some standards for fabrics intended for consumer use.

The Flammable Fabrics Act is administered by the **Consumer Product Safety Commission.** The commission, upon the advice of a nine-member panel composed of manufacturers, distributors, and consumers, promulgates standards regarding the flammability of fabrics intended for consumer use. Generally, flammability refers to how quickly a fabric will catch fire upon being subjected to a source of ignition and how swiftly the fire will spread throughout the fabric. Because virtually all fabric will burn if exposed to sufficient heat, the standards are not designed to eliminate the danger of fire entirely. However, they are designed to prohibit the use of fabrics that catch fire unusually quickly, spread unusually quickly, burn with an intense heat, or are difficult to extinguish. The Consumer Product Safety Commission is charged with testing the fabrics for these properties. Fabrics that do not conform to the standards are prohibited from sale in interstate commerce for use as clothing, bedding, or other intimate uses. The Flammable Fabrics Act presently is concerned with burn injuries caused by the ignition of fabric. Injuries caused by toxic fumes that are released by the burning of fabrics are the purview of the **Hazardous Substances Act,** also administered by the Consumer Product Safety Commission.

Standards promulgated under the Flammable Fabrics Act preempt [see **preemption**] any state laws that are designed to protect against the same danger of fire. The Flammable Fabrics Act does not provide for a **private right of action** against the **seller** of a fabric that does not conform to the standards. However, the fact that a fabric that caught fire and caused injury did conform to the federal standards does not preclude the injured consumer from suing the manufacturer for **negligence** or **strict tort liability** under state **common law.** A jury may well find that the federal standards create only a minimum level of safety, and that the special circumstances of the case require a higher **standard of care** from manufacturers or a less dangerous product.

FOOD   Any substance consumed primarily for nutritive value or for taste or aroma. Today, national standards for food purity and safety are set by the **Food and Drug Administration** (FDA). Regulation of the sale of foods and beverages occurs mainly in two areas: safety and economic fairness.

By far the most active area of regulation is food safety. The FDA sets standards for sanitation in food processing and is empowered to inspect foods for bacteria or filth that might cause disease if ingested. Offending processors may be closed down.

Perhaps more importantly, the FDA sets tolerances for a wide variety of contaminants that may exist in food products and that may be harmful if ingested. These include naturally occurring toxins, pesticide residues, chemicals added incidentally during processing, and substances that are deliberately introduced into food products in order to preserve freshness or improve taste or visual appeal. These last types of substances are known as *food additives.* Unless they are **generally recognized as safe,** they must go through a rigorous approval process in which the food manufacturer desiring to use them must prove that they are safe for human consumption.

In the area of economic fairness, the FDA dictates the type of information that must appear on the labels of food products in order to ensure that the **consumer** knows what he or she is buying. This includes ensuring that the name of the product is descriptive of its contents, that contents are listed, that weight and volume are accurately stated, and that correct nutritional data are included. Any health claims included on a product's label must be corroborated by scientific research. Economic **adulteration** is forbidden. See also **misbranding.**

The FDA is empowered to enforce its rules through confiscation of unsafe food products, injunctions on the distribution or sale of food, and criminal sanctions on offending food sellers. Individual **consumer**s, however, do not have a **private right of action** under the **Food, Drug & Cosmetic Act.** Consumers who have been injured by harmful objects or deleterious substances in food products must seek other forms of redress.

Consumer Remedies for Harmful Food Products

Consumers who have been injured by ingesting a harmful food product have several remedies available to them under the **common law.** They may sue the seller of the food for **negligence** in its preparation, packaging, or sale. A suit for breach of **warranty** may also be appropriate, particularly breach of the **implied warranty of merchantability.** In addition, a suit based on **strict tort liability** may be possible.

Unresolved Issues in Food Product Safety

In the years following passage of the Food, Drug & Cosmetic Act, food safety in the United States has improved dramatically. The United States today may enjoy the safest food supply in the world. Nevertheless, the drive to exploit new methods of food production has also spurred the development of more artificial foods and beverages. The safety of synthetic foods, genetically engineered produce, and irradiation as a preservative technique are likely to be continuing issues in the law of consumer protection.

FOOD AND DRUG ADMINISTRATION   The federal agency responsible for enforcing federal laws that regulate **food**s, **drug**s, **medical device**s, **cosmetic**s, and certain other **consumer products** that are sold in interstate commerce.

History

The forerunner of the Food and Drug Administration (FDA) was created in 1906 when Congress passed the Pure Food and Drug Act. At that time the public was reeling from disclosures of tainted foods and fraudulent patent cures that were purveyed with shameless zeal all over the country. Instrumental in disclosing widespread fraud and the presence of untested additives in food was Dr. Harvey Wiley [**Wiley, Harvey**], head of the Bureau of Chemistry at the Department of Agriculture. Wiley was instrumental in lobbying for the 1906 act and his agency was given the task of enforcing it when it passed. Later the Bureau of Chemistry was renamed the Food, Drug and Insecticide Administration. In 1931, the name was shortened to the Food and Drug Administration. Today, the FDA is part of the Department of Health and Human Services.

Activities

The major law that is enforced by the FDA is the **Food, Drug & Cosmetic Act.** Passed in 1938, it replaced and supplemented the provisions of the 1906 Pure Food and Drug Act. The act gives the FDA broad powers to regulate the sale of food, drugs, medical devices, and cosmetics.

To this end, the FDA sets standards for purity in food products, including designating tolerance levels for pesticides, additives, and colorings. It oversees inspections of these products and has the power to prevent their sale if they are adulterated or misbranded [see **adulteration; midsbranding**]. The FDA may also set and enforce sanitary standards for facilities that manufacture, store, or sell food products. The agency may also prohibit the importation of food products from other countries that do not meet its standards. The FDA is also in charge of regulating the content of labels and information accompanying food products to ensure that lists of ingredients are accurate and that no unproved health claims are made. Regulation of food advertising, however, comes under the jurisdiction of the **Federal Trade Commission.** Areas of future active concern for the FDA in food regulation are likely to involve the use of irradiation to improve the shelf life of agricultural products and the use of genetic engineering to improve the abundance or quality of food products.

The Food and Drug Administration has the broadest powers to regulate drugs and medical devices, including the power to grant initial approval for their sale. The power to approve or reject a product prior to its entry on the market is unique among federal agencies, and is evidence of the extreme importance and extreme risks that drugs and other medical products entail for the public. All new drugs must be approved for sale by the Food and Drug Administration after the results of extensive testing and laboratory research are presented concerning their safety and efficacy. The burden of proving a drug safe and effective rests with the drug company rather than the agency. However, the FDA conducts extensive research of its own to substantiate claims and set standards for efficacy. After a drug has been approved for sale, the FDA continues to monitor its quality, efficacy, and safety. The agency may set standards relating to a drug's content and the processes by which it is manufactured. The agency may also determine what warnings and instructions must be included on the labels and packaging of drug products. It regulates prescription drug advertising to ensure accuracy. In addition, the FDA assigns generic names to new drugs that must be placed on product labels so that the public is aware of the true identity of trademarked drug products. The FDA also has authority over drugs for animals, including feeds for animals that contain drugs. Similarly, the agency approves the sale of medical devices and may set standards for their efficacy.

The FDA may revoke its approval of a new drug or medical device if it is later proven to be unsafe or if the original application for approval was inaccurate.

In recent years, the FDA has been criticized for its failure to streamline the new drug approval process, or as an alternative, to relax proscriptionss on the use of some experimental drugs for use by patients whose conditions are terminal. In particular, the pressure to find a cure for AIDS has nudged the FDA into relaxing certain standards for the use of experimental drugs on AIDS patients.

The FDA is also empowered to regulate the sale of cosmetics. However, perhaps because the dangers associated with cosmetic products are generally less serious than those associated with the other products within its jurisdiction, the agency has been relatively inactive in this area.

Among the many other laws enforced by the FDA is the Radiation Control for Health and Safety Act. Under this act, the FDA is empowered to set standards for the emission of radiation from electronic products. This includes various types of electromagnetic radiation as well as sonic vibrations that may be emitted from products as diverse as televisions, microwave ovens, electronic oscillators, and computers. Because of the increasing dependence of modern life on electronic devices of all sorts, it is likely that this area of FDA regulation will increase in activity in the years to come. Of particular concern for the agency is likely to be continuing research into the effects of magnetic fields generated by electric currents on human beings.

Procedures

The process under which regulations are issued by the FDA begins with a proposal for a rule, which may come from staff members, industry representatives, or the general public. After internal investigation and development, a proposed rule will be published in the *Federal Register*, a government publication. Reaction is then solicited from the public. After a certain period allowed for comment, the FDA will make a final draft of the rule. In some cases it may hold a formal hearing to consider the pros and cons of the rule. After the final version of the rule is published, at least another 30 days is allowed to elapse before enforcement of the rule may begin.

In order to enforce its rules, the Food and Drug Administration may seize products that violate its regulations, issue **injunction**s against the further sale of such products, take violators to court and obtain fines from them for contempt, and even institute criminal actions against violators that may result in prison terms for individual company representatives. In some cases, the agency may obtain an order from a court for the recall of a product that has been found to violate the agency's regulations.

The Food and Drug Administration welcomes the interest of the individual **consumer** in the affairs of the agency. The agency has 21 district offices within six regions around the country at which consumers may obtain information or file complaints. However, the FDA is not empowered to aid individuals in gaining redress of particular grievances. The agency is more concerned with using individual consumer complaints as a first step towards enforcing existing rules or creating new rules to prevent the specific type of abuse reported from occurring to others.

FOOD, DRUG & COSMETIC ACT   Federal legislation [21 U.S.C. §§301–392] designed to protect **consumer**s from harmful, unhealthy, or deceptively marketed **food, drug**s, **cosmetic**s, and **medical device**s.

The Food, Drug & Cosmetic Act was passed in 1938. It replaced and supplemented the provisions of the Pure Food and Drug Act of 1906. The 1906 law was hailed as a social landmark, being the first attempt by the federal government to regulate abuses in the trade of food and drugs. However, by 1938 it was clear that there were serious flaws in the administrative and enforcement mechanisms of the old act. Some have argued that its actual effect was to diminish the quality of both food and drugs and to leave the agency charged with its enforcement with little power. An incident in 1937 in which over 100 persons died from taking an untested patent drug shocked the nation by revealing the impotency of the act to protect the nation from harmful substances sold as medicines [see **sulfanilamide tragedy**]. Opposition to the Food, Drug & Cosmetic Act, then pending in Congress, was swept away.

The new Food, Drug & Cosmetic Act added important rule-making and enforcement provisions to the powers of the federal government to regulate the sale of the goods within its purview. The definition of **adulteration** was expanded. The power to obtain **injunction**s against the sale of goods found to violate agency rules was granted to the government for the first time. Cosmetics and medical devices were added to the list of products subject to government regulation. Also, the government was given veto power over the marketing of new drugs, although it could not require proof of their safety or efficacy.

Over the years, the Food, Drug & Cosmetic Act has been amended several times. The most important amendments were the Pesticide Chemicals Amendment (1954), which empowered the government to set tolerance levels in foods for various pesticide residues; the Food Additive and Color Additive Amendments (1958), which brought into the regulatory scheme various chemicals added to food for purposes other than nutrition; the New Drug Amendments (1962), which required that all new drugs be proved safe and effective before they could be marketed; and the Medical Devices Amendment (1976), which increased the federal government's oversight of medical devices and subjected certain types to the same requirements of presale approval as drug products.

Today, the Food, Drug & Cosmetic Act is administered by the **Food and Drug Administration** (FDA), an agency within the Department of Health and Human Services. The act itself is relatively general in scope. It states which products are subject to regulation and which types of deceptive or dangerous practices with respect to selling them are prohibited. However, it does not define these with specificity. It is up to the FDA to make very detailed rules about what is and is not allowed in the marketing and sale of products within the act's scope. The FDA also is empowered to enforce its own rules and standards. The Food, Drug & Cosmetic Act does not provide a **private right of action** to individual consumers; a consumer may not privately sue the seller of a food or drug for violations of the act or to enforce the act. Only the FDA may do that. However, a consumer may generally use FDA standards as evidence in a civil trial against the seller of such products to show that the seller or manufacturer was negligent, was guilty of **fraud,** or that the product was unreasonably dangerous.

FOREIGN-NATURAL TEST   A test employed by courts to determine whether substances or objects found in food or beverages are defects [see **defectiveness**] and, hence, whether compensation must be paid to **consumer**s who are injured by them.

Basically, the rule holds that if an object or substance is one that might normally be found in the food or beverage it is not a defect. Food sellers are not required absolutely to ensure the safety of their products. Even with the most careful methods, some inedible items will slip by in the food manufacturing process. For example, a cherry pit would normally be expected to surface from time to time in a cherry pie. Thus, even though a consumer might break a tooth on it, the cherry pit would not legally be considered a defect in the pie. Similarly, an occasional chicken bone in chicken soup or fragment of clamshell in clam chowder are simply risks that the diner must accept.

By contrast, an open safety pin in a piece of cherry pie is not something that a consumer would normally expect to encounter. The pin is entirely foreign to the pie. It would, therefore, be a defect in the pie and the injured consumer may receive compensation for it.

These examples of foreign and natural objects are quite obvious. However, sometimes the status of a substance or object in a food or beverage is unclear. For example, fish bones are to be expected in fish. But, what of a bone in a fish fillet? By definition, a fillet of fish is supposed to be boneless. Is the bone, therefore, a foreign object? Or, what about a plastic decoration on a frosted birthday cake? Clearly, plastic is not normally a component of birthday cakes. However, plastic decorations are frequently used on such cakes and the normal consumer surely has come to expect them.

Because of these ambiguities, the foreign–natural test for determining defects in food products is falling out of favor. In its place, courts often use the **consumer expectation test.** This test makes the determination of whether foods or beverages are defective dependent on whether a reasonable consumer would expect occasionally to find a particular object or substance in the product. In the cake decoration case, for example, the clearly foreign plastic object might not be a defect because a reasonable consumer would expect to find it there. On the other hand, the bone in a fish fillet, though natural to fish, may be a defect because a consumer who buys a fillet expects it to be boneless.

FORESEEABILITY The quality of being predictable by average human beings. Foreseeability underpins the legal principle that one should only be required to compensate others for harm that is the *foreseeable* result of one's actions. The foreseeability of harm plays a major role in **tort** cases, both in defining the existence and scope of a duty to be careful [see **duty of care; standard of care**] and in determining when a particular action has caused harm [see **proximate cause**].

Foreseeability affects **consumers** involved in **products liability** lawsuits brought to determine whether the **seller** of a product will be required to pay for harm caused by it. In **negligence** cases, the seller of a defective product will only be required to compensate an injured consumer for harm if the risk of that type of harm happening because of the product was foreseeable—or to be expected—when the product was sold. For example, it is reasonable to expect that consumers might accidentally cut themselves with a chain saw that is not equipped with a safety guard. The seller of such a saw would probably be required to compensate consumers for cuts caused by the product, because such injuries are foreseeable. On the other hand, the seller would probably not be required to compensate a consumer who was injured because the lack of a safety guard allowed water to contact the chain when the saw was left outside in the rain, resulting in rust that weakened the chain and caused it to break. Such an injury is probably not the foreseeable consequence of failing to supply a safety guard with the saw.

Deciding what is or is not foreseeable generally depends on how judges or juries believe that an average, reasonable person [see **reasonable person test**] would think in a situation like the one they are considering. If an average, reasonable person would be likely to foresee the danger of harm occurring from particular conduct, the harm is foreseeable and, hence, compensable.

Generally, it is not necessary to be able to predict exactly what the consequences of particular behavior will be in order for harm to be foreseeable under the law. In a case involving a caustic paint product, for example, the paint manufacturer claimed that it was not liable for a boy's blindness because it could not have foreseen that the boy would run into the dripping paintbrush his father was holding. The court disagreed. It was not necessary for the manufacturer to foresee exactly how paint might get into a consumer's eyes to be liable for the injury, the court said. Rather, it was enough to be able to imagine that the paint might somehow come in contact with a consumer's eyes—something that was quite possible and could have been predicted. The paint company was found liable for the boy's injuries.

See also **misuse; strict tort liability.**

 FRAUD　A general term for any deliberate deception practiced in order to achieve unfair gain.

The use of the term *fraud* is so all-pervasive today to describe unlawful or unfair schemes of deception of all sorts that it has virtually lost any technical legal meaning. However, it is perhaps most frequently used to refer to the ancient **tort** of **deceit,** which involves deception by deliberate false representations made with the intention of inducing one to act in **reliance** on them. Often the terms *fraud and deceit* or *fraudulent* **misrepresentation** are used to describe this wrong. See also **nondisclosure.**

FTC v. Sperry & Hutchinson Company   The Supreme Court case *FTC v. Sperry & Hutchinson Company* [405 U.S. 233 (1972)] first recognized the power of the **Federal Trade Commission** (FTC) to declare certain business practices illegal merely because they were "unfair" under criteria set by the commission itself. Prior to this time, courts had interpreted the word *unfair* in the **Federal Trade Commission Act**'s prohibition against "deceptive or unfair practices" to mean only those practices that were deceptive or had already been declared a violation of **antitrust law** by the U.S. Supreme Court.

Sperry & Hutchinson (S & H) was the largest of many companies that sold trading stamps to various retail **sellers** for distribution to **consumers** upon purchase of the sellers' goods. The stamps were redeemable for merchandise at S & H stores. S & H made money largely because not all the stamps given away were redeemed. Sellers who distributed the stamps with sale of their goods justified the price they paid for the stamps by the increased sales that the stamps attracted. Moreover, many sellers raised their prices slightly overall in order to pass the cost of the stamps on to the consumers. Over time, independent dealers in trading stamps began to appear. They bought stamps from consumers who had collected them and sold them to other consumers who needed them to amass sufficient numbers for redemption. For a small fee, they also facilitated trades between consumers who wanted to swap the stamps of one company for those of another. The S & H company tried to stop the independent dealers by a series of lawsuits. S & H claimed that allowing independent dealers to buy and sell the stamps would reduce the incentive for consumers to visit the retail stores that gave the stamps away. These retail stores would then have no incentive to buy the stamps from S & H. This would put S & H out of business.

Conversely, the FTC believed that independent dealers in trading stamps should be allowed to continue their business. According to the FTC, by helping consumers acquire enough stamps to redeem for merchandise, the independent dealers ensured that consumers could get their full money's worth from purchases made where stamps were given away. Moreover, allowing independent dealing in the stamps would promote price and quality competition among the companies that issued the stamps. The FTC declared the effort by S & H to put the independent dealers out of business to be "unfair" and illegal because it was not in the best interest of consumers. However, there was no evidence that S & H's practice was deceptive. Nor did it violate any antitrust laws. S & H challenged the FTC ruling as being beyond the agency's powers. The fight went all the way to the Supreme Court.

The Supreme Court sided with the FTC, finding that the FTC may declare any practice unfair and illegal if the agency decides the practice offends public policy, is unethical, or causes substantial injury to consumers or competitors. This decision is important to consumers because it significantly expanded the powers of the FTC to act in their interests. By giving the agency the flexibility to ban new practices without having to fit them into established molds of illegal conduct, the FTC can quickly minimize the detriment such practices cause to consumers.

Some examples of the FTC's use of the so-called "unfairness doctrine" announced in the *Sperry* case were the abolishment of the **holder-in-due-course doctrine** in consumer transactions and the banning of **creditors'** suits in forums that are inconvenient for consumers.

FURNESS, ELIZABETH MARY (BETTY) (1916–1994)   Actress, television personality, and industry spokeswoman turned **consumer** activist. Furness's most conspicuous service to the consumer protection movement occurred when she served as Special Assistant to the President for Consumer Affairs under President Lyndon Johnson from 1967 to 1968.

Born in New York City in 1916, Furness's first job was for a modeling agency. In the 1930s, she moved to Hollywood and landed roles in some 35 movies, most of them forgettable. After a similarly undistinguished stint on the stage, Furness returned to New York where the infant television industry was waiting to make her a star.

A distinctive vocal quality, a good memory, and wholesome good looks helped Furness land the role for which she was indelibly imprinted in the minds of a whole generation of American consumers: the "Westinghouse Girl." Beginning in 1949 for nearly 12 years Betty Furness demonstrated Westinghouse products in television commercials. In an age when women's careers were restricted to teaching or nursing, a woman of less mind might have been content to bask in her celebrity and collect her $100,000 yearly salary—one of the highest in the industry at the time. However, partly as a result of Westinghouse's sponsorship of the national political conventions in the late 1950s, Furness had become interested in politics and public affairs. She accepted a **contract** as moderator of a daily television panel show that featured experts from various fields responding to questions from viewers. For the first time audiences were treated to the quick, alert, and probing mind behind the glamorous TV presence. A critical and popular success, the show established Furness as a capable professional with a point of view and a command of the facts to back it up.

In 1963, Furness left television to pursue political interests and became a tireless and effective campaigner for Democratic candidates. In February 1967, her loyal work was rewarded. She was appointed by President Johnson to be Special Assistant for Consumer Affairs. The Furness appointment was initially greeted with skepticism from mainstream consumer protection groups. Inexperienced in consumer matters, Furness herself confessed that she never even did her own shopping. Some critics saw in the appointment of a television celebrity a suggestion that the administration did not take consumer affairs seriously. After a shaky start, Furness proved herself to be an opinionated, informed, and able spokeswoman for the administration on consumer matters. A quick study, she testified convincingly before investigatory hearings on proposed legislation for flammable fabrics, truth in lending bills, prohibition of unsolicited **credit cards**, and mandatory federal meat inspection. By late 1967, consumer activists and legislators alike were praising her work.

After leaving her federal post in 1968, Furness continued to be active in consumer affairs. She served as the head of the New York State Consumer Protection Board in 1970–1971, and New York City's Department of Consumer Affairs in 1973. She appeared as a consumer affairs expert on NBC's *Today Show* for 16 years until 1992, and served on the board of **Consumers Union.**

GARNISHMENT A legal procedure whereby a **consumer**'s earnings may be withheld in order to pay off a debt. Typically, the consumer's employer is ordered to deduct a specific amount from the consumer's wages and pay it to the consumer's **creditor.**

Federal law regulates the amount of a consumer's wages that may be garnished and prohibits employers from dismissing employees who are subject to garnishment orders. This law is important both to prevent predatory creditors from virtually enslaving consumers who get themselves too deeply in debt and to protect consumers from discharge because of a garnishment order, resulting in deeper financial woes.

Generally, the federal law provides that a garnishment to repay a consumer debt may not exceed 25 percent of a consumer's disposable earnings per week, or it may not exceed the amount by which the consumer's disposable earnings for a week exceed 30 times the minimum hourly wage. These limits apply to all debts combined. Once the limit is reached, no more garnishment orders may be executed. The law applies only to garnishment to repay consumer debts. Garnishment orders designed to collect child support or alimony, or state and federal taxes, are not subject to these limits. Employees of the federal government are not subject to garnishment at all.

The most significant feature of the **Consumer Credit Protection Act**'s regulation of garnishment is the prohibition of discharge for having one's wages garnished for any one indebtedness. Dismissal of the affected employee used to be a standard reaction of employers to garnishment orders. Perhaps employers perceived that an employee subject to garnishment would lose incentive to work, or they were reluctant to become entangled in nasty legal procedures from which they could derive no benefit. However, employers may discharge an employee if a second garnishment order is received and the first order has not already reached the maximum amount allowed to be taken from the employee's wages.

The federal restrictions on garnishment are administered by the federal Department of Labor. Violators are subject to a fine of $1,000 and/or imprisonment for up to one year. The federal law does not specifically grant a

private right of action to consumers who have been the victims of violations of the garnishment law. However, courts in a number of states have interpreted the law to allow such private suits.

GENERALLY RECOGNIZED AS SAFE A special term given by the **Food and Drug Administration** to substances that have been established by custom, long usage, or scientific research to be safe for human consumption under specific conditions and in specific amounts. These substances may be added to food products without undergoing the rigorous testing for safety required of each new chemical proposed as a food additive. Generally recognized as safe (GRAS) substances include common spices, natural flavorings and seasonings, essential oils, common synthetic flavorings, chemical preservatives, nutrients, anticaking agents, coatings, gums, stabilizers, and dietary supplements.

Today, approximately 200 substances fall into the GRAS category. Some substances are placed on the list on an interim basis until more information can be gathered as to their possible health risks. An example of an interim GRAS substance is caffeine when used as an additive in soft drinks. Occasionally, new information may be brought to light casting doubt on the safety of a substance that has already achieved GRAS status. In such a case, the substance may "fall from GRAS" and be removed from the Food and Drug Administration's list. An example of such a substance is the artificial sweetener, cyclamate.

Sellers of food products frequently request that the Food and Drug Administration declare that a substance is generally recognized as safe, because this saves them the great expense of having to prove the safety of a substance every time they want to incorporate it into a new food product.

GREEN SEAL A testing and endorsement organization dedicated to the goal of environmental protection through the promotion of environmentally benign **consumer products**. Founded in 1990, Green Seal represents a step beyond traditional **consumer** organizations, with their primary emphasis on the personal safety and satisfaction of individual, ultimate consumers. Instead, Green Seal is concerned with the wider effects of the product on the environment for all consumers.

The idea of promoting products made with "favored" manufacturing methods is not new. In 1899, the first American group to style itself a consumer organization, the **National Consumers League,** urged citizens to buy goods made by companies with fair labor policies. In many respects the mirror image of a **consumer boycott,** this tactic entails less risk of infringing on the rights of **sellers** because of the emphasis on praise of products that meet certain standards rather than disparagement of those that do not.

Essentially, manufacturers and sellers pay Green Seal a fee to be examined by the organization for compliance with its product standards. The standards are developed by Green Seal in conjunction with **Underwriters Laboratories Inc.,** a nonprofit product testing company, to discover the least environmentally damaging products in various categories. Every aspect of a product's existence is taken into account—including the effects on the environment of its manufacture, its use, and its ultimate disposal. If a product meets the standards, the seller is permitted to display Green Seal's logo on its packaging. This is a signal to consumers concerned with environmental degradation not only that their use of the products will cause as little harm as possible, but also that they are rewarding the sellers of benign products with their patronage. Theoretically, as more companies see the commercial advantages of an endorsement by Green Seal, they will alter their products in order to comply. Green Seal also provides a special endorsement for those sellers who, in turn, strive to procure their raw materials from sellers engaged in environmentally benign manufacturing.

As of 1994, Green Seal had established standards for some 20 products, with a major emphasis on improving energy efficiency, preventing toxic chemical pollution, protecting air quality, wildlife, and wilderness areas, and mitigating the effects on global warming of product manufacture.

Green Seal is a nonprofit organization funded primarily by the fees paid by sellers for testing and certification. Donations from foundations and individuals make up the remainder. Pledged to independence, Green Seal has no financial interest in the success or failure of any particular product. It is governed by a board of directors composed of representatives of business and major consumer and environmental organizations. It is based in Washington, D.C.

GREENMAN V. YUBA POWER PRODUCTS INC. A landmark case that recognized the doctrine of **strict tort liability** as an avenue of recovery for **consumers** who have suffered injury or loss as a result of defective [see **defectiveness**] products. Although strict tort liability was known in ancient times, *Greenman v. Yuba Power Products Inc.* [59 Cal. 2d 57, 377 P.2d 897, 27 Cal. Rptr. 697 (1962)], decided in 1962, was the first modern case in which the doctrine was explicitly reintroduced into American jurisprudence.

The plaintiff in *Greenman* was injured when a piece of wood he was turning in his lathe flew out and hit him in the head. He sued the manufacturer of the lathe for breach of **warranty,** stating that he had relied [see **reliance**] on statements made in the manufacturer's brochure that the lathe was designed to hold wood securely. A jury found in favor of the plaintiff. However, the manufacturer appealed the decision on the grounds that the plaintiff failed to give it notice that the warranty had been breached—a requirement for recovery in any warranty case [see **notice in warranty**].

The court first noted that the notice requirement for warranty lawsuits was a "booby trap" for unwary consumers who, having bought a product from a retailer, have no idea that it is also necessary to notify the distant manufacturer when the warranty is breached. Recovery for personal injuries suffered by consumers should not depend on the intricate rules of warranty lawsuits, said the court. It then proceeded to apply the new rule of strict tort liability to the case, stating:

> A manufacturer is strictly liable in tort when an article he places on the market, knowing that it is to be used without inspection for defects, proves to have a defect that causes injury to a human being. [*Greenman v. Yuba Power Products, Inc.*, 377 P.2d at 900]

In the years since *Greenman,* the doctrine of strict tort liability has been increasingly used by consumers seeking compensation for personal injuries in **products liability** cases. See also **negligence.**

GRIMSHAW V. FORD MOTOR COMPANY The most prominent of a number of lawsuits brought against the Ford Motor Company in the 1970s and 1980s alleging a **design defect** in the placement of the fuel tank in Ford's small subcompact Pinto automobile. Decided in 1981, *Grimshaw v. Ford Motor Company* [119 Cal. App. 3d 757, 174 Cal. Rptr. 348 (1981)] is noteworthy for its allowance of punitive **damages** against Ford based on a finding that Ford's marketing of the car with knowledge of the danger posed by the placement of the fuel tank was reprehensible.

Punitive damages, as the name implies, are monetary payments exacted from a losing defendant in a lawsuit in order to punish him or her for the behavior that led to the suit. Prior to 1976, awards of punitive damages in **products liability** cases were very few and the amounts of the awards were small. Many courts took the view that punitive damages were not allowed at all in cases based on the theory of **strict tort liability.** Theoretically, the conduct of the defendant in such cases is not supposed to be an issue. Rather, only the condition of the product that caused injury is relevant. Nevertheless, many courts recognized even in strict liability cases that the behavior of some **sellers** in putting unsafe products on the market was so unethical that it should be deterred by any means available. Large punitive damage awards could provide such a deterrent.

In *Grimshaw*, the 13-year-old plaintiff was riding with an adult companion in a Pinto automobile on a highway in California. The car stalled suddenly in a lane of traffic and an automobile traveling behind it was unable to stop in time to avoid hitting the Pinto in the rear. Upon impact, the Pinto burst into flames and the car's occupants were badly burned before it had even come to a stop. The adult driver died of her injuries and young Grimshaw suffered severe, permanent, debilitating, and disfiguring burns. The surviving family members of the driver and Grimshaw sued Ford Motor Company.

At trial a jury found that the automobile was defective [see **defectiveness**] because its gas tank was especially vulnerable to collapse and puncture due to its position behind the rear axle, and the lack of other safety features such as an interior "bladder" in the tank or reinforcement of the car's bumpers. In addition to the car's defectiveness, the evidence in the case revealed that persons in authority at the highest levels of Ford had known of the dangers posed by the Pinto's fuel tank design. The automobile had consistently failed Ford's own crash tests, and the crash results were alarmingly like the real-life accident in which the plaintiff was burned. Moreover, the evidence showed that, for as little as $100 per vehicle, the fuel tank assembly could be completely redesigned or fitted with safety-enhancing equipment. Internal corporate documents revealed that the management of Ford had deliberately decided to forego any remedial measures for the car's design in order to save $20.9 million over two years.

Observing that the company had deliberately engaged in a cost-benefit analysis that balanced "human lives and limbs against corporate profits," the court approved a $3.5 million award of punitive damages against Ford. The mentality at Ford constituted callous indifference to public safety, which equated with the type of "malice" California law required before punitive damages could be assessed. To Ford's objection that the amount of the award was excessive, the court pointed out that it represented only .005 percent of the company's net worth and any less would not provide any deterrent to such behavior in the future. Similarly, when Ford objected that the amount of the award was far greater than state and federal fines it was required to pay for selling an automobile that failed government crash standards, the court responded that it is "precisely because monetary penalties under government regulations prescribing business standards . . . are so inadequate and ineffective as deterrents against a manufacturer and distributor of mass produced defective products that punitive damages must be of sufficient amount to discourage such practices." [*Grimshaw v. Ford Motor Company*, 174 Cal. Rptr. at 389]

The *Grimshaw* case was but one prominent example in what later proved to be a flood of products liability **action**s in which large punitive damage awards have been issued since 1976. As the twentieth century draws to a close there is some concern that the pendulum may have swung too far in favor of such awards. The result may be less product choice for **consumers** and less innovation because large sellers fear departure from standards and small manufacturers cannot afford even to enter the market.

GUARANTY The words *guaranty* and *warranty* are the same in origin, both deriving from the old Norman French language in which the letter *g* had a *w* sound.

Today, the noun *guaranty* is commonly used interchangeably with the noun *warranty* to mean a promise about the quality of goods that is legally enforceable. When used in this sense, it may also be spelled *guarantee*. It is technically preferable to use the word *warranty* when this meaning is intended, because the word *guaranty* has another legal meaning as well, which is exclusive to it. See **warranty** for further discussion of this topic.

The word *guaranty* in its most technical sense refers to an obligation to make good on the promises of another. For example, banks frequently ask for a *guaranty* before loaning money to someone with a less-than-sterling credit rating. This guaranty is a promise by some third party to pay back the loan to the bank if the borrower fails to do so.

The word *guaranty* or *guarantee* may also be used as a verb meaning both to create a warranty on a product and to stand ready to perform someone else's promise if he or she fails to do so. Technically, it is more correct to use the verb *warrant* when referring to the first meaning.

HAZARDOUS SUBSTANCES ACT A federal law [15 U.S.C. §1261 et seq.] administered by the **Consumer Product Safety Commission** (CPSC), the purpose of which is to determine substances that present a substantial risk of harm to **consumers** and to regulate the sale of products that contain them.

Substances that fall into the category of "hazardous" are those that are toxic, flammable, or corrosive or that are irritants or strong sensitizers (i.e., those that induce allergies) to human beings. Radioactive substances and those that generate pressure through decomposition, heat, or other chemical reactions are also included. Toys that present hazards because of electrical, mechanical, or thermal features are covered by the act as well.

Products made with these types of substances are subject to stringent labeling regulations under the act. In addition to requiring the name and place of business of the manufacturer of the product, the regulations require detailed statements of the product's contents, the hazards they present, and instructions for the product's safe use. A statement of first aid measures to be applied if a chemical product is accidentally spilled or ingested is also required. Some products require additional labeling, such as the addition of the word "poison" or a skull-and-crossbones emblem. See also **warning defect.**

Under the act, the CPSC is empowered to declare as misbranded [see **misbranding**] any product that does not comply with regulations applicable to it and to seek fines and penalties against the product's manufacturer or **seller.**

If the CPSC finds that a substance is so dangerous that it cannot be used safely even with extensive warnings and instructions on the label, it may have products containing it banned from sale.

HENNINGSEN V. BLOOMFIELD MOTORS, INC. *Henningsen v. Bloomfield Motors, Inc.* [32 N.J. 358, 161 A.2d 69 (1960)] represented a significant step in **consumer** protection by (1) allowing a nonpurchaser

171

who was injured by a defective product to sue for breach of an implied **warranty,** and (2) invalidating a standard industrywide disclaimer [see **disclaimer of warranty**] because it was unfair to consumers.

The plaintiff in *Henningsen* was injured when a defect in a new automobile purchased for her by her husband caused it to crash. She sued both the dealer from whom the car had been purchased and the manufacturer of the car. In their defense, both defendants maintained that the rule of **privity of contract** prevented warranty suits against them by anyone with whom they did not have direct contractual relations. Since the plaintiff herself had not purchased the car, she was a stranger to the contract of sale and, according to the rule, not allowed to sue.

Moreover, the manufacturer and the dealer pointed out that the contract of sale of the automobile contained **limitations of warranty remedies** that basically limited the companies' responsibility under the warranty to the replacement of defective parts. The contract also contained a disclaimer that stated that there were no other warranties. Therefore, even if the plaintiff could sue the companies, she could not recover for her personal injuries.

The court disagreed, holding that the plaintiff could sue both the dealer and the manufacturer for breach of the **implied warranty of merchantability.** On the privity issue, the court reasoned that a defective automobile was really no different than tainted food or drink for which the privity requirement had been abolished long ago: "The unwholesome beverage may bring illness to one person, the defective car, with its great potentiality for harm to the driver, occupants, and others, demands even less adherence to the narrow barrier of privity." [*Henningsen v. Bloomfield Motors, Inc.,* 161 A.2d at 83].

The court also struck down the companies' warranty disclaimer as void against public policy. In making this ruling, the court considered the changes in the manner in which products are manufactured, marketed, and sold that had occurred in the years since the turn of the century. Previously, **sellers** and consumers dealt directly with each other and were roughly equal in their ability to bargain for better terms. In the modern age, consumers and producers of goods are separated by many layers of distribution. Products have become increasingly complex, and the consumer has less and less opportunity to inspect them before purchase. Moreover, the huge disparity in bargaining power between a giant corporation and the consumer means that the terms of sales contracts frequently are unilaterally dictated by the seller. The consumer has no leverage to change the contract and must trust the manufacturer to deliver a safe product, especially since there is often no real alternative product to which to turn.

Recognizing these realities, the court found it most unfair to allow an entire industry, such as the automobile industry, to impose a single standard contract on consumers. It was unconscionable to allow an industry to spend millions of dollars advertising features of its products and then to deny any responsibility for the absence of those features by disclaiming all warranties in the contract of sale. Therefore, said the court, "[w]hen the manufacturer puts a new automobile in the stream of trade and promotes its purchase to the public, an implied warranty that it is reasonably suitable for use as such accompanies it into the hands of the ultimate purchaser from the dealer." [*Henningsen v. Bloomfield Motors, Inc.*, 161 A.2d at 83] Thus, the implied warranty of merchantability survived the attempt to disclaim it in *Henningsen* and served to allow the plaintiff to recover for her injuries caused by the defective automobile.

HOLDER-IN-DUE-COURSE DOCTRINE   A rule that one who purchases a negotiable instrument before it is due and without knowledge of any defenses or claims against it has an absolute right to demand payment on it. Simply stated, a negotiable instrument is a signed IOU note that contains an unconditional promise to pay its bearer on demand or at a certain time. **Consumers** frequently pay for goods or services with such IOU notes, also called *promissory notes.* **Sellers** who receive these notes in payment then sell them, in turn, to financial institutions and **creditors**. Under the holder-in-due-course doctrine, the purchasers of these IOUs have an absolute right to demand payment from the consumers who originally made them. This means that the consumer loses his or her right to withhold payment because of some defect in the goods or services received.

For example, A buys an air conditioner from B, and gives B an IOU note in payment. B sells this note to C. C has no reason to believe that there may be a legitimate reason for A not to pay. Later, before A finishes paying all the installments agreed to in the note she signed, she discovers that the air conditioner was defective and cannot be repaired. Meanwhile, B has gone out of business and moved away. A stops payment. C sues A for the rest of the payment due on the IOU note. If C is a holder in due course, A must make the payments regardless of the fact that the merchandise received was defective.

Promissory notes that are negotiable are distinguished from nonnegotiable obligations. A promissory note is negotiable only if it is unconditional and payable to whoever holds it. If a promise to pay is part of a contract in which performance by either side is subject to any kind of condition, the document is not negotiable and the holder-in-due-course doctrine does not apply to it. Many sales contracts fall into this category. These obligations may also be sold to third parties, but in this case the third party takes only those rights that the original signer of the contract held. This means that any legitimate defenses a consumer may have against making payment under the contract (such as receipt of defective merchandise) also are valid against a third party to whom the seller sold the contract. See also **waiver of defense clause.**

The holder-in-due-course doctrine has been part of the **common law** since the eighteenth century. Historians speculate that it was created at a time when there was a shortage of currency. Therefore, it was useful to treat the promissory notes of individuals like cash, allowing them to be circulated freely and relied upon as payment for goods and services. If merchants and others had to worry whether the original signer of a promissory note had some legitimate reason not to pay it, they would be reluctant to accept the note in exchange for anything of value. Therefore, it was important to make the notes absolutely payable once they had been sold to the first buyer who had no notice that there was any defense against paying them. In addition, in the early days of the doctrine, most makers of promissory notes were large institutions, well able to ensure that they would not be taken advantage of in trade.

Apologists for the doctrine point out that the holder-in-due-course doctrine has played a role in making consumer goods widely available. Without the ability to sell promissory notes that buyers could have faith in for cash, sellers—particularly small businesses—might be unable to extend credit to buyers. Without credit, buyers would buy less. The result, according to these theorists, would be few sellers, fewer buyers, and less material prosperity.

Notwithstanding this argument, the holder-in-due-course doctrine had become the bane of consumers by the mid-twentieth century. Sellers found that they could avoid responsibility for the quality of their goods by accepting a promissory note in payment and selling the note to a third party. The consumer was then left with the burden of defective goods and the obligation to pay the third party who now held the promissory note. Of course, a disappointed consumer could still seek satisfaction from the seller for shoddy goods. However, he or she had lost the powerful weapon of withholding payment. If negotiations with the seller broke down, the only recourse against the seller was a lawsuit. However, lawsuits were generally too time-consuming and costly for many consumers. Sellers, therefore, had little incentive to make good on breached warranties or replace faulty merchandise.

Because of the manifest unfairness of this result, states began restricting the applicability of the holder-in-due-course doctrine in consumer transactions. These restrictions showed up first in court decisions that became part of the common law. Later, states passed statutes embodying the restrictions. Some states abolished the rule altogether. Finally, the federal government acted through the **Federal Trade Commission** to ensure that the holder-in-due-course doctrine was rendered toothless in transactions involving consumers. Today, the holder-in-due-course doctrine is generally applicable only in commercial transactions between businesses and large institutions who are able to defend themselves in the marketplace. See also **close-connectedness doctrine;** *Commercial Credit Company v. Childs;* **preservation of defenses rule; waiver of defense clause.**

HYPERSENSITIVE CONSUMER DEFENSE A defense to a **products liability** suit based on the argument that the injured **consumer**'s hypersensitivity to the product that caused harm was the cause of the injuries and not a defect [see **defectiveness**] in the product itself.

To establish this defense, the **seller** of the product must prove that the consumer's allergic reaction was not foreseeable [see **foreseeability**]. In other words, the reaction must have been so unusual and idiosyncratic that it could not have been discovered by the most advanced testing methods available. If the reaction was predictable because tests showed—or would have shown if they had been conducted—that a small number of consumers had the same allergy, the seller may be liable for the consumer's injuries. However, if the seller provided a warning with the product regarding known hypersensitive reactions, no liability may be found. See **unavoidably unsafe product; warning defect.**

IMPLIED WARRANTY OF FITNESS FOR A PARTICULAR PURPOSE A **warranty** that goods are fit for a special or particular purpose that arises automatically under certain conditions when the goods are sold. This warranty is the reverse of the **implied warranty of merchantability,** which guarantees that goods are fit for the usual purposes of goods of like type. Like any implied warranty, the existence of an implied warranty of fitness for a particular purpose on a product does not depend on the intentions or expectations of the parties to the sale.

Certain conditions must be met before the implied warranty of fitness for a particular purpose will come into existence. First, there must be a sale of goods. Therefore, there can be no implied warranties of fitness for a particular purpose on leased or borrowed goods. However, unlike the implied warranty of merchantability, there is no requirement that the **seller** of the goods be professionally engaged in the regular sale of goods of the same type in order for this warranty to arise. Thus, the private citizen who sells a single bicycle at a onetime-only garage sale may be required to make good on an implied warranty that the bicycle is fit for a particular purpose.

Second, for an implied warranty of fitness for a particular purpose to arise, the buyer of the goods must have a particular purpose in mind when purchasing them. This purpose must be different than the ordinary purpose to which the goods are usually put. The buyer must have the special use in mind before making the purchase. No warranty will arise if the buyer decides to put the goods to a special use after buying them.

Third, the buyer of the goods must rely on the seller's skill, knowledge, or expert judgment to provide goods that are suitable for the buyer's special purpose. The buyer must be prepared to prove this **reliance** if he or she hopes to recover in a lawsuit based on a breach of the warranty. See **express warranty; implied warranty of merchantability.**

Fourth, the seller of the goods must know, or have reason to know, both about the particular purpose for which the buyer intends to use the product and about the fact that the buyer is relying on him or her to select an appropriate product for that use.

177

This last requirement is often the most difficult to establish. Of course, if the buyer specifically tells the seller about his or her special purpose there will be no question about the seller's knowledge of it. However, this is not the only way for a seller to have knowledge of a buyer's particular purpose. If the buyer is known by the seller to be in a particular business or to have a particular hobby, the seller may have reason to know of the buyer's special purpose even without being told. For example, if a world-famous motorcycle stunt rider comes into the seller's sporting goods store to buy a helmet, the seller may have reason to know that the buyer has a special purpose in mind and needs an especially heavy-duty model. Similarly, other circumstances surrounding the sale may tip the seller off that a special purpose is contemplated for the product. A customer wearing a jacket with the name and logo of a local mountaineering club who comes into a hardware store asking for rope may be presumed to need the rope for the special purpose of climbing rocks and not just to walk his dog. In this case, the seller may be required to ask if a special purpose is contemplated or face the possibility of breaching the implied warranty of fitness for a particular purpose if he sells the customer clothesline rope and the fellow plunges to his death when using it to climb rocks.

Proving the seller's knowledge that the buyer was relying on his or her special knowledge to furnish an adequate product for a special purpose may also be difficult. In the case of the world-famous motorcycle stunt rider, for example, it is reasonable for the seller to assume that the customer knows as much or more about motorcycle helmets as he or she (the seller) does and, therefore, is not relying on the seller's expertise in selecting a suitable product. On the other hand, it may be obvious that a customer is not an expert and is probably relying on the seller's greater knowledge in selecting a suitable product for a special purpose. The prim little old lady who enters a sporting goods store and announces that she intends to start stunt riding will clearly be relying on the expertise of the burly clerk with the Harley-Davidson tattoo to recommend a helmet.

If all of the above requirements are met, an implied warranty that the goods will be fit for the particular purpose will be created. If the goods then prove not to be fit for that purpose, the warranty will be breached and the buyer may recover **damages** for injuries or losses caused by the breach.

Importance to Consumers

The implied warranty of fitness for a particular purpose is of somewhat less importance to **consumer**s than other types of warranties. The reason for this may be the relative difficulty of proving that the warranty exists and that it was breached. After all, "fitness" for a special or even an ordinary purpose is a rather vague concept and must be proved with reference to other products and standards in the trade. In addition, it is rare that a transaction between a seller and a consumer takes place entirely without any express statements as to appropriate uses for the product being sold. Typically, the consumer will ask for and receive express assurances that a particular product is suitable for the consumer's planned use. In such a case, an express warranty will come into being and it is generally easier to prove the breach of an express warranty than an implied one.

The implied warranty of fitness for a particular purpose is of greatest use to professional and commercial buyers who deal with suppliers on an ongoing basis. In this context, the seller is more likely to have knowledge of the commercial buyer's business and the uses to which that buyer intends to put the product without the necessity for express statements regarding the products' uses.

IMPLIED WARRANTY OF GOOD AND WORKMANLIKE PERFORMANCE   Theoretically, a **warranty** that is automatically implied in **contracts** for **consumer** services. The law is undecided about what this warranty covers—and even whether it exists at all—making it a strange, wraithlike figure on the legal landscape.

Generally, consumers of products enjoy much greater protection under the law than consumers of services. The reason for the distinction harkens back to the basic justification for the consumer movement as it arose in the nineteenth century: Products were increasingly manufactured by large, faceless corporations at a distance from the ultimate consumer. Lost was any special compunction for honesty fostered by a personal relationship between **seller** and consumer, which had existed in days gone by. Moreover, the product consumer could not be expected to know much about manufacturing processes and frequently was not even able to examine the goods before purchase because they were contained in sealed packages. The product consumer was, therefore, considered to be at a special disadvantage vis-à-vis the product seller. The same was not true for services. Even today, most services are provided by professionals in solo practice or small, local shops. The consumer has a face-to-face relationship with the service provider and is able to observe and inspect his or her work. Thus, it has been perceived that the consumer of services does not need the same level of protection as the consumer of products.

For this reason, the majority of states adhere to a traditional view that the implied warranty of good and workmanlike performance guarantees only that the seller of services will perform them in a manner that is consistent with the normal care and skill practiced by an average provider of similar services in the same community. It does not mean that any particular result is guaranteed. This is really only the same thing as requiring that a service provider avoid being negligent. Thus, under this view the same issue is involved in any alleged breach of the implied warranty of good and workmanlike performance as in any ordinary **negligence** case: Did the conduct of the seller of the service measure up to the **standard of care** for providing the type of service at issue? To adherents of this traditional view, the implied warranty of good and workmanlike performance does not really exist. Instead, it is only another name for the **tort** of negligence. In addition, some very strict jurisdictions hold that not only is the implied warranty of good and workmanlike performance to be judged by a negligence standard, but, if the warranty exists at all, only the consumer who actually purchased the services may take advantage of it [see **privity of contract**].

A more consumer-friendly view is taken by a minority of jurisdictions. Under this view, the implied warranty of good and workmanlike performance guarantees that the results of the services performed will conform to what a reasonable consumer would expect [see **consumer expectation test**]. Thus, the implied warranty of good and workmanlike performance should do for consumer services the same thing that the **implied warranty of merchantability** has done for consumer products: That is, judge them on the quality of the outcome (the tangible product in the case of products) rather than on the quality of the effort that went into providing them. For example, a consumer who hires a chimney sweep would expect that the chimney would be free of dangerous soot buildup after the sweep had done his work. If the house later burns down because soot in the chimney caught fire, the consumer might naturally assume that the implied warranty of good and workmanlike performance had been breached. However, the chimney sweep may have performed his duties competently and the fire may have resulted from a buildup of soot in a crevice that could not have been discovered by even the most expert eye. Under the traditional view of the implied warranty of good and workmanlike performance, the chimney sweep would not be liable for any **damages** caused by the fire because he had performed his work with adequate skill. However, under the progressive view of the warranty he would be liable, since the results of his efforts were not what a normal consumer would expect.

Proponents of the progressive view of the implied warranty of good and workmanlike performance argue that the distinction between products and services is outdated. They maintain that the consumer is at just as great a disadvantage when contracting for services as when buying products. Typically, he or she knows nothing about how the service should be performed and must rely totally on the special skill and honesty of the service provider. Additionally, he or she lacks the expertise to judge the quality of the result. Moreover, service contracts are often presented in standardized form, which the consumer must either sign or reject. There is frequently no real opportunity for bargaining between the parties.

While all these things may be true, traditionalists still believe that it is inherently unfair to force providers of services to guarantee certain results. If a service provider feels confident enough of an outcome to make an **express warranty** about the results of the work, he or she is free to do so. However, the provider of services is not in control of the results of his or her work in the same way as the maker of a product. The maker of a product is responsible for the initial decision to make the product. He or she designs it, tests it, and markets it with appropriate instructions and warnings. Typically, a service provider is called on to affect things already in existence or to step into a situation already unfolding and alter the course of events. He or she is not responsible for the present state of affairs into which he or she is thrust. Moreover, the number of known and unknown variables over which the service provider has no control makes prediction of results difficult, if not impossible. For these reasons, some jurisdictions that recognize the implied warranty of good and workmanlike performance confine it to services that affect tangible things only, such as the repair of appliances or the like. In some states, the implied warranty of good and workmanlike performance is further restricted to those providing services for products they themselves have sold.

IMPLIED WARRANTY OF HABITABILITY   A **warranty** that arises automatically in a **consumer** lease or purchase of housing. Generally, the warranty ensures that the leased or purchased premises are habitable; that is, that they are safe and healthy for dwelling.

The implied warranty of habitability is a relatively recent development in consumer law. Prior to the mid–twentieth century, the sale or lease of real estate (land or buildings) did not entail any of the types of warranties normally available for **consumer products**. Traditionally, the rule of *caveat* *emptor,* or "let the buyer beware," was strictly applied to the conveyance of any rights in land. At the time the rule was invented, real estate was mostly rural and agrarian. The land itself was the focus of the transaction and buildings on the land were likely to be simple and easy to inspect. However, as agrarian society gave way to industrial society, the structures on land became more important and more complex. By the mid–twentieth century, huge apartment buildings and mass-produced houses in developments with scores of separate dwellings had became the norm. Such property was far more difficult to inspect, and the average consumer lacked the expertise to judge its quality. In addition, parity in bargaining power between large corporations owning scores of developments or apartment houses and the average consumer trying to house a family did not exist. Thus, the average consumer was entirely in **reliance** on the skill and honesty of the seller of the property, who typically held himself or herself out to be competent to provide adequate housing. Moreover, the purchase of a house, or even a lease of an apartment, represented one of the most important economic transactions an average consumer was likely to make. These considerations, and growing instances of grossly substandard housing foisted on tenants with little or no recourse, prompted the development of the implied warranty of habitability.

Like many developments in consumer law, the warranty evolved as part of the **common law.** It was first invented by judges as they tried cases involving consumers stuck with defective dwellings. Today, most states recognize some form of the warranty in their common law. Others have written the implied warranty of habitability into their **statutory law.** In all states that recognize it, the warranty applies to the sale of new residential houses. In most states, it also applies to the lease of a dwelling. A minority of states also recognize the warranty in the sale of existing homes.

Generally, the implied warranty of habitability applies only to latent defects; that is, defects that are not obvious or could not be discovered by routine, casual inspection. The warranty typically covers only major defects in a dwelling. Usually, these defects must affect health and safety in some way. For example, defects in the integral structure of the house, such as the foundation, walls, or the electrical, plumbing, and heating systems may breach the warranty. Thus, a defective joist system, improper elevation causing flooding, and nonpotable well water are all conditions that may breach the warranty. By contrast, the misplacement of an air-conditioning unit, sloppy application of wallpaper, or an obstructed view from the living room probably are not serious enough to be called breaches of the warranty.

Usually, breaches of the warranty are judged on an objective basis: That is, would most reasonable people consider the defect serious enough to endanger health or safety? Of course, defects may vary by degrees of seriousness. Noisy neighbors in an apartment building may result in a breach of the warranty of habitability depending on how disturbing the noise is to most reasonable people.

A consumer who proves that the implied warranty of habitability has been breached may have the right to collect money **damages,** to insist on repairs, or to rescind [see **rescission**] the contract of sale or lease.

IMPLIED WARRANTY OF MERCHANTABILITY   A **warranty** that a product will conform to certain minimum standards of quality for products of the same type. The warranty arises automatically upon the sale of a product by anyone in the business of selling that type of product.

As its name suggests, the implied warranty of merchantability does not depend for its existence on any intention or statement of a product's **seller.** It also does not depend on any expectations of the buyer for the product. The law simply *implies* the existence of the warranty, unless it has been specifically disclaimed [see **disclaimer of warranty**] by the seller. This differs from express warranties [see **express warranty**], which depend on an expression by the seller about the quality of the goods and the **reliance** (in some form) of the buyer on the truth of the expression when deciding to purchase them.

A seller will be liable for a breach of the implied warranty of merchantability even though he or she is in no way at fault for the defect in the goods. Thus, for example, the seller of a cow that turns out to have a fatal disease will be liable to the farmer who purchased it, even though the presence of the disease could not be detected or prevented by any means prior to the sale.

The origin of the implied warranty of merchantability can be traced to England, where in 1815, a certain Lord Ellenbourgh declared that there must be an implied warranty of quality because a "purchaser cannot be supposed to buy goods to lay them on a dung hill." [*Gardiner v. Gray*, 4 Camp. 144, 145, 171 Eng. Rep. 46, 47 (KB 1815)] The American courts rejected this view, however, and held fast to the rule of *caveat emptor* until into the twentieth century. According to American legal theory of the time, if a purchaser required assurance that goods were of a certain quality, he or she could bargain with the seller for an express warranty to that effect, and very likely pay extra for the security. Nevertheless, the widely adopted Sales Act of 1906 revealed that the idea of an implied warranty of merchantability was becoming an accepted doctrine of American jurisprudence.

Definition under the Uniform Commercial Code

Today, the implied warranty of merchantability of goods is largely defined and regulated by the **Uniform Commercial Code.** Certain requirements must be met under that law in order for the warranty to come into existence.

First, there must be a **contract** for the sale of goods. This requirement is easy to meet, since virtually any transaction in which money is exchanged in return for something qualifies as a contract of sale. A contract for the sale of goods can even come into existence before the purchaser pays for the item if it is clear that purchase is intended. A shopper who is standing in line to pay for a bottle of soda may sue for breach of the implied warranty of merchantability if the bottle explodes in his hands before he gets to the cashier. The circumstances of the incident make clear that the customer took possession of the item with the intent to purchase it.

The definition of goods subject to the implied warranty of merchantability is also broad: Virtually any tangible, movable thing that can be sold will qualify. Food and drink that are to be consumed on the premises are also "goods" within the Uniform Commercial Code definition. In addition, there is a trend to make services subject to the implied warranty of merchantability as well [see **implied warranty of good and workmanlike performance**]. Excluded from the warranty of merchantability are real estate and intangible property, such as financial securities, and intellectual property like copyrights and patents.

The second requirement for an implied warranty of merchantability to arise is that the seller of the goods must be a *merchant*. Under the Uniform Commercial Code, a *merchant* is someone who sells the type of product at issue in the regular course of his or her business or profession [see **seller**]. Thus, a used bicycle purchased at a private citizen's garage sale does not come with an implied warranty of merchantability if the seller is not normally in the business of selling bicycles out of his or her garage.

Standards

If the above requirements are met, a warranty that the goods are *merchantable* will be created. This means that the goods must conform to certain minimum standards of quality. The Uniform Commercial Code offers six quality standards that must be met before the goods will pass as merchantable. The most important of these is that the goods must be "fit for the ordinary purposes for which such goods are used."

Of course, this definition is itself very vague. The determination of what makes a product fit for ordinary purposes may ultimately depend on common sense. For example, an automobile that quits running after a few thousand miles is intuitively not fit for the ordinary purposes for which automobiles are used and, therefore, is not merchantable. Likewise, a food product that makes the **consumer** ill is not merchantable.

Not all cases are this clear, however. For example, what if the automobile quit running after 40,000 miles? Is this unreasonably few? For tough cases like this one, comparisons with similar products made by other manufacturers are crucial to help determine whether a product is merchantable. In this case, one would look to other automobile manufacturers to see if the life spans of their products are roughly the same or considerably greater. One might also check to see if the automobile conforms to government standards and regulations with regard to mileage. In addition, there may be some industry standards by which professionals in the automobile manufacturing business measure automobile performance. This is known as *usage in the trade* and can be very valuable in determining the fitness of a product for its normally intended use. Finally, one might check relative prices of automobiles. If the price paid for the automobile that quits after 40,000 miles is roughly equal to the price paid for a type of automobile that regularly gets 200,000 miles, the former is probably not merchantable.

It is important to note that products do not have to be perfect or of the highest quality in order to be merchantable. Generally, it is only necessary that they be within the bounds of average quality for the type and price range of product to which they belong. The fact that a cherry pie may contain a cherry pit does not make it unmerchantable. It is to be expected that imperfections such as this will arise in the normal course of manufacture. However, a cherry pie that was found to contain rat droppings would not be merchantable. By any standards, this type of contamination makes a food worthless, even though it may not actually cause illness to the consumer.

A more difficult issue is posed by products that are inherently unsafe [see **inherently dangerous product**], such as cigarettes. Are they unmerchantable because they can cause cancer? Generally, courts have said they are not. Merchantability is determined by a product's relative quality in comparison to other like products on the market. Because all cigarettes—

even those of the highest quality—share this unfortunate characteristic to approximately the same degree, it is not possible to say that any are unmerchantable for that reason. Nevertheless, this issue is still unsettled. It would not be surprising for courts to reverse rulings on this issue in the future as the demand for safer products for the public continues.

Importance to Consumers

Implied warranties of merchantability are of particular importance in protecting consumers from losses due to inferior products because they impose a type of *strict liability* on the professional seller of goods. Since implied warranties arise automatically and without regard to any conduct on the part of the seller or reliance on the part of the buyer, it is easier to prove that an implied warranty of merchantability exists than it is to prove that an express warranty exists.

On the other hand, while it is easy to prove that an implied warranty of merchantability exists, it is harder to prove that the implied warranty has been breached. Because the terms of express warranties are just that— *expressed*—the parties generally know what was promised and whether it was delivered. But in the case of the implied warranty of merchantability, it is necessary to make reference to a host of other factors to determine if a particular product is *unmerchantable.*

Also unfavorable to consumers is the fact that an implied warranty of merchantability may be disclaimed by the seller in some states [see **disclaimer of warranty**]. Moreover, states are divided as to whom an implied warranty of merchantability applies. In some, only the person who actually purchased the defective product may claim the benefit of this warranty [see **privity of contract**]. In others, anybody who suffers physical injury as a result of a defective product may claim the benefit of the implied warranty of merchantability and recover damages, whether or not they were the actual purchaser. Persons who have suffered only economic losses, however, may not recover in these states unless they were the actual purchaser of the defective product. Still other states extend the protection of the implied warranty of merchantability on goods to anyone for any type of loss, regardless of whether that person was the purchaser of the product.

A consumer who proves that an implied warranty of merchantability on a product has been breached will generally be able to recover for his or her losses in terms of monetary **damages.**

IMPLIED WARRANTY OF TITLE A **warranty** arising automatically when goods are sold that the seller really owns them and is passing a good title to them on to the buyer [see **sales law**]. If it later turns out that the seller did not own the goods he or she sold, the warranty will be breached. It is irrelevant to the creation of the warranty whether the seller knew at the time of the sale that he or she did not really own the goods.

The most extreme situation of a breach of the implied warranty of title occurs when the seller has no legitimate claim to the goods at all, as, for example, when the goods are stolen property. The huckster trying to sell the Brooklyn Bridge fits into this category as well. More frequently, the seller does have a legitimate claim to the goods, but some third party claims them as well. Often, the third party has a *security interest* in them. A security interest arises when goods have been used as collateral for a loan and gives the lender a right to repossess them if the loan is not repaid. A seller who owns goods subject to such a security interest does not own them "free and clear." In other words, he or she does not have good title to them.

If the seller of goods sells them without having good title to them, the true owner will typically sue the buyer of the goods to get them back. The buyer of the goods must then defend the lawsuit by showing that good title to the goods was passed to the buyer during the sale. If the buyer loses the lawsuit, and the goods revert to the third party who claimed ownership of them, the buyer may sue the seller for breach of the implied warranty of title. In this case, it is clear that the warranty was breached because a court has determined that the true owner of the goods was a third party and the seller sold them without having good title.

A more difficult issue arises when the buyer wins a lawsuit brought by a third party claiming true ownership of the goods. In this case, a court has determined that the third party did not own the goods and the seller did pass good title to them to the buyer after all. However, does the mere fact that a third party claimed ownership to the goods and sued the buyer to get them back mean that the implied warranty of title was breached? This question has not been completely resolved. Some courts say that the implied warranty of title includes a warranty that the buyer of goods will not be disturbed by third parties claiming ownership of them, whether or not the third party claim is justified. Under this view, the warranty is breached whenever a third party starts trouble by claiming ownership and suing the buyer for return of the goods.

Other courts have held that the warranty of title is breached only when a third party has a *plausible* claim to the goods, even though the claim may ultimately be denied. However, if the third party's claim is frivolous from the start, there will not be a breach of the implied warranty of title.

Another unresolved issue surrounding the implied warranty of title is the type of **damages** to which the buyer is entitled if the warranty is breached. It seems clear that a buyer who is deprived of goods because the seller did not have full ownership of them should be entitled to a return of the purchase price of the goods. The buyer should also be reimbursed for legal expenses spent in an effort to defend ownership. Unresolved is what other types of compensation for the disappointed buyer might be recoverable.

The implied warranty of title may be disclaimed by the seller by specific language that makes clear that the seller is conveying only such ownership interest in the goods as he or she actually has, and that the seller does not promise that this represents full ownership [see **disclaimer of warranty**].

INHERENTLY DANGEROUS PRODUCT   A product that is naturally dangerous as a result of being effective for its intended use. For example, a knife is an inherently dangerous product. In order to be effective in its intended use—cutting—a knife must be sharp. Since it is sharp, it also presents a risk of harm to **consumers** that cannot be eliminated.

An inherently dangerous product is not defective [see **defectiveness**] just because it is dangerous. Like all products, an inherently dangerous product must be in an **unreasonably dangerous condition** before it will be found defective. For example, guns are inherently dangerous products. However, the fact that guns can kill people does not mean that they are automatically unreasonably dangerous. A consumer who is injured by a gun must generally show that the gun was more dangerous than other guns of its type. For example, perhaps its safety latch was weak or nonexistent, its barrel of uneven thickness, or its trigger too easily set off.

It has been argued that under the **risk–utility test,** inherently dangerous products present more risk than utility and should, therefore, automatically be found defective regardless of flawless workmanship in their manufacture. This argument has most often been presented with regard to guns and cigarettes. For example, the risk of contracting cancer from cigarettes is alleged to outweigh the pleasure derived by smoking them. They should, therefore, be declared defective and the cigarette manufacturer strictly liable in tort [see **strict tort liability**] for injuries caused by them. While the argument has some force when applied to cigarettes, it is less obvious in the case of knives or scissors that are of such everyday utility as to be indispensable.

Up to the present, courts have resisted this argument. Basically, it is necessary to prove that an inherently dangerous product is defective just like any other product before compensation for injuries caused by them will be allowed. However, because of the extreme risk of harm from inherently dangerous products, the **seller** of such products must exercise a high **standard of care** in making and selling them. In the case of guns, for example, a seller may have to take special precautions to ensure that they are not sold to minors or mentally unstable persons. See also **negligence.**

An inherently dangerous product should be distinguished from an **unavoidably unsafe product.** An unavoidably unsafe product is universally recognized as being of very great utility and little or no danger to most people, but possessing a significant risk of harm to some people that cannot be eliminated by any known means. Some drugs fall into this classification. By contrast, the inherently dangerous product presents the same danger to everyone, the danger is not insignificant, and the utility of the product is not so obvious.

INJUNCTION   An order issued by a court that directs an individual, a group of individuals, or a legal entity—such as a company or corporation—to cease doing something. Less frequently, an injunction, sometimes called a *mandatory* injunction, directs individuals or legal entities to take some positive action.

Injunctions are important to **consumers** because they represent one of the primary ways the government acts to ensure that defective [see **defectiveness**] products are kept off the market. Numerous federal agencies are specifically authorized to go to court and procure injunctions in order to force **sellers** to comply with their regulations. Injunctions may also be sought by private citizens in lawsuits seeking compensation for injuries or losses resulting from defective products or services.

INTERLOCKING LOAN   A loan made to a **consumer** in order for the consumer to buy goods or services from a **seller** with whom the lender is affiliated. Also called *all-in-the-family loans,* interlocking loans are a way a seller may attempt to isolate a consumer's obligation to pay for goods and services from the seller's obligation to deliver them. Normally, a consumer's duty to pay depends on the seller's delivery of acceptable goods, and vice versa. If the goods are not delivered or are defective in some way, the buyer may be justified in stopping payment. However, if the buyer's obligation to pay is owed to someone other than the seller of the goods, defenses against having to pay (such as undelivered or defective goods) may not be applicable.

Frequently, a consumer wishing to buy goods from a seller lacks sufficient cash. Instead of extending credit directly to the consumer, the seller refers the consumer to a **creditor** (lender). The creditor, in a separate transaction, lends the consumer the amount of money necessary for the consumer to purchase the goods from the seller. The creditor may give this money to the consumer or may pay the money directly to the seller. In any case, the loan agreement is between the consumer and the creditor only. The consumer's obligation to pay the money back to the creditor is, therefore, absolute. The fact that the goods purchased from the seller may later turn out to be defective does not in any way concern the creditor, since he or she is not a party to the sales transaction. Of course, the consumer could turn to the seller to get the purchase money back in order to pay it back to the lender, but this may involve a time-consuming and costly lawsuit. By the time any suit is settled, the seller might have gone out of business, moved, or gone bankrupt. Meanwhile, the consumer's obligation to keep paying back the creditor remains.

An interlocking loan arises when the seller and the creditor are affiliated with each other. Sometimes this relationship can be so close that one is virtually the alter ego of the other. In other cases, the relationship may be merely one of accommodation: The seller refers consumers who need loans to make purchases to a particular creditor. In either case, the insidious aspect of interlocking loans is that the seller and the creditor have conspired to strip the consumer of his or her rights to avoid paying for defective or undelivered merchandise. The seller gets immediate full payment for the goods sold to the consumer, and the creditor has the right to collect the full amount of the loan from the consumer without any excuses or justification for nonpayment. The consumer is left with the risk that the goods or services are unsuitable or defective.

Of course, loaning a consumer money to buy goods is not illegal, even when the lender and the seller are affiliated with each other. The unfair aspect of the arrangement is depriving the consumer of his or her defenses that might justify a refusal to pay for shoddy or undelivered goods and services merely because the source of the purchase money is nominally a third party. Therefore, it is necessary to balance the consumer's right to assert defenses against payment for defective goods with the legitimate rights of third party creditors to have their loans repaid. Many states' laws address this problem by making all of the consumer's possible defenses against payment applicable against any lender that is affiliated with the seller from whom the goods are to be purchased. Creditors that are truly independent, unaffiliated third parties are unaffected: They have the right to collect on loans absolutely.

When is a loan "interlocking"? Elaborate criteria have been set up for determining whether creditors and sellers are sufficiently affiliated with one another to justify imposing the consumer's defenses on the creditor. Some factors that indicate sufficiently interlocking relationships include:

- the creditor pays the seller a commission or referral fee for referring consumers to the creditor
- the seller guarantees the loan given to the consumer
- the creditor supplies the seller with a loan contract document that the seller then helps the consumer fill out
- the loan is conditioned on the purchase of goods or services from a particular seller
- the seller and the lender have a joint advertising campaign

Generally, state laws restricting interlocking loans apply only to consumer loans; that is, loans made for the purpose of purchasing goods or services for personal, family, or household use. Loans made for business and commercial reasons are not included.

Interlocking loans raise another legal problem. Generally, laws protecting consumers' rights to stop payment to creditors on loans used to purchase goods or services that turn out to be defective allow only for the consumer to cease payment. They make no provision for the consumer to get back from a creditor amounts already paid. However, the **Federal Trade Commission's preservation of defenses rule** and the laws of some states do allow the consumer to get back amounts already paid, including down payments, from the creditor extending an interlocking loan.

INTERSTATE LAND SALES FULL DISCLOSURE ACT Federal law [12 U.S.C. §2616] designed to curb deceptive sales practices by real estate developers. Specifically, the Interstate Land Sales Full

Disclosure Act was intended to address the problem of developers selling land sight unseen to consumers in distant states by means of false or misleading descriptions. The classic example is the property described as "waterfront" that turns out to be underwater.

The act exempts a large number of real estate transactions from its effect. Generally, it applies only to developers who sell undeveloped, subdivided land. It protects purchasers as well as persons who lease such land. The act requires real estate developers within its scope to file a statement with the Department of Housing and Urban Development regarding the proposed subdivision and development plan. In addition, the developer must furnish each prospective buyer of lots with a detailed and truthful property report. This report must contain information about the land for sale, including its geographic location, its present condition, the plan for the subdivisions around it, and the availability of essential amenities, such as water and electricity. It must disclose the status of the title to the real property and provide information about the financial condition of the property's **seller**.

The Interstate Land Sales Full Disclosure Act generally prohibits any practices that employ artifice, **fraud,** or **misrepresentation** in the sale of real property. This includes statements that roads, sewers, water, gas, or other amenities will be provided, unless the developer at the same time makes a written, enforceable promise that the amenities described will be completed. Stating that a lot has good investment potential is also prohibited, unless the developer furnishes written evidence of this based on ascertainable facts.

A consumer may rescind any contract to buy land covered by the act for any reason within 7 days of signing. In addition, the consumer has up to two years after signing the contract to rescind the transaction if the consumer did not receive a property report prior to signing the contract or if the contract of sale itself did not contain disclosures required by law. However, this right of **rescission** is lost if the consumer receives a warranty deed within 180 days after signing the contract to purchase the land.

The act provides a **private right of action** to consumers who have been defrauded by forbidden sales practices. In addition, criminal penalties of up to five years in prison or $10,000 in fines or both may be meted out to a developer who willfully violates any of the act's provisions.

Many states have laws governing practices involving the sale of real estate as well. State laws providing greater protection to consumers than the Interstate Land Sales Full Disclosure Act will take precedence over it. Less protective laws are preempted [see **preemption**].

INTERVENING CAUSE An action or event that intervenes in a chain of events already in progress and changes the outcome. Sometimes called *superseding cause,* intervening cause is often claimed as a defense in **tort** cases based on theories of **negligence** or **strict tort liability.**

Arguing that an intervening cause changed the outcome of a chain of events already in progress may be used to negate a finding that an action or failure to act was the **proximate cause** of harm. For example, F, whose failure to secure a lock on the ocelot enclosure he was installing allowed the animal to escape, may argue that he is not responsible for injuries a driver sustained when she hit a tree to avoid the ocelot after a child chased the loose animal into the street. In F's view, the action of the child was an intervening cause that interrupted the chain of events set in motion by his shoddy workmanship.

Like many concepts developed by the **common law,** it is not possible to define *intervening cause* exactly. It depends for the most part on a common sense evaluation of the particular circumstances of each case. However, there are a few guidelines for deciding whether an action or event was an intervening cause of some later event.

First, the action or event must be a *cause in fact* of the later event: That is, the later event would not have happened but for the action or event at issue. In the above example, it is possible that the ocelot may have run into the street anyway, but maybe not at the precise moment that the driver appeared. Unless the ocelot was already heading into the street at the time, it is probable that the accident would not have happened if the child had not chased the animal.

Second, the action or event must not be the natural or probable consequence of the original action or failure to act that sets a chain of events into motion. For example, F will argue that having a child come along and chase the loose ocelot into the street was not the natural and probable consequence of leaving the lock unsecured. He will say that the child's action was an independent force that was entirely unforeseeable [see **foreseeability**] and was the real cause of the accident. On the other hand, the driver of the automobile who wishes to hold F liable for her injuries will argue that the presence of the child was foreseeable, and the action of chasing an animal is typical of a child. She will argue that the chasing of the ocelot was, in fact, the natural and probable consequence of F's careless workmanship. In other words, she will say that the child's action did not break the chain of events set in motion by F when he failed to secure the lock on the ocelot enclosure. Typically, in such a case as this, a judge or jury will decide who is right based on their own notions of reasonable probabilities.

Importance to Consumers

Intervening cause may be an issue in a **products liability** case in which a **consumer** seeks compensation for harm allegedly caused by a defective [see **defectiveness**] product. The **seller** of the product at issue will claim that some independent action or event broke the chain of events set in motion by the seller's conduct, or by the defective condition of his or her product, that culminated in the consumer's injury. Most typically, this argument will center around alteration of the product [see **alteration of product**] after it was sold or **misuse** of the product by the consumer. See also **strict tort liability.**

JOINT AND SEVERAL LIABILITY A legal doctrine applicable in **tort** cases under which each of several parties who have concurrently caused harm are liable to pay compensation for all of the harm caused, regardless of their relative fault in causing it. For example, if C was harmed because both A and B were negligent [see **negligence**], C could recover the full amount of compensation due to her from either A or B, or from both together. This is true regardless of which of them was more negligent. C may sue B for the full amount of her **damages,** even though A was 90 percent at fault and B was only 10 percent responsible. From C's standpoint, there may be good reasons to sue B alone, even though A's conduct was the major cause of the harm. For example, A may be bankrupt or have fled the state.

Joint and several liability applies only where the conduct of each of the defendants was a *cause in fact* of a single incident of harm. This means that it will apply only if the harm would not have occurred but for the wrongful actions of both of the defendants. See **proximate cause.**

Sometimes called *entire liability,* joint and several liability is now the subject of some controversy. Despite its ancient roots (it was recognized in England in some forms before the United States existed), some 33 states have found it unfair to defendants and have moved to abolish or modify it. Critics of the doctrine say that it is unjust to require one whose fault is minimal to pay for the full amount of injury that was caused mostly by another. On the other hand, supporters of the doctrine point out that, as between a defendant who was only a little bit at fault and an injured plaintiff who was not at fault at all (or whose fault only contributed to the injury but did not invite it), it is better to make the one at fault pay. Otherwise, the injured plaintiff may not be able to recover for his or her injuries at all. In addition, a defendant who has been forced to pay for a harm for which he or she was only minimally to blame has the right to sue the other defendants whose fault was greater to recover a proportional amount of the judgment. Moreover, supporters argue that defendants are better able to spread the costs of judgments against them to society at large by charging higher prices for their goods and services. This acts as a form of insurance for all **consumers** who might be injured by the negligence or defective products of **sellers**. In response, critics say that this is a type of insurance that society has not agreed to pay, but has been forced upon it by an outdated legal doctrine.

In states that have abolished joint and several liability, plaintiffs are able to collect from each defendant only an amount proportional to the extent to which each caused the harm. Thus, if the above example occurred in such a state, C could only collect 10 percent of the amount necessary to compensate him or her from B, because B's negligence was only 10 percent of the cause of the injury. If A has gone bankrupt or moved away, C must be content with the mere 10 percent judgment against B.

LANHAM TRADEMARK ACT A federal law [15 U.S.C. §§1051–1127] granting sellers exclusive rights to the use of a particular trademark, tradename, or trade dress (the distinctive "look" of a product's packaging or design) in the marketing and sale of their goods and services. Generally, the Lanham Trademark Act is viewed as protecting sellers from unfair competition by other sellers who seek to trade on their goodwill by adopting similar trademarks and packaging.

However, one of the stated purposes of the act is to prevent confusion among **consumer**s as to the source of a particular product or service. Thus, the Lanham Act is a consumer protection statute as well as a fair competition statute. Specifically, the law forbids sellers from making "false designations of origin" for their products and services. This generally means that a seller may not copy the trademarks, logos, packaging, or design of a competitor in order to make consumers believe that the copier's product was made by the copied seller, or vice versa.

The Lanham Act also forbids false descriptions or **misrepresentation**s in commercial advertising as to the "characteristics or qualities" of a seller's goods or services. When the original 1946 version of the act was amended in 1988, language was inserted to the effect that "any person" who believes he or she has been harmed by a seller's false descriptions may sue the seller to recover **damages.** Currently, courts are divided as to whether this means that individual consumers themselves have a **private right of action** for **false advertising** against a seller who violates the act. For the present time, the majority of courts appear to say that they do not. However, as the **common law** evolves to interpret the law in this area, there may be more successful attempts by consumers to recover damages for false advertising by invoking the protection of the Lanham Act.

LEMON LAW A law adopted in most states to provide additional **warranty** protection for purchasers of automobiles. Automobile sales were singled out for special treatment by such laws because, aside from the purchase of a home, they represent the single largest commercial transactions in which the average **consumer** is involved. Moreover, unequal bargaining power between individual consumers and the giant corporate manufacturers and franchise empires that sell most automobiles in the United States means that even an informed consumer is little able to influence the shape of a contract to purchase an automobile.

The general purpose behind lemon laws is to inject some standardized, objective **contract** terms into every contract for the sale of an automobile. These contract terms are first negotiated between industrial representatives and consumer interest groups, whose combined bargaining power enables them to win a fairer deal for the consumer. Then, these prenegotiated terms are enacted into law—the so-called *lemon law*. They then are considered to be part of any contract for the sale of an automobile in the state in which the law is in force.

A typical lemon law will provide these types of protection to the purchaser of a new automobile: First, provided the purchaser has notified the **seller** within the warranty period [see **notice in warranty**] of defects that do not conform to an **express warranty,** the seller must repair the automobile to make it conform to the warranty. The seller must make these repairs even if the warranty has expired. Second, if the seller is unable to repair the vehicle after a reasonable number of attempts, the seller is obligated to replace the automobile with a new one or refund the purchase price of the vehicle, less a reasonable amount representing the use the purchaser made of the vehicle.

Lemon laws vary in defining what is a "reasonable number" of attempts to repair a vehicle. Typically, this may be four attempts to repair the same problem within the term of the express warranty, or a period of one year following the date of original delivery of the car to the consumer, whichever comes first. Sometimes, the lemon law will define attempts at repair in terms of the total number of days that the car is out of service in the warranty period due to the problem. Typically, if the automobile is out of service for a period of 30 or more days during the warranty period, or during the first year following delivery, it may be declared a "lemon" and the replacement or refund provisions of the law will come into play. Generally, however, before this point is reached the consumer must submit to some form of informal settlement procedure with the seller to try to work out their differences about the vehicle. Frequently, lemon laws will set guidelines for this informal settlement procedure. If no agreement between the parties can be worked out during the settlement procedure, the remedy of replacement or refund may be ordered.

Generally, lemon laws apply only to sales of new passenger vehicles. A few states have lemon laws covering the sale of used vehicles, and some protection for purchasers of used automobiles derives from the **used car rule** promulgated by the **Federal Trade Commission.**

The remedies provided by lemon laws also usually only apply to defects in a vehicle that impair its function or value as a means of transportation. Minor problems that defy repair usually do not come under the protection of lemon laws. Lemon laws vary as to whether they apply to defects that affect the safety of a vehicle.

Other issues addressed by lemon laws include whether notice of defects must be made in writing to the seller, whether the parties to a contract for the sale of an automobile may waive or modify the provisions mandated by the lemon law, and which party (seller or purchaser) chooses between the remedies of replacement or refund if repairs cannot be made.

In spite of their touted benefits to consumers, lemon laws have come under fire in recent years for lack of any real effectiveness. Generally, lemon laws do not affect other remedies that a consumer may have under other existing state laws or the **common law.** They merely supplement these existing laws by defining more precisely the conditions under which the traditional remedies may be had. For this reason, some consumer rights activists see little benefit for the consumer in lemon laws over laws already in existence.

LIMITATIONS OF WARRANTY REMEDIES A method by which a **seller** may limit responsibility for defects in products under **warranty** by restricting the remedies available to the buyer if the warranty is breached.

Offering warranties is an effective marketing technique for sellers because **consumer**s are always anxious to limit their risks of purchasing defective goods. A warranty is basically a promise made by the seller that a product will conform to certain descriptions or standards of quality. Typically, a warranty will also specify what actions the seller will take if the product does not conform to the promise. These are the buyer's remedies.

Because warranties are considered part of the **contract** of sale for goods, the parties to the sale are free to bargain over their terms. It is perfectly legitimate for the seller to limit the types of remedies available to the buyer in case of breach of the warranty, provided the buyer has notice of the limitations and agrees to them.

Distinguished from Disclaimers

Limitations on warranty remedies and disclaimers of warranty are frequently confused. The reason is that they both serve the same purpose: relieving sellers of legal responsibility for defects in their products. However, the mechanisms by which they accomplish this are different.

Basically, a **disclaimer of warranty** is a denial that any promises or warranties were made. In effect, the seller is saying to the buyer: "I have made no promises about the quality of this product. Therefore, you assume the risk that the product may turn out to be defective."

By contrast, a limitation of warranty remedies does not deny the existence of a warranty, but it limits what the seller will do for the buyer if the warranty is breached. The result can be the same as a disclaimer. For example, imagine the seller says: "I promise you that the product has no defects. But, if it does turn out to have defects after all, the only remedy I will offer to you is a written apology." Clearly, this situation is no better for the buyer than having no warranty at all. It is the same as if the seller had disclaimed the warranty entirely.

To provide an example more true to life, a warranty disclaimer may provide, "There is no warranty as to any of the moving parts in this clock." The same result may be accomplished by a limitation on warranty remedies: "The exclusive remedy for defects in this clock is limited to repair or replacement of the clock's stationary parts."

Given the similarity between the effects of warranty disclaimers and remedy limitations, it would seem that there would be no reason for the law to distinguish between them. Oddly, however, the law regulates them differently. Under the **Uniform Commercial Code,** disclaimers are subject to a whole array of rules and regulations about the language the seller must use and the size, appearance, and placement of the text of the disclaimer in any written document of sale. By contrast, limitations of warranty remedies are virtually unregulated as to their form and placement. There are no specific words that must be used to create a valid limitation of warranty remedy and there is no requirement that such limitations be made conspicuous. Limitations of remedies may be buried in the fine print of a written document of sale with nothing to call attention to them.

Limitations on Remedy Limitations

While it may appear that an unscrupulous seller could entice a buyer with a warranty only to strip it away by the perfectly legal device of limiting warranty remedies, there are some legal restrictions on the seller's ability to limit remedies.

First, any warranty remedy limitation must be part of the bargain of sale between the parties. Basically, this means that the buyer must be given notice of the limitations at the time of sale. This does not mean that the buyer must actually have knowledge of the limitations. It is enough if they are provided in the written contract of sale. The law assumes that a buyer is aware of any limitations in the contract of sale for a product or its accompanying documents, even if the limitations are included in the fine print.

Second, a limitation on warranty remedies is effective only if it does not "fail of its essential purpose." A remedy limitation will fail of its essential purpose if the buyer is substantially deprived of the value of his or her bargain after the remedy has been applied.

Determining whether a warranty remedy has failed of its essential purpose will depend on the product and the extent of the defect. Consider the example in which a warranty remedy is limited to a written apology. Suppose the product was a clock and the defect was the absence of an hour hand. In that case, the product would be essentially worthless to the buyer even after receiving the written apology. In that case, the warranty limitation would fail of its essential purpose. However, suppose the product was a personalized biography of the buyer and the defect was a false statement that the buyer had been convicted of a felony. In this case, the product— the biography—would not be worthless to the buyer after receiving the written apology. The apology could be shown to readers of the book and would essentially cure the defect. In that case, the limitation of remedy would not fail of its essential purpose.

Third, a remedy limitation will be invalid if it is *unconscionable*. *Unconscionable* means so extremely unfair as to "shock the conscience" of a reasonable person. For example, sellers frequently try to limit warranty remedies in order to exclude *consequential damages* resulting from defects in their products. Consequential damages means damage that occurs to other things as a result of a defect in a product. For example, if a defect in an automobile engine causes the car to explode and the explosion causes the automobile owner's house to catch fire and burn down, the damage to the house is consequential; it happened as a consequence of the defect in the car. If the seller of the automobile successfully excluded warranty remedies for consequential damages arising as a result of defects in the car, the seller would be responsible only for repairing or replacing the car itself and not the house.

Under the Uniform Commercial Code, it is unconscionable for a seller of consumer goods to try to exclude remedies for consequential damages resulting in personal injuries. For example, imagine that a cigar explodes and singes the smoker's eyebrows and at the same time chars his shirt. The seller of the cigar may not limit warranty remedies to exclude compensation for the smoker's medical bills to treat his singed eyebrows. However, the same rule does not hold true for mere property damage. In this case, the cigar seller may exclude compensating the smoker for his ruined shirt.

LOAN FLIPPING   The practice of refinancing a loan without allowing for the refund of prepaid interest or finance fees so that the borrower ends up incurring a greater debt burden than expected.

In a typical flipping situation, a **consumer** takes out a loan to pay off an old loan and to get additional cash. Since the old loan is being paid off early, the consumer should receive credit for any prepaid interest and finance charges for the remainder of the loan period. For example, if a consumer borrowed $100 for ten months with precomputed interest of 10 percent, the consumer is given $100 and must make ten payments of $11 each in order to total the full $110 at the end of the loan period. If the consumer refinances this loan with another lender five months before it is due, the consumer should be credited $5 in interest, since the loan is being repaid in half the time. However, in "flipping," the new lender pays off the old lender with the $50 that is still due, but adds the $5 remaining originally due as interest on the old loan as a new interest charge on the new, refinanced loan. In addition, the lender adds this $5 to the amount of the new loan and computes interest on the total sum. Thus, the consumer ends up paying interest on interest, often resulting in payments in excess of the state **usury** rate.

This practice is illegal under the laws of all states. Generally, in the refinancing of a loan with precomputed interest and fees, the balance owing must be treated as though it has already been paid. The consumer will then be credited with all the refunds computed. Thus, in the above example, the new lender would be lending the consumer only the $50 that was necessary to pay off the old loan (not the $55 necessary to repay the old loan with interest), plus any new loan amount. Interest and finance charges are added only on the sum of the old and new loan amounts.

MACPHERSON V. BUICK MOTOR COMPANY   A landmark case, *MacPherson v. Buick Motor Company* [217 N.Y. 382, 111 N.E. 1050 (1916)] established the **tort** doctrine of **negligence** as a widely available basis for **consumer**s to recover compensation for injuries caused by defective [see **defectiveness**] products of all types.

In *MacPherson*, the plaintiff was injured when a wheel of his automobile collapsed. Evidence established that the manufacturer of the automobile was negligent in failing to inspect the wheel, which was made of defective wood. Under the law of the day, the plaintiff would have been precluded from recovering compensation for his injuries because of the rule requiring **privity of contract.** Under that rule, the buyer of goods could recover tort damages for injuries caused by the goods only from the goods' immediate **seller** and not from a manufacturer far removed in the chain of distribution, as was the manufacturer in the *MacPherson* case.

In deciding to ignore the rule of privity, the *MacPherson* court likened the situation to cases involving injuries caused by tainted food products, in which the rule had long been abolished. In those cases, the rationale for doing away with the privity requirement was that the products were inherently dangerous and presented a likelihood of harm to a great many people. What was the difference, asked the court, between those products and a product like an automobile, which, if defective, was also dangerous? Moreover, the manufacturer of the automobile was aware that it was to be used by persons other than its immediate purchaser, the retail dealer:

> If the nature of a thing is such that it is reasonably certain to place life and limb in peril when negligently made, it is then a thing of danger. Its nature gives warning of the consequences to be expected. If to the element of danger there is added knowledge that the thing will be used by persons other than the purchaser, and used without new tests, then, irrespective of contract, the manufacturer of this thing of danger is under a duty to make it carefully. . . . We have put aside the notion that the duty to safeguard life and limb, when the consequences of negligence may be foreseen, grows out of contract and nothing else. We have put the source of the obligation where it ought to be. We have put its source in the law. [217 N.Y. at 390, 111 N.E. at 1053]

The rule developed in *MacPherson* was gradually adopted by all of the states. From it, the modern rule of negligence has evolved: If a risk of injury from a defective product is reasonable to expect, a duty to take care in manufacturing the product extends to any foreseeable user of the product regardless of the lack of a contractual relationship between the manufacturer and the user. See also **foreseeability; negligence; proximate cause.**

MAGNUSON-MOSS WARRANTY ACT A 1975 amendment to the **Federal Trade Commission Act** that was designed to eliminate deceptive and confusing warranties [see **warranty**] on **consumer products**.

Generally, the Magnuson-Moss Warranty Act [15 U.S.C. §§2301–2312] requires **sellers** to (1) disclose the terms and conditions of written warranties for their products by means of clear and simple language, and (2) provide **consumers** with reasonable and effective remedies if a warranty is breached.

Provisions

Under the act, a seller who chooses to offer a written warranty with a product must conform to certain rules. First, the warranty must be embodied in a single document, not intermingled with other literature about the product. The warranty must answer the following questions in simple, easy-to-understand language:

- To whom is warranty protection extended? Is it limited to the original purchaser of the product, or does it also apply to persons who receive the product from the original purchaser?

- Which parts or components of the product are covered by the warranty? Which are not?

- How long will the warranty be in effect?

- What event will trigger the warranty obligation? Is purchase alone sufficient, or must the purchaser perform some action (such as sending in a registration card) in order to activate the warranty?

- What are the seller's obligations in case the product proves to be defective under the warranty? Will the seller repair the product or replace it?

- What procedure must the consumer follow in order to receive performance of the warranty obligation? This must include step-by-step instructions about whom to contact and how and when to return the defective product.
- What informal procedures are available in order to resolve any disputes about the warranty that might arise between the seller and consumer?
- Are there any limitations on the duration of implied warranties for the product? Because some states' laws do not allow such limitations, the warranty must also include the statement: "SOME STATES DO NOT ALLOW LIMITATIONS ON HOW LONG AN IMPLIED WARRANTY LASTS, SO THE ABOVE LIMITATION MAY NOT APPLY TO YOU."
- Are there any limitations or exclusions on the type of losses or **damages** that the warranty covers in case the product is defective under the warranty? Because some states' laws do not allow such limitations, the warranty must also state: "SOME STATES DO NOT ALLOW THE EXCLUSION OF INCIDENTAL OR CONSEQUENTIAL DAMAGES, SO THE ABOVE LIMITATION OR EXCLUSION MAY NOT APPLY TO YOU."
- The warranty must provide a statement that it confers special legal rights on the holder.

The terms of any written warranty provided with a product that costs more than $15 must be available to consumers prior to purchase. If the product is sold in a store, the seller must display the warranty with the product or have the warranty available for the consumer to read if he or she requests it. If the product is sold through a catalog, the seller must print the text of the warranty in the catalog or send it through the mail to any consumer who requests it.

Types of Warranties Allowed

Under the act, a written warranty on any product costing over $15 must clearly be designated either *full* or *limited*. This is to remedy the frequent practice of making up fanciful names for warranties that confuse consumers because they have no standardized meanings.

In order to qualify as a *full* warranty, a warranty must obligate the seller to repair a covered defect without charge and within a reasonable time. If repeated attempts at repair have failed, the seller must allow the consumer to choose between a refund or replacement of the product.

A *full* warranty must cover any owners of the product during the warranty period—not just the original purchaser.

Generally, a seller who offers a *full* warranty may not condition the performance of its warranty obligations on any act of the consumer. There are three exceptions to this rule. A seller may require the consumer: (1) to provide proof of when the product was purchased, (2) to notify the proper party that a defect exists, and (3) to take reasonable steps to return the product so that the defect may be remedied. The seller who offers a *full* warranty may not require the consumer to send back a warranty registration card as a condition for performance of the obligations imposed by the warranty.

A *full* warranty may be limited by duration. For example, it may be a *full two-year warranty.* However, a *full* warranty may not limit the duration of any implied warranties.

If a written warranty does not meet the requirements for a *full* warranty, it must be called a *limited* warranty.

No written warranty, either *full* or *limited,* may impose any "unreasonable" duties on the consumer in order to receive the benefits it promises. Moreover, no warranty may grant the seller the final authority to decide disputes arising out of the warranty's promises. With limited exceptions, it is forbidden to require the consumer to buy any other specific products or services in order to receive the benefits of a warranty. If the warranty specifies that repairs must be done by an "authorized service representative," both the service and any replacement parts must be provided free. See **tying agreement.**

Remedies under the Act

The Magnuson-Moss Warranty Act is unusual among federal consumer laws because it provides an injured consumer with a **private right of action** to sue directly to enforce its provisions. Thus, a consumer may bring a case in federal or state court for noncompliance with any of the act's provisions, as well as for breach of warranty. A consumer who wins his or her case by showing that damages were incurred as a result of the seller's violation of the act is also entitled to payment of attorney's fees. Without this feature, many aggrieved consumers might not consider a lawsuit under the act worthwhile, since the value of most consumer goods is small compared to the cost of paying an attorney. In addition to the consumer, the

Federal Trade Commission is authorized to bring suit against violators of the act.

Issues

Despite its many advantages for consumers, the Magnuson-Moss Warranty Act has been relatively underutilized as a basis for obtaining direct redress of consumer grievances involving warranties. The reason may be that the interaction between the act and state laws concerning warranties is quite complicated, making it difficult to manage a private action brought under its auspices.

The Federal Trade Commission has been far more active in using the act as a basis for suing violators and enjoining practices that are deceptive under its terms. Because of the relative complexity of the Magnuson-Moss Warranty Act, it seems likely that this pattern of government, rather than private, enforcement will continue.

MAIL-ORDER RULE A rule promulgated by the **Federal Trade Commission** setting certain requirements for **sellers** of mail-order merchandise.

Under the rule, mail-order merchandise must be shipped within the time period promised by the seller, or within 30 days if the seller does not state a time for shipment. If a shipping delay is expected, the seller must notify the **consumer** who placed the order and allow him or her the option of agreeing to the delay or canceling the order. The seller must provide a cost-free means for the consumer to reply to the notice.

If the consumer agrees to the delay, or does not reply at all, the seller has another 30 days in which to ship the ordered merchandise. If a further delay is expected, the notice procedure must be repeated. If the consumer decides to cancel the order, a full refund of any payment already made must be returned to the consumer within 7 working days after the cancellation is received.

Some types of mail-order transactions are exempt from the rule. These include telephone orders charged to a **credit card,** C.O.D. (collect-on-delivery) orders, magazine subscriptions after the first issue, sales of seeds and live plants, and photo-finishing services. So-called "negative option" sales are also exempt. Under these arrangements, the consumer agrees to periodic shipments of merchandise, which he or she has the option of accepting or sending back upon arrival.

Under the **Federal Trade Commission Act,** it is illegal to bill a consumer for merchandise sent through the U.S. mail that the consumer did not expressly order. Unordered merchandise received through the mail may be considered a gift. It is not necessary for the recipient to pay for it or return it.

Manufacturing Defect A defect [see **defectiveness**] in a product that arises as a result of some accident during the manufacturing process.

The distinguishing feature of a product with a manufacturing defect is that it does not conform to the manufacturer's own specifications. This is in contrast to a product with a **design defect,** which conforms perfectly to the manufacturer's plan. In the former case the defect lies in the deviation of the product from the plan. In the latter case, the plan itself is flawed because it is not reasonably safe or effective.

It is relatively easy to prove that a product has a manufacturing defect because there is an objective standard with which to compare it: the manufacturer's own design. If the product does not conform to the design, it is likely to be found defective. For example, a drill that comes off the assembly line with an ungrounded wire, a chair with a missing screw, and a hair dye solution with more peroxide than the formula called for are all examples of manufacturing gone awry.

However, the mere fact that a product deviates from the manufacturer's specifications for it will not automatically mean that it is defective in the eyes of the law. Manufacturers are not required to make perfect products. In fact, it is an impossibility. Some deviations that occur during the manufacturing process are to be expected in an imperfect world and do not make the product defective under the law. For that, it must be shown that the manufacturing anomaly in the product caused it to be unreasonably dangerous or unfit for a purpose for which it was intended. See **consumer expectation test; foreign–natural test; products liability; risk–utility test.**

Market Share Liability A method by which an injured **consumer** who does not know who made a product that caused an injury may recover compensation from a majority of all the **sellers** of that type of product. Recovery from each defendant seller is based on the percentage of market share each had at the time the defective product was sold. Generally, a consumer who has been injured by a defective product must establish the identity of the seller who was responsible for putting the product on the market before he or she can recover compensation in a **products liability** lawsuit. Usually, this will not be difficult because the consumer remembers who sold the product or the product label will list its manufacturer. However, in some cases the product may have been purchased long before the injury occurred and the source of the product forgotten. Market share liability is a way for injured consumers to circumvent this difficulty.

Market share liability was first invented to help the second-generation cancer victims of the defective drug diethylstilbestrol, or DES. The victims' mothers had all taken the drug during their pregnancies in order to prevent miscarriages. Only after their daughters became adults did the tragic side effects of the medication begin to appear: Exposure to the drug *in utero* could cause cancer in adulthood. By that time decades had passed. The victims' mothers could not recall in most cases exactly which company had sold the DES they had taken. Rather than let the cancer victims go without a remedy, courts fashioned the market share liability doctrine.

Because market share liability may, and probably will, result in a seller having to pay some compensation for an injury he or she did not cause, the requirements for its application are very strict.

First, the defective product must have been the **proximate cause** of the consumer's injuries. In the case of DES, the victims all developed rare cancers that virtually could only have been caused by exposure to the drug. A *signature injury* of this type is usually necessary to apply the doctrine, because speculation as to whether the product at issue caused the injury will not be allowed. For example, victims of retardation have had difficulty recovering from the makers of lead-based paint to which they were exposed in childhood because there are simply too many other possible causes of retardation to single out the lead-based paint as the cause.

Second, the product that caused the injury must be identical, or *fungible,* from maker to maker. In the DES case, the drug was essentially made from the same formula by all of the manufacturers.

Third, the injured consumer must sue enough sellers of the product to account for most of the market. This is to increase the chances that the maker of the product that actually caused the injury does not escape liability because he or she was not sued.

Fourth, the injured consumer must genuinely be unable to tell who the seller of the defective product was. A consumer may not, for example, throw away the containers of injurious products he or she used and then claim not to know who made them. In the DES cases, the victims had a perfect excuse: They were still unborn when the injury occurred to them.

If all the above prerequisites are met, the doctrine of market share liability may be applied. However, the defendant sellers of the defective product must be allowed to prove that they did not cause the injury. In the DES cases, for example, some manufacturers of the drug escaped liability by showing that they had not started to manufacture the drug until after the injured consumers were born.

If a seller is unable to prove that his or her product did not cause the injury, the seller will be required to pay compensation to the injured consumer based on the share of the market for the product that the seller had at the time of the injury. For example, if a company making DES had 70 percent of the market for the drug at the time a consumer was exposed to the drug, that company must pay 70 percent of the total amount of compensation due to the injured consumer.

Importance to Consumers

Market share liability and some other variations of it are important to consumers who, through no fault of their own, do not know who made the particular products that injured them. However, courts are reluctant to impose it if all of the conditions are not met because it represents a significant departure from a concept of fairness basic to American jurisprudence: namely, that one will only be required to compensate another for injuries he or she actually caused.

MEDICAL DEVICE   Any article intended for use in diagnosing, preventing, treating, or curing diseases or medical conditions in human beings. An amendment to the **Food, Drug & Cosmetic Act** in 1976 brought medical devices into the group of products subject to strict regulation by the federal government through the **Food and Drug Administration** (FDA). Prior to that time, regulations involving medical devices were largely ineffectual and quackery flourished. The 1976 amendments give medical devices the same importance as **drugs** in the effort to protect **consumers** against harmful or ineffective products.

Generally, medical devices differ from drugs only in the manner in which they affect the body. Drugs affect body structures or functions through chemical changes. Medical devices affect body structures or functions through mechanical manipulation. An article is subject to regulation as a medical device if it is intended to have a medical or therapeutic effect on the body, even if it has no effect at all. This is to protect the public from claims for products that may have no effect at all, but serve to mislead or raise false hopes.

Many types of products qualify as medical devices. They include products that are placed within the body, such as pacemakers, heart valves, artificial joints, surgical pins, or even tampons. Or, they may be products that are placed on the body, such as artificial prostheses, casts, braces, hearing aids, glasses, or even antisnoring contraptions. Medical devices also include products intended for the delivery of drugs or other substances into the body, such as hypodermic needles, feeding tubes, catheters, and breathing machines. Products that don't actually touch the body, but are used in making diagnoses or designing treatments are also medical devices. Examples include home pregnancy test kits or blood sugar testing kits for diabetics. Even such items as towels, chairs, and hot-water bottles may be considered medical devices if they are intended to treat a medical condition.

Sometimes there is a question whether a product is a medical device or a drug. The answer is important to consumers, because laws affecting a consumer's ability to sue the seller of such products differ depending on whether the product is a drug or a medical device. One product whose status has been at issue is the intrauterine contraceptive device, or IUD. Because some IUDs work by releasing copper or other substances into the body where it has a chemical effect, they have been classified as drugs in some instances.

Given the very broad spectrum of products classified as medical devices, the FDA divides them into three categories, which are subject to different levels of regulation and control. The FDA generally decides to classify a device as one or another type on the basis of the risks associated with its use or the extravagance of claims as to its effectiveness.

Medical devices are placed in the FDA's first category if they are relatively safe and make only modest claims. These devices are subject only to the requirement that they be properly labeled. The label must make no false or misleading claims about the efficacy of the product and must have instructions for its safe and effective use.

The second category of medical devices entails greater risks to consumers. These devices must meet standards for effectiveness, manufacturing quality, and truthfulness in advertising. Devices that fail to perform as intended may be taken off the market.

Devices placed into the FDA's third category are those that entail considerable risks unless used properly. These so-called Class III devices are subject to the most intense regulation, including the requirement that they pass safety and efficacy tests *before* they are marketed. Their use is also restricted to prescription by a licensed physician. These requirements are similar to those established for marketing new prescription drugs.

The Food, Drug & Cosmetic Act provides that federal regulations dealing with Class III medical devices preempt any other laws passed by the states [see **preemption**]. Practically speaking, this means that a Class III medical device that has passed the stringent requirements of the FDA is deemed safe and may not be regulated further by state laws. There is some controversy as to whether this rule is intended to preclude private lawsuits brought by individual consumers based on **common law tort** claims, such as **negligence** and **strict tort liability,** to recover for injuries caused by using a particular medical device that has passed the FDA's requirements. The courts are divided on this issue.

MEETING-THE-COMPETITION DEFENSE   A **seller**'s defense to the charge that he or she is engaged in **predatory pricing** in violation of the **antitrust law**s of the United States based on the argument that a price cut was necessary to meet the prices of competitors.

In order to use this argument successfully, a seller must show that competitors were actually offering lower prices and that the seller believed in good faith that it was necessary to match those prices in order to compete effectively.

In order to prove that a competitor was offering lower prices, a seller generally must present circumstantial evidence. This might consist of complaints from customers that they now can buy comparable goods from someone else at a lower price. Ironically, evidence gathered from the competitor himself or herself—as, for example, from a phone call inquiring about prices—may itself result in a violation of the **Sherman Antitrust Act.** Contact with competitors about their prices coupled with setting one's own prices to match creates a strong implication of illegal **price fixing.**

In order to prove his or her good faith in lowering prices, the seller must show that the competitor's goods or services were of like quality, although they need not be identical. A showing that customers have threatened to buy from competitors also bolsters the impression of good faith in setting prices to match.

The meeting-the-competition defense is very important in antitrust cases today. If the defense is proven, a seller's pricing is lawful even if it injures competition. This was not always so. In early cases, courts greatly restricted the availability of the defense. For example, a seller could only lower prices to *match* a competitor's prices, but not to *beat* them. Similarly, a seller was not allowed to lower prices in order to attract new customers, but only as a defensive measure to keep old ones from defecting to the competition. This strict interpretation actually served to foster rigid, identical pricing—precisely the opposite of the general purpose of antitrust laws. In recent years, allowance of the defense has broadened, resulting in enhanced price competition and generally lower prices for **consumers**.

MERGER   Occurs when independent **sellers** come under common control. Mergers may violate the **Clayton Antitrust Act** and other **antitrust laws** if they have a detrimental effect on competition. For antitrust purposes, it does not matter exactly how a merging of sellers takes place. The rules apply whether the merging occurs through the acquisition of stock or assets or some other procedure. The rules also apply to joint ventures by sellers who come together only temporarily.

Mergers may occur between direct competitors (horizontal mergers), between sellers and their distributors and suppliers (vertical mergers), or between sellers that have no logical association with each other at all (conglomerate mergers).

The law requires that mergers between sellers with over a certain amount of assets must be announced beforehand to the **Federal Trade Commission** and the Justice Department. Details of the proposed joining are then studied for their possible effects on competition. If these authorities decide that competition will be damaged, they may challenge the proposed merger in court on the grounds that it will violate the antitrust laws. This sort of prior review of planned mergers is considered preferable to challenging them after they have occurred. At that time it is more difficult to undo the tangled webs of ownership and control.

When deciding whether a proposed merger is likely to damage competition, the authorities will consider the type of products or services involved and whether there will still remain significant independent competitors providing the same product or service in the relevant geographic area. They will also examine whether there will still be significant independent competitors providing products or services that can substitute for the ones at issue. The market share of the product or service at issue that is ultimately commanded by the new entity will generally be crucial in determining whether a merger will have harmful effects on competition.

The avowed purpose of the Clayton Act in regard to mergers is to prevent large economic power from becoming concentrated in relatively few business entities. The provisions of the Clayton Act with regard to mergers are important to **consumers** because they guard against **monopolization** and the resulting rise in prices and decline in innovation. However, the Clayton Act was also designed to protect small businesses purely because they are considered a desirable feature of the economic life of the country. Ironically, by protecting small businesses, which are frequently inefficient and must charge higher prices to stay in business, the Clayton Act's merger provisions may harm consumers in the short run. In many cases, a proposed merger would result in a new seller that could afford economies of scale that could be passed on to consumers in the form of lower prices.

MISBRANDING The placement of false, misleading, or incomplete information on the label of a product in violation of standards set by federal or state laws. A product that is misbranded under federal law may be ordered off the market unless the label is changed to comply with the regulations.

The federal agencies most active in setting labeling requirements on **consumer products** are the **Food and Drug Administration** and the **Consumer Product Safety Commission.** These agencies have promulgated many rules for the labeling of **foods**, **drugs**, **medical devices**, **cosmetics**, hazardous substances, and other types of products in interstate commerce. The rules may be very detailed, specifying not only the type of information necessary on a product label but also the size, placement, and even color of the typeface used to convey it.

Typically, there are three types of misbranding: *compositional, economic,* and *safety.*

Compositional misbranding refers to inaccurate information as to the manufacturer of the product, the quantity, weight, or measure of the product in the container, the ingredients in the product, and even the product's name. The name of a product may be subject to detailed regulation in order to avoid misleading the **consumer.** For example, if there is a "common" or "usual" name for the product, it may have to be used instead of some fanciful made-up name.

Economic misbranding refers to false, misleading, or unproven claims as to product quality. This includes claims in reference to health benefits, nutritional value, or effectiveness. If the product is a food, any analysis of the nutritional value of the ingredients that appears on the label must be accurate. Moreover, descriptions of the product, its uses, and the effects users can expect are subject to very high standards of accuracy. Generally, anything that creates a false impression may be found to be misleading and the product it describes will be misbranded. For example, the claim that a vegetable oil "contains no cholesterol" may be misleading because, while true, it implies that some vegetable oils do contain cholesterol, which is not the case. A label prominently emphasizing an ingredient that is present in the product only in very small amounts might also be found to be misleading. A product named "Whole Wheat Crackers," for example, may be misbranded if it, in fact, contains only small amounts of whole wheat.

Safety misbranding refers to false, misleading, or incomplete information in warnings or instructions that accompany products.

A product is misbranded only if it fails to comply with specific labeling requirements set by law. Generally, a consumer may not sue privately to enforce the provisions of federal or state labeling laws [see **private right of action**]. However, a consumer who has suffered loss or injury when using a product that is subject to federal or state labeling requirements may present evidence that the product was misbranded when bringing a civil lawsuit against the product's **seller.** The fact that the label failed to comply with applicable laws will tend to show that the product was defective [see **defectiveness**] or that its seller was negligent [see **negligence**] in marketing it. On the other hand, the fact that a product did comply with federal or state labeling requirements does not preclude a seller's liability, because such laws set minimum standards only for safety and truthfulness. See also **Fair Packaging and Labeling Act; Nutrition Labeling and Education Act; warning defect.**

MISREPRESENTATION   A general term for any words or conduct that can reasonably be interpreted in a way that is not consistent with the truth. A misrepresentation may be a direct lie, an ambiguous statement, or even an impression made by conduct alone. It may be made intentionally, negligently, or entirely innocently.

Misrepresentation can be a **tort,** or private wrong, for which the law will provide a remedy. In **consumer** protection law, the misrepresentation will generally concern conduct by a **seller** that misleads a consumer about aspects of a product or service for sale. Sometimes it involves information provided by professional advisers, such as accountants, financial consultants, or attorneys. If the information provider intended to deceive the consumer with false or misleading information, the matter is known as *fraudulent misrepresentation* and is the same as **deceit.**

If the information provider did not intend to mislead the consumer and did not even know that the impression he or she gave was false, the misrepresentation involved may be what is known as the tort of *negligent misrepresentation.* Negligent misrepresentation is a far more complicated subject than fraudulent misrepresentation. As its name implies, negligent misrepresentation is a form of **negligence.** The wrong involved is the seller's failure to be as careful as he or she should have been in making a statement or conveying an impression about the product or service at issue.

At least since 1908 and *Cunningham v. CR Pease House Furnishing Company* [74 N.H. 435, 69 A. 120], American law has recognized a consumer's right to recover for physical injuries or damage to property resulting from a negligent misstatement by a seller. However, the requirements for proving the seller's liability in these cases are onerous. In order to win a **products liability** lawsuit based on negligent misrepresentation, the consumer must prove not only that the statement or impression made by the seller about the product was false, but that a reasonable person [see **reasonable person test**] in the seller's position would not have made the statement because he or she knew there was not enough reliable information to make it with confidence of its truth. Only statements or impressions about a *fact* may be the subject of a negligent misrepresentation lawsuit. Mere *opinions* do not qualify.

The consumer must also prove that the seller made the misleading statement or impression with the intent of influencing the consumer's conduct. The consumer must show that he or she acted in **reliance** on the false information, that the reliance was reasonable, and that it caused the injury or damage at issue. These requirements are frequently difficult to establish.

The question of whether a seller may be liable for negligent misrepresentation when the harm suffered as a result is only economic or monetary loss is more problematic than when physical harm has occurred. When physical harm has occurred because of a misrepresentation, courts consider that the harm done to the injured party outweighs the concern that the seller's fault in making the misstatement was very slight. However, courts are reluctant to allow consumers to recover where the only harm done was financial loss because of the almost limitless responsibility it would mean for sellers—responsibility far out of proportion to the extent of the wrong. After all, the person who negligently misrepresents something does not intend to deceive anyone. Then there is the issue of who would be entitled to compensation. Would anyone who heard the misleading information through any source whatsoever have a right to recover compensation? For example, could C sue A for negligently making an untrue statement if C only heard about the statement secondhand from B?

Today, the majority of states recognize an **action** for negligent misrepresentation when only financial losses have occurred. However, they all put significant restrictions on recovery. There are basically two different approaches to the issue. In the most restrictive states, only persons who the information provider knows will rely on the information can sue for negligent misrepresentation if the information turns out to be false. In the less restrictive states, anyone who foreseeably [see **foreseeability**] might rely on the faulty information has a right to sue. In this latter situation, an information provider might be liable for negligent misrepresentation if he or she did not know, but should have known, that someone was relying on the accuracy of the information.

In general, a lawsuit for negligent misrepresentation is not the most effective way for a consumer to achieve redress for harm caused by false or misleading statements. The requirements for proving a breach of **warranty** or a **strict tort liability** action for a **warning defect** are frequently much less burdensome. Nevertheless, a negligent misrepresentation lawsuit may be the most expeditious avenue for redress in some cases, particularly those involving the sale of stocks, securities, or other financial services.

MISUSE   A defense raised by the **seller** in a **products liability** suit brought by a **consumer** to recover compensation for harm caused by a defective [see **defectiveness**] product. The defense is based on the argument that a seller should not be responsible for injuries caused by improper use of his or her products.

Misuse may be found in cases in which a consumer uses a product for a totally unintended purpose, or in cases in which a consumer uses a product for its intended purpose but in an unintended manner. An example of the former type of misuse would be using a chlorine-based tile cleanser to brush teeth. An example of the latter type of misuse might be using the tile cleanser to clean tile—after mixing it with ammonia.

The mere fact that a consumer uses a product for an unintended purpose or in an unintended manner is not enough to establish misuse. The seller may still have a duty to protect against the consumer's injuries if the particular misuse of the product was foreseeable [see **foreseeability**]. Therefore, in order to establish the defense of misuse, the seller must also prove that the way the injured consumer was using the product was not predictable. In the above example, using tile cleanser to brush teeth would probably not be foreseeable. This use of the product would be misuse and the defendant would not be liable for injuries caused by it. On the other hand, there is greater likelihood that an uninformed consumer might mix a chlorine-based cleanser with ammonia or another product containing ammonia. Such a misuse may be foreseeable and the seller might be held liable for injuries caused by it.

In cases in which a misuse is foreseeable, a defendant may still escape liability for the resulting injuries by providing an adequate warning to the consumer to refrain from using the product in this way [see **warning defect**]. In the cleanser example, a warning that the product could be dangerous if mixed with ammonia or ammonia-based products would probably absolve the defendant of liability for injuries caused by such an act. Generally, a defendant is entitled to assume that consumers will read and heed warnings placed on products. Use of a product in contravention of an adequate warning is considered to be misuse. The argument that it is foreseeable that consumers will disregard adequate warnings is not effective—not because it is not true, but simply because liability for injuries caused by products must end somewhere.

In order for the defense to be effective, the particular misuse of the product must have been the cause of the consumer's injuries. In the cleanser example, the fact that the consumer misused the product by mixing it with ammonia would not relieve the defendant of liability if the consumer was not claiming injury from the resulting toxic fumes, but rather because she cut herself on a defect in the container when she was pouring it.

The defense of misuse may also be called *abnormal use* or *unexpected use*. See also **negligence; strict tort liability.**

MONOPOLIZATION   The possession of monopoly power by a **seller** with the intent to acquire, use, or maintain that power. Monopolization is illegal under the **antitrust law**s of the United States. A seller may be guilty of monopolization whether he or she acts alone or as part of a group of sellers acting together.

Monopoly power arises when a seller, or group of sellers acting together, has the power to control prices or exclude competition. A monopolist is able to set prices for goods or services far above the cost of producing them. Depending on the type of product or service, this price could be very high indeed—limited only by the point at which **consumers** would opt not to buy the product at all. If the product or service is very essential, consumers may be willing to pay a very high price. In addition to allowing the monopolist to charge high prices, the existence of monopoly power also discourages improvements and innovations in the monopolist's products and services. Thus, consumer interests are always threatened by the existence of monopolies.

Interestingly, however, American law does not prohibit the mere possession of monopoly power. After all, a monopoly may result from an accident, from superior skill and efficiency, or from the fact that no one else wishes to sell a certain product or service. A seller of sculptures made of bat guano, for example, may have a monopoly through no effort of his or her own! A monopoly may also result from the grant of a patent that entitles its holder to the exclusive use of a certain process or design. Generally, so long as the possessor of monopoly power has no intention to exclude competitors by using his or her power, there is no illegal monopolization. In the case of patent holders, this would mean no intention to exclude competitors beyond the rights to do so granted by the patent.

The law also does not prohibit the mere intention to acquire monopoly power. A small seller in a large market with much competition may have all the intention in the world to acquire a monopoly. However, although he or she might be guilty of other illegal acts performed in an effort to monopolize, he or she cannot be charged with the offense of monopolization. A violation of the law occurs only when a seller commands enough of the market that monopoly power is plausible and the seller has an intention to acquire, use, and maintain that power and more. It is generally accepted that this point is reached when a single seller, or a group of sellers acting together, has control of more than 65 percent of the market for a particular good or service.

The reason the law is careful to require both possession of monopoly power and the intent to use it has to do with the particular paradox of antitrust law in general: The policy of encouraging vigorous competition may be undermined if competitors have no rewards to look forward to for winning. As one prominent jurist put it, "The successful competitor, having been urged to compete, must not be turned upon when he wins." [Judge Learned Hand in *United States v. Aluminum Company of America*, 148 F.2d 416 at 430 (2nd Cir. 1945)]

In any case in which a seller is accused of monopolization, a crucial task will be to determine the relevant market for the goods or services at issue. The relevant market includes both geographic area and product or service categories. The relevant geographic market is generally the area in which the seller operates and in which consumers could reasonably turn for substitutes. For example, the relevant market for a computer dealer may well be national, since buyers can easily turn to mail order if the only computer dealer in town is charging exorbitant prices. However, the relevant market for a trash collection service may well be confined to the municipality in which it operates. Consumers in that town cannot easily turn to out-of-town companies for substitute service. Even if an out-of-town company agreed to collect trash in the community, it would probably have to charge very high prices to make up for its increased travel costs.

Similarly, the relevant product or service market is that category of product or service in which individual, unique products may be substituted and still meet the needs of the consumer. For example, in one famous case, a company that controlled 75 percent of the national market for cellophane was found not guilty of monopolization because the court defined the relevant product market as including all "flexible packaging materials." With the market defined this broadly, the cellophane maker had only 20 percent of that market—well below having monopoly power. [*United States v. E. I. du Pont de Nemours & Company*, 351 U.S. 377 (1956)]

Monopolization cases are extremely difficult to prove for another reason: It is necessary to find that the accused monopolist intended to discourage competition by his or her actions. Since sellers rarely admit this was their intent, intention must be inferred from the seller's behavior. However, some actions send mixed signals at best. For example, the classic maneuver of a seller who wants to use monopoly power is to raise prices after the competition has been driven out of business. Yet, when prices are raised, competitors are attracted back into the market. Recently, there has been a trend away from finding monopolization if the accused seller has acquired and kept monopoly power through legitimate competitive means and has not engaged in other acts that are considered illegal under other antitrust laws.

MUCKRAKERS A group of investigative journalists who specialized in exposing industrial and political corruption in the early twentieth century.

The group was given this nickname after President Theodore Roosevelt, in expressing his disapproval of them, invoked the seventeenth-century Puritan allegory *Pilgrim's Progress* by John Bunyan. That work alludes to a "Man with the Muck-rake," happier raking "the filth of the floor" than looking upward to nobler things. The moniker "muckraker" stuck. Roosevelt tolerated the muckrakers' activities reluctantly. Although they provided valuable support for many of his reforms, he believed that they distorted the truth and stirred up dangerous public unrest.

The muckrakers' influence on public policy was magnified by innovations in printing that greatly reduced the cost of magazine publishing and allowed in-depth analyses of popular topics to reach the masses for the first time. In fact, most of the muckrakers worked for popular magazines of the day.

The work of the muckrakers covered a broad swathe of topics of popular concern. Long suspicious of the power of big business and politicians, the public devoured the muckrakers' detailed and often hotly indignant accounts of industrial fraud and political corruption. Many topics were of direct concern to **consumer**s, especially the accounts of **adulteration** of the nation's food supply and harmful patent medicines. In addition, exposés on how large business interests were destroying free competition were important to consumers because of the implications such monopolies had in creating unfair pricing and shoddy merchandise.

Some of the most prominent writers on these topics included the novelist, Upton Sinclair [see **Sinclair, Upton Beall**], whose novel *The Jungle* (1906) alarmed middle-class Americans about unsanitary methods in food production. Ida Tarbell [see **Tarbell, Ida Minerva**] wrote a famous account of how the Standard Oil trust had crushed its competition with unfair methods (1904). And Samuel Hopkins Adams produced an electrifying account of fraud in the patent medicine business in 1905.

The muckrakers were responsible for helping galvanize popular support for reforms that directly benefited consumers. Most notable were the passage of the Pure Food and Drug Act of 1906, which imposed nationwide standards of purity and safety on foods and drugs, and the breakup of some of the most notorious trusts that were threatening the competitive system of free enterprise.

The age of the muckrakers waned after 1912, perhaps because a jaded public felt complacent with the measures that had been taken to remedy the greatest abuses. However, the legacy of the muckrakers lives on in the tradition of investigative journalism that Americans have come to expect. Among the most prominent "neo-muckrakers" for consumer interests is

Ralph Nader [see **Nader, Ralph**], whose book *Unsafe at Any Speed* (1965) forced reforms in the automobile industry and whose continuing activism still incites consumer pressure for safer products.

NADER, RALPH (1934–)   A lawyer and **consumer** activist whose name is virtually synonymous with the modern consumer movement in the United States. Nader, together with legions of disciples throughout the nation, has formed and staffed over 40 consumer protection organizations. He has exposed countless instances of consumer **fraud** and corporate **negligence,** as well as provided crucial lobbying for the passage of most of the major federal consumer protection legislation in the past 30 years. Nader, alone and with others, has written or sponsored scores of books and reports on consumer issues. His organizations publish numerous newsletters, pamphlets, brochures, and manuals on consumer issues.

Nader was born in Winsted, Connecticut, in 1934. He was the youngest of four children born to Nadra and Rose Nader, Lebanese immigrants who earned their living running a family restaurant. The senior Naders fostered an atmosphere of intellectual stimulation and inquiry at home. The family dinner table became the forum for nightly discussions on social issues of the day. As a child, young Ralph already had a reputation for studious intensity. It is said that he read back issues of the Congressional Record for recreation. By the age of 14 he had also read the works of the early **muckrakers,** which profoundly influenced his thinking on social ills and the citizen's duty to confront them.

Nader entered Princeton University in 1951. In an age of silent conformity, he was already notorious for his outspoken advocacy. After finding numerous dead birds on campus following spraying with DDT, Nader tried unsuccessfully to have the chemical banned by the university. This experience and other failed attempts to stir up popular support on campus for social causes impressed Nader with the appalling apathy with which most Americans view their world. Nader graduated in 1955 and entered Harvard Law School. More disillusionment awaited him there. Nader viewed the school as awash in moral complacency and preoccupied with narrow intellectualism. He complained that the law school was no more than a "high-priced tool factory," producing lawyers to be the corporate tools of the nation's rich and powerful. [Bollier, page 2]. An interest in social issues was considered a sign of a soft intellect. However, while still at Harvard, Nader began an investigation into the safety of automobiles, an interest that would later lead to his career as a consumer activist.

After graduation from Harvard, Nader spent several years in private practice in Hartford, Connecticut, where he handled automobile accident cases, among other things. Between 1961 and 1964, he worked as a freelance journalist and traveled the world, learning how other countries dealt with consumer issues. In 1964, Nader returned to the United States to serve as a consultant for Daniel Patrick Moynihan, then an Assistant Secretary of Labor. In that post he wrote an official critique of the federal highway safety program. The following year, 1965, Nader published the book that would make him a household name, *Unsafe at Any Speed*, an indictment of the General Motors Company (GM) for negligence in the design of the Corvair sports car.

Nader's book evoked only modest interest at first. It was GM's reaction to it that catapulted both it and Nader into national prominence. Irritated by the book and the possibility that Nader would testify against the company in civil lawsuits, GM hired a private investigator to tail Nader and unearth discrediting details about his life. The plan backfired when the spying and dirty tricks became public. Senator Ribicoff, before whose committee on automobile safety Nader was to testify, summoned the president of General Motors to explain his company's harassment. Public attention was focused on automobile safety as never before. Adverse publicity and Nader's invasion of privacy lawsuit against the company induced GM to offer Nader $425,000 in settlement of his claims. Nader used the money to fund the start-up of dozens of consumer organizations, beginning with the Center for the Study of Responsive Law in 1968.

In the mid-1960s, Nader's popularity soared. He was likened to David slaying Goliath—an underdog who prevailed against enormous odds in the age of impersonal, unaccountable bureaucracies. Perhaps the most admired man in the country at the time, Nader was even mentioned as a possible presidential candidate. His celebrity inspired legions of the young and idealistic to descend on Washington, D.C. Many of them found jobs in Nader's newly created consumer organizations. There, working long hours for little pay, the bright young activists pushed their way into government offices and corporate suites, researching issues, writing reports, and bullying staid old bureaucracies, such as the **Federal Trade Commission,** to act in the consumer's interest. Their sometimes hair-trigger zealotry earned them the sobriquet "Nader's Raiders."

Nader's leadership and the energy of his followers helped push through much of the major consumer legislation of the 1960s and 1970s, including the **National Traffic and Motor Vehicle Safety Act,** the **Federal Cigarette Labeling and Advertising Act,** the **Truth in Lending Act,** the **Fair Credit Reporting Act,** the **Fair Credit Billing Act,** and the **Fair Packaging and Labeling Act.** Nader's activities were instrumental in the creation of a number of new government agencies, including the **Consumer Product Safety Commission,** the Environmental Protection Agency, and the Occupational Safety and Health Administration.

In spite of Nader's success in lobbying for legislation and the government regulation of business practices, Nader's own philosophy remains decidedly in favor of the free market. In his ideal world, numerous aggressively competing businesses would increase efficiency and improve quality without the necessity of government intervention. Instead, a countervailing force of committed, active, informed, and intelligent consumers would, through the power of their informed spending, encourage **sellers** to improve the safety, effectiveness, and economy of their products. It is the unfortunate fact of public apathy that has made greater government intervention necessary. Nader's commitment to personal activism is reflected in his major umbrella organization, **Public Citizen,** which oversees the activities of Nader's groups. The name of the group refers to Nader's conviction that each individual should care enough to take active part in shaping the world for the better. One should not seek to be a private citizen, says Nader, but an engaged, questioning "public citizen." [Bollier, page 3]

In the 1980s, Nader's influence seemed to wane. The reasons were multifarious—not the least of which was Nader's very success. Many of Nader's protégés were appointed to government posts during the Carter administration in the late 1970s. Complacency set in once again as consumers naively assumed that consumer problems were being taken care of by the new legislation and agencies formed by Nader's initiative. Idealistic baby boomers were aging and settling down to make their personal fortunes, instead of working for public causes. The Reagan administration began pursuing deregulation, and a consumer spending binge characterized the era. Nader and consumerism were old hat, even tiresome. One journalist dubbed Nader the "national nag." Personal tragedy also diverted Nader's energy. He suffered the death of his brother and bouts of personal illness. Critics, ironically taking their cue from Nader's own tactic of investigating the powerful, began to inquire into Nader's personal affairs. Though conceding his brilliance, detractors described Nader as driven, intense, humorless, and even hypocritical. Staffers at his organizations frequently complained that Nader expected them to live the same ascetic lifestyle as he did and to keep pace with his own frenetic work schedule. Rumors surfaced about Nader's property holdings and investments in some companies that would have benefited from negative revelations about other companies made by Nader groups. None of the vague allegations was proven.

As the 1980s waned, Nader began making a quiet comeback. His efforts at reform late in the decade included lobbying to repeal the exemption from the nation's **antitrust laws** enjoyed by the insurance industry, increased automobile safety, and a plan to encourage government to use its vast purchasing power to reward companies that cut down on waste and provide quality products. In the 1990s, Nader has also turned his attention to investigating Congress and the activities of particular lawmakers.

NATIONAL CONSUMERS LEAGUE Founded in 1899, the first private, national organization to style itself a **consumer** protection group in the United States. Initially most concerned with ensuring fair treatment for workers, the National Consumers League soon joined the cause of improving the safety of the nation's **food** supply and lobbied for passage of the Pure Food and Drug Act and the Meat Inspection Act in 1906. The league also operated a product endorsement program for food manufacturers by setting standards for sanitary procedures and wholesome ingredients and inspecting factories for compliance. A label certifying compliance was awarded to those manufacturers that met the standards.

The National Consumers League was also an important supporter of the **Food, Drug & Cosmetic Act** of 1938. Subsequently, it has kept up pressure on both the food and **drug** industries by alerting consumers to contaminated foods and the dangers inherent in many over-the-counter and prescription drugs. In recent years, the concerns of the National Consumers League have expanded to include such diverse consumer concerns as telemarketing **fraud,** deceptive advertising, health care, financial services, and telecommunications access. Much of its focus continues to be trained on fair labor issues and workplace conditions.

True to its slogan "investigate, educate, and advocate," the National Consumers League commissions numerous surveys and studies on consumer and fair labor issues. It publishes the results in numerous newsletters, brochures, and manuals, many of which are available in languages other than English. It also maintains a telephone hotline on consumer fraud, with bilingual (Spanish/English) services. The league conducts conferences, seminars, and workshops on issues within its sphere of interest. It lobbies in state legislatures and Congress for changes in the laws affecting consumers. It frequently sends representatives to testify before federal agencies concerned with consumer protection.

The National Consumers League is a nonprofit organization governed by a board of directors with broad experience in law, business, labor, and consumer protection issues. In 1994, its membership was approximately 8,000. It is based in Washington, D.C.

NATIONAL HIGHWAY TRAFFIC SAFETY ADMINISTRATION

An agency within the Department of Transportation that is charged with administering certain federal laws pertaining to motor vehicle safety, including the **National Traffic and Motor Vehicle Safety Act** and the Motor Vehicle Information and Cost Saving Act.

As part of its efforts to reduce the number of injuries and fatalities resulting from motor vehicle accidents, the National Highway Traffic Safety Administration prescribes standards for safety features and safety-related performance for automobiles sold in the United States. The agency is empowered to order manufacturers to repair or redesign noncomplying vehicles. In addition, the agency has the power to order a recall of vehicles found to have safety problems. The agency also provides **consumers** with information concerning the relative safety of various automotive features as well as soliciting information from consumers about safety concerns regarding automobiles. The agency establishes safeguards for preventing **fraud** by **sellers** of automobiles who turn back the odometers on used vehicles.

Among its other activities, the National Highway Traffic Safety Administration conducts extensive testing and research on motor vehicle safety features in order to encourage manufacturers to adopt advanced safety designs. It evaluates various automobiles and automobile equipment on the basis of safety. It also develops and promulgates mandatory fuel economy standards. The agency operates the National Center for Statistics and Analysis, where it maintains a large database containing information about, and analysis of, accidents on the nation's highways.

NATIONAL TRAFFIC AND MOTOR VEHICLE SAFETY ACT　The federal law [15 U.S.C. §§1381–1431] that created the **National Highway Traffic Safety Administration** and empowers it to establish and enforce motor vehicle safety standards.

The National Traffic and Motor Vehicle Safety Act prohibits the manufacture and sale of vehicles that fail to comply with regulations issued by the National Highway Traffic Safety Administration. It also prohibits modifications by **sellers** of automobiles that would render required safety features inoperative. Each automobile manufactured or sold that does not comply with safety standards represents a separate violation of the act, which may be punished by penalties of up to $1,000 each. Under the act, the National Highway Traffic Safety Administration may prohibit the sale of vehicles that do not comply and order the recall of vehicles already sold.

When a recall is ordered, the seller of the vehicle must notify **consumers** who purchased it by first-class mail. An explanation of the reason for the recall must be included in the letter, including a description of the defect and the possible risk it presents. The letter must explain the measures to be taken to remedy the defect. It must notify the consumer that the remedial measures will be undertaken free of charge and explain the procedure for obtaining the remedy. The remedy may be repair of the defect, replacement of the defective part, replacement of the entire vehicle, or a refund. Generally, the seller may determine which remedy it will offer.

Remedies for defects in recalled motor vehicles need not be offered free of charge beyond eight years from the first sale of the car, or three years beyond the first sale of a tire.

The obligations of sellers of motor vehicles under the act do not affect any other obligations they may have to honor a **warranty** or to comply with other state or federal laws.

NEGLIGENCE　A **tort**, or private wrong, that occurs when a person causes harm to another by failing to be as careful as conditions require. Negligence represents one of the most momentous developments in the **common law** and an important avenue of redress for **consumers** who have suffered harm caused by defective [see **defectiveness**] products.

History

The idea that one's legal liability for causing harm to another should depend on whether one's conduct was in some way blameworthy is not of great antiquity in the Anglo-American legal tradition, going back at most 1,000 years. Prior to that time the basic rule was one of *strict liability:* A person who caused harm was required to pay compensation to the injured party regardless of whether the harm was intentional or purely accidental.

In theory, this rule in civil disputes [see **civil law**] continued into the nineteenth century. However, by that time so many complicated exceptions to it had developed—particularly in the case of accidentally caused harm—that it was virtually impossible to assess the chances of prevailing in a lawsuit. Casting about for a more workable system, judges seized on a then little-known legal theory under which one's legal responsibility for accidentally caused harm depended on the degree of care one took to prevent it. This was negligence liability.

Legal historians are divided on the reasons for the sudden rise to prominence of the negligence concept in the nineteenth century. Some see it as a way of simplifying legal responsibility in a period when so many exceptions had virtually swallowed up the old strict liability rule and left no avenues for injured persons to recover compensation. Conversely, others view the emergence of negligence liability as a way to protect the risky, but important, new enterprises of the Industrial Revolution from the financial ruin that might have resulted if the old rule of compensation for harm regardless of fault was enforced.

Whatever the reason, the novel idea that it was necessary to prove that a person acted carelessly, or *negligently,* in order to establish his or her legal liability for accidental harm first appeared in a legal case in the United States in 1850. [*Brown v. Kendall,* 60 Mass. 292 (6 Cush 292) (1850)] By the end of the century it was the dominant legal theory upon which recovery for accidental harm was based.

Unfortunately, however, the necessity of proving the negligence of a **seller** as a prerequisite to recovery for harm caused by defective products was a great disadvantage to consumers. The average consumer rarely had the specialized knowledge to show that a seller had not been sufficiently careful in designing or making the products that caused harm. Moreover, many other restrictions were established that made it hard for injured persons to recover on negligence grounds [see **contributory negligence; privity of contract;**].

However, restrictions on recovery in negligence cases began to erode in the twentieth century as the era of mass marketing of consumer goods led to grave inequities in bargaining power between individual consumers and the giant corporations that made their goods. Today, complaints based on negligence are probably the most frequently litigated of all consumer claims involving harm caused by products. See also **strict tort liability.**

Application

As its name suggests, the tort of negligence involves careless or inadvertent behavior. However, legal responsibility for such behavior depends on additional factors beyond merely an inattentive state of mind.

First, some actual harm must have resulted from the allegedly careless conduct before a case of negligence can be made. The law does not compensate mere potential victims of harm.

Second, the careless conduct must have caused the harm. The causal link between the conduct and the harm must be sufficiently strong to justify holding the perpetrator responsible for it [see **proximate cause**].

Third, the person who caused harm must have had a **duty of care** to look out for the welfare of the person who suffered the harm. In the early days of negligence law, legal responsibility for harm depended greatly on the relationship between the person who caused the harm and the injured party. For example, an innkeeper had a strong duty of care to look out for the safety of his or her guests, while a landowner had only a slight duty of care to watch out for the safety of trespassers. Today, this duty is less dependent on formal relationships between the harmer and the harmed and simply depends in most cases on what amount of care and foresight would reasonably be necessary to avoid the type of harm that occurred. The amount of carefulness reasonably necessary to avoid foreseeable harm—and, hence, liability for negligence—is called the **standard of care.** See also **foreseeability; reasonable person test.**

Fourth, the conduct of the person who caused the harm must have fallen below this standard of care under the circumstances. In other words, that person must have "breached" his or her duty of care.

Therefore, a court will ask two questions: Did the defendant act reasonably with regard to the safety of the plaintiff under the circumstances? And, if not, did the defendant's failure to act reasonably cause the harm suffered by the plaintiff? If the defendant did not act reasonably and his or her conduct caused the harm, he or she will be required to pay for it.

Importance to Consumers

Today, consumers who have suffered injury because of a defective product may be able to recover compensation from the product's seller by bringing a lawsuit based on negligence in any aspect of the product's manufacture and sale. This includes negligent design, negligent testing, negligent manufacture, negligent inspection, negligent misrepresentation, negligent marketing, and negligence in any number of other processes necessary to making and selling products. Negligence as a basis for imposing legal responsibility in **products liability** cases has somewhat declined in recent years with the rise of strict tort liability, which favors consumers by doing away with the necessity to evaluate a manufacturer's or seller's conduct. Nevertheless, negligence principles continue to be important in product **design defect** cases and cases in which defective warnings [see **warning defect**] are alleged, even when these cases are based on the doctrine of strict tort liability.

NEGLIGENCE *PER SE*   A rule of law in some states under which violation of a statute is automatic proof that the violator was negligent and may be held liable in a civil lawsuit for the **tort** of **negligence.** The rule is helpful to **consumer**s by making it unnecessary to prove what degree of carefulness [see **standard of care**] the **seller** of a product that caused injury was required to meet. Under the rule, the statute that was violated itself prescribes the minimum degree of care necessary to avoid liability. If the seller violated the statute, it also means that he or she did not meet the required standard of care and is liable for negligence.

For example, suppose a statute specifies that cider may not contain over a certain percentage of alcohol. A cider manufacturer makes cider of greater alcoholic content, thereby violating the statute. A consumer drinks the cider, becomes drunk, and wanders onto a busy highway, where he is struck by a car. The consumer sues the cider manufacturer for negligence. Under the negligence *per se* rule, the fact that the cider seller violated the statute is proof *per se* (in itself) that the seller was negligent and must compensate the injured consumer. Without the rule, the injured consumer would have to prove that the cider's alcoholic content was unreasonably high by showing that a large number of people could not drink it without becoming dangerously intoxicated, or other such scientific evidence on its harmful effects. The need for this type of complex, detailed, and speculative evidence is avoided by the negligence *per se* rule.

States differ in how they apply the negligence *per se* rule. In some states the rule makes violation of a statute conclusive in a civil lawsuit on the issue of the violator's negligence. In other states, it merely raises a presumption that the violator was negligent, which he or she may rebut with other evidence.

Also, even though the negligence *per se* rule may conclusively establish that one who violated a statute was negligent, it will still be necessary to prove that the negligence was the **proximate cause** of the injury. For example, suppose the consumer in the above example was an inexperienced drinker and would have become drunk even if the cider had not contained excessive alcohol. Even though the cider seller was negligent in making a cider with excessive alcohol, the excessive alcohol was not the cause of the injury.

In addition, in order for the rule to apply, the statute that was violated must have been designed to protect people in the same situation as the injured consumer. For example, if the cider statute was passed in order to prevent bottles of cider from bursting during fermentation, it was not addressed to the problem of intoxication at all. In this case, the rule would not be applicable to help the consumer who became intoxicated and wandered onto the roadway. It would only apply to help the consumer who was injured by a bursting bottle.

Another aspect of the rule that is favorable to consumers is that while the violation of a statute results in negligence *per se,* the opposite is not true. Compliance with a statute does not necessarily mean that the one complying was sufficiently careful to escape liability for negligence. Statutes set *minimum* requirements only. An injured consumer may still be able to prove that the circumstances of the case required the seller to be even more careful than the statute required.

NONDISCLOSURE   A failure to disclose facts of which one is aware. Nondisclosure may be a form of **misrepresentation,** a **tort** for which the law will provide a remedy.

In the **consumer** law context, nondisclosure generally occurs when a **seller** fails to inform a consumer about facts concerning a product or service that would be important for the consumer to know in order to decide whether to buy it. It is easy to see how conduct designed to conceal product defects is a form of misrepresentation. For example, plastering over cracks in a foundation or turning back the odometer on a used automobile is active conduct that makes a representation or impression about the product. The representation is that the product does not have a foundation problem or that the car is less used than it is.

A far more difficult situation occurs where there is no conduct or representation made at all. Suppose the seller takes no measures to conceal the condition of a product, but merely passively remains silent about certain defects of which he or she is aware. Will the consumer have a remedy if the product turns out to be defective? Generally, the answer is "yes" if certain circumstances are present. The seller will have a duty [see **duty of care**] to disclose facts about a product in any of the following circumstances:

- the fact is about something that is important to a reasonable consumer, or known to be important to the particular consumer.

- the fact concerns a latent condition of the product. If the condition is obvious and a reasonable consumer would discover the condition himself or herself prior to the sale, the seller has no duty to disclose it.

- the seller is asked a direct question about the possibility of the existence of the fact that the seller knows. For example, if a seller knows that the odometer on an automobile is inaccurate and the consumer asks directly about the accuracy of the odometer, the seller has a duty to disclose what he or she knows. In general, the consumer's question need not be exactly about the specific undisclosed fact in order to create a duty of disclosure on the part of the seller. For example, if the consumer asks whether a house has a "water problem," the seller will probably have a duty to disclose that the basement floods every time it rains. The consumer does not have to ask, "does the basement flood?" in order to trigger the duty to disclose. On the other hand, a question like "Is there anything else I should know about this product?" may be too general and vague to trigger a duty to disclose facts about the product.

- the seller receives information that directly contradicts a representation about the product that he or she has already made. In such a case, the seller has an affirmative duty to correct the representation that was already made.

- the seller learns that a third party has made an untrue representation about the product to the consumer. In such a case, the seller has a duty to correct the misimpression that he or she knows the consumer has.

- the seller stands in a fiduciary relationship with the consumer. That is to say, the seller already has a legally recognized duty to be scrupulously honest in his or her dealings with the consumer. For example, an attorney has a legally recognized duty to be completely honest with a client.

- in general, whenever the seller's knowledge of the product is considerably greater than the consumer's.

If any of these conditions are met, a seller's failure to disclose facts about a product or service may amount to a misrepresentation for which the law will provide a remedy in the form of a tort lawsuit. However, there may be rare circumstances in which none of the above circumstances are present. In such cases, a seller generally does not have an affirmative duty to come forward with information about a product for sale. Suppose, for example, that the seller of a house knows that a Siberian elm tree on the property is a nuisance, getting into the sewers, dropping leaves and sticks, and attracting annoying insects that have infested it to the point of weakening it. If a prospective buyer does not ask about the tree or the sewer, the seller probably does not have to say "By the way, this tree is a nuisance." The existence of a duty to disclose may also depend on whether the seller is in the business of selling the particular product, or whether he or she is merely making a "onetime only" sale.

Even assuming that all of the conditions are met that give rise to a seller's duty to disclose facts about a product he or she is selling, an **action** for misrepresentation may not be necessary. Generally, the law implies that the seller of goods has made certain representations about the condition of the goods he or she sells that amount to a **warranty** that they will be useful and not defective. If the goods turn out to be defective, this implied warranty may be breached and the consumer can use that avenue for redress. See **implied warranty of merchantability.**

NOTICE IN WARRANTY Under the **Uniform Commercial Code** [§2-607(3)(a)], a buyer who believes that a product does not conform to its **warranty** must inform the **seller** of this fact in order to preserve his or her warranty rights. If the buyer does not give the seller notice within a reasonable time after the sale that a product warranty has been breached, the buyer will be barred from any remedy.

Three reasons justify this rule: (1) Notifying the seller that a warranty has been breached gives the seller an opportunity to repair the defect and save the goodwill of the **consumer** before the matter ends up in court. This also saves public resources by encouraging a private settlement of the matter. (2) Notice gives the seller an opportunity to know what the buyer's complaint will be if the matter is taken to court. (3) The requirement that notice be given within a reasonable time provides a seller with some security against being called to account for defects in a product sold in the distant past. It would simply be unfair to allow a buyer to complain about a defect years after purchasing the product, by which time it might be substantially altered.

Generally, a consumer is required to give notice that a warranty has been breached only to the immediate seller of the goods. It is not necessary to notify the manufacturer of the goods, even if the manufacturer was the one who extended the warranty. After being notified of the problem by the buyer, the immediate seller then has the duty to inform the manufacturer or whoever extended the warranty.

Notice that a warranty has been breached may be oral or in writing. It is not necessary to actually use the words "breach of warranty." Nor is it necessary for the buyer to demand compensation or to threaten a lawsuit when notifying the seller that a warranty has been breached. It is enough to tell the seller in a general way that the goods do not conform to the terms of the warranty. However, merely stating that there may be a "problem" with the goods might not be enough. Also, the filing of a lawsuit against the seller for breach of warranty does not count as "notice" to the seller because one of the purposes of requiring notice to sellers about breaches of warranty is to avoid lawsuits.

The issue often most difficult to resolve with regard to notice in warranty is what counts as "within a reasonable time." The law does not define this term. Rather, it depends on the circumstances of each case. One factor to consider is the obviousness of the defect in the product. If the defect is very obvious, it seems reasonable to require the buyer to notify the seller very soon. For example, if a sports car was supposed to be red and the car that was delivered was blue, it would be reasonable to require the buyer to notify the seller immediately and not drive around for several months before complaining that the car was not red as promised. On the other hand, if the defect in the sports car was a brake problem that only showed up when the weather was cold, the buyer might reasonably be allowed to notify the seller of the problem after the first cold spell in which the defect was obvious, even if it was six months or more from the time of purchase.

In general, the buyer's obligation to notify the seller of a breach of warranty begins only when the buyer knows, or should know, that the goods do not conform to the warranty. The buyer will then be allowed a "reasonable time" from that point to comply with the notice requirement. By no means may the buyer delay notifying the seller in order to allow damages resulting from the breach of warranty to mount. For example, if a pesticide warranted to be effective against grasshoppers turns out to promote their growth instead, the buyer will not be allowed to wait until giant grasshoppers have totally consumed his or her crops before notifying the pesticide's seller of the problem.

Another unresolved issue concerns the identity of the person who must give the notice. It is clear that the buyer of the defective product is under an obligation to notify the immediate seller of the defects in the product and the possible breach of warranty. However, are other people who might use the product and be injured by its failure to conform to a warranty also required to notify the seller in order to qualify for a remedy? Generally, if the injured nonbuyer is a private citizen (not a commercial dealer) who has suffered physical injury (not just economic loss), the rule is that no notice of the breach of warranty is necessary.

Nutrition Labeling and Education Act A federal law passed in 1990 [Pub. L. No. 101-535, 104 Stat. 2353] requiring detailed nutritional labeling on most food products. Although the **Food, Drug & Cosmetic Act** of 1938 gave the **Food and Drug Administration** (FDA) broad powers to regulate food labeling, it was clear by the 1980s that the old regulations did not address changes in nutritional needs for average Americans. The old labeling requirements were designed during the Great Depression, when malnutrition was a serious problem; information regarding the vitamin content of foods was vital at that time. Moreover, official government dietary guidelines of the period were recommending large amounts of fat in the diet—the opposite of today's view. As the nation became less concerned with malnutrition and more concerned with problems caused by overeating, the old label requirements did not change. While a **consumer** could find out how much niacin a product contained, for example, he or she was at a loss to discover the amount of fat, saturated fat, cholesterol, fiber, or other constituents recently implicated in causing disease. In typical fashion, food producers were quick to respond to new information about nutritional needs with fanciful, but unsubstantiated, claims for the health benefits of their goods. While the FDA could simply have revamped their rules regarding food labeling in response to the new concerns, Congress felt that an entirely new law was needed to lend added authority to the agency's undertaking.

The Nutrition Labeling and Education Act has four major effects on food labeling:

First, it applies to the vast majority of food products, not just the 60 percent addressed by the old labeling rules.

Second, it requires labels to contain information of more concern to health conscious consumers in light of recent research. For example, the fat content of foods must be listed, including the amount of saturated fat. The number of fat calories per serving size must be listed, as well as the percentage of total calories that fat represents. Serving size must be designated, for example, in terms of how many servings are in the package. The FDA has authority to issue detailed regulations about the size and placement of this information.

Third, the act empowers the FDA to work out a standard definition for commonly used "descriptors" in the food industry, such as "lite," "reduced," "natural," "low," or "organic." Food **sellers** will be required to use these adjectives only if their products actually comply with the standard definition. This will eliminate deception.

Fourth, the act gives official authority to the FDA to allow food sellers to make nutritional claims for their products without subjecting them to the rigorous investigations required for new drugs. However, the health claims must comply with rigorous requirements for clarity and reliability. The claims will only be allowed where research has overwhelmingly established a link between the type of ingredient at issue and a health effect. The mere fact that a few studies have suggested such a link is not enough. In 1995, the only claims allowed were those linking fat consumption with cancer and cardiovascular disease, calcium intake with osteoporosis, and sodium consumption with high blood pressure.

The new labeling requirements under the Nutrition Labeling and Education Act are well designed to enable the consumer to purchase healthy foods. However, there is some concern that food sellers will comply with the letter of the labeling requirements, but shift their deceptive claims to advertising of the foods. Food advertisements are regulated by the **Federal Trade Commission.**

The Nutrition Labeling and Education Act generally preempts [see **preemption**] any state laws that are not exactly identical. However, provided the labeling requirements are the same, provisions in state laws for particular penalties for violation of the laws are not preempted. Thus, violation of the labeling requirements set out in the act may subject the violator to penalties provided by state law as well as those under federal law.

OPEN AND OBVIOUS DANGER   A defense raised by a **seller** in a **products liability** case. Also called the *latent-patent rule*, the defense is based on the premise that an injured **consumer** should not be allowed to recover compensation if the dangerous defect in the product that caused injury was obvious.

The defense of open and obvious danger is used most often in cases based on a theory of **strict tort liability.** Depending on the circumstances of the case, the defense can resemble either **assumption of the risk** or **contributory negligence.** Generally, in cases involving alleged design defects [see **design defect**] in products, the open and obvious danger defense is virtually the same as an assumption of the risk defense. The defendant seller must prove that the injured consumer saw and subjectively appreciated the risk presented by the defective product and then voluntarily proceeded to encounter that risk. For example, a carpenter who notices that there is no safety guard on a table saw but proceeds to use the machine anyway might be denied recovery for injuries in a lawsuit on the grounds that the dangerous defect in the saw (i.e., its lack of a guard) was open and obvious.

The use of the open and obvious danger defense in design defect cases has been criticized because it lets the makers of dangerous products off the hook too easily. Critics argue that just because a dangerous defect is readily apparent should not exonerate the maker of the product for injury caused by it—particularly if a safer design or safety feature could easily and cheaply be provided. In the above example, such critics might argue that a saw without a safety guard is so dangerous that it should not be marketed at all. The fact that consumers can see the product is dangerous does not make the danger of using it any easier to avoid. The argument is strengthened by the fact that safety devices for saws are simple and cheap to provide. This type of criticism has prompted some states to outlaw the use of the open and obvious danger test in design defect cases.

In cases involving alleged **warning defect**s in a product, the open and obvious danger test more closely resembles the defense of contributory negligence. The standard for determining whether the danger is obvious in warning cases is an objective one: If most reasonable people would see and appreciate the danger, it is open and obvious and the seller of the product is not obligated to warn about it. For example, an adult who injures himself by diving into an aboveground swimming pool with a depth of four feet will probably not prevail in a lawsuit against the pool's maker for failure to provide a warning against diving. The depth of the pool is obvious to anyone using it, and the dangers of diving into shallow water are so well known that it would be an injustice to hold the manufacturer liable for the folly of the few who might not appreciate it.

The rule that a seller is not required to warn of obvious dangers in a product may also be prompted by a practical consideration: Lengthy warnings listing every possible way a product might cause harm, even obvious ones, might detract attention from warnings about serious hidden dangers.

ORDINARY USEFUL LIFE A defense to a **products liability** lawsuit that is based on the argument that a **seller** should not be held accountable for a product's failure to perform properly after it has passed the period of its expected ordinary useful life.

The obvious fairness of this argument belies some problems. First, how is the ordinary useful life span of a product determined? A jury may decide this based on evidence as to how long similar products have typically lasted. Or it may simply be assumed that a product is beyond its ordinary useful life if it is extraordinarily old and/or has been used extensively. See also **statutes of repose.**

Second, since products typically do not wear out all over all at once, the defect in a product that causes injury may be in a component that has not yet reached the end of its normal lifespan. To preclude an injured **consumer** from receiving compensation merely because the product as a whole is beyond the normal span of its useful life seems unfair if the actual injury is caused by a component that is still serviceable. See also **proximate cause.**

Because of these problems, the defense of ordinary useful life is relatively little used. This is especially true in cases based on **strict tort liability,** in which the injured consumer is required to prove that the product was in substantially the same condition when it caused injury as when it left the control of the seller. If a product has been used beyond the span of its ordinary useful life, it is hard to show that it is in the same condition as when it left the control of the seller.

PERTSCHUK, MICHAEL (1933–) Lawyer and activist chairman of the **Federal Trade Commission** (FTC) from 1977 to 1981.

Born in 1933 in London, England, Pertschuk was five years old when his family moved to the United States. He attended Yale University, where he majored in English, and Yale Law School. After graduation Pertschuk clerked for federal judge Gus J. Solomon, whom he later credited with instilling in him a zeal for social and political causes. Pertschuk later practiced law in Portland, Oregon. In 1962, he moved to Washington, D.C., to become a legislative assistant and eventually joined the staff of Senator Warren Magnuson, a Democrat from Oregon.

Thus began a 13-year career as staff counsel with the Senate Commerce Committee, which Magnuson chaired. Eventually assuming the post of staff director for the committee, Pertschuk was involved in drafting many of the laws that have served as the backbone of the modern **consumer** protection movement. These included the **Magnuson-Moss Warranty Act,** the **National Traffic and Motor Vehicle Safety Act,** and the **Federal Cigarette Labeling and Advertising Act.** During his tenure on the committee, Pertschuk also prepared many of the investigatory hearings on consumer issues and kept the press apprised of their findings. No less a consumer champion than Ralph Nader [see **Nader, Ralph**] praised Pertschuk's work in the Congress as diplomatic yet determined to have the consumers' interests heard.

In 1977, President Jimmy Carter named Pertschuk to head the FTC. Pertschuk proved an active administrator in the interest of consumers. During his tenure, the FTC lost its moniker of the "little old lady of Pennsylvania Avenue," which had been bestowed on it by consumer groups critical of the agency's alleged lassitude and coddling of industries it was supposed to regulate. In the face of Pertschuk's regulatory zeal, industrial representatives dubbed the agency the "Mad Queen" instead.

Pertschuk sought especially to strengthen the antitrust arm of the FTC, declaring that "the **antitrust law**s are the strongest consumer protection we have." [1986 Current Biography Yearbook, page 428] Under Pertschuk, the FTC vigorously investigated anti-competitive practices by the nation's largest companies and examined proposed **mergers** of corporations for anti-competitive effects. For the first time, the agency made extensive use of the so-called "shared monopoly" theory, under which the conduct of a small group of large corporations was scrutinized closely for collusive effects, such as signaling price hikes. See **price fixing.**

Pertschuk also vigorously championed a more active role for the FTC's consumer protection division, taking particular interest in the energy, health, transportation, and **food** industries. Under Pertschuk's leadership, the agency utilized its power to issue industrywide regulations, which was granted as part of the Magnuson-Moss Warranty Act that Pertschuk had helped write a decade earlier. Regulations were issued to curtail unfair practices in the used car, funeral, health insurance, and over-the-counter **drug** industries. The FTC challenged the policies of organizations for doctors and lawyers and other professionals that unduly restricted entry into those professions and prohibited the competitive advertisement of fees. He believed that such practices artificially inflated the prices of such services.

Pertschuk's personal crusade at the FTC concerned television advertising aimed at children. Television, he believed, was "a trusted companion, a teacher, a window on the world" for the country's smallest and most impressionable citizens. [1986 Current Biography Yearbook, page 429] Because they often lacked the ability to distinguish programs from advertisements or to understand the selling purpose of advertising, children needed particular protection, in Pertschuk's view. Accordingly, he launched what was dubbed the "Kidvid" investigation into the ways advertising manipulated children in order to reach their parents' wallets.

With the election of Ronald Reagan to the presidency in 1980, Pertschuk's leadership of the FTC came to an abrupt end. The new conservative administration was hostile to more government regulation of business and a new chairman was appointed who shared those views. Though no longer chairman, Pertschuk continued as a member of the FTC board of commissioners until 1984, often serving as the minority voice for regulation in consumers' interest.

In 1984, Pertschuk left the FTC to form Advocacy Institute, a private lobbying organization representing consumers. He also authored several books on the history of government consumer regulation, including *Revolt against Regulation: The Rise and Pause of the Consumer Movement* (1982) and *Giant Killers* (1986), a memoir of consumer lobbying during the Reagan administration.

PETERSON, ESTHER (1906–) Labor leader, **consumer** activist, and Special Assistant to the President for Consumer Affairs for Presidents Johnson and Carter.

Born Esther Eggersten in Provo, Utah, in 1906, Peterson grew up on a farm near Brigham Young University. Her father was a school superintendent and a teacher at a Mormon seminary. In keeping with Mormon tenets, a sense of mission informed all the family's activities. Esther's sense of purpose led her to become a teacher. She graduated from Brigham Young University in 1927 and accepted a teaching position at Cedar City, Utah.

A decision to attend graduate school at Columbia Teachers' College in New York changed the course of Peterson's life. While there, Esther met Oliver Peterson, already a union activist. He took his future bride to see the sweatshops and poverty of New York City in the late 1920s. After graduation, Esther took a teaching position near Boston while Oliver was attending Harvard. Although it did not square with her duties at the exclusive private school, Esther soon found herself involved in helping poor working women in the garment trade form a union. Success in that endeavor led to an invitation to help form a teachers' union. Peterson realized her true calling and left the teaching profession. Over the next 20 years, in the United States and abroad, she continued to immerse herself in the fight for wage equality and working women's issues. Back in the United States, she became director of the Woman's Bureau at the Department of Labor.

Peterson's interest in wage issues led directly to concern for consumers, particularly since the typical image of a consumer in her day was of a woman: usually a housewife who had to make her family's dollar go as far as possible. Peterson also might have seen another image: a single working woman, who—paid less than a man for the same work and forced to pay inflated prices for poor quality goods—was cheated twice. In 1964, President Johnson named Peterson to the newly created post of Special Assistant to the President for Consumer Affairs. At first, the position was largely window dressing. So cautious was the White House at the time that Peterson was not even given permission to speak out against the used automobile industry's fraudulent practice of rigging odometers. However, Peterson persevered and succeeded in bringing some real influence to the post for the benefit of consumers.

During the Nixon and Ford years, Peterson worked as a consumer consultant to private business. At first she harbored concern that her position with the giant Grant food chain would appear to be a sellout to the enemy. However, the company proved enlightened and was anxious to develop a true "in-house" consumer advocate. At Peterson's urging the company was at the forefront in developing and marketing foods free of chemical additives that were suspected of causing disease.

In 1977, President Carter again appointed her to the post of Special Assistant to the President for Consumer Affairs. The intervening years since she had last held the position had seen consumerism become an important force in politics. Accordingly, Peterson had increased clout the second time around. Among her foremost concerns were expanding unit pricing for commodities and labeling reform for food products.

After she left the presidential advisory post in 1980, Peterson continued to represent consumer interests on the boards of a number of consumer organizations, including the **Center for Science in the Public Interest, Consumers Union,** and the **National Consumers League.**

POISON PREVENTION PACKAGING ACT Passed in 1970, this federal law [15 U.S.C. §§1471–1476] empowers the **Consumer Product Safety Commission** to regulate the packaging of household substances in order to protect children from the danger of accidental poisoning.

Household substances subject to regulation include any that have already been classified as hazardous under the federal **Hazardous Substances Act,** as well as pesticides, **drug**s, **cosmetic**s, and fuel stored in portable containers.

These substances, or products containing them, must be supplied to **consumer**s in child-resistant packages. They may also be supplied in standard packages for the benefit of elderly or handicapped adults for whom the child-resistant packaging is difficult to open. In such cases, the package must clearly indicate that it is intended only for households without young children.

PREDATORY PRICING Occurs when a **seller** sets the price of goods or services at below the average variable cost of producing them, with the intention of driving competitors from the market. Variable costs are costs that vary with changes in output. They include such things as materials, labor, fuel, and repair of capital equipment. Predatory pricing is illegal under the **antitrust law**s of the United States, because it allows the seller engaging in the practice to raise prices to artificially high levels after competition has been eliminated. Ultimately, the interests of **consumers** are hurt.

Predatory pricing does not occur every time a seller is able to price products or services below the competition. In fact, lower prices that result from a seller's efficiency in production are encouraged, even if it means that less efficient competitors will not be able to stay in business. The difference is that the seller's low price resulting from extra efficiency represents the lowest price for which the product or service can be produced and, therefore, is beneficial to consumers. Moreover, other competitors are encouraged to streamline their operations to be as efficient, resulting in more competition rather than less.

Generally, a seller must be large and wealthy enough to have the ability to price others out of the market before below-cost pricing is considered predatory. If a small seller temporarily prices a product or service below cost in order to encourage consumers to try it, predatory pricing will not be found.

Genuine predatory pricing occurs relatively rarely because it entails extreme risks for any firm that undertakes it. First, the potential predator must have sufficient resources that it can afford to lose money for the period it may take to drive less-wealthy rivals out of business. Second, the predatory seller must believe that it can quickly recoup the losses sustained in the period of predation by raising prices again after the competitors are eliminated. As soon as a seller raises prices, however, other sellers are encouraged to enter the market because they believe they can now successfully compete. Therefore, real predatory pricing occurs only in those industries where very high start-up costs discourage competitors from re-entering the market.

PREEMPTION   The rule that federal laws have priority over state laws and may completely invalidate them. This rule is derived from the Supremacy Clause of the United States Constitution, which provides that "the Laws of the United States . . . shall be the supreme law of the land." [U.S. Const., art. VI, cl. 2]

Preemption is important for **consumers** because of the complicated web of laws and regulations, both federal and state, that purport to govern consumer issues. Often federal and state laws on particular consumer issues coexist and are both valid. However, federal laws will preempt and invalidate state laws on a subject in three circumstances: (1) the federal law explicitly states that it preempts any state laws in the area, (2) the federal law directly conflicts with the provisions of the state law, and (3) federal legislation in an area "occupies the field." The first two of these instances are fairly easy to determine. However, the vagueness of the third circumstance has given rise to much litigation.

Frequently, federal preemption is an argument made by **sellers** in **products liability** cases order to escape responsibility for injuries caused by their products. First, they argue that federal law alone establishes whether their products are defective [see **defectiveness**], and that all state laws in the same area are preempted and invalid. They then try to show that the product or service at issue conformed with federal regulations. If preemption is found, the injured consumer may lose his or her chance to show that the product did not conform to more stringent state or common-law [see **common law**] requirements.

A typical outcome in such cases is that a court will find that some types of state law claims are preempted by federal regulations, but that others are not. See, for example, *Cipollone v. Liggett Group, Inc.* Moreover, unless the Supreme Court has spoken on the issue, lower courts are free to disagree about whether a particular claim is preempted by federal law. This all makes for a very sticky procedural quagmire through which consumers seeking redress for product-caused injuries must wade.

PRESERVATION OF DEFENSES RULE   A rule created by the **Federal Trade Commission** (FTC) to prevent **sellers** from immunizing themselves against **consumers'** defenses to payment for defective goods and services by means of the **holder-in-due-course doctrine, interlocking loans,** or **waiver of defense clauses.**

Generally, all three of these seller tactics sever a consumer's obligation to pay for goods and services from the seller's obligation to deliver them. This is done by transferring the right to receive payment for the goods and services to someone other than the seller—either a third party to whom the consumer's obligation to pay has been sold or assigned, or a third party who was induced to give the consumer a direct loan for the purpose of paying for the goods and services. Either way, the effect is that the consumer's obligation to pay is absolute, even if the goods are defective, were not delivered, or there is some other good reason to withhold payment. The justification for this result has traditionally been that the third party who now owns the right to collect payment from the consumer either had no notice that the consumer might have a good reason not to pay (for example, because the goods were not received or were defective) or had reason to believe that the consumer had waived rights to avoid payment (for example, by signing a waiver of defense clause). It would be unfair—goes the reasoning—to subject this "innocent" third party to the risk that the debt would not be paid.

Basically, this FTC rule abolishes all of these devices in consumer transactions by requiring that a notice be placed in all **contract**s, promissory (IOU) notes, and loan agreements made for the purpose of extending credit for consumer purchases. The notice states:

> Any holder of this consumer credit contract is subject to all claims and defenses which the debtor could assert against the seller of goods or services obtained pursuant hereto or with the proceeds hereof. Recovery hereunder by the debtor shall not exceed amounts paid by the debtor hereunder.

The effect of the notice is to warn any third parties who might buy the consumer's obligation to pay the seller, or who might lend money to the consumer for the purpose of buying consumer goods and services, that the consumer may have valid reasons not to pay. Because such third parties have now been warned of this possibility, they are no longer "innocent" and deserving of protection in case the possibility of nonpayment comes to pass. Thus, with this simple requirement, all of the traditional devices used by sellers to avoid consumers' defenses against payment have been swept away.

The FTC rule applies only in cases involving credit extended to a consumer for consumer purposes; that is, for personal, household, or family use. The rule does not apply to credit sought for commercial or business purposes. Moreover, the rule applies to lenders making purchase money loans (loans for the purpose of buying consumer goods or services) only if the lender is affiliated with the seller of the goods or services or the seller has referred the consumer to the lender for the purpose of getting a purchase money loan.

Under the FTC rule, a consumer is entitled not only to stop payment to a third party creditor, but to get back money already paid if the consumer has a valid reason to withhold payment.

PRICE DISCRIMINATION   Occurs when a **seller** varies the price charged to different buyers of identical goods that are intended for resale. Price discrimination is illegal under the **antitrust law**s of the

United States when it tends to limit competition and drive up prices charged to the ultimate **consumer**s of the product. If a seller is able to charge different prices for identical goods, he or she is able to influence which resale distributors and even retail dealers will thrive and which will fail. Ultimately, this could lead to a monopoly in a single product line.

Many factors must be considered before a determination is made that a seller is engaged in price discrimination. Practices such as charging buyers different rates based on the cost of delivery to their different locations is not illegal. Neither is charging less per unit for large volume orders than for smaller orders. As long as lower rates are offered to all potential buyers on the same terms, there is no illegal price discrimination.

The law prohibiting price discrimination is broken only when there has been an actual injury to competition resulting from price differences. Therefore, a buyer who feels disadvantaged by prices that are higher than those charged by a certain seller to others must prove that his or her ability to compete with other buyers has been diminished. This might be accomplished by showing that, because of the higher prices for a particular raw material, the buyer cannot make his or her own products as cheaply as the competition. The buyer is then forced to charge higher prices for the finished product and, as a result, lose sales to competitors.

PRICE FIXING An agreement among competing **sellers** to control or stabilize prices for their goods or services. Price fixing is illegal under the **Sherman Antitrust Act** and other **antitrust laws** of the United States. This prohibition is beneficial to **consumers** since, by eliminating price competition among themselves, a group of sellers could maintain prices at artificially high levels.

Virtually any attempt to tamper with the normal effect on prices of the law of supply and demand is illegal. Agreements to set maximum prices, as well as minimum prices, are outlawed. Practices that only indirectly affect prices are also illegal. Some of the less obvious illegal practices that result in price fixing include the following:

- agreements limiting production or sales. By controlling the supply of a product to the market, producers can more or less control the price of the product. This includes agreeing to stockpile raw materials necessary for making a product.

- agreements to refrain from discussing price with potential consumers until the consumers have chosen a seller. This practice is illegal
because it eliminates competitive price bidding.

- agreements to eliminate discounts or other cost incentives to
distributors. Discounts can be seen as a component of the price of
goods. Tampering with the freedom to grant discounts is, therefore,
affecting prices.

- circulation of uniform list prices for use as a common starting point
to begin to bargain with consumers. Even though each seller is free
to come to any agreement with a consumer on the final price of the
product, the uniform price list affects prices since it is used as a
starting point for bargaining.

Under the Sherman Act, it is not necessary to find an explicit agreement
between sellers to fix prices, or to control factors that affect prices, in order
to find a violation of the law. A violation may be found if a seller sets prices
at a certain level with knowledge that others will do the same. This is known
as *tacit collusion*. Frequently, such collusion results when subtle signals are
sent to competitors suggesting price adjustments. These may be no more
than publishing planned price changes. Illegal price fixing results if other
competitors, hearing of their rival's price change, understand that they are
being invited to change their own prices and then do so.

There are other practices that are not themselves illegal, but are sometimes used by sellers to signal an invitation to fix prices. Ironically, many of
them seem at first to be favorable for consumers. However, they end up
encouraging artificially high prices in the long run. Therefore, the **Federal
Trade Commission** and other agencies charged with enforcing antitrust
laws look carefully at these to ensure that they are not being used improp-
erly. The following are examples of such signals:

- *Meeting-the-competition clauses.* This arrangement works like this:
Seller A promises to match any price offered by a competitor. Seller
A then raises its own prices. It does not lose any business by this
tactic because a consumer can still get the lowest price of any of A's
competitors just by demanding that A match that price. However,
all the other competitors are now encouraged to raise their prices to
match A's new price, because that way they will no longer be
penalized by consumers buying from A and demanding their lower
prices. If everyone's price matches A's, no one is disadvantaged by
A's offer to consumers. In other words, A's offer to match any price

will no longer attract consumers, because everyone's price is the same. Moreover, the new price is now higher than it was before, so all the sellers benefit. However, all the consumers lose.

- *Lowest price guarantees.* Under this arrangement, Seller A offers not only to meet the lowest prices of its competitors, but to go lower still. Consumers naturally flock to A. A raises its usual prices, but no consumers are driven away by this because they can always demand a price lower than A's lowest-priced competitor. However, all the other competitors are losing business to A in droves. There is great pressure on them to raise their own prices to match A's new higher price and to offer the same lowest price guarantee that A did. Only in this way can they win back their customers. Lowering prices will no longer attract customers to them as it normally would in a free market situation, because A has promised to go even lower.

PRINTER'S INK MODEL STATUTE   Represented the first widespread effort to regulate the truthfulness of advertising [see **false advertising**] through **statutory law.** Drafted in 1911 for the industry trade journal, *Printer's Ink,* the model law was ultimately adopted by 44 states and the District of Columbia. It makes it a misdemeanor to disseminate any advertisement that contains "any assertion, representation, or statement of fact which is untrue, deceptive, or misleading."

Despite its broad language and widespread adoption, the Printer's Ink Model Statute has not been an effective means of regulating advertising practices. The fact that the statute prescribes criminal [see **criminal law**] rather than civil [see **civil law**] penalties means that it is interpreted very strictly. Some states make conviction dependent on proof that a **seller** intended to deceive or mislead **consumer**s by means of an advertisement. Since proving someone's intent is very difficult, few prosecutions in these states have ever resulted. Moreover, because the statute is criminal in nature, proceedings to enjoin false advertising practices and punish perpetrators must be instituted by a state attorney general or other public figure. An injured consumer has no **private right of action** to sue a seller directly for violation of the statute. Moreover, many practices, such as **bait-and-switch advertising,** are excluded from the statute's coverage.

PRIVATE RIGHT OF ACTION   The right of a private citizen to sue the violator of a law in order to make sure that the law is enforced or to recover **damages** for injury caused by the violation.

Any private citizen of the United States has the right to sue another private citizen or corporate entity in a civil action [see **civil law**] based on tenets of the **common law.** However, a private citizen's right to sue in other cases may be, and often is, restricted. For example, a private citizen may not initiate a criminal prosecution. A private citizen may, of course, file a criminal complaint. However, it is up to the public authorities, through the public prosecutor, to bring the alleged criminal to court.

The same is true of a number of regulatory laws passed for the purpose of protecting **consumer**s. Typically, in addition to outlawing certain conduct, such laws will establish a government regulatory agency to monitor compliance and enforce the law's provisions. Where such regulatory agencies exist, the law frequently does not allow private citizens to sue violators independently in order to see that the law is enforced. Instead, the right to bring violators to court belongs exclusively to the government agency. An example of a law allowing no private right of action is the **Food, Drug & Cosmetic Act.**

Generally, it is presumed that there is no private right of action to enforce a statute unless that statute explicitly grants one. Some consumer protection statutes do explicitly grant consumers a private right of action to enforce their terms. One such law is the **Consumer Product Safety Act.**

The type of relief a consumer may seek when a law does grant a private right of action will vary. Sometimes, the consumer is entitled only to an **injunction** to order the violator to stop the violating conduct. Other laws grant the consumer a right to sue for damages as well.

A private right of action should not be confused with a right to proceed to trial. Rather, a private right of action merely means that a court is allowed to entertain a lawsuit brought by a private individual in a certain case. The court may then decide whether to dismiss the action on other grounds (e.g., insufficient evidence to proceed) or to hear the case.

PRIVITY OF CONTRACT   The state of having a direct contractual relationship with a party, which is a prerequisite to bringing certain types of legal claims against that party.

The concept of privity of **contract** was developed in the early nineteenth century. Arguably, it was a way to restrict the number of lawsuits brought against **seller**s of goods and thus encourage the nascent Industrial Revolution. Basically, the rule held that only a buyer who had direct contractual relations, that is, who was *in privity of contract,* with a seller could sue the seller for losses incurred as a result of purchasing defective goods.

For example, if sausage turned out to be tainted, only the immediate buyer could sue his or her immediate seller for injuries caused by the poisoning. Only the buyer was in privity of contract with the seller. The buyer's wife and children who also became sick from eating the sausage were left without a remedy. Moreover, the buyer could sue only his immediate seller. If the seller was merely a retail dealer with no responsibility for making the sausage, it made little sense to sue him or her. Yet the buyer would be precluded from suing the manufacturer of the sausage, who was really responsible for its unwholesomeness, because the buyer was not in privity of contract with the manufacturer.

At the beginning, the rule of privity applied both to lawsuits based on **tort** and those based on **warranty** principles. However, as **consumer** products were increasingly mass-produced by distant corporations, the inherent unfairness and even absurdity of the rule began to be apparent. The twentieth century has seen the sometimes slow and sometimes fast erosion of the rule, which one legal commentator poetically termed "the assault on the citadel" of privity. [Prosser, *The Assault upon the Citadel,* 69 Yale L.J. 1099 (1960)]

First to go was the rule of privity in regard to the tort of **negligence.** Early on, the law recognized certain classes of products that were automatically excluded from the rule. These were products such as adulterated foods and beverages or mislabeled poisons that entailed the likelihood of serious and widespread harm to many persons besides the immediate buyer. It simply seemed unfair to preclude the innocent victims of a manufacturer's negligence from recovery merely because they did not happen to be the direct purchaser of the product. Gradually, the rule was abolished in all lawsuits based on the alleged negligence of a seller. Presently, the responsibility of a manufacturer for negligently made products extends to all those who might foreseeably be injured by the product. See *MacPherson v. Buick Motor Company.*

The rule of privity has lingered longer in the area of warranties. Warranties are considered to be part of the **contract** of sale, about which the parties to the sale can bargain. Theoretically, the buyer of a product should be able to bargain for more inclusive and far-reaching warranties that would protect individuals other than the buyer and ensure recovery from more than just the immediate seller. The reality, of course, is that the consumer has very little bargaining power over the terms of warranties supplied with the mass-produced articles he or she buys.

For this reason, the rule of privity has been abolished in warranty cases under many circumstances. Generally, whether or not privity will be required for a **consumer** to recover for a breach of a product warranty will depend on the type of warranty, the type of injury suffered, and the type of privity involved.

There are two kinds of privity. *Vertical privity* is the relationship of the buyer of goods to **sellers** up and down the chain of distribution for the product. *Horizontal privity* is the relationship of the seller of goods to persons outside the chain of distribution of the product. Questions involving vertical privity relate to whether the buyer may sue the distant manufacturer or distributor of a product rather than just the product's immediate seller. Questions of horizontal privity involve whether a person who was not the buyer of the product may sue the seller because the product did not conform to a warranty.

Generally, if the type of injury involved in a breach of warranty lawsuit is personal physical injury, no privity of contract is required for any type of warranty. Thus, a physically injured buyer may sue any seller of the defective product up the chain of distribution all the way up to, and including, the manufacturer.

The degree to which horizontal privity has been abolished in cases of personal injury depends on the state where a case is heard. In some states, only the immediate family of the buyer of a product may recover for personal physical injuries caused because the product did not conform to its warranty. In other states, anyone who might reasonably be expected to use, or be affected by, the product may sue to recover for personal injuries.

Generally, if the type of injury involved in a breach of warranty suit is property damage or financial injury only, the rules of privity are more strictly applied. Some states allow the buyer to sue only the immediate seller of a defective product. Others allow the buyer to sue up the chain of distribution of the product. In some states, the ability of the buyer to sue up the chain of distribution of a defective product may depend on whether the warranty was express or implied [see **express warranty; implied warranty of merchantability**]. Usually, however, if the buyer relied on express statements made by the manufacturer of the product in advertisements and labels, no privity is required. These types of representations are considered to be express warranties directed at the ultimate purchaser.

The trend in the latter half of the twentieth century has been towards eliminating the rule of privity altogether. Even now it is largely irrelevant to consumers because of the continuing development of negligence and **strict tort liability** as alternatives to breach of warranty lawsuits when personal injury or property damage has resulted from defective products.

PRODUCTS LIABILITY The name given to a branch of law that deals with compensating **consumer**s for injuries or losses caused by defective products.

For the most part, products liability law is a phenomenon of the latter half of the twentieth century. Essentially, its emergence reflects the view that society, as well as business, is better served by placing the burden of paying for injuries and losses caused by defective products on the makers of those products. The added pressure thus generated to produce ever safer and more effective products has undoubtedly accounted for much of the technical innovation in products on the market today. The fact that the cost of developing these better products is often spread to all consumers through increased prices does not diminish this salutary effect. The alternative might well be a population of crippled and cynical citizens, who—when not impoverished by paying for their own product-caused injuries—would lack the confidence to purchase new products for which they would bear the risk of any defects.

Strictly speaking, products liability law deals only with cases in which a product has caused physical injury or property damage to a consumer or some other person. Thus, it clearly encompasses both **tort** and **warranty** types of lawsuits when these are based on physical injuries or property damage. Most important within the field of products liability law are the tort **action**s known as **negligence** and **strict tort liability.**

Technically, products liability does not refer to lawsuits to compensate for a consumer's disappointment or monetary loss because a product does not perform as expected. These types of situations are considered to be **contract** or warranty issues that are covered by the **sales law.** However, recovery of compensation in these situations depends on the same sort of proof that is necessary in physical injury and property damage cases. Since there is a great deal of overlap in proof, these "disappointed consumer" cases are also frequently included in the products liability category.

Products liability law, for the most part, evolves slowly through the processes of the **common law.** However, some states have passed special products liability statutes that regulate the issues typically covered in this area of the law.

Like many trends in society, products liability law depends on a metaphorical pendulum that swings from one extreme point of view to another. The biggest issue currently facing products liability law is whether it may now be too easy for consumers to recover for all sorts of injuries and losses, real and imagined. The ability of the producers of products to pay the judgments and respond with new innovation may be taxed to the limit. For this reason, proposals to cap the amount of compensation recoverable by plaintiffs in products liability cases have been making headway.

PROXIMATE CAUSE An action, or failure to act, without which a later event would not have occurred, and which is significant enough in its magnitude or proximity in time or space to the later event to be fairly assigned legal responsibility for it. Sometimes called *legal cause*, proximate cause is one of the most debated concepts of the **common law.**

Basically, proximate cause reflects a simple rule of fairness: One must have caused harm before one will be made to pay for it. However, because all events influence later events in an endless chain stretching into infinity, there must be some practical cutoff point at which an action or failure to act simply becomes too remote in time or too small in significance to be considered a cause of some particular later event. It is where to draw this line that creates the confusion surrounding the concept of proximate cause: At what point is an action or failure to act significant enough in causing a later event to justify imposing legal liability on one responsible for it?

Like many legal concepts, proximate cause does not have a rigid formula but depends on common sense under particular circumstances for a definition. However, there are some guidelines for determining when an action or failure to act is the proximate cause of some other event.

First, in order for Event A to be the proximate cause of Event B, Event A must be a *cause in fact* of Event B. Generally, this means that Event B would not have occurred without Event A. Sometimes courts call this the *but-for test:* That is, Event B would not have occurred *but for* the occurrence of Event A. If Event B would have occurred anyway—even without Event A occurring—Event A cannot be the proximate cause of Event B.

For example, J stops to tell a joke to F, who is installing an enclosure for a homeowner's pet ocelot. Laughing at the humor, F neglects to secure the lock in the enclosure. Later, the ocelot discovers the unlocked gate and escapes from the yard. It wanders out into the street, causing an automobile driver to swerve and run into a tree, where she sustains a broken arm.

Clearly, all of the events related are causes in fact of the driver's broken arm: (1) the telling of the joke; (2) the failure to secure the lock; and (3) the wandering into the street of the ocelot. The driver's decision to drive on that particular street is also a *cause in fact* of the accident. However, the fact that the driver was going ten miles over the speed limit at the time was not a cause in fact of the accident if the driver would not have been able to stop the car in time even if she had been driving at the speed limit.

Second, Event A must be a *substantial factor* in bringing about Event B. In the above example, it is intuitively clear that the telling of the joke was not a substantial factor in bringing about the accident. Any number of things might have distracted F and caused him to leave the lock unsecured in the fence. By contrast, the failure to secure the lock greatly facilitated the ocelot's escape and, of course, the ocelot's decision to run into the street was the major factor in causing the driver to swerve.

Third, Event B must be the *natural and probable consequence* of Event A. Generally, this means that Event B must be foreseeable [see **foreseeability**] under the circumstances. It is not necessary that the exact sequence of events be foreseeable in order to find Event A the proximate cause of Event B. For example, it is not necessary to be able to predict exactly how a loose ocelot might cause harm. It is enough to be able to see that if the enclosure lock is not secured the ocelot may get out and cause damage to someone's person or property. Moreover, the test of whether Event B is the natural and probable consequence of Event A is usually considered from hindsight. In other words, looking back, does what actually occurred seem unlikely, unusual, or bizarre? If not, it was probably the natural and probable consequence of Event A. In the above example, while a poorly secured fence naturally and probably leads to the escape of an animal confined behind it, the telling of a joke does not naturally and probably lead the hearer to neglect his or her work.

Fourth, the natural chain of events between Event A and Event B must be *unbroken*. Imagine that the ocelot had slipped out of the yard and was innocently trampling the flower beds when a child came along and deliberately chased it into the street. A reasonable interpretation might be that this deliberate action intervened in the chain of events between the leaving open of the gate and the automobile accident. The child's chasing the ocelot into the street thus took over as the effective cause of that accident. See **intervening cause.**

Assuming that no child came along to chase the ocelot, two events remain that meet all of the criteria for proximate cause of the accident: F's bad workmanship and the ocelot's running into the street. Logically, either or both could be the proximate cause of the subsequent automobile accident. However, since an ocelot is not responsible for its actions, it can be seen as nothing more than a natural phenomenon that exhibits certain tendencies. Therefore, it is probable that in the sight of the law, the poor workmanship on the fence was the proximate cause of the automobile accident. Whether F will be liable to pay for the driver's injuries and losses will depend on some other factors as well. See **duty of care; negligence; standard of care; strict tort liability.**

Importance to Consumers

The concept of proximate cause is of great importance to any **consumer** involved in a **products liability** dispute in which a defective [see **defectiveness**] product has allegedly caused harm. In any such case, it will be necessary for the consumer to prove that the defect in the product was the proximate cause of his or her injury or loss. The relevant factors in such cases are frequently many times more complex than the simple example above. Technical evidence as to how the product was designed, how it was manufactured, how it was supposed to work, how it did work, as well as medical or technical evidence about how its malfunctioning caused the consumer's injury or loss will often be indispensable before any recovery may be had.

PRUDENT MANUFACTURER TEST   A test used by courts to determine whether a product is defective [see **defectiveness**] and, therefore, whether compensation must be paid to **consumer**s who have suffered injury or damage caused by it.

Under the test, a product is defective if a prudent manufacturer, knowing of all the hazards presented by it, would not have put the product on the market. In practice, the test is a variation of the **risk-utility test,** because it requires the balancing of a number of factors related to product safety and utility. Thus, it is important to determine the usefulness of the product and weigh this against its dangers, including the severity and frequency of the injuries that might be caused by it. It will also be important to determine whether there are other, safer designs that might be used for the product instead.

The hypothetical prudent manufacturer in the test is presumed to know all of the risks of the product involved. The test is not based on what a prudent manufacturer would do if he or she knew only what the actual manufacturer in the case knew about the product. Therefore, the prudent manufacturer test is particularly suited to lawsuits brought on a theory of **strict tort liability** in which the condition of the product rather than the behavior of the manufacturer determines the manufacturer's liability for injuries caused by it.

Public Citizen   A nonprofit advocacy group founded by Ralph Nader [see **Nader, Ralph**] in 1971, Public Citizen is an umbrella organization for numerous other Nader groups, including the Health Research Group, the Critical Mass Energy Project, Buyers Up, Congress Watch, and the Public Citizen Litigation Group. Public Citizen gets its name from Nader's philosophy that each individual should become involved in public affairs for the common good.

The Health Research Group, headed by Dr. Sidney Wolfe [see **Wolfe, Sidney**], is concerned with the safety of **food** and **drug** products and **consumers**' access to quality health care.

Critical Mass is an environmental group dedicated to the demise of nuclear power and the promotion of more benign energy sources.

Buyers Up is a consumer's cooperative, in which individual consumers band together to pressure **sellers** for the lowest prices and best quality. It is devoted to realizing the theoretical condition known as *monopsony* or *oligopsony*—in which a single buyer or group of buyers use their economic power to counter the monopoly or oligopoly power of a single seller or small group of sellers. The group presently is organized to purchase home heating oil. The national office hires managers to negotiate with sellers of the oil for the best bulk prices to pass on to its members in various parts of the country.

Congress Watch is devoted to monitoring the process of government to make sure it operates fairly and in the open. Congress Watch keeps an eye on individual lawmakers' votes and attempts to "follow the money" from special interests to see if it is unduly influencing them. The group publicizes embarrassing votes or corporate ties in an effort to keep legislators accountable to the public who elected them. Congress Watch is far more than a glorified "tattletale," however. It also is vitally involved in lobbying for the passage of laws or at least the inclusion of salutary procedural provisions in them. For example, Congress Watch activists helped ensure that the rule-making procedures for a number of federal agencies would be kept informal. Informal proceedings are accessible to all, while formal proceedings would have excluded all but wealthy interested parties. Skilled professionals with knowledge of the arcane rules of give-and-take in the legislative process, Congress Watch activists have managed to link consumer protection measures with legislation certain to pass for other reasons.

The Litigation Group specializes in taking legal action on behalf of the other organizations under the Public Citizen umbrella. It was also the first organization to make extensive use of the Freedom of Information Act as a tool for citizens to become informed about the processes of their government. Much of its litigation centers around forcing disclosures under that law. The litigation group has filed and won numerous lawsuits designed to protect the principles of separation of powers under the Constitution. In a case that went all the way to the Supreme Court, the litigation group challenged the validity of the so-called *legislative veto*. This was a device by which Congress presumed to halt specific actions by authorized regulatory agencies by declaring a "veto" of particular regulations issued by the agencies. The litigation group persuaded the Court that this was an unconstitutional usurpation of the executive branch's power. Essentially, the veto allowed lawmakers to vote for popular regulatory measures and then quietly squelch the actual implementation of them. The victory in this case has had profound effects on the successful enforcement of numerous regulations involving **fraud,** product safety, and environmental hazards. The litigation group also successfully challenged the Gramm-Rudman-Hollings deficit reduction law of 1985 on constitutional grounds. Under that law, unelected bureaucrats in the executive branch of government were to have the task of implementing automatic cuts in federal programs in order to balance the federal budget. The scheme amounted to an abdication of legislative responsibility for necessary, but unpopular budget restraints. Once again, the Supreme Court struck it down. By making legislators themselves vote on the provisions of the budget, the process is opened to public view and ultimately oversight through the election process.

Public Citizen is a full-service consumer organization, involved in numerous causes and engaged in working in various forums—from the halls of Congress, to the suites of corporate America, to courtrooms all over the country. By sharing a central administration, which is responsible for fundraising for all the groups, the individual organizations that make up Public Citizen can more effectively concentrate on advocacy and political activism in their respective areas. Moreover, the experts employed in each group may more easily collaborate with each other for effective action, whether it is lobbying before Congress or litigation in the courts.

PUFFERY A **seller**'s exaggerated statements of opinion about the quality of his or her goods or services.

Basically, puffery, or *puffing,* is a seller's defense to a **consumer**'s claim that he or she was mislead by the seller's advertising or sales talk regarding a product. The law recognizes that merchants are prone to overblown praise of their wares in attempting to induce sales. Consumers are expected to recognize this as well. Therefore, the law does not provide a remedy to consumers who complain that a product they have purchased does not live up to the grandiose claims of its seller.

However, some statements made by sellers do amount to legally enforceable promises, or warranties [see **warranty**], about the quality of their products. The law provides compensation for consumers who have suffered **damages** as a result of relying on these types of false statements. The important question, therefore, is: When does a seller's statement about a product acquire legal significance for a consumer who hears it, and when is the statement merely harmless puffery? See also **reliance.**

Generally, in order to be harmless puffery, a statement must be a statement of opinion and not of fact. Opinions are easy to recognize if they are expressed with adjectives that cannot be measured objectively. For example, superlatives such as "great" or "wonderful" are clearly opinions because there is no standard for greatness or wonderfulness upon which everyone agrees. The statement that a car gets "great gas mileage" is mere puffery.

Conversely, statements that a product is "red," "brand new," and "equipped with a V-8 engine" are clearly statements of fact. They can be objectively verified by looking at the product or its documentation. A statement that a car got "55 miles to the gallon in road tests conducted last year" is also a statement of fact. The law will provide a remedy under certain circumstances if a statement like this turns out to be false.

However, there are many statements that do not fall so neatly into either category. For example, descriptions such as "large capacity," "well-tuned," or "quick acceleration" may be opinion or they may be fact, depending on the circumstances under which they are made. A statement that a car will "probably get 55 miles to the gallon" falls within this gray area.

The following factors are important in determining when a seller's statements constitute puffery and when they do not:

- A vague statement is more likely than a specific one to be considered puffery. The word "large" is vague, while "25-gallon capacity" is specific and more likely to be a statement of fact.

- Statements about future events are more likely to be puffery than statements about the present or past. The reason for this, of course, is that present and past circumstances are more subject to verification. Everyone knows that the future cannot be predicted with certainty.

- Statements that are qualified by words expressing uncertainty, such as "probably," "maybe," or "possibly," are more likely to be mere puffery than statements of fact.

- The more obvious a defect is in a product, the more likely a seller's statements about it will be considered puffery.

- Oral statements are more likely to be considered puffery than written ones. The reason is simply that written statements are more likely to be deliberate than oral statements, which are frequently spontaneous and exuberant.

- If certain words have acquired customary meanings in the seller's trade, they are more likely to be found to be statements of fact and not puffery. If, for example, "large" is a word commonly used by sellers of hot-water heaters to mean having a capacity of over 40 gallons, describing a hot-water heater as "large" is likely to be a statement of fact and not mere puffery.

- Unfavorable statements about a competitor's product are less likely to be considered puffery than a seller's flattering statements about his or her own product.

- Statements about the safety of a product, even if vague or dosed with superlatives, are less likely to be considered puffery and more likely to be considered statements of fact. The reason may be that consumers are particularly gullible about the important issue of product safety.

- Inequality in expertise between the seller and the consumer regarding the product being sold will tend to indicate that the seller's statements about it are statements of fact and not puffery. Particularly if it is clear that a consumer is relying on the expertise of the seller in recommending a product, the seller's statements are less likely to be considered puffery and more likely to be considered statements of fact.

PYRAMID SALES   In theory, a pyramid sales plan is a method by which a company distributes its products through several layers of distributors. The distributors sell the products at a percentage of their retail price to distributors in the layer below them until the products are finally sold at their full retail price to **consumer**s. Typically, distributors pay a sum of money to the company for a supply of the company's products and the right to recruit distributors at the next lower level of the distribution chain, for which they receive a "finder's fee" or "commission."

Pyramid sales plans are frequently found to violate consumer protection laws because their true purpose is not to sell goods but to recruit new paying participants by misrepresenting the income potential of participation. High-pressure sales tactics and subtle psychological manipulation are employed to disguise the fact that participants at the lower levels of the chain have little, if any, prospect of making any money. At some point the market for distributorships will become saturated and those distributors at the bottom of the pyramid will not be able to recruit new participants. Moreover, the revenue these bottom-level distributors might be able to generate from sales of the company's product to consumers is not enough to cover their costs of joining the company.

In most pyramid distributorships, the actual sale of goods to consumers is mere window dressing to make the scheme look legitimate. In fact, the income generated in such plans depends on the sale of false hope to those buying a chance to participate at lower levels of distribution. In actuality, nothing of value is being exchanged for a participant's entrance fees except the chance to collect commissions from the sale of false hopes to other gullible investors.

Because of the inherently misrepresentative nature of pyramid sales schemes, the law has sought to regulate them, if not flatly outlaw them. The **Securities and Exchange Commission** (SEC) has determined that some pyramid sales schemes are, in fact, sales of "investment contracts" or "profit-sharing plans" because they involve the payment of a fee for the chance to make money on the efforts of others without any direct involvement in the running of a business. The SEC is, therefore, entitled to regulate them like other **seller**s of securities. Because SEC regulations are very strict, pyramid sales schemes that fall within the SEC's jurisdiction are frequently unable to comply and are quickly put out of business.

State laws also are used to close down pyramid schemes. Because all that is really being sold in such plans is a chance to make money based on the happening of an event (recruitment of another) over which the participant has little control, some states define pyramid schemes as lotteries. They may, therefore, be banned under statutes prohibiting lotteries.

Other state laws against **fraud** may be used to close down pyramid operations based on the deceptive way that distributors are recruited. Prospective participants in pyramid schemes invariably are not told about the real potential to make money from participating. Nor are they informed about other dues and fees that the operators of the enterprise require in addition to the distributor's initial fee payment. Finally, prospective participants are frequently not informed that they must pay their own expenses in their efforts to recruit new participants. See also **referral sales.**

REAL ESTATE SETTLEMENT PROCEDURES ACT A federal law [12 U.S.C. §§2601–2617] designed to standardize disclosures of settlement costs in real estate transactions and to eliminate kickbacks or "commissions" among the various professionals providing services to **consumer**s purchasing real estate.

Generally, the Real Estate Settlement Procedures Act (RESPA) applies to residential property purchased with the proceeds of loans from institutions insured by the federal government. Loans to build homes or to purchase empty lots are excluded.

RESPA requires **creditor**s to provide applicants for real estate loans with basic information about the types of settlement costs they face when purchasing a home. Consumers frequently do not realize that, in addition to the cost of the home, they may be required to pay fees for the origination of the loan, appraisals, and title searches, and to make deposits for real estate taxes and insurance. To minimize unpleasant surprises, RESPA first requires lenders to give loan applicants a booklet with a detailed description of how a real estate transaction is consummated and an explanation of each settlement cost item likely to be encountered. At the same time, the creditor must provide a good faith estimate of what each of those cost items will be in the planned transaction. Then, at or before the time of closing the real estate sale, the consumer must be provided with a list of the actual settlement costs on a standardized form known as the Uniform Settlement Statement. The consumer must also be informed that the right to collect mortgage payments on the property may be sold or assigned to another creditor. If this occurs, the consumer must be notified again at the time of the transfer.

In addition to requiring disclosures to the consumer, RESPA also prohibits the payment of "commissions" to brokers for referring a consumer to a certain creditor, title insurance company, or other provider of real estate services. Such payments between the professionals who arrange real estate transactions only increase costs to consumers without benefiting them. Moreover, they are anti-competitive because they encourage real estate professionals continually to bid up the commissions they pay referrals in order to compete for clients. RESPA, therefore, forbids all agreements between professionals providing real estate services to refer business to each other in exchange for anything of value. In order to prevent real estate professionals from getting around the prohibition on "commissions" for referrals by inflating the fees they charge for their actual services, RESPA also prohibits charging more than the reasonable value of the services actually performed.

Notwithstanding RESPA's stated purpose of eliminating charges that do not benefit the consumer, it specifically recognizes a number of exceptions to the referral fee prohibition. These include the traditional brokers' fee sharing that occurs between the listing and selling agents of real property; referral arrangements in which one real estate professional refers a consumer to another professional who is affiliated with, or owned by, the referring professional; and arrangements whereby the consumer agrees to pay for services of real estate professionals chosen by the creditor to represent the creditor's interests. There are other exceptions as well, leading to the impression that RESPA's antikickback provisions have little real effect. In fact, this charge is frequently levied at RESPA by consumer advocates.

RESPA also outlaws some other practices, such as requiring a consumer to use a particular title insurance company. Title insurance is required in most real estate transactions in order to ensure that ownership of the property is clear of any third-party claims. RESPA also limits the amount of money creditors may require a consumer to pay in advance into escrow accounts to cover anticipated periodic charges on the property, such as taxes and insurance premiums.

RESPA provides consumer victims of kickback agreements between real estate professionals with the award of a civil penalty against the guilty professionals in the amount of three times the charge on which the kickback was levied. However, beyond this, RESPA does not provide consumers with a **private right of action** to sue for other **damages** caused by nondisclosure of required terms or kickback arrangements. A consumer might be able to sue for a violation of the **Truth in Lending Act,** however, since that law also mandates certain disclosures in real estate transactions and does provide a private right of action. RESPA gives certain federal and state officials the right to impose criminal penalties on violators and to enjoin future violations.

REASONABLE PERSON TEST   A test used by courts to determine whether an individual was negligent [see **negligence**] and must compensate one who was injured as a consequence. The test compares the conduct of the individual under consideration with that of a hypothetical "reasonable" person who embodies the average qualities of knowledge, experience, and reason prevalent in the community. In applying the test, the court will engage in a type of "make believe" by imagining what this "reasonable person" would have done under circumstances similar to the ones in the case before it. If the individual under examination in the case does not measure up to what the "reasonable person" would have done under similar circumstances, he or she was negligent.

The reasonable person test has been part of the **common law** for at least 200 years. According to tradition, the mythical creature known as the "reasonable person" shares the physical attributes of the individual whose conduct is being examined. For example, if the individual is blind, the standard against which his or her conduct is to be measured is that of a reasonable blind person. On the other hand, the "reasonable person" shares the mental characteristics—the intelligence, insight, and prudence—of an average member of the community. Thus, the individual being examined must conform to the average **standard of care** of the community in which he or she lives, but need not exceed it.

There are two exceptions to this objective mental standard under the test. First, if the individual whose conduct is at issue is a child, he or she will generally be judged on his or her own subjective mental abilities. For example, if a 10-year-old is mentally slow for his age, his conduct will be compared with his own slow standard to determine whether he was negligent, and not with that of other, average 10-year-olds.

Second, if the individual whose conduct is at issue is an expert of some sort, his or her conduct will be compared to that of a minimally qualified "reasonable expert" of the same type. For example, the conduct of an architect in designing a building for fire safety will be compared with that of a hypothetical, minimally qualified "reasonable architect" given the same task.

The reasonable person test is also used to determine whether the victim of someone's negligence was also negligent in causing his or her own injury. See **comparative fault; contributory negligence.**

Importance to Consumers

Generally, any **consumer** who is involved in a lawsuit to recover compensation for harm caused by the negligence of a **seller** will encounter the reasonable person test. The test will be applied to determine if the seller's conduct in making or marketing the product measured up to what a "reasonable person" would have done in similar circumstances. See also **misuse; open and obvious danger; prudent manufacturer test; state-of-the-art defense.**

REFERRAL SALES These occur when a buyer of goods is promised discounts or commissions for referring new customers to the **seller.** Referral sales are considered deceptive practices and are illegal in many states.

There are three reasons why these arrangements are considered unfair to **consumer**s:

- First, in order to get the promised discounts or commissions, a buyer is typically required to buy the goods at inflated prices. Thus, even if the buyer does later get "discounts," he or she is really not getting any benefit at all. Instead, the buyer is merely paying a price closer to the real value of the merchandise.

- Second, the discounts or commissions are usually offered only for referrals to the seller that actually result in sales. This, in effect, makes the discounts or commissions contingent on events over which the buyer has no control.

- Third, the terms of the referral agreement are frequently stated orally or are written in a **contract** separate from the contract for sale of the product. This makes it difficult for the buyer to prove that the agreement to pay a rebate or a commission was ever made. In the meantime, the buyer is still obligated to pay the inflated price for the merchandise he or she purchased subject to the agreement.

To penalize sellers who practice these unfair sales tactics, the **Uniform Commercial Code** provides that the buyer of goods under an illegal referral agreement may keep the goods without paying for them. State laws vary in their definitions of, and penalties for, illegal referral sales.

Some types of referral sales practices are not illegal. For example, the Uniform Commercial Code allows referral sales in which discounts or commissions are offered to the buyer of goods in return for the names of prospective customers. Under this type of arrangement the buyer is entitled to a discount or commission even if the referred customers do not buy anything.

REFUSAL TO DEAL A **seller**'s refusal to do business with other sellers. Depending on the reason for the refusal and the number of sellers involved, a refusal to deal may violate the **antitrust law**s of the United States.

Generally, the decision of a single seller to refuse to do business with another seller or sellers is not illegal. However, if the refusal is combined with some other illegal activity, the refusal itself may become illegal. For example, if a seller refuses to do business with another seller unless the other seller agrees to an illegal **tying agreement,** the refusal to do business is itself illegal. However, a seller's refusal to allow a certain distributor to distribute his or her goods is not generally illegal. A seller has a right to distribute his or her own goods as he or she wishes.

The law views agreements among more than one seller to refuse to deal with other sellers differently. This is called a *concerted refusal to deal* or *group boycott.* Such an arrangement is illegal if its purpose is to drive competing firms out of business or to coerce them to join a wider conspiracy to violate antitrust laws.

Group boycotts can arise in a variety of situations. For example, a group of retail sellers may agree among themselves not to buy goods from a certain wholesale dealer because the wholesaler also sells directly to the public. The purpose of the boycott is to force the wholesaler not to sell to the public. If the boycott is successful, the retailers will have succeeded in reducing their competition. Ultimately, this will injure **consumer**s by resulting in higher prices.

Another classic group boycott situation occurs where a powerful seller induces a competitor's suppliers to agree not to sell to the competitor unless they do so at inflated prices. The suppliers are likely to agree to this arrangement because they do not want to lose the powerful seller as a customer. The result is that the smaller competitor is driven from business.

Group boycotts are not illegal if they are for a legitimate business purpose. For example, it may be a legitimate business purpose for a seller to agree with others not to do business with a supplier whose products do not meet certain industrywide standards of quality. However, courts are likely to scrutinize such agreements carefully to make sure that they are not concealing an anti-competitive purpose.

Concerted agreements not to deal with other companies for completely noncommercial reasons are also legal if there are no hidden reasons for them that are anti-competitive. For example, a refusal by many companies not to buy from a supplier with discriminatory hiring practices may be a legitimate group boycott.

Reliance One of the factors a **consumer** must prove in a number of types of lawsuits in order to recover compensation based on a **seller**'s failure to supply goods of the type or quality promised.

Generally, reliance is the consumer's belief in the truth of the seller's descriptions of a product that induces the consumer to buy it.

Reliance involves two separate aspects. First, the consumer must show that he or she believed the representations made about the product by the seller. If the statements made by the seller about the product are too preposterous, it will be difficult to show that the consumer believed them. Such statements are generally considered mere **puffery,** for which there is no consumer remedy. For example, if a rug salesman tells a consumer that a carpet is guaranteed to fly, the statement is too preposterous to be believed. However, there is also a subjective element to a consumer's reliance on statements made by sellers. Some consumers are more gullible than others. For example, if the consumer is a child it may be possible to convince a court that the statement about a flying carpet was actually believed.

Second, the consumer must show that the seller's description of the product actually convinced him or her to buy it. This will be easiest to prove if the statement was about some aspect of the product that is considered by most consumers to be important. For example, statements about the safety of automobiles are usually considered to be important to consumers' decisions to buy them. It would be easy, therefore, to show that a consumer relied on such a statement when purchasing an automobile.

A consumer may also prove that a seller's statements about a product convinced him or her to buy it by showing that the statement was about some aspect of the product that he or she personally considered to be important. For example, a consumer whose hobby is collecting fine carpets could probably convince a court that a seller's statement that a particular carpet was a rare antique was important in the consumer's decision to buy it. However, a consumer who only wanted to buy a carpet to cover a bare spot on her living room floor would have a harder time convincing a court that a statement that the carpet was a rare antique was important in her decision to buy it.

It is necessary for the consumer to prove reliance on the seller's descriptions or promises in lawsuits alleging various **tort**s, including **deceit** and negligent **misrepresentation.**

In lawsuits based on an alleged breach of **warranty,** the necessity for the consumer to prove reliance has generally been relaxed. If the complaint involves an **express warranty,** the **Uniform Commercial Code** requires only that the promises in the warranty were part of the "basis of the bargain." Although the law is not entirely clear on the meaning of this phrase, any statements made by a seller about a product prior to sale appear to be part of the bargain. Hence, the consumer need not prove that he or she relied on them in order to recover for a breach of express warranty.

It is generally settled that a consumer need not prove reliance on any representations about a product in order to recover for breach of an **implied warranty of merchantability.** However, if the consumer alleges that the seller breached an **implied warranty of fitness for a particular purpose,** it is generally necessary to show that the consumer actually relied on statements made by the seller that the product was fit for the purpose for which the consumer wanted to use it.

RENT-TO-OWN CONTRACT A lease, usually of durable goods such as automobiles, furniture, and home appliances, that has a short renewable term and offers the leasing **consumer** the right to purchase the goods at the end of a specific number of terms for a slightly more than nominal fee.

Traditionally, rent-to-own **contract**s are most attractive to poor consumers who are unable to get credit through conventional lenders. Rent-to-own contracts typically offer easy credit and low periodic payments. Often these arrangements present the only opportunity for a poor consumer to own major necessities such as refrigerators and furniture. Moreover, a consumer who leases goods incurs no long-term debt. Instead, the consumer can return the leased goods at any time with no further obligation.

On the other hand, rent-to-own transactions are notorious for abuses and exploitation. Frequently, the amount ultimately paid by a consumer who exercises the option to buy the goods at the end of a certain number of lease terms will be much greater than normal retail cash prices for similar goods, or even than the price plus interest on a normal credit sale of the same item.

The opportunity for abuse in rent-to-own contracts arises because they are not regulated by consumer protection laws. Most consumer protection laws are triggered only when a "sale" is involved. Since there is no absolute obligation for a consumer in a lease agreement to buy the goods, there is no "sale" in the eyes of the law. Consumer advocates contend that rent-to-own contracts are nothing more than credit sales in disguise and should be regulated as such. A credit sale occurs when a **seller** allows a buyer to buy goods or services and pay on installment. Rent-to-own dealers disagree, and so far the courts have agreed with them. In a true credit sale, they say, a buyer is absolutely obligated to pay the full amount of the sale price, plus interest for the privilege of deferring payments. The buyer does not have the option of simply returning the goods and avoiding further payments, as does the consumer in a rent-to-own transaction.

Because rent-to-own agreements are not "sales" in the eyes of the law, they are exempted from the provisions of most consumer protection legislation. This results in three major disadvantages for consumers.

First, the disclosure requirements of the federal **Truth in Lending Act** and many similar state laws do not apply to rent-to-own transactions. Therefore, rent-to-own dealers can, and frequently do, obscure the true cost to the consumer of the transaction. This involves failing to state what the goods would normally cost at prevailing retail prices and what the consumer will have paid at the end of the rent-to-own period. In addition, all sorts of late payment fees and penalties may be hidden in the lease contract.

Second, payments made pursuant to rent-to-own contracts are characterized as a fee for the use of the goods, not "interest" on a loan. Therefore, rent-to-own contracts are exempt from state **usury** laws. Frequently, the amount a consumer eventually pays to exercise the option to buy rented goods is many times the legal usury limit.

Third, a rent-to-own customer accumulates no ownership interest in the rented goods until he or she exercises the option to buy at the very end of the rent-to-own period. This is unlike normal credit sales in which the consumer gradually accumulates ownership in the goods as he or she makes installment payments. If the credit-sale consumer suddenly is unable to make payments, the seller may repossess the goods. However, the seller must reimburse the consumer for the amount of the retail price of the goods that he or she has already paid. Moreover, the purchaser of the goods may redeem them by paying the total amount due. By contrast, the rent-to-own consumer is only paying for the use of the goods and does not accumulate an ownership interest with each payment. Consequently, the rent-to-own dealer is still the absolute owner of the goods. If the consumer defaults on rent payments, the dealer may repossess the goods without giving any credit to the consumer for the amount already paid. Moreover, the consumer has no right to pay off the remainder of the purchase price and get the goods back.

Because of these inequities, many states have enacted laws specifically directed at the rent-to-own industry. These laws typically mandate the disclosure of terms in rent-to-own agreements, such as the overall nature of the transaction, the expected costs to the consumer including any fees that could be assessed during the contract term, and the consumer's rights against the dealer during and after the lease. Other provisions of these laws regulate the dealer's right to repossession in case the consumer stops paying the rent. They prohibit some intrusive practices, such as late night "raids" of the consumer's home and bullying. They also give delinquent consumers rights to reinstatement on the lease with no penalty. That is, if the consumer pays the amount owing on late or unpaid rent payments, he or she is entitled to have the goods back with credit towards ownership for all previous payments he or she made prior to delinquency.

State laws also regulate the types of fees that may be charged on rent-to-own contracts. Typically, fees to pick up goods after a consumer has terminated the lease or fees to purchase property insurance from the dealer are forbidden. However, the dealer may require a security deposit to pay for damage to the goods, or require that the customer have property insurance from another source. Delivery fees are also allowed, as well as fees for reinstatement after a delinquency in paying rent. Fees to collect payment from the consumer at his or her home are allowed, as are fees for late payment, although they are subject to a maximum amount.

States' efforts to regulate rent-to-own contracts contain surprisingly few limits on the actual amount of rent to be charged over the course of the contract. One reason is that rent-to-own contracts are, in fact, valuable to consumers unable to qualify for credit because of low income or unstable employment. Moreover, rent-to-own dealers are justified in charging higher prices to these customers because they represent an increased risk of default or delinquency. States also realize that such limits are easy to evade. For example, when a number of states made rent-to-own contracts subject to the usury limit, rent-to-own dealers responded by raising the stated price of the rental goods so that the rental payments added together would stay within the legal usury rate.

Res Ipsa Loquitur An evidentiary rule used under certain circumstances in **negligence** cases that makes it easier for the injured party to prevail when the exact cause of an accident is not clear. Pronounced *race-ipsa-LAW-quitter*, the phrase is Latin for "the thing speaks for itself." Before the advent of **strict tort liability** in the United States, injured **consumers** used the rule of *res ipsa loquitur* in **products liability** cases with some success to make **sellers** responsible for explaining how accidents involving their products happened.

The basic premise of the rule is that some events usually do not occur unless someone is negligent. For example, dead mice are not usually found in sealed cans of beer. It may be safe to assume that the manufacturer of the beer was negligent in some way. Generally, it is necessary for the one bringing a lawsuit, the plaintiff, to explain the cause of the accident and how it was the fault of the defendant in the case. However, if the defendant in a case involving the type of event that only occurs because of someone's negligence had exclusive control of the object that caused the plaintiff harm, it seems fairer to require him or her to explain the cause of the accident.

By shifting the burden of explanation to the defendant, the plaintiff in such a case is usually assured that the case will not be thrown out of court for lack of evidence as to how the accident happened [see **proximate cause**]. Rather, the court will usually leave it to the jury to determine whether the defendant adequately explained how the accident happened. Since juries are traditionally more sympathetic to plaintiffs, the plaintiff in such a case will find this strategically favorable.

In order to apply the doctrine of *res ipsa loquitur*, certain factors must be present: (1) the event at issue must be of a type that usually does not happen in the absence of someone's negligence, (2) the defendant must have had exclusive control of the object that caused the plaintiff harm, (3) the plaintiff must not have contributed to causing the accident, and (4) the explanation for how the accident happened must be more accessible to the defendant than to the plaintiff.

It usually is fairly easy for a consumer injured by a product to establish the criteria necessary to invoke the rule of *res ipsa loquitur*. If a product did not perform as it was supposed to do and harm was caused as a result, there is at least a suspicion that someone's negligence is to blame. Because the manufacturing processes of most products are beyond the understanding of ordinary consumers, it is logical to assume that the manufacturer has greater knowledge of why the product did not function correctly. Moreover, unless a defect in a product is fairly open and obvious, it is hard to argue that the consumer himself or herself caused the harm.

Only the requirement that the product have been within the exclusive control of the seller when the accident occurred presents problems for consumers. Courts have resorted to a stretch of imagination here: If the product had not been altered in any way between the time it left the possession of the seller and the time the injury occurred, it is reasonable to assume that the seller had exclusive control over it at the time the defect came into being.

The most famous products liability case in which the *res ipsa loquitur* rule was used serves as a good example of its application. In *Escola v. Coca-*

Cola Bottling Company [24 Cal. 2d 453, 150 P.2d 436 (1944)], the plaintiff consumer was injured by an exploding bottle. Since the explosion of bottles was a rare occurrence even then, it could be assumed that someone's negligence had caused it. A review of the evidence established that, not only had the bottle been untouched since it left the defendant bottler's possession, but the defendant was responsible both for filling and inspecting the bottles. The plaintiff had done nothing out of the ordinary in selecting and holding the bottle. Also, the intricacies of the bottling plant were far better known to the defendant. Thus, the case was appropriate for the application of the doctrine.

Despite its advantages for injured consumers, the rule of *res ipsa loquitur* has never become widely used in products liability cases. The reason may be that the doctrine's application and effect are confusing, even to legal experts. Also, the rise of strict tort liability as an option for recovery by injured consumers beginning in the mid-1960s has made the rule unnecessary in most cases. Indeed, the *Escola* case, described above, is remembered today not for the holding but rather for a judge's concurring opinion that advocated the new theory of strict tort liability.

Nevertheless, the rule of *res ipsa loquitur* is still useful in cases in which a product that causes injury is itself destroyed in the accident, leaving no way for the injured consumer to determine how it may have been defective.

RESALE PRICE MAINTENANCE   The dictating by a **seller** of the prices that independent distributors may charge for the seller's products. Resale price maintenance is similar to **price fixing,** except that it involves an agreement between a seller and his or her distributors instead of an agreement between a seller and his or her direct competitors.

Resale price maintenance is generally illegal under the **antitrust laws** of the United States because it prevents a distributor from independently responding to competition in his or her own selling area by adjusting prices. This can mean higher prices for **consumers** for several reasons. First, if the dictated price is higher than the price would normally be on the free market, the consumer will pay more than is necessary. Second, if the set price is lower than the price that the free market would establish in responding to the laws of supply and demand, the distributor might be tempted to cut back on servicing or repairing the product in order to make up the difference. Ultimately, the consumer would pay more in repair costs. There is also a temptation for a distributor to make the dictated maximum resale price a minimum price as well, in order to even out the losses that occur when the natural market price fluctuates above or below the dictated level. Resale price maintenance may also facilitate price fixing among direct competitors.

Despite the prohibition on setting prices for independent distributors, there are many legal ways for a seller to influence the prices at which a distributor will sell his or her products. For example, a seller may arrange for a distributor to sell goods on consignment. The distributor in a consignment arrangement is not independent but is rather merely an agent of the seller. A seller may always set the price at which his or her agents or employees will sell products or services.

A seller may also suggest resale prices. No violation of the law results if a distributor decides to sell at the suggested price. However, there must be no coercion on the part of the seller that would interfere with the distributor's freedom to set his or her own prices. A seller may not condition the price of goods sold to the distributor on the distributor's agreement to resell the goods at a suggested price.

Likewise, it is permissible to grant rebates or reductions in prices charged to a distributor in an effort to allow the distributor to meet the prices his or her own competition is charging.

Finally, some states' laws specifically allow resale price maintenance. In those states, the practice is legal.

RESCISSION The annulling or canceling of a **contract**. Rescission is a remedy available to a **consumer** who has entered into a sales contract as a result of **fraud** or **misrepresentation**. Rescission may also occasionally be granted when one or both parties are simply mistaken as to the contract's terms.

When a contract is rescinded, the goal is to put both parties back in the position they would have been in if the contract had never existed. Naturally, this is easier to do if little time has passed or if neither party has yet performed his or her side of the bargain. In most cases involving the sale of **consumer product**s, it is sufficient if the consumer returns the product and the **seller** gives the consumer his or her money back. However, in some cases, something besides the mere exchanging of product for money may have occurred because of the sale. The law will make an attempt to put these peripheral matters back in the precontract position as well. For example, suppose a seller induces a consumer to buy a defective television by misrepresenting that it is in working order. In **reliance** on the seller's promises and before the new set is delivered, the consumer goes home and gives his old television set away. When the consumer discovers that the new set is defective, it is not sufficient merely for him to return the defective set and get his money back because this does not place him in the same position he would have been in had the contract never existed. He now has no television set at all. Moreover, it may now cost him more to purchase another new, working television. In such a case, the consumer may be entitled to money **damages,** as well as a rescission of the contract of sale. The money damages are necessary in order to pay for the difference between the cost of the defective set and the new, working set he is now forced to buy because he gave his old television away.

It is fairly obvious that a contract should be rescinded when fraud, **deceit,** or misrepresentation on the part of the seller is involved. However, when one or both of the parties is mistaken through no fault of the other about important aspects of a contract, the right to rescission is less clear. Generally, the law favors enforcing contracts, because commercial relationships would be very unstable if parties could cancel contracts merely by claiming that they were mistaken about the meaning of one or more of its terms. Of course, if both parties were mistaken about the meaning of the same terms when they made the contract, it is clear that there was no real agreement between them. Therefore, if both seller and consumer were mistaken about an important aspect of the contract, rescission is appropriate.

The more difficult issue arises when just one of the parties is mistaken about the terms of the contract. There are many complicated rules as to when rescission may be allowed in such circumstances. Generally, however, one does not have the right to rescind a contract just because one suddenly discovers he or she was mistaken about some aspect of it. However, if the other party to the contract knew, or suspected, that the first party was under a mistaken impression when the contract was signed, a rescission may be appropriate.

In rare circumstances a court may allow a party to rescind a contract because of a mistaken understanding about its terms, even though the other party had no reason to know about the mistake. Generally, the circumstances under which rescission will be allowed in this situation must be very dire. As a rule, failure to read the contract is not a sufficient excuse to allow rescission.

RESTITUTION Strictly speaking, the restoring of a thing or money to its rightful owner. More recently, the word has achieved a broader meaning to include payments to compensate one for losses or injury caused by another.

Restitution in its narrow sense is a remedy that may be available to **consumer**s who have paid for a product that proves to be defective or does not conform to the **seller**'s statements about it. The purpose of the remedy is to place the parties as nearly in the position they would have been in if the transaction at issue had never occurred. Usually, this merely means that the seller must return the consumer's money and the consumer must return the seller's product.

However, restitution may become more complicated if the defective product has been used or broken, or when the provision of services is involved. In such a case, in order to place the parties in the same position they were in before the product or service was provided, it may be necessary for the consumer to pay the seller some compensation. For example, if the consumer used the product for a period of time before discovering its defects, the seller may be entitled to some compensation for the wear and tear on the returned product. Likewise, if the seller has performed some service for the consumer, it is likely that the consumer has received some benefit from it, even though it might not be what he or she expected or paid for. Moreover, when a service is involved, it is impossible to "return" it to the seller. It would be unfair to allow the consumer to keep the benefit he or she received from free use of the product or service. This is known as *unjust enrichment*, and the seller is entitled to be compensated for the reasonable value of the benefit conferred on the consumer.

When restitution is used in its broad sense, it means the same thing as **damages.**

RESTRAINT OF TRADE   A joint practice of **seller**s that restricts or limits competition among them and is, therefore, illegal under U.S. **antitrust laws**, particularly the **Sherman Antitrust Act.**

Numerous practices may be categorized as restraints of trade. Generally, they are divided into two types: so-called *horizontal restraints* and *vertical restraints*. Horizontal restraints involve agreements between directly competing sellers. Vertical restraints of trade are those that result from agreements between a seller and his or her distributors or suppliers in the chain from manufacturer to ultimate **consumer.**

RISK-UTILITY TEST   A test used by courts to determine whether a product is defective [see **defectiveness**] and, therefore, whether compensation is required for **consumer**s who suffer injury or damage as a result of using it.

The risk-utility test is used mainly in **tort** cases involving personal injuries caused by products. It is most useful where a product allegedly has a **design defect** that has made it unsafe.

Under the test, a product is defective if its inherent dangers outweigh its usefulness to consumers. In order to make this determination a court must consider many different factors, including:

- the usefulness of the product to consumers and to the public as a whole;
- the seriousness of the injury the product is likely to cause;
- the likelihood that the injury will occur;
- the feasibility of making the product safer;
- the present availability of a safer product;
- the obvious nature of the product's dangers;
- the ability of the consumer to avoid injury by using the product carefully; and
- the expectations of consumers in general as to the safety of the product.

In considering the feasibility of alternative, safer designs for a product, a court will take into account not only the technical possibility of making a new design, but also its cost. Under the law, a manufacturer is not required to make a product perfectly safe. Nor is a manufacturer required to use the safest possible design for a product if that design is so costly as to be unprofitable. Moreover, a manufacturer is not even required to use a safer, more cheaply produced design for a product if the safer design detracts from the utility of the product.

For example, a pair of scissors may easily and cheaply be made safer by blunting the ends. However, the utility of the scissors is thereby impaired. The final determination of whether the scissors are defective would depend on balancing these facts with the rest of the criteria listed above. How important is it for consumers to have sharp scissors available? What uses might they have that could not be done with blunt scissors? How serious are injuries caused by sharp scissors likely to be? How often do such injuries occur? How significant is it that the danger presented by sharp scissors is obvious and fairly easy to avoid? Finally, how important is it that scissors with blunt ends are also available from other manufacturers for those consumers who do not want to take the risk presented by the obvious hazards of sharp scissors?

The large number of factors that must be considered, balanced, and weighed makes the risk-utility test complex and often unpredictable. Judges and juries who use the test to decide whether products are defective are likely to decide differently on similar facts simply because of differences in personal opinions on each factor. Nevertheless, the risk-utility test is perhaps the most effective way of determining whether a product is defective and, thus, whether society will require the product's **seller** to bear the burden of compensating individuals who are injured by it. See also **consumer expectation test; defectiveness; prudent manufacturer test.**

RULE OF REASON   A rule applied by courts when determining whether a **seller**'s business practices violate the **antitrust laws** of the United States that allows for consideration of any legitimate reasons for the practices as well as their actual effects on competition.

Under Section 1 of the **Sherman Antitrust Act,** any contract that "restrains trade" is illegal. Very soon after the passage of the act, the courts realized that, taken literally, this provision would outlaw almost every business contract in existence. After all, if A agrees to sell a horse to B, A's freedom to sell the same horse to C has been "restrained." If the act were taken literally, even this type of normal contract would be illegal. Since this was clearly not the intended effect of the act, courts invented the *rule of reason,* which allows them to consider a variety of factors in deciding whether a particular business practice violates the spirit of the antitrust laws.

The rule of reason does not apply in all antitrust **action**s. Some practices, such as **price fixing,** are so clearly damaging to competition that the rule of reason does not apply to them. These practices are *per se* illegal because there is no legitimate reason for their existence except to restrict competition. It is necessary only to determine that the practice exists in order to find that it violates the laws.

However, other practices may have some legitimate justification. The *rule of reason* does apply to them. For example, setting the price of a product lower than the cost to make it for a period of time may be vigorous competition, something that the antitrust laws are designed to encourage, or it may be **predatory pricing.** For these business practices in the "gray area" of antitrust law, the rule of reason is important. Courts will consider all the possible legitimate reasons for the practice, the intention of the seller in adopting the practice, and the actual effect that the practice has on competition before deciding whether the Sherman Act has been violated. The burden of proving that trade is unreasonably restrained in such cases falls on the complaining party.

 **SALES LAW** The branch of law that deals with the relationship between **seller**s and buyers of goods and the rights and duties of each.

The modern law of sales is descended from *law merchant,* which developed in Renaissance England to govern the activities of merchants. It became part of the heritage of the American legal system when the colonists came to this continent.

Law merchant bequeathed two important concepts to the law of sales that persist to this day. The first was the concept of title to goods. Title is the sometimes mysterious, abstract device signifying ownership of goods. When ownership changes, it is said that title to the goods *passes.* Ownership is important because it determines what rights and duties each of the parties has with respect to the goods. For example, ownership will determine who bears the risk of loss of the goods if they are stolen and accidentally destroyed. Interestingly, title to goods does not always pass when money is exchanged for them.

The other legacy of law merchant to the modern law of sales was the concept of the *good faith purchaser,* or *bona fide purchaser.*

This is the rule that a purchaser of goods who does not know that the seller did not have title to them (did not really own them) would nevertheless end up being their rightful owner. This rule has been modified under the modern law of sales, but still persists under some circumstances. See **holder-in-due-course doctrine.**

Today, sales law in the United States is an amalgam of these and other old law merchant rules blended with a heavy dose of modern **contract** law. Sales law, for the most part, is spelled out in the **Uniform Commercial Code,** a comprehensive compilation of rules that has been adopted—with some modifications—by all the states except Louisiana.

Sales law deals with many rights and duties that are important to **consumer**s, such as how a contract for the sale of goods is formed and what remedies are available if the contract is breached. It defines and regulates different types of sales agreements, including sales of goods made on credit.

However, for the most part, the law of sales is more important to commercial buyers and sellers. An exception is the law of **warranty,** which is part of the law of sales. Warranties are a major source of rights for consumers.

SCHLINK, FREDERICK JOHN (1891–1995)   Engineer, product testing pioneer, author, and cofounder of the **Consumers' Research** organization, which he headed for 55 years.

Born in Peoria, Illinois, in 1891, Schlink was the son of German immigrants. He graduated from the University of Illinois in 1912 and two years later earned a master's degree in mechanical engineering from the same school. Schlink's first professional work was designing machines and supervising plant maintenance at the United States Bureau of Standards in Washington, D.C. He spent several years working for private industry, acquiring experience in designing methods and apparatuses for testing the machines used by those industries, as well as the products they produced.

With his experience in testing products for **sellers,** Schlink became concerned that the **consumers** of such products should have the same objective information in order to make rational purchasing decisions. He and a community church in White Plains, New York, set up an experimental product testing station. The results of the testing were compiled in lists of recommended and not-recommended products. During this period, Schlink and coauthor Stuart Chase [see **Chase, Stuart**] wrote the book *Your Money's Worth,* which appeared in 1927. *Your Money's Worth* was a frank revelation of how the average consumer was being misled by slick advertising and cheated by prices far in excess of the real cost to produce products. The book was an instant sensation. Consumers inundated the authors with queries about the White Plains organization and how they could get similar information about other products. Schlink and Chase realized that the demand for objective information on product performance would support a national organization. In 1929, the new national organization was incorporated under the name Consumers' Research. The goal of the group was to apply impartial laboratory tests to the advertised claims of brand products and sell the results in published reports. For the next 55 years, the nonprofit organization steadfastly adhered to this mission under Schlink's leadership.

In 1933, Schlink coauthored with Arthur Kallet *100,000,000 Guinea Pigs: Dangers in Everyday Foods, Drugs and Cosmetics.* Another best-seller, this book revealed to consumers how they were unwittingly exposed to unwholesome, untested, and sometimes downright poisonous foods, medicines, and cosmetics. The book detailed how arsenic and lead pesticides were sprayed onto vegetables, resulting in numerous deaths and cases of illness. It explained the use of the poison sodium sulfite to restore fresh red color to meat and disguise the odor of decay. It told how raw milk was still sold from tubercular cows, resulting in transmission of the disease to humans. It revealed how an ingredient in a popular toothpaste was so poisonous that "a German army officer committed suicide by eating a tubeful." Schlink himself wrote another book on the same topic in 1935, *Eat, Drink, and Be Wary,* which also enjoyed wide audiences. Reaction to these books and the **sulfanilamide tragedy** that occurred a few years later led directly to the passage of the **Food, Drug & Cosmetic Act** in 1938.

The Consumers' Research organization reached the zenith of its influence in the early 1930s. But in 1935, a bitter labor dispute broke out at the company. Schlink fired the union activists and a strike was called. Schlink resorted to strike breakers and **injunctions** to remain in operation. He maintained that the labor union had Communist sympathies and refused all its demands. Seventy of the strikers, led by Arthur Kallet and including Colston Warne [see **Warne, Colston E.**], broke away and formed their own organization, the rival **Consumers Union.** Consumers' Research survived the strike, but at a smaller, less influential level. Consumers' Research was soon eclipsed by Consumers Union, which took a more activist, all-inclusive view of the consumer movement.

Schlink remained at the helm of Consumers' Research until retiring in 1983. During the 55 years of his tenure, he maintained that the best service a consumer organization could render was to keep consumers informed with objective data about products on the market. He distrusted laws to regulate industry, believing that the government was too far corrupted by the businesses it purported to regulate to be effective in protecting consumer interests. For this reason, Consumers' Research never became an advocacy or lobbying force, and consequently receded from the public eye.

Frederick Schlink continued to publish occasional articles of interest to consumers in *Consumers' Research Magazine* and other publications after his retirement. He lived quietly in Washington, New Jersey, until his death at the age of 103 in 1995.

SEALED CONTAINER DEFENSE A defense sometimes available to intermediate and retail **sellers** in **products liability** and **warranty** lawsuits. The defense is based on the argument that sellers should not be held legally accountable for defects in products that they cannot inspect prior to sale to the ultimate **consumer.** Generally, these are products that come directly from the manufacturer in sealed containers and are not designed to be opened before sale. The defense can also apply to products with component parts in sealed housings that cannot easily be opened and inspected without dismantling the entire product.

The sealed container defense is most applicable in **negligence** cases, where the reasonableness of the seller's conduct is at issue. Clearly, it is not reasonable to expect a retail seller to open or dismantle every product that comes through his or her store in order to inspect for defects. Therefore, unless there is some reason to suspect that a ready-made or sealed product is defective, a retail seller has no duty to inspect it and is not negligent for failing to do so.

The defense is less adaptable in **strict tort liability** cases, where the condition of the product rather than the conduct of the seller is relevant. For this reason, most courts have held that the **common law** does not allow the sealed container defense in cases based on this theory. These courts justify this result by reasoning that, as between an innocent injured consumer and a retail seller with no opportunity to inspect a product, it is the retail seller who should bear the burden of paying for product-caused harm. After all, the consuming public relies on retail sellers to supply them with adequate, safe goods. Moreover, the retail seller is compensated for the risk that he or she might have to pay for harm caused by an uninspected product by elevated retail prices. In addition, the retail seller who is sued for harm caused by a defective product that he or she could not inspect is not without recourse. He or she may, in turn, sue the manufacturer who made the defective product for indemnity.

Despite these powerful arguments against applying the sealed container defense in strict tort liability cases, some states have passed statutes that override the common law and specifically allow it. Nevertheless, most of these statutes provide that the defense will not be available if the retail seller commissioned the product to be made to specification or if the retail seller advertised the product as his or her own without naming the true manufacturer. The defense also may not be available if the manufacturer of the product has become insolvent or has gone out of business.

SECURITIES AND EXCHANGE COMMISSION The federal agency that regulates the sale of financial securities to protect investors by promoting fair trading and preventing **fraud.**

Pursuant to the Securities Exchange Act of 1934, the Securities and Exchange Commission (SEC) requires the **sellers** of financial securities, such as stocks and bonds, to register with the agency and disclose certain information about themselves and the stocks or bonds they are offering for sale. Registration does not imply government approval of any security. Nor does it mean that the government vouches for the accuracy of the information disclosed. It especially does not mean that investors are insured from losses. The disclosure requirements exist mainly to assure that investors have sufficient information upon which to make reasonable decisions regarding the purchase or sale of financial securities.

In addition to maintaining a register of securities and their sellers, the SEC has broad regulatory powers over how trading on securities markets is conducted. For example, the commission may set rules for how and when certain types of securities may be sold. The SEC also oversees the many self-regulatory organizations set up voluntarily by representatives of the securities' industry. The commission has the power to approve, reject, or modify rules adopted by these organizations for their members.

Under the Securities Exchange Act, the sellers of securities are required to file annual reports with the SEC regarding the financial health of the companies whose stocks or bonds are for sale. They must also disclose the stock and bond holdings of the directors and officers of the companies whose stock is for sale. Any purchases of stocks or bonds that result in a single buyer owning more than 5 percent of the outstanding shares of a company must be reported.

The SEC also regulates the practices of financial consultants who sell advice about investing. The agency may obtain court orders to enjoin the activities of securities traders that are deceptive or unfair to investors. It may suspend the registrations of companies and brokers engaged in such activities, effectively removing them from the market. The SEC may also initiate criminal prosecution of persons who violate its rules or other securities laws.

The SEC offers assistance to **consumers** wishing to invest in securities by answering questions about particular companies or the investing process in general. The commission also assists investors in resolving specific problems that might arise between them and their brokers or the companies in which they invest.

 SELLER Generally, anyone who provides a product or service in exchange for remuneration. For purposes of determining the rights of **consumers**, however, the definition of *seller* will vary depending upon which law is involved.

As consumers' rights have expanded, so has the number of parties from whom consumers can demand satisfaction for defective products. Today, a *seller* may be anyone in the chain of distribution of a product—manufacturer, distributor, or retail dealer. These may be individual natural persons or legal entities such as partnerships and corporations. A manufacturer of component parts that are incorporated into a finished product may also be considered a seller of the product. Moreover, successor companies that take over the operations of other companies may be held accountable under some circumstances for defective products made by their predecessors.

Within this broad spectrum of sellers who may be held responsible for harm or disappointment caused by products, modifications may be applicable depending on the theory of recovery pursued by an aggrieved consumer. For example, if the consumer sues for a breach of **warranty,** the number of potentially liable sellers may be restricted to the one who actually sold the product directly to the injured consumer. See **privity of contract.**

By contrast, if an injured consumer sues to recover compensation under the theory of **strict tort liability,** the number of sellers who are potentially liable may include everyone from the manufacturer to the retail dealer. Persons who lease or repair products for hire may also be sellers under this theory. Moreover, a party who has provided goods for free may still be considered a seller with responsibility to compensate an injured consumer if he or she normally is in the business of selling the type of product at issue.

Generally excluded from the definition of *seller* under the doctrine of strict tort liability are occasional sellers: persons who are not in the business of selling the type of product at issue or who may be making a onetime only sale. However, individuals who make sales occasionally may be liable to make good on any warranties they make with regard to the product.

Statutory laws that regulate product safety or the fairness of sales practices generally include a specific definition of *seller* that may be different from the definitions under **common law.** Therefore, in seeking redress for any product-caused harm or disappointment, a consumer must know who qualifies as a *seller* from whom compensation may be sought under the law.

 SHERMAN ANTITRUST ACT The major federal legislation [15 U.S.C. §§1–7] in the United States designed to curb monopolistic practices and promote competition among **sellers** of goods and services. The law was passed in 1890 in response to increasing concentrations of economic power in ever fewer companies that began with rapid industrialization after the Civil War. The lock these combinations of companies, or *trusts,* held on several key industries worked gravely to the disadvantage of **consumers**, because prices and production could be set arbitrarily by the trusts entirely to maximize their own profits.

The actual text of the Sherman Antitrust Act, named for U.S. Senator John Sherman (1823–1900), is remarkably spare and general. Its two major sections prohibit (1) **contracts**, combinations, and conspiracies in **restraint of trade,** and (2) **monopolization** and attempts and conspiracies to monopolize. Because of the importance of the Sherman Act in the commercial life of the country, it has been characterized as the "economic constitution" of the United States.

Although the language of the act has remained virtually unchanged for over a century, the federal courts have been ceaseless in interpreting the details of the broad principles set out in it. The result is a devilishly complicated fabric of judge-made law [see **common law**]. The difficulty faced by these interpreting courts is to promote vigorous competition among sellers without completely depriving winning competitors of all their hard-won advantages—since this would, in turn, stifle the incentive to compete. In interpreting the law, the courts are guided by the **rule of reason,** which allows some flexibility in balancing legitimate business interests against the harm a particular practice may entail to competition.

The prohibitions of Section 1 of the act apply only to joint action by more than one business entity. It is generally permissible for a single seller to do any of the things that are illegal under this section if done in combination. This raises two thorny problems for courts considering Section 1 cases: (1) Is there only one or more than one seller involved? and (2) If there is more than one seller involved, was there an agreement between them to act jointly in taking the action at issue?

Generally, a parent corporation and its wholly owned subsidiaries are considered to be a single business entity. The same is true of a company and its unincorporated divisions. A company and its own officers and directors are also considered a single entity, unless the officers and directors have a personal, noncompany interest in the questioned activity. However, there are so many forms of organizing business ventures today that a court reviewing a Sherman Act case must frequently engage in a complicated analysis of the business structure of the sellers named as parties before determining that one or more than one is involved.

Explicit agreements between separate sellers to violate the Sherman Act are rare. However, implicit agreements may be inferred from circumstantial evidence. For example, correspondence or telephone contacts between sellers who later engage in anti-competitive practices may be enough to infer an agreement. Even a unilateral announcement by one company that it intends to take certain action may result in an agreement with other companies if those other companies understand that they are being invited to take the same action and then do so. Even mere awareness of a competitor's actions followed by a decision to act similarly may lead to charges of *conscious parallelism* and result in a violation of the Sherman Act.

Over the years a number of specific practices have been found to violate the Sherman Act. Some of these include **price fixing, monopolization, tying agreements, division of markets,** and concerted **refusals to deal.** Because new and creative arrangements that restrict competition are always arising, a complete listing of actions forbidden by the Sherman Act is not possible.

The Sherman Act is enforced by the Department of Justice's antitrust division and the **Federal Trade Commission.** Criminal prosecutions involving fines and imprisonment for responsible corporate executives may be pursued. **Injunctions** against activities found to violate the act may also be ordered. This may include court-ordered divestitures of stock or assets that give one seller control over another, or the undoing of corporate **mergers** that are found to injure competition. A **private right of action** may be available in some cases to persons injured by anti-competitive activities found to violate the act. Most antitrust lawsuits are brought by sellers against other sellers for injury to their ability to compete. However, individual consumers may also bring lawsuits to recover for overcharging or unfairly high prices resulting from Sherman Act violations. Successful plaintiffs may receive treble the amount of actual **damages** they can prove.

SINCLAIR, UPTON BEALL (1878–1968)   Writer and muckraker [see **muckrakers**] whose 1906 novel *The Jungle* shocked the public with graphic descriptions of unsanitary conditions in the nation's meatpacking plants and helped increase pressure for the passage of pure **food** legislation.

Born in Baltimore to a broken-down southern aristocrat and a prim Methodist mother, the young Upton endured a childhood of itinerant poverty as his father sank into alcoholism. The family moved to New York

City in 1886. Much under the influence of his mother, Upton was a sensitive youth upon whom the air of vice and corruption in the big city made a big impression.

At the age of 14, Upton entered the City College of New York. He also embarked on his career as a writer, first contributing jokes and puzzles to children's magazines and then writing fiction for juveniles that appeared in New York newspapers. Sinclair often boasted that he began to earn his living with the pen at age 16 and never earned a cent any other way thereafter.

In the early years, this living with the pen was meager at best. Convinced of his genius and filled with fervent idealism, Sinclair determined to be a writer at any cost. Plans to go to law school were abandoned. Sinclair was very prolific, writing hundreds of stories for juveniles and several serious novels between the years 1900 and 1904. His serious work was not well received, however, and he and his new wife and child were reduced to living in a tent in the woods when royalties ran out.

In 1902, Sinclair was introduced to socialism by a chance meeting with a socialist in his publisher's office. The utopian appeal of the movement was perfect for Sinclair's idealistic bent. He threw himself into his new passion with unparalleled zeal. While writing polemics for a socialist newspaper, Sinclair conceived of the idea for the novel that would change his life and that of the country as well.

An unsuccessful strike of packing plant workers in Chicago in 1904 suggested to Sinclair the idea of writing a novel documenting the dreary hopelessness of the lives of thousands of laborers doomed to toil for subsistence in the giant factories that were inexorably swallowing up small business in America. He hoped thereby to win supporters to the cause of socialism.

In preparation for his writing, Sinclair spent seven weeks investigating the Chicago packing plants that were to be the setting for his story. He toured the plants officially and also disguised himself as a worker so that he could see the unofficial side of the business as well. Because of his credentials as a socialist, workers confided to him appalling stories of filth and danger in the factories. He interviewed dozens of workers, doctors, lawyers, and others who knew something of the conditions in the plants.

The work that resulted from this was *The Jungle*, published in 1906. In it, Sinclair follows the story of a young Lithuanian immigrant whose vision of America as a land of opportunity is shattered when he finds himself a hopeless thrall in a giant beef-packing plant. Sinclair's on-site investigations allowed him to describe with appalling clarity the conditions in which the nation's meat products were made. He described how filth swept from the packing room floors made its way into the sausages and how moldy meat rejected in Europe was sent back and mixed into products for the American breakfast table. He told how workers themselves would sometimes fall into vats of lard and be processed and packaged along with the animal fat.

The portion of *The Jungle* actually devoted to an exposé of conditions in the Chicago plants is rather small. Most of the book details the protagonist's conversion to socialism. However, it was enough to turn the stomach of the nation. Even President Roosevelt said that it put him off his breakfast. Some historians maintain that it took decades for Americans to regain their appetite for meat. [Root and de Rochemont, *Eating in America: A History* (New York, 1976), pages 210–211]

In any event, public outrage over the revelations was enormous. Already primed by the reporting of other muckrakers about **adulteration** in the nation's food, the public was moved to demand reform. The Pure Food and Drug Act of 1906 came about largely because of this phenomenon.

Publication of *The Jungle* made Upton Sinclair an overnight success. From then on he would never lack for a publisher or readers for the many other books and articles he would write until his death at 90 in 1968. He maintained his utopian outlook and fervor. He became active in politics, even making an ill-fated run for the governorship of California in 1934.

Sinclair later said that he found the reaction to *The Jungle* ironic. His purpose, after all, was to incite sympathy for workers and advance the socialist cause. "I aimed at the public's heart, and by accident I hit it in the stomach," he said. [Sinclair, *What Life Means to Me*, page 594]

STANDARD OF CARE   That degree of carefulness that one must exercise in order to avoid creating an unreasonable risk of harm to others for which compensation may be required under the law. The determination of the standard of care and whether it has been met is the central issue in any **tort** case based on **negligence.** For **consumer**s, this is usually a **products liability** lawsuit against a **seller** to recover compensation for harm caused by a defective [see **defectiveness**] product.

Determining the standard of care depends first on the nature of the alleged negligent conduct. A seller may be negligent in any phase of creating, producing, and marketing a product. The seller's conduct in any of these areas will first be compared with that of a reasonable person in the same situation [see **reasonable person test**]. To the extent that the seller was less careful than this imaginary reasonable person, he or she will have breached the standard of care.

A number of factors are relevant when determining what a reasonable person would do in the seller's place. First, how easy would it have been to prevent the type of harm that came to pass? If preventative measures were relatively easy and cheap to take, and the likelihood of serious harm from not taking the preventative measures was relatively great, a reasonable person would probably have taken the preventative measures. Therefore, taking the preventative measures will be part of the standard of care. If the seller failed to do so, he or she probably breached the required standard of care.

Second, what is the custom in the seller's industry? It can be assumed that the great majority of sellers act carefully in making and marketing their products. The normal practices of similar sellers are also part of the standard of care. If a seller deviated from these practices, it is likely that he or she breached the standard of care.

Third, are there any government-imposed rules for making or selling the product at issue? These, too, will be part of the standard of care required of a seller under the circumstances.

If the seller breaches the standard of care based on these factors, he or she may be held liable for the tort of negligence and will be required to compensate a consumer who was injured as a result.

STATE-OF-THE-ART DEFENSE A manufacturer's defense in a **products liability** lawsuit alleging that a defective [see **defectiveness**] product caused injury or loss. The essence of the defense is that the product at issue embodied the most advanced technology and design available at the time it was made, or was *state of the art*. According to the defense, the fact that more recently developed technology has made safer or more effective products feasible is not relevant in determining the manufacturer's liability.

The state-of-the-art defense is particularly effective in **negligence** cases involving the design of a product. There, the focus of inquiry is on the conduct of the manufacturer in making the product. If the manufacturer used the most advanced methods and designs available at the time, it is hard to say that the manufacturer was negligent in making the product.

The state-of-the-art defense is more problematic in **strict tort liability** cases. There, the focus of inquiry is on the condition of the product when it caused injury to the **consumer,** not on the manufacturer's conduct in making it. Theoretically, it is irrelevant how the product was made. The only thing relevant is what the product's condition was at the time it caused injury. In other words, was it unreasonably dangerous at that time?

States are divided on whether to allow the state-of-the-art defense in strict tort liability cases. The ones that allow it do so because they consider it unfair to hold the manufacturer of a product made in the past to standards for products made in the present. The states that do not allow the evidence justify their rule by pointing out that there really would be no difference between negligence and strict tort liability lawsuits if they were to allow the state-of-the-art defense in both. See **negligence; strict tort liability.**

Assuming that the defense is allowed, another problem is determining just what constitutes state of the art. It is clear that state of the art is not the same thing as ordinary industry custom. In other words, it is not good enough for the manufacturer to say that its product was not defective because everyone else was making their products in exactly the same way at the time. State of the art involves something more. It is, of course, safe to assume that if the manufacturer was using methods on the most cutting edge of technology at the time, the product embodied the state of the art. It is not clear whether something less than this may still be considered state of the art. Under the law, manufacturers are not required to make the most safe and effective products. They are only required to make products that are reasonably safe and effective for the purposes for which they are intended.

STATUTE OF LIMITATIONS   A law that limits the period of time during which a lawsuit may be brought. The purpose behind statutes of limitations is to promote certainty in human affairs by placing some limit on the time one will be legally accountable for one's actions or omissions. Moreover, principles of fairness dictate that one should not be required to defend a lawsuit long after witnesses and evidence may have become unavailable.

Importance to Consumers

Statutes of limitations are important to any **consumer** intending to bring a lawsuit to recover compensation for harm or disappointment caused by a defective [see **defectiveness**] product. Statutes of limitation vary depending on the type of injury suffered or the theory upon which the lawsuit is based. For example, statutes may prescribe a certain time limit for lawsuits to recover for personal injuries, or for cases based on **tort** theories in general. Some states have special **products liability** statutes that specify a limitations period for any lawsuit involving harm caused by defective products. If the lawsuit is based on a breach of **warranty,** most states follow the four-year limitations period allowed in the **Uniform Commercial Code** (UCC).

Generally, statutes of limitations for personal injuries begin to run from the time that harm occurs. Thus, the period will begin to run from the time that a product causes injury. Sometimes, a product-caused injury may take a long time to develop or may remain undiscovered for a long period. Most statutes of limitations allow for this by commencing to run from the time that a consumer discovered, or should have discovered, that a product had caused injury. Moreover, some events will suspend, or *toll,* the running of a statute of limitations. For example, if the **seller** of a product conceals defects or misleads consumers as to the cause of an injury, the running of the limitations period may be suspended until the consumer discovers, or should have discovered, the true state of affairs.

Generally, the statute of limitations for bringing a lawsuit based on a breach of an **express warranty** will begin to run from the date of delivery of the product to the consumer. However, if the warranty specifies a period of time during which the product is warranted to perform properly, the limitations period will begin to run from the time the consumer discovers, or should discover, that the product is not working properly. For example, if a product carries a two-year warranty and stops working on the last day of the second year after delivery to the consumer, the consumer will have another four years (the UCC limitations period) to sue for breach of the warranty. Warranties that promise "lifetime" freedom from defects are included in this category of products. Thus, the period of limitations on a product with a lifetime warranty will begin to run from the time the consumer discovers the defect. See also **statutes of repose.**

STATUTES OF REPOSE   Laws that limit the time period within which a lawsuit may be brought to recover for harm caused by a defective [see **defectiveness**] product, starting from the date of sale or manufacture of the product. A statute of repose is similar to a **statute of**

limitations, except that under the latter, the period within which a lawsuit must be brought begins to run from the time the harm occurs.

Statutes of repose are favored by **seller**s because they cut off legal responsibility for malfunctioning products based on the time the product has been in use. Thus, they are consistent with the view that a seller should not be responsible for the way a product performs after it has passed the period of its **ordinary useful life.** By contrast, under typical statutes of limitations, a lawsuit may be brought at any time during the existence of a product even though the harm it caused occurred long after the product should have been retired because of ordinary wear and tear.

Statutes of repose differ from state to state. Time periods vary, as well as the event that will trigger the running of the period. In some states, the period begins to run from the time the product is manufactured; in others, from the time the product is sold to a **consumer.** In some states, the expiration of the period of repose does not cut off a consumer's right to bring a lawsuit, but merely raises a strong presumption that the product involved was not defective. The injured consumer may still bring his or her case, but will have a heavy burden of proof to show that the product was defective at the time it left the seller's control.

States that have statutes of repose may also have ordinary statutes of limitations. In such states, an injured consumer wishing to file a lawsuit must make sure that he or she does so within the time periods prescribed by both types of statutes. For example, if a statute of repose requires filing within six years of the sale of a product and a statute of limitations requires filing within three years of a product-caused injury, the injured consumer will be barred from bringing suit if either of these periods has already passed.

STATUTORY LAW   A law, or body of laws, formulated and passed by a legislature and promulgated in written form. Together with **common law,** statutory law is a major source of protection for **consumer**s in the United States.

Unlike common law, from which general principles may be inferred from a gradual accretion of judicial decisions in specific cases, statutory law represents an attempt to state general principles directly in a straightforward, prospective way. This approach has the advantage that it allows those affected by the laws to know exactly how they are expected to behave without having to guess from the often vague and contradictory pronouncements of judges in specific cases. On the other hand, stating general principles that fit the peculiarities of every situation that may arise is virtually impossible. Courts are frequently called upon to interpret how statutory law should be applied in specific cases. Thus, judges still have a great role in shaping statutory law in the United States.

Statutory laws affecting consumers are found at all levels of government, from the federal laws enacted in Congress to state and local laws passed by legislatures and town councils. Frequently, these laws state general goals for protecting consumer rights and safety. They then create administrative agencies that are empowered to develop very specific rules for meeting these goals. A statute of this type is the **Food, Drug & Cosmetic Act,** which enables the **Food and Drug Administration** to create regulations for ensuring the safety of the nation's **food** supply. Some of these statutes specifically provide that only the government has a right to sue violators to enforce them. Others allow consumers who have been harmed by violation of the statute to seek enforcement and compensation through a private, civil lawsuit [see **private right of action**]. Generally, federal regulatory statutes of this type preempt [see **preemption**] statutes of state or local governments.

STRICT TORT LIABILITY A doctrine that imposes legal responsibility on one who causes harm without regard to his or her fault. Strict tort liability—as its name implies—is a type of lawsuit to recover compensation for a **tort,** or private wrong. It represents both an innovation and a throwback in the evolution of Anglo-American **common law.** Strict tort liability is of great importance to **consumer**s who have suffered harm as a result of defective products [see **products liability**].

History

In the very early days of English common law, from which American law is derived, a person was held to be legally responsible for any harm he or she caused to another, even if the harm was entirely accidental and did not result from any carelessness. This rule of *strict liability* applied to everyone, including **sellers** of goods that caused harm.

For reasons best left to legal historians to sort out, by the mid–nineteenth century the rule of strict liability had disappeared in favor of liability based on some sort of "fault," or "blameworthy" conduct. Under the new system, if harm occurred accidentally it was necessary to prove that the perpetrator had acted at least negligently in causing it [see **negligence**]. This shift in policy had the result of making it very difficult for consumers to recover compensation for harm caused by defective [see **defectiveness**] products.

A solitary consumer rarely had sufficient knowledge of the sophisticated industrial processes used to make the products he or she purchased through distributors far removed from the actual manufacturer to be able to show that the manufacturer had acted carelessly in making the product. Moreover, the traditional defenses to a negligence action put the injured consumer at a grave disadvantage [see **contributory negligence**].

This state of affairs represented the zenith of the *caveat emptor* (buyer beware) philosophy. Since the beginning of the twentieth century, the policy pendulum has gradually swung back towards placing the burden on sellers to ensure that the products they put on the market are safe and effective. A new high point on this retrograde swing was reached in 1962, when the famous case of **Greenman v. Yuba Power Products Inc.** was decided. In that case the court stated that a seller who places a defective product on the market is liable for injuries caused by that product regardless of how careful he or she was in making or marketing it. Thus, the ancient rule of strict liability in the absence of fault or blameworthy conduct had made a comeback. The only difference between this new strict tort liability announced in *Greenman* and the old strict liability rule is that it is now necessary for the consumer to prove that the product that caused injury was defective [see **absolute liability**]. However, proving that the product is in a defective and unreasonably dangerous condition is generally easier than proving that the seller was negligent in making or marketing it.

Today, most states recognize some form of strict tort liability as an avenue of redress for consumers harmed by defective products.

Features

The distinguishing feature of strict tort liability is that it focuses on the condition of the product itself and not on the behavior of the seller in making or marketing it [see **negligence**]. Specifically, a product must be proved to be defective [see **defectiveness**] and unreasonably dangerous [see **unreasonably dangerous condition**] before its seller will be liable for harm caused by it. If the product is defective and unreasonably dangerous, the fact that the seller had taken all measures possible to ensure that it was safe will not relieve him or her of liability for the consumer's injuries.

In addition to proving that the product is defective, there are three other requirements for recovery under a strict tort liability theory. First, the doctrine only applies to those who are in the business of selling the type of product at issue [see **seller**]. Strict tort liability cannot provide a basis for recovering compensation from an individual who sells a product in a one-time transaction.

Second, the product must be in substantially the same condition it was in at the time it left the control of the seller. It would be unfair to hold the seller responsible for alterations in the product that he or she did not make. See **alteration of product; misuse; ordinary useful life.**

Third, the defective and unreasonably dangerous feature of the product must have been the **proximate cause** of the harm suffered by the consumer.

Importance to Consumers

Strict tort liability presents the most favorable legal theory for consumers to recover for injury or loss caused by a defective product. Gone is the necessity of proving that the seller's conduct was negligent, often a daunting task given the complexities of product design and manufacture. Gone also is the necessity of proving the existence of a valid **warranty** on the product that would cover the contingency at hand. Another advantage to the strict tort liability **action** is that the conduct of the injured consumer is also not generally at issue. The defense of the consumer's contributory negligence is not available to a seller trying to defend against a strict tort liability lawsuit. The defenses of **assumption of the risk,** misuse, **open and obvious danger,** as well as ordinary useful life may still be used in appropriate cases, however.

SUBSEQUENT REMEDIAL MEASURES RULE A rule in **products liability** cases that bars the introduction of evidence that the **seller** of a defective product attempted to make it safer after it injured the plaintiff **consumer.**

Naturally, an injured consumer would like to show that the seller improved a product's safety after learning of the consumer's accident in order to prove that the product was defective [see **defectiveness**] to begin with. The subsequent remedial measures rule was created to prevent the use of this type of evidence for two reasons. First, if sellers knew that their attempts to make products safer after accidents could be used against them as an admission that there was something wrong with the product in the first place, many of them might choose not to make the changes—thereby leaving the product in its dangerous condition. Second, sellers make changes to products for many reasons. The mere fact that a change was made to a product after it injured someone does not necessarily mean that the product was defective before the changes.

There are many exceptions to the subsequent remedial measures rule. For example, evidence of remedial measures performed on a product subsequent to an accident in which it was involved might be used to prove that safer products were feasible at the time of the accident. Feasibility of safety features is one of the factors considered in determining whether a product is defective [see **risk-utility test**]. In addition, evidence of subsequent remedial measures might be allowed to refute a seller who maintains that he or she believed the product was safe.

SULFANILAMIDE TRAGEDY An incident in 1937 in which more than 100 people died from taking a patent medicine containing a poisonous solvent. The tragedy swept away political obstacles that had been holding up passage of the **Food, Drug & Cosmetic Act** of 1938.

Medicine in the early decades of the twentieth century was a curious mixture of genuine good science and outrageous quackery. Unfortunately, the laws of the period did not always enable the two to be distinguished. Basically, any nostrum could be touted as a cure for any ailment. There was no legal requirement that medicines be proven either safe or effective before they were sold. The only labeling required under federal law was to list any alcohol or narcotics in the mixture. As a result, illness or death resulting from taking such remedies was not uncommon. Activists railed against the purveyors of these harmful substances and public pressure was building for strengthening the old Pure Food and Drug Act of 1906. A bill for this purpose was introduced in Congress early in President Roosevelt's administration.

However, the Great Depression was in full swing. Business interests argued that tougher laws would kill struggling companies and throw more people out of work. They pointed out that promising new medicines, such as the sulfa-based **drugs** then appearing in Germany, might be delayed by increased governmental regulation. Research might be stifled. Meanwhile, the press was discouraged from reporting on incidents of harm caused by patent medicines as manufacturers threatened to withdraw their advertising—often the difference between survival and failure for small papers. The legislation was stalled in Congress.

It was against this background that a tragedy of such enormous proportions occurred that it could not be kept from the public. Ironically, sulfanilamide was an effective treatment for bacterial infections. However, it was hard to swallow as a tablet and difficult to dissolve into a liquid. The S. E. Messengill Company of Bristol, Tennessee, developed an effective method of dissolving the medicine into what it called "elixir of sulfanilamide." Unfortunately, the solvent, diethylene glycol, was a deadly poison similar to substances used for antifreeze. Amazingly, the company had tested its product for fragrance and flavor, but it had never tested it for safety. The product was placed on the market and advertised nationally.

On 11 October 1937, the first reports of deaths associated with the drug began to trickle in. Patients who had taken it suffered intense pain, urine stoppage, vomiting, convulsions, stupor, and coma. The agony often lasted a week or more before death ensued. Most of the victims were children. As the death toll mounted, the **Food and Drug Administration** (FDA) finally took action. Absurdly, the only legal justification for ordering a recall and forbidding sale of the product was to charge that use of the term "elixir" on the label constituted **misbranding** when used in a drug that did not contain alcohol. If the drug had been labeled properly, it would not have been illegal!

The FDA's agents, numbering no more than the police department of Philadelphia, fanned out across the country to track down bottles of the poison. Physicians who had prescribed it went to heroic efforts to get it back from their patients before they swallowed it. The Associated Press reported that a "nationwide race with death" was under way. One agent spent four days trying to reach a family named Long who had purchased the drug in rural Arkansas. He arrived too late. The funeral of the family's seven-year-old daughter, who had taken the drug, was just getting under way. Before the ordeal was over 107 people would die from taking the drug. Only six gallons of the elixir were responsible. Miraculously, of the 700 pints remaining in circulation when the recall was ordered, 99% of it was found and destroyed. The chemist at the Messengill Company who developed the elixir committed suicide. The company itself was fined $26,000, the highest fine allowed under the law. But it was not enough to placate an outraged public.

The magnitude of the sulfanilamide tragedy galvanized support for the new law stalled in Congress. A majority of newspapers, many businesses, advertising groups, and various professional associations were finally persuaded to endorse it. President Roosevelt signed the bill into law on 25 June 1938. In the future, the safety and efficacy of drugs would have to be proved before they were marketed.

In an odd postscript to history, one of the researchers who helped discover which component of the elixir sulfanilamide was responsible for the deaths was Dr. Frances B. Kelsey, then a young graduate student at the University of Chicago. Later, hers would be the only voice at the FDA to object to the approval of another dangerous drug, thalidomide [see **thalidomide incident**]. Her persistent doubts prevented the drug's sale in the United States.

TARBELL, IDA MINERVA (1857–1944) Writer and journalist whose epic *History of the Standard Oil Company*, published in 1904, helped ignite public sentiment for regulation of powerful trusts then threatening free enterprise in the United States. The taming of the trusts was important for **consumers** in that it preserved competition among **sellers** of goods and services. Competition operates to keep prices for goods and services reflective of the actual costs of producing them, thus ensuring a generally "fair deal" for consumers.

Tarbell was born on her grandparents' Pennsylvania farm in 1857. When oil was discovered in northwestern Pennsylvania in 1860, the family moved to the future city of Rouseville, where Ida's father went into the infant oil business. Her father's own struggles to remain independent against the pressure of the Standard Oil trust to sell out left a lasting impression on a teenaged Ida.

After a brief stint as a schoolteacher, Tarbell returned to her alma mater, Allegheny College, where she earned a master of arts degree. In 1883, she joined the staff of *The Chautauquan*, a monthly educational magazine. There she learned the craft of magazine publishing, from copywriting and production to promotion.

In 1890, bored with her position as managing editor at *The Chautauquan*, Tarbell quit her job and went to Paris. She studied historiography at the Sorbonne while supporting herself writing articles about Paris for American newspapers.

Tarbell returned to the United States in 1893 and joined the staff of *McClure's Magazine*, a literary and current affairs journal. S. S. McClure, the magazine's founder, showed genius for mass-marketing. By using cheaper production methods than other periodicals, he was able to offer accessible, quality articles on popular topics for budget prices. Readership soared. Tarbell contributed a number of biographies on popular historical figures that ran in serialized form, including Napoleon and Abraham Lincoln.

McClure assembled an impressive stable of writers and journalists for his magazine. These included many of the original **muckrakers** examining

301

the seamy side of American industrialism. Looking for new directions for the magazine in 1900, it was McClure who hit upon the idea of a series of articles on industrialists, the labor movement, and political corruption. From this came Ida Tarbell's assignment to write a history of the Standard Oil Company, much in the public eye at the time.

Tarbell warmed to the task, doubtless fired by the memory of her own father's struggles against the giant trust. The *History of the Standard Oil Company* ran in serialized form in *McClure's* from 1902 to 1904. In it, Tarbell gave a vivid account of the methods used by the oil trust to drive its competitors out of business, including secret rate agreements with the railroads that allowed Standard to undercut competitors' prices and networks of holding companies that snapped up the competitors as they reeled towards bankruptcy.

Long suspicious of trusts like Standard Oil, the public for the first time had a lively, understandable, and superbly documented account of how they really worked. The effect was electrifying. Public pressure increased to enforce the **Sherman Antitrust Act,** passed in 1890 but little used. In 1911, the U.S. Supreme Court ordered the Standard Oil trust dissolved, thereby corroborating much of Tarbell's accusations against it. See *United States v. Standard Oil Company.* Ida Tarbell thus became one of those rare journalists who not only record history but also help make it.

In the years following her triumph over Standard Oil, Tarbell continued to write and lecture widely on many topics. Her views on big business softened towards the end of her life, causing many to accuse her of naïveté about just how successful reforms had really been. Nevertheless, Tarbell's *History of the Standard Oil Company* remains a landmark in the effort to ensure fair business practices to benefit competitors and consumers alike.

THALIDOMIDE INCIDENT An incident in which a dangerous **drug** was nearly approved for sale in the United States, providing an important impetus to strengthen the protective function of the federal **Food and Drug Administration** (FDA).

Thalidomide was a tranquilizer developed in Germany in the early 1960s. It was in wide use in Europe as a sleeping aid and for relief of morning sickness in pregnant women. Except for experimental use, the drug had not been approved in the United States. However, because requirements for marketing new drugs were not very stringent at the time, approval was imminent. Only the doubts of Dr. Frances B. Kelsey, an employee at the

FDA, were standing in the way of opening a wide new market for the drug in the United States. Representatives of the Merrell Company, which intended to sell the drug in the United States, were pressing the FDA to override Dr. Kelsey's decision to delay approval when reports began to filter in from Europe of birth defects in children whose mothers had taken the drug. A large number of these children were born with seal-like flippers in place of limbs as a result of their mothers' use of the drug during pregnancy.

The understanding that a similar tragedy in the United States had been averted only by the misgivings of a single government employee helped galvanize support for increased control of the sale of new drugs in the United States. This support led to the passage in 1962 of the New Drug Amendments to the **Food, Drug & Cosmetic Act.** Those amendments expanded the FDA's power to require proof of the safety and effectiveness of any proposed drug prior to its approval for sale.

Oddly, however, the book has not closed on thalidomide. New research suggests that thalidomide may be of benefit to AIDS patients by halting the extreme weight loss that many experience in the latter stages. Thalidomide has also shown promise in treating leprosy. Renewed calls to legalize its use are posing new challenges for the FDA to balance the drug's known devastating effects on human embryos against its possible efficacy for these other heartbreaking conditions. Some suggest that, with stringent safeguards, it may be possible to have the benefits of the drug without its disastrous consequences. For others, even the remote possibility of a child born without arms or legs is enough to ban the drug forever.

TIME-PRICE DOCTRINE   A legal fiction that exempts **sellers** of goods and services on credit from normal **usury** laws. The doctrine applies whenever a seller establishes a higher price for goods sold on credit than the price for the same goods sold on a cash basis. The difference between the two prices is considered to be neither a finance nor an interest charge and, hence, not usury.

First adopted in the United States in 1861 [*Hogg v. Ruffner*, 66 U.S. (1 Black) 115 (1861)], the time-price doctrine is justified by the argument that the higher cost of goods sold on credit reflects the price of the seller's forbearance to insist on full payment at once. The seller considers having to give up the goods while waiting for payment to be such a detriment that extra payment is required, while the buyer considers immediate possession of the goods with deferred time to pay such a boon that the premium is worth the price. Thus, each party has given up something and gotten something in return.

The time-price doctrine does not differentiate between seller credit (i.e., credit given directly by the seller to the buyer to finance the goods sold by the seller) and lender credit (i.e., credit given by a third party so that a **consumer** may buy goods directly from a seller). For example, suppose a seller extends credit to a buyer to purchase goods, charging what amounts to a higher rate than the normal usury ceiling, and then assigns the buyer's debt to a third party. In this way, the third party ends up collecting more in interest than he or she legally could have done by extending a loan directly to the buyer to purchase the goods from the seller. Or, imagine that a third party advances funds to a seller so that the seller may extend credit to a consumer to purchase goods. The seller then pays the third party the proceeds of the sale with the higher price of the extended payback period. Again, the third party sidesteps the usury laws. In each case, the consumer pays the same amount.

In truth, the time-price doctrine is merely a device invented by courts to allow sellers to charge rates above the unrealistically low ceilings established by state usury laws. The assumption is that requiring sellers of consumer goods to comply with the low lending rates established by usury laws would tighten credit, causing a slowdown of consumer sales and the entire consumer economy. However, today most states have passed special laws setting ceilings on the rate sellers can charge for retail installment credit sales. These laws apply variously to different types of sales. However, they all have one thing in common: The effective rate of interest allowed on a credit installment sale is higher than the normal usury limit.

TORT   In societies organized under a common-law system [see **common law**] of jurisprudence, such as the United States, a citizen is expected to act with a certain degree of care towards the physical and emotional integrity of others. This **duty of care** goes beyond the prohibitions on harmful conduct established by criminal laws. If this extra duty of care is not observed and a person suffers injury as a result, a private wrong, or tort, has been committed. The law will provide a remedy to compensate the victim of a tort.

The private nature of the wrong is important in understanding torts. A tort is not the same thing as a crime, even though the latter is also a wrong. Technically, a crime is a wrong that is an offense to the public order that may, in addition, cause injury to a private individual. Therefore, the public, through its authorities, first declares the type of activity constituting the crime to be against the law. Then the public, acting through its law enforcement authorities, undertakes to enforce the law and prosecute violators who engage in the forbidden activity. Under criminal laws, violators are punished by fines or incarceration and the public order is restored. However, the victim of the injurious activity is not compensated.

Frequently, the type of activity that constitutes a crime will also be a tort. For example, there are criminal laws against **fraud.** Fraud is also a tort. The perpetrator of a fraud may be prosecuted by the public authorities for the crime of fraud. He or she may also be sued privately by the victims of the activity for the tort of fraud. The plaintiffs in the tort lawsuit will be entitled to compensation from the perpetrator if they prevail.

Crimes also differ from torts in that the criminal must have an intent to engage in the activity that is illegal. A person who causes harm purely by accident is not usually guilty of a crime. However, the person may be liable for a tort. Of course, there are many torts that do require proof of intent before liability will be found, including fraud, malicious prosecution, and battery. But many torts do not require proof of intent to cause harm as a prerequisite for compensation. Under tort law, a person may be required to compensate another for injuries that were entirely unintended. However, it will be necessary to prove that the person did not act as carefully as society thinks is proper towards others and an injury occurred as a result. This is the tort of **negligence.** Victims of negligence may sue privately for compensation for their injuries.

Importance to Consumers

Along with the law of **contract**s, tort law is one of the great pillars of the common law upon which the rights of **consumer**s rest in the United States. There are many different types of torts that consumers may encounter. Among so-called *intentional* torts, fraud, **deceit,** and **misrepresentation** regarding products for sale are most frequently encountered by consumers.

However, consumers are usually most concerned by the unintended negligence of **seller**s who produce and market products that are unsafe. The crux of the wrong in such cases is that the seller could have discovered the unsafe nature of the product through the exercise of proper care and prevented the injury by altering the product or taking it off the market. Because of the seller's negligence in failing to do so, the seller may be liable to pay the injured consumer compensation for his or her injuries.

As the age of the consumer has progressed, another type of tort liability has developed that is of great importance to consumers who are injured by defective [see **defectiveness**] products. This is liability without fault, or **strict tort liability.** Under this legal theory, the seller of a product that is unsafe will be required to compensate a person who was injured by the product, even though the seller was as careful as possible in making and marketing it. It may seem somewhat unfair to force a seller of a product to pay for injuries caused by the product even though the seller was not negligent or careless in any way. The law justifies this result by reasoning that the seller, who is reaping profits from the sale of the product, is in a better position than the injured consumer to pay for the injury caused by the product. The seller may then spread the cost of paying for such injuries throughout society by raising the price on the product. This way the society as a whole shares both the risk of injuries caused by useful products as well as the benefits they bring.

TRUTH IN LENDING ACT A federal law [15 U.S.C. §1601 et seq.] that requires a **creditor** to make certain disclosures about the terms of any **consumer credit transaction** in which credit is extended to a **consumer** to purchase goods or services for household, family, or personal use. This includes the purchase of a home. Credit extended for business purposes is excluded.

The Truth in Lending Act applies only to transactions in which the credit extended is to be repaid in at least four installments or in which a finance charge is to be imposed. Basically, a finance charge is any fee, including interest, that is imposed on a borrower for the privilege of deferring payment.

Purpose

Prior to the act's passage in 1968, consumer credit agreements were frequently couched in terms that obscured the true cost of borrowing. To curb abuses by unscrupulous lenders and to make credit transactions more comprehensible to ordinary consumers, the act requires that certain types of information be conveyed prior to the consummation of any credit agreement. Moreover, the information must be conveyed in a standard form in order to facilitate comparison with terms offered by other creditors. Informed in this way, the consumer may choose the lender with the best terms or decide to forego assuming credit obligations altogether.

In any consumer credit transaction the Truth in Lending Act requires the following:

- All necessary disclosures must be made before consummation of any credit agreement. This includes inserting the required disclosures in any advertising of credit availability if the ads use certain "triggering" phrases.

- Required disclosures must be made in writing in a form the consumer may keep.

- The terms of all finance charges must be clearly stated in language understandable to average adults. The words *required finance charge* must be used and must be more conspicuous than other type.

- The annual percentage rate of interest must be clearly stated with the words *annual percentage rate* more conspicuous than other terms.

- The creditor or creditors extending the loan must be clearly identified.

These disclosures must be made to all the consumers involved in the transaction. If any term becomes inaccurate, the creditor must communicate corrections to all of the consumers involved.

Other disclosures are also required, depending on the type of credit extended. For example, if the credit is open-ended—that is, the type used for **credit card** charge accounts—the creditor must provide the customer with periodic statements of the account's status. These statements must list all purchases made on the account during the billing period, all payments made by the consumer to pay down the outstanding debt during that period, and must explain how the periodic interest rate and finance charges were applied to the unpaid balance.

If the credit is closed-ended—that is, a specified amount for a single transaction, such as the purchase of a home—the creditor must also include a payment schedule showing the amounts and timing of payments to be made, and a summation showing the total amount the consumer will have paid when all the scheduled payments have been made. This way the consumer can quickly compare the cost of an item purchased with credit with the item's cash price.

The Truth in Lending Act also requires an explanation of the circumstances under which a creditor who has not been paid may take a *security interest* in the consumer's home. A security interest, also known as a *lien on property*, is basically a legally recognized claim of part ownership in a debtor's property that will be relinquished upon repayment of the debt. A security interest is a particularly serious consideration because it gives the creditor the right to have the consumer's home sold in order to satisfy an unpaid debt.

The act provides a consumer with the right to rescind transactions in which the creditor takes a security interest in the consumer's dwelling. The creditor must notify the consumer that a security interest has been taken and explain that the consumer has the right to cancel the transaction that led to the creation of the security interest. The creditor must tell the consumer how the transaction can be canceled and provide the proper form for the consumer to sign. The consumer then has three business days to exercise the right to rescind the transaction by sending the signed form back to the creditor. If the creditor fails to provide this information to the consumer, the consumer may rescind the transaction any time within three years after its consummation. The right of **rescission** is granted to anyone whose ownership rights would be affected by the creation of a security interest even if that person is not the consumer who applied for credit. For example, the spouse of a consumer whose credit agreement allowed the creditor to take a security interest in a jointly owned home would also have a right to rescind the transaction that led to the creation of the security interest. The right of rescission does not apply to home purchases in which a mortgage is taken out on the acquired home in order to pay for it, or to transactions in which a state agency is a creditor.

The most important of the federal agencies responsible for enforcing the Truth in Lending Act is the **Federal Trade Commission.** If a violation involves intentional deception by a creditor, a criminal prosecution by the U.S. Attorney General's office may follow. The Truth in Lending Act also provides consumers with a **private right of action.** Thus, an individual consumer may sue a creditor to enforce the law and may receive up to $1,000 from the creditor if a violation of the act is proved. The act also allows for **class action**s brought jointly by a number of aggrieved consumers. A creditor found liable in a class action may be forced to pay up to 1 percent of its net worth in fines, or $500,000, whichever is less. In addition, the fact that a creditor violated the Truth in Lending Act may, in some circumstances, be used as a defense by a consumer in a lawsuit brought by the creditor against him or her to recover the amount of the debt.

Many states have enacted laws similar to the Truth in Lending Act. Provisions of such laws are valid if they do not conflict with the act. However, if the state law provisions are inconsistent with the act, the act will preempt them. See **preemption.**

TRUTH IN SAVINGS ACT A federal law [12 U.S.C. §4301 et seq.] requiring banking institutions to disclose certain information about the terms on which they accept and keep deposits. Its purpose is to aid **consumer**s in choosing banks that are most advantageous for keeping their funds.

Under the Truth in Savings Act, a bank must disclose the following information to prospective depositors:

- the annual percentage of interest it will pay on deposits;
- how the annual percentage rate will be applied to determine the amount of interest to be paid on an account;
- the period of time the annual percentage yield is in effect;
- any minimum balance requirements on accounts for which interest is payable;
- any minimum time period the deposit must remain in the account in order to qualify for the interest payment;
- any fees that may be imposed that would reduce the yield; and
- a statement that an interest penalty will be imposed for early withdrawal, if this is the case.

The Truth in Savings Act also requires that banks provide depositors with periodic statements showing the status of their accounts, including the amount earned and the amount of any fees or charges incurred.

Consumers may sue violators of the act directly, either as individuals or in a **class action.** A banking institution found liable in such a lawsuit may be required to pay up to $1,000 to an individual plaintiff, or up to 1 percent of its net worth in a class action. The Truth in Savings Act is administered by the Federal Reserve Board in Washington, D.C.

TYING AGREEMENT An agreement that arises when a **seller** refuses to sell a product or service unless the buyer agrees to purchase another product or service. Such agreements are primarily used by companies to try to limit competition between themselves and other companies. Therefore, they are matters of most concern to the **antitrust law**s.

Occasionally, sellers try to condition the validity of a product's **warranty** on the buyer's use of another product or service. Such arrangements are illegal under the **Magnuson-Moss Warranty Act.** Under that law, a seller may not require that a **consumer** buy any other product or service in order to validate a product's warranty. However, a seller may condition the warranty on the use of specific replacement parts or "authorized service representatives" as long as both the parts and the service are provided to the consumer free of charge.

Occasionally, the **Federal Trade Commission** may allow a company to require that consumers use replacement parts of a certain brand when making repairs under a warranty. Generally, the company must show that the product will only work with those parts or some other compelling reason for requiring them. This is rarely possible. However, a luxury automobile company was able to justify a tying agreement in its warranty that required the use of its own brand of replacement parts. The company argued that lower-cost parts of another maker might prove inferior and fail, thus injuring the company's reputation for quality.

It should be noted that a seller may always set specifications for replacement parts to be used in its products under warranty. What it may not do is specify a particular brand of parts or service to be used.

UNAVOIDABLY UNSAFE PRODUCT   A product of great utility that also presents a significant risk of harm that cannot be eliminated by any known means. Such products are not considered defective [see **defectiveness**] under the law because their utility so greatly outweighs the risk they present. The argument that a product is unavoidably unsafe is usually presented as a defense in a **products liability** case based on **strict tort liability.**

The best example of unavoidably unsafe products are prescription **drug**s. Because of their ability to fight disease, drugs are among the most useful products known. At the same time, drugs present the potential for harmful side effects that may even include death. Such side effects generally arise because of individuals' slightly different biological responses to different chemicals. Therefore, these side effects cannot be completely eliminated. Nevertheless, society considers drugs so important that it frequently is willing to tolerate the risks presented by them by exempting their **sellers** from liability for injuries caused by their unavoidable hazards.

Of course, not all prescription drugs may claim to be unavoidably unsafe products. If a drug's utility in treating disease is less than the likelihood of serious side effects it causes, it may be found defective even though it might also be of benefit to a certain segment of the population. Moreover, even when a drug clearly qualifies as an unavoidably unsafe product, a **consumer** who has suffered injury from one of the drug's unavoidable, dangerous side effects may still recover compensation if he or she was not adequately warned about such hazards [see **warning defect**].

Unavoidably unsafe products should not be confused with **inherently dangerous product**s. Such products are also dangerous by nature. However, they are not considered so useful by society that they cannot be found to be defective.

UNDERWRITERS LABORATORIES INC.   An independent, not-for-profit organization dedicated to setting safety standards for products and testing them for compliance.

Underwriters Laboratories (UL) was founded in 1894 by William Henry Merrill. As a 25-year-old electrician, Merrill was hired to investigate and repair problems with the "Electricity Building" display at the 1893 World's Fair in Chicago. The more than 100,000 incandescent lightbulbs in the display were drawing huge crowds curious about the relatively new phenomenon of harnessed electricity. However, the display was also a fearsome, jury-rigged mass of dubious electrical connections that was continually sparking fires. The problem was so severe that the future of electricity as a useful force was in doubt. Numerous insurance companies had already voiced fears that an increased incidence of fire at large buildings was caused by recently installed electrical devices. Inspired by his experience at the World's Fair, Merrill saw a need for careful scientific investigation of the era's new electrical inventions in order to determine how they might best be made safe. In this way, the obstacles to utilizing the awesome power of electricity for the public good could be surmounted.

Underwriters Laboratories was initially funded by insurance underwriters with the purpose of recommending to insurance companies which electrical products were good risks for insurance protection. However, under Merrill, the organization asserted its absolute independence early on. Merrill was devoted to unbiased, thoroughly objective reporting, based on proven scientific tests. In 1936, UL was incorporated as an independent company, eliminating any trace of suspected influence by its original patrons. Today, the company is funded primarily by fees paid by its "clients," the manufacturers of the products it tests. These **sellers** bring their products to UL for safety testing. In 1995, UL's client base included over 40,000 manufacturers worldwide.

Underwriters Laboratories initially concentrated on evaluating products for electrical hazards, which today include harmful electromagnetic emissions, as well as the possibility of shock and ignition of fires. Later, UL expanded its mission to analyze fire-prevention and fire-fighting products, such as fireproof doors and fire extinguishers. Gradually, the company began to consider other types of risks posed by products, from the stability of ladders to the environmental risks of refrigerant recycling devices. Today, UL evaluates more than 16,500 different types of products, and components of products, for safety.

Products specifically intended to promote safety are evaluated for efficacy and reliability. For example, smoke detectors may be tested for how well they work detecting smoke, as well as for any separate dangers they may pose. Underwriters Laboratories is continually expanding its expertise to meet the safety challenges of new technologies. Now in its second century, UL has recently begun testing the safety and efficacy of computer systems, including software.

When testing a product for safety, UL considers potential risks posed by the product's design and then subjects a sample unit of the product to stresses on the targeted design feature in excess of those likely to be encountered by the product in actual use. For example, among other tests, UL will bake an electric iron in an oven for seven hours at 18 degrees higher than the product's own maximum operating temperature in order to evaluate its structural integrity. It is unlikely that this type of stress will ever be encountered by an iron in everyday use. However, its ability to withstand these excessive stresses correlates directly with the degree of safety a typical **consumer** can expect from the product.

The standards that products must meet to pass the UL tests are set after input from all interested parties is received, including opinions from manufacturers, government agencies, and consumer groups. The actual standards may be derived from these parties' knowledge of the type of use typically expected for the product, the manufacturers' claims for the product, engineering expertise regarding the degree of safety feasible in similar products, and also from empirical data collected from the testing of numerous similar products. Standards for various products are published and are available to anyone who requests them for a subscription fee. Most of UL's standards have been approved by the American National Standards Institute.

In addition to testing samples of the product, UL also conducts periodic inspections of clients' manufacturing facilities to verify that their production continues to comply with safety standards. Samples of the product may also be brought back to UL's laboratories periodically for retesting. This is to ensure continued compliance and protect the integrity of UL's product marks.

Products that meet UL standards are authorized to display a UL mark. The organization has numerous marks that vary in appearance. Each type of mark indicates that the product has met safety standards for a certain type of hazard. For example, the familiar "UL Listed" mark indicates that the product has been evaluated for electrical hazards, such as shock and fire.

Underwriters Laboratories and other product certification services are of unique value to consumers. The presence of the UL mark indicates to the consumer that the product embodies a certain degree of safety and can be purchased with confidence. This, in turn, is of value to the client sellers who are rewarded for their dedication to safety by increased sales. Insurance companies are also able to pass on better rates to sellers whose products have passed UL's safety testing. In addition, government agencies, including local building code authorities, use UL standards in the regulations they draft, thus increasing the overall safety of the public.

UNFAIR OR DECEPTIVE ACTS OR PRACTICES STATUTE A generic name for laws passed in all states to protect **consumers** from a number of common unfair commercial tactics. These statutes vary in the type of transactions they regulate, the persons they are designed to protect, and the remedies that they provide.

Generally, unfair or deceptive acts or practices statutes codify prohibitions on types of unfair commercial conduct that are already recognized by the **common law.** Many are patterned after the general language in Section 5 of the **Federal Trade Commission Act.** Some of the state statutes are very specific in the conduct that they proscribe. However, most merely outlaw "deceptive," "misleading," or "unconscionable" trade practices, leaving it to the courts and administrative authorities to decide whether or not a violation has occurred in a specific case. A court or other adjudicative body will usually take into consideration the age, education, literacy, handicap, or other infirmity of the consumer involved when determining whether a particular commercial practice violated an applicable state unfair or deceptive acts or practices statute.

Typically, unfair or deceptive acts or practices statutes prohibit **misrepresentations** by **sellers** as to the nature of the goods or services they are offering and the terms for their sale. Misleading statements about the quality, grade, style, or model of goods, prior use, recommended uses, the reasons for the availability of goods, or the seller's intention to supply a quantity of goods are prohibited. Also proscribed are misrepresentations about the identity or affiliation of the manufacturer or seller and the existence or extent of any price advantage for the consumer [see also **deceptive pricing**]. Gross overpricing, **bait-and-switch advertising, referral sales, pyramid sales** schemes, and deceptive warranties [see **warranty**] and disclaimers [see **disclaimer of warranty**] are also typically outlawed by state unfair or deceptive acts or practices legislation.

Unfair or deceptive acts or practices statutes usually apply only to the sale of **consumer product**s or services. Other types of transactions are usually exempted from the scope of these statutes because they are subject to regulation by other laws. Exempted transactions include those involving credit, insurance, leases, or utilities. State statutes vary in their applicability to the sale of real property.

Retail sellers are the main target of state unfair or deceptive acts or practices statutes. Wholesalers and casual, nonprofessional sellers are usually not subject to these statutes. Also typically excluded are insurance companies, printers, and representatives of the media.

Many statutes provide a **private right of action** for consumers to sue a violator directly. Usually, only the consumer who was actually a party to the unfair sales transaction is protected under these statutes; however, some states do provide that third parties who are intended to benefit from sales transactions are covered as well.

A consumer who has been injured by a violation of a state's unfair or deceptive acts or practices statute typically has a variety of remedies. These may include **damages** or injunctive relief [see **injunction**]. A group of state statutes allow for **class action**s to be brought by a number of disappointed consumers acting together. In addition, all state statutes award attorney's fees to consumer litigants who are successful in proving their cases.

The titles of state unfair or deceptive acts or practices statutes can vary. Usually the words "unfair," "deceptive," or "consumer sales" will appear in their names.

UNIFORM COMMERCIAL CODE A comprehensive code of law regulating transactions involving the sale of goods. The Uniform Commercial Code (UCC) was conceived in 1940 by a group of legal scholars promoting the cause of uniformity in the commercial laws of the states. Drawing on principles of the **common law** as well as **statutory law** in many states, these scholars drafted a model comprehensive law that standardized commercial practices with regard to sales. This draft law was then circulated among the legal community for comment and revision. A first, semifinal version of the law was presented to the public in 1952. Over the course of the next 30 years, every state, with the exception of Louisiana, adopted the Uniform Commercial Code as its own state law. Many of the states added their own amendments to the code, and even Louisiana has adopted some of its provisions.

The UCC represents a great improvement over the past, when every state had special rules for the sale of goods. Now, in spite of some local variations, parties to sales transactions involving goods are secure in knowing what rules will apply to their dealings, even if they reside in different states.

Although it was especially designed for commercial dealers, the UCC is also important to **consumers** because it governs the rights and duties they have as buyers of goods. Of particular importance to consumers are the code's provisions regarding **warranty** and the buyer's remedies for non-delivery of goods, for the delivery of defective goods, or for the **seller**'s failure to deliver the goods that the buyer ordered.

The UCC does have some limitations. First, as noted above, the code varies somewhat from state to state due to amendments that each state added when it adopted the law as its own. Second, the UCC is written in broad language. Therefore, it is subject to interpretation. Much interpretation occurs when parties litigate disputes involving the meaning of words used in the code. The decision of the court in such a case supplies the interpretation for the disputed word. Therefore, in order to know exactly what rights the code offers to consumers, it is also necessary to know the decisions of courts that have interpreted the words used in the law [see **common law**]. Fortunately, there are many books and commentaries that discuss this "judge-made" law with regard to the UCC. Third, the code does not cover numerous types of transactions at all. For example, it does not cover real estate transactions or **contracts** to buy insurance.

UNITED STATES RULE The rule prohibiting the compounding of interest on consumer loans. Interest may be charged only on outstanding principal. A lender may not add other charges, such as unpaid interest or late fees, into the loan amount and charge interest on the entire sum. This practice would soon result in rates exceeding the **usury** limit. Therefore, on consumer loans, all such charges must be kept separate from the unpaid principal.

UNITED STATES V. STANDARD OIL COMPANY The landmark case [221 U.S. 1 (1911)] in which the U.S. Supreme Court announced the **rule of reason** as a basis for determining violations of the **Sherman Antitrust Act,** and simultaneously struck a blow for increased competition by breaking up the most notorious of the nineteenth-century trusts, the Standard Oil Company trust.

The Sherman Antitrust Act was passed in 1890. It prohibited "all contracts, combinations, and conspiracies in restraint of trade" and "monopolization, or attempts and conspiracies to monopolize." However, 20 years after its passage, the act still lacked teeth. One problem concerned its general language. It was unclear which specific behaviors "restrained trade." The other problem was the law's injunction against *all* **contracts** or combinations that restrained trade. If taken to its logical extreme, this prohibition would outlaw virtually any business agreement at all. After all, if A contracts to sell hay to B, A's freedom to sell the same hay to C is "restrained." Nevertheless, some jurists believed that the plain meaning of the words "all" and "restraint of trade" should be adopted by the courts. The upshot would be that any contracts between businesses to ship products across state lines would probably have been illegal. Moreover, many of these same jurists believed that a specific limit for largeness should be set for corporations beyond which they would be considered monopolies and found illegal.

On the other hand, more moderate jurists believed that the Sherman Act was meant to prohibit all contracts or combinations that *unreasonably* restrained trade. Under this view, a court of law would examine the actual effect on competition of the practices that allegedly restrained trade. If the effect of a practice on competition was minimal, it would be allowed. Moreover, the same jurists believed that monopolies in themselves were not illegal under the act. Rather, they believed that a violation of the law ensued only when a company with sufficient strength to successfully drive competitors out of the market acted with the intent to do so.

The standoff between these ideological factions was the backdrop to the lawsuit brought against the Standard Oil Company in 1911 for alleged violations of the Sherman Antitrust Act. The Standard Oil Company trust, headed by John D. Rockefeller, was initially formed in 1882. In 1899, newly consolidated yet again, it became the Standard Oil Company of New Jersey. The company represented the classic trust organization: Various corporations transferred their stock to trustees who, having a controlling interest in all of the corporations, ran them as one company. By 1911, the trust had cornered 90 percent of the market for kerosene and lubricating oils. It had done so by purchasing over 120 of its competitors, frequently after softening them up for takeover by engaging in **predatory pricing.** In addition, the Standard Oil Company was accused of securing discriminatory freight rates for its own goods, buying up pipelines and refusing to allow competitors to use them, operating bogus independent companies, dividing markets among its subsidiaries [see **division of markets**], and engaging in corporate espionage. Many of these activities were first disclosed by Ida Tarbell [see **Tarbell, Ida Mirnerva**] in her 1902–1904 series of articles in *McClure's Magazine* on the history of the Standard Oil Company. A full 57 pages of the court's record were needed to list the anti-competitive practices of which the company was accused.

In its defense, the company argued that its activities were not in restraint of trade. Since the company with all its many subsidiaries was but a single entity, how could it be accused of contracting, combining, or conspiring with itself? Moreover, the company took the view that since an individual may purchase property, he or she may purchase a competitor. And, because he or she may purchase one competitor, he or she may purchase all of them. Then, since a corporation could do anything a natural person could do, it also was privileged to purchase all of its competitors.

The high court ruled against Standard Oil, but the outcome of the case was greeted skeptically by the public. On the one hand, the court did find that the practices of the Standard Oil Company were in violation of both sections of the Sherman Antitrust Act and ordered the company broken up into its constituent parts. On the other hand, the moderate view of the act's meaning prevailed. The rule of reason was adopted. In the future, corporate acts would be analyzed for their effects on competition and would be found to violate the act only if, in the reviewing court's opinion, those effects were deleterious.

The triumph of the rule of reason incensed many **consumer** and antitrust advocates. Despite the victory over Standard Oil, they believed that the rule would water down the effect of the Sherman Antitrust Act and give too much power to courts that were sympathetic to businessmen. Their agitation was instrumental in getting the **Clayton Antitrust Act** and the **Federal Trade Commission Act** through Congress, which were partly intended as a way to undo the Standard Oil decision's adoption of the rule of reason.

In spite of the fears of activists of the time, the rule of reason in **antitrust law** has not proved to emasculate the Sherman Act. On the contrary, by ensuring that only practices that actually damage competition are illegal under the act, the rule clears the way for prosecutions but does not hamstring legitimate business dealings. The conservative viewpoint, by outlawing virtually any combination, might have seriously hurt the ability of American business to bring consumers the plethora of relatively cheap and high-quality goods and services that they enjoy today.

UNKNOWABLE DEFECT   A defense raised by a **seller** in a **products liability** case based on the argument that hazards in a product that caused injury were beyond scientific knowledge at the time the product was produced and that it would be unfair to hold the seller responsible for them.

This defense very closely resembles the **state-of-the-art defense,** since both defenses are based on insufficiently advanced scientific or technical knowledge at the time the product was made. However, the unknowable defect defense is based on the idea that the seller could not have even known that the product presented a danger, while the state-of-the-art defense argues that, while the danger may have been known, there was no known way at the time to avoid it. The unknowable defect defense is used most often in cases involving substances, the dangers of which are apparent only after long periods of exposure. The defense has been used with some success by the manufacturers of cigarettes in cases involving **consumer**s who began smoking before the mid-1950s, when the first scientific studies linking cigarette smoking and cancer began to appear.

The unknowable danger defense is not favored by courts because it may be seen as rewarding the sellers of products for failing to take all measures to test their products for safety before marketing them. For this reason, some courts require the seller using this defense to show not only that his or her own testing of the product failed to reveal any safety hazards, but also that there was no other scientific data available anywhere else at the time that suggested the presence of any danger in the product. See also **negligence; strict tort liability.**

UNREASONABLY DANGEROUS CONDITION   A prerequisite to recovery of compensation in a **products liability** case based on **strict tort liability** is proof that the product was in an unreasonably dangerous condition when it caused harm. This requirement derives from wording in the widely respected *Restatement (Second) of Torts,* section 402A, which states that one injured by a product must prove both that the product is defective [see **defectiveness**] and that it is unreasonably dangerous before the doctrine of strict tort liability will apply.

To some jurists, the requirement seems redundant, since a product is deemed to be defective precisely because it is unreasonably dangerous. Others point out, however, that a product might be defective, in the sense that it fails to work properly, and yet not present any danger to a user. In their view it is important first to show that the product has a defect and then that the defect made the product unreasonably dangerous. On the other hand, since it is necessary in any case to show that the defect in the product was the **proximate cause** of the **consumer**'s injury, the two requirements amount to the same thing. This is particularly true in cases involving **design defect**s and defective warnings [see **warning defect**]. It is hard to imagine a product in which there is a defect that causes injury that is not also unreasonably dangerous.

Nevertheless, the phrase *unreasonably dangerous condition* continues to be employed by courts considering products liability cases based on strict tort liability. Some courts insist that the language be used in court pleadings, briefs, and arguments, even though the court itself would be hard pressed to explain the difference between a *defect that causes injury* and an *unreasonably dangerous condition.* In any event, the same types of tests that are used to determine whether a product is defective are also used to determine whether it is unreasonably dangerous. See **consumer expectation test; risk–utility test.**

USED CAR RULE   A regulation promulgated by the **Federal Trade Commission** governing **warranty** disclosures on used cars. The rule applies only to dealers who sell more than five used vehicles per year.

The used car rule requires dealers to display a sticker, called the *Buyers Guide,* on the window of any used car offered for sale. It must identify the vehicle, including its make, model, model year, and vehicle identification number. The guide must indicate what type of warranty, if any, is included. If a warranty is extended, the provisions of the warranty must be explained on the guide.

Many dealers offer service **contract**s on used vehicles for an additional charge. The used car rule prohibits dealers from disclaiming [see **disclaimer of warranty**] any implied warranties [see **implied warranty of merchantability**] on systems covered by a service contract. This is to prevent dealers from making warranty coverage that is normally required by law at no charge dependent on the **consumer** paying for a service contract.

Information in the *Buyers Guide* overrides any contrary provisions in the contract of sale for a used vehicle. See also **conflict of warranties.**

USED GOODS   The law provides many avenues for a **consumer** to pursue compensation when new products prove to be defective. However, the law is still unsettled regarding the rights of consumers who purchase defective used goods. See **defectiveness; negligence; strict tort liability; warranty.**

The liability of the **seller** of used goods generally will depend on how much control he or she has over the condition of the product. By definition, a used product has been first under the control of its manufacturer, distributor, and retail seller, and then under the control of one or more consumers—all of whom may have introduced a defect into it. Therefore, it seems unfair to many courts to burden the seller of such a secondhand product with liability for a defect he or she might not have created. This is particularly true since the used product dealer may not have recourse to sue the consumer from whom he or she acquired the product if it proves defective. A retail seller of a new product may always sue the manufacturer or distributor of the product if the retailer is found liable to pay a consumer for the product's defects. Moreover, resale of used products should be encouraged since it is the only way poorer members of society may acquire some consumer goods. Making sellers of used goods liable for defects in them may result in many of them going out of business. Despite these arguments, the seller of a defective secondhand product may be found legally responsible when (1) the secondhand dealer made statements about the condition or quality of the product that later proved untrue, or (2) the secondhand dealer modified, repaired, altered, or reworked the product in any way.

In the first situation, the seller may be liable for breaching an **express warranty** about the used product. In the second situation, a court may decide that an **implied warranty of merchantability** has come into existence because the dealer has taken more responsibility for the product's condition by repairing or altering it. In either situation, a court might also find that the dealer is liable for defects in the product under a theory of strict tort liability.

In situations in which the dealer neither made any statements about the used product nor changed it in any way, liability is less certain. If the dealer is in the business of selling used products of the same type, strict liability in tort for the product's defects may be imposed. The reasoning here is that one who sells only used goods of a certain type will know more about them and a consumer will be more justified in relying on the seller's expertise regarding their condition. If the seller sells many different types of used goods, it is less reasonable to expect he or she has expertise regarding any of them.

Regardless of the theory of liability pursued by a consumer who has been injured by a used product, courts are likely to judge the defectiveness of the product in relation to other used products of the same type. In other words, a used product will be found defective only if it compares poorly with other used products of the same type that are on the market. It will not be compared with new products.

Of course, no consumer expects a used product to be as free of defects as a new one. The problem facing the court in a used product case is to determine just what is reasonable for a consumer to expect from a used product. Generally, it has been held that a consumer may expect more in the way of safety than quality from a used product. Here again, though, the court must decide how much safety a consumer may rightfully expect from a product he or she knew was in less-than-perfect condition when it was purchased. The answer typically depends on the unique facts of each case.

Generally, the seller of used products may place the risk of defects in those products entirely on the consumer by stating at the outset that the product is sold "as is." This "as is" language operates as a **disclaimer of warranty.** Or, a consumer who buys a used product marked "as is" may be presumed to have assumed the risk [see **assumption of the risk**] of the product being defective and causing harm.

USURY The granting of a loan, or the forebearing to demand repayment of a loan already due, in exchange for a rate of interest in excess of that allowed by law. Originally, the word *usury* meant only the charging of a fee for the *use* of money, a practice that was recognized even in the earliest times as legitimate. Only in relatively recent times has the word *usury* come to denote something illegal in itself.

Today, although the charging of interest on loans is a legitimate and even indispensable mode of conducting business, there is still a debate about whether interest rate ceilings should be imposed. Those against such regulation argue that the marketplace itself will set prices (rates) for the use of money based on supply and demand, just like any other commodity. They point out that when legal interest rates are set lower than legitimate suppliers of credit are willing to accept, the supply of legal credit dwindles. Many consumers are then forced to resort to loan sharks who not only charge excessive interest, but often engage in other oppressive tactics.

Despite these arguments, every state in the union, in addition to the federal government, has adopted some sort of usury law imposing limits on the price of credit, i.e., the amount of interest **creditor**s may charge for making a loan. Proponents argue that the limits are necessary to ensure that consumers pay fair prices for the money they borrow, particularly since some unsophisticated consumers may be pressured into loan transactions that could be ruinous for them otherwise.

Technically, in order to be usury, a creditor lending money must intend to charge a rate that is higher than that allowed by law. This does not mean that the creditor must intend to violate the law, but only that he or she intend to charge interest that turns out to violate the law. For example, a creditor who intends to charge 10 percent interest but does not know that the legal rate is 8 percent is guilty of usury, because the intent was to charge an amount that turned out to be over the legal rate. On the other hand, a creditor who intends to charge 8 percent but accidentally miscalculates in setting payments so that the actual rate paid by the consumer is 10 percent will not be guilty of usury, because he or she intended to charge an amount that would have been legal but for the miscalculation.

In addition, in order to be usury, the repayment of the loan must not be subject to any contingencies. In other words, the right to repayment must be absolute. If the loan is not repayable unless a certain event takes place, a creditor may charge more than the rate set by usury laws because he or she is taking a bigger risk by making the loan. Of course, if the contingency is utterly implausible, charging a higher rate than the legal limit may still be usury. For example, if the contingency under which a loan need not be repaid is the sun rising in the west, charging a higher rate for the loan would be still usury because the creditor is not really incurring any risk at all. On the other hand, if the loan is for a risky investment and will only be repayable if the investment proves successful, charging a higher rate of interest will be justified. The test used by courts in such cases is whether a reasonable person [see **reasonable person test**] would take a risk in loaning the money under the particular circumstances for the legal amount of interest only. If not, the loan will not be usurious.

Generally, the remedy for a victim of usury is the return of the amount of interest charges in excess of the legal maximum. Some state laws require payment of some multiple of the excess interest. In some cases, state laws may allow a consumer to avoid paying back any part of a loan on which usurious interest is charged. Moreover, courts may refuse to enforce consumer loan agreements if any of their terms, including interest, are *unconscionable*. This means that the terms are so one-sided in favor of the lender as to shock the conscience of a reasonable person.

In spite of the universal view that laws setting maximum legal rates of interest are necessary, usury laws are of surprisingly little uniformity. States typically enact different usury limits for different types of loans. For example, many states have so-called *small loan laws* that allow higher rates of interest for loans under a certain modest maximum. Other state laws set separate loan rates for pawnbrokers, credit unions, home improvement loans, check loans, installment loans or industrial or business loans. Frequently there are many exceptions to the rules for these types of loans depending on different conditions in the loans. In addition, many types of loans are excluded from usury laws altogether. Among the most important of these are loans made by sellers to finance consumers' purchases of their goods. See **time-price doctrine**.

To complicate matters further, certain creditors are allowed to charge higher interest than the legal state limit. These so-called *supervised lenders* may apply for a license to charge over 18 percent interest, in exchange for submitting to supervision by a government agency. Banks and lending institutions chartered by the federal government are allowed by federal law to charge the maximum rate allowed to state lenders in the state in which they are doing business. States, in turn, have laws allowing state lending institutions to charge the same rates as federal institutions. The result of all of these various rates is a crazy-quilt of laws governing interest rates. The consumer generally finds that a state's basic usury law rarely applies to the particular loan for which he or she is applying.

 WAIVER OF DEFENSE CLAUSE A clause inserted in a **con-tract** of sale stating that the **consumer** agrees to give up, or *waive,* his or her normal right to withhold payment for defective [see **defectiveness**] or undelivered goods if the contract is sold or assigned to a third party.

Normally, the responsibilities of each party to a contract of sale are mutually dependent. This means that the consumer's duty to pay is dependent on the **seller**'s delivery of acceptable goods, and vice versa. It is a common practice for a seller to sell or assign a contract of sale to a third party after the consumer has signed it. The third party then has the same right to collect payment from the consumer as did the original seller. Usually, this also means that the consumer can assert any defense against payment (such as nondelivery or delivery of defective goods) against the third party that he or she could have asserted against the original seller. In order to make these sales contracts more attractive to third parties who might buy them, sellers sometimes attempt to make consumers of their goods or services waive their rights to assert defenses against payment by signing a contract with a waiver of defense clause. This means that the consumer could be stuck with defective goods (or no goods at all) and still have to pay the third party to whom the contract of sale was assigned or sold. Of course, the consumer could sue the seller to get his money back, but lawsuits are expensive, time-consuming, and exhausting, and few consumers have the resources to mount such efforts. Moreover, the seller could be out of business or have fled the state.

Because of the manifest unfairness of waiver of defense clauses to consumers, they are banned or restricted in most states. The federal **preservation of defenses rule** makes them invalid as well in consumer contracts. See also **holder-in-due-course doctrine.**

 WAIVER OF TORT LIABILITY A method by which a **seller** may limit legal responsibility for harm caused by his or her defective [see **defectiveness**] products by inducing the **consumer** to agree to give up, or *waive,* the right to sue the seller to recover compensation for such harm. The validity of such waivers varies depending on the type of harm excluded and the state in which a claim is made.

Generally, a seller may not use waiver agreements to limit **tort** liability for personal injuries caused as a result of the seller's **negligence** or the defective condition of his or her products. Unlike legal responsibility arising from warranties [see **warranty**], which concern voluntarily made promises, tort liability is based on a duty automatically imposed by law to act with regard for the safety of others. It would entirely defeat this important public policy and encourage negligent and reckless behavior to allow individuals to simply bargain away their responsibility to act with care.

However, on rare occasions the seller of a product and an individual consumer may agree that the seller will assume no responsibility for injuries caused by the product, whether through the seller's negligence or a defective condition in the product. In order to be valid, such agreements must be expressly stated, using the words "negligence" and/or "**strict tort liability.**" The consumer must be fully apprised of the consequences of waiving his or her right to sue the seller for a tort, including the seriousness of possible injuries and the likelihood of their occurrence. In addition, the parties must be roughly equal in their bargaining power. This type of waiver of tort liability is virtually the same as **assumption of the risk.**

If physical injury is not involved, waivers of tort liability for harm caused by a product to the property or economic interests of a consumer may be valid in some circumstances. Generally, in order to be valid the agreement to waive tort liability must be voluntary. It is not sufficient merely to bury a waiver of tort liability in the **contract** of sale, even if the consumer is made aware of it. The waiver must be stated in clear language using the actual words "negligence" or "strict tort liability." In addition, the parties must be relatively equal in their power to negotiate and bargain over the terms of the sale. This generally means that the seller and the consumer must be equally experienced and knowledgeable, and there must be alternative products available to the consumer. Because of the stringency of these requirements, it is very rare that a consumer will be found to have waived his or her right to hold the seller of a defective product accountable in tort for negligence or strict liability. Usually, waivers of tort liability are only found valid in sales between two business entities when no physical injury is involved.

WARNE, COLSTON E. (1900–1987)   Economist and co-founder and president of **Consumers Union** (CU) for 43 years. Born in Romulus, New York, in 1900, Warne originally planned to be a banker. He majored in economics at Cornell University and completed his Ph.D. at the University of Chicago with a dissertation on the **consumer** cooperative movement. He also became interested in labor issues.

In 1936, Warne was one of a group of employees, led by Arthur Kallet, who left **Consumers' Research** in a labor dispute and founded their own product testing organization, Consumers Union. Perhaps because of its turbulent beginning, Consumers Union reported on the labor conditions of the companies whose products it tested as well as on the products themselves. Warne served as president of Consumers Union until retirement in 1979.

Described as gentlemanly in demeanor, deliberate and cautious in his actions, Warne is credited with guiding Consumers Union through difficult times in the 1940s, when the organization was branded "subversive" by representatives of business interests and the federal government. Warne later commented that the highly publicized negative assaults on his organization helped it survive by keeping it in the public eye and attracting new members. "If we had been left alone and ignored, we might not have stood the test. By making such an outcry, we became forbidden fruit," he later explained. [*Washington Post*, 2 January 1980, section D, page 14] In 1954, Warne successfully fought to have Consumers Union removed from a list of "subversive" organizations prepared by the House Un-American Activities Committee of the United States Congress.

Warne was described as a driving force in Consumers Union who nevertheless was able to delegate the authority for day-to-day operations to his subordinates. In 1960, he helped found the International Organization of Consumers Unions, which consists of approximately 175 separate consumer groups. He served as that organization's first president. Warne was particularly concerned about product advertising, stating in 1962 that "artificial product differentiation and romantic fantasies may for a time capture unthinking consumer loyalty, but these techniques are no substitute for the unadulterated truth." [*New York Times* Biographical Service, 7 May 1987, page 494]

In the 1970s, Warne and Consumers Union were criticized by Ralph Nader [see **Nader, Ralph**] and others for being timid and slow to join in political activities such as lobbying government for change. Nader had resigned his position on the board of directors of the organization in protest.

Although CU responded by becoming more involved in political issues concerning consumers, Warne resisted the urgings of Nader and others to make Consumers Union more activist. Instead, he steadfastly stuck to his original vision of Consumers Union as primarily an objective testing service that would allow consumers to make judicious economic decisions. Although Consumers Union was much more politically active than Consumers' Research, Warne believed that most of the lobbying should be left to others.

In addition to his duties as president of CU, Colston Warne also taught economics at a number of prestigious universities. He died in Bedford, Massachusetts, in 1987.

WARNING DEFECT   A product defect resulting from a lack of effective warnings or instructions to enable a **consumer** to use the product safely. Warnings and instructions are considered an integral part of any **consumer product.** A product marketed without adequate warnings and instructions may be defective [see **defectiveness**] and the **seller** liable to pay compensation for injuries or losses caused by it.

In order to be adequate, warnings accompanying a product must inform the user of hazards the product presents. This includes a description of the way in which the product may cause harm, the type of harm that may result, and the seriousness of the harm. For example, a warning that merely states that exposure of a product to the eyes "may cause irritation" is not adequate if exposure may actually result in blindness.

The product must also include instructions on how it is to be used so that it will be effective for its intended purpose and enable the user to avoid the hazards listed in the product's warning. It may also be necessary to explain why certain procedures are advised. For example, a product warning that states that paint should be used with "adequate ventilation" may be defective because it does not explain why the ventilation is necessary. A user of this product might reasonably think that the need for ventilation is to avoid exposure to poisonous fumes. He or she might don a respirator to ensure a supply of fresh air to breathe without realizing that the true need for ventilation is to prevent the buildup of explosive fumes. In this case, the admonition to use the product with "adequate ventilation" is insufficient to ensure that the user will be able to avoid the real danger posed by the product.

Instructions accompanying products should also be specific. In the paint example above, directions that say to use the product with "adequate" ventilation may also be defective because a user will not know exactly what type of ventilation is "adequate."

It may also be necessary to warn the consumer against uses of a product that are not intended by its manufacturer but might foreseeably be tried by an average user. See also **misuse.**

Warnings and instructions accompanying products must be written in language that is easy to understand for the average consumer. Language that is too technical may be inadequate and result in a warning defect. A seller may be required to provide warnings and instructions in languages other than English if the seller anticipates that a significant proportion of consumers will not speak English. In some instances, it may be necessary to provide illustrations or other graphic devices in order to impart the necessary warnings. For example, a skull-and-crossbones device is commonly used to warn that a substance is poisonous. It may be necessary to place such a device on a product, particularly if children may be exposed to it.

Warnings and instructions must be placed on the product they accompany in such a way as to be readable and conspicuous. Warnings or instructions that are particularly important may have to be printed in larger type or contrasting colors in order to be adequate to warn the user of dangers posed by the product. However, it is not necessary to provide warnings about every possible way in which the product may cause harm. In fact, to do so may result in a product with a warning defect. If there are too many warnings or instructions, important information might be overlooked in the confusion.

Generally, a seller must ensure that any warnings or instructions are imparted to the ultimate consumer of the product. It is generally not sufficient merely to warn the distributor or the retail dealer in hopes that he or she will pass the information along [but see **bulk supplier defense**]. Moreover, a seller has a continuing obligation to inform consumers of any hazards associated with the product that are discovered after it is sold. This may mean that it will be necessary to disseminate the new information in the advertising media, or even to trace the consumers of the product and inform them directly.

Generally, the adequacy of warnings or instructions is a question that must be determined on a case-by-case basis with regard for all the facts. Sellers have a duty to provide adequate warnings and instructions whenever they know, or should know, that a danger presented by the product will not be appreciated by the consumer, or that the consumer will not know how to use the product in order to avoid the danger.

In order for a consumer to recover compensation for harm caused by a product with a warning defect, it is also necessary to prove that the lack of warnings or instructions was the **proximate cause** of the harm. If a consumer already knows about the dangers posed by a product before using it, the lack of a warning cannot be the cause of any harm that results. Likewise, if a consumer would not read warnings even if they were provided, their absence cannot be the cause of harm resulting from the product's use.

WARRANTY A seller's express or implied promise or statement of fact about a product that induces a buyer to purchase it, and for which the law will provide a remedy if it proves to be untrue.

Despite its simple definition, no more difficult question exists under the law than what makes a warranty. This complexity is reflected in the history of the warranty concept.

History

In the very early days of the **common law,** society imposed a duty on sellers to make their goods conform to their statements about them. This duty was absolute and was owed to anyone who suffered damage or injury because of the goods, not just the buyer. The breach of this duty, or warranty, was a private wrong, which is called a **tort.** This strict policy was a reflection of the church-imposed morals and tightly knit guild system of production characteristic of the Renaissance.

By the seventeenth century, the guild system was losing ground to free competition among many producers. A new merchant class had sprung up. Perhaps in order to promote the tender roots of capitalism, the law began to look differently at the relationship between seller and buyer. As a result, a seller was no longer subject to an absolute duty to make his or her goods conform to statements made about them. Rather, statements made about goods would be legally significant (i.e., enforceable) only if they were part of the bargain, or **contract** of sale, struck between the seller and the buyer.

This change reflected the philosophy that buyers and sellers were equal in the ability to appraise the quality of goods and to bargain for the most favorable terms of sale. Thus was born the doctrine of *caveat emptor,* or "let the buyer beware," that has so dominated **sales law** into the twentieth century. Because a seller's statements about goods were now enforceable only if they were made part of the bargain, or contract of sale, between the parties, warranty was viewed as a contract issue. This view has prevailed into modern times.

As part of a contract of sale, a warranty could arise only if certain conditions were met. Most importantly, the statements about the product that made up the supposed warranty had to be a part of the bargain between seller and buyer. Legally, this means that the buyer had to have relied on the statements when making the decision to purchase the goods. Or, stated another way, the seller's statements about the goods had to have induced the buyer to purchase them [see **reliance**].

The view of warranty as part of the contract of sale had another, negative, implication for consumers: Only the immediate buyer of the warranted goods could claim the benefit of the warranty. Thus, if a buyer and his wife became sick from eating green apples that were guaranteed to be ripe, he could sue the seller for a breach of warranty, but she had no remedy. This was known as the rule of **privity of contract.** It required that the maker of the warranty and the injured **consumer** have direct contractual relations with each other in order for the warranty to be enforceable.

As the Industrial Revolution matured in the nineteenth century and the age of mass-consumption dawned in the twentieth, the law's insistence on viewing a warranty as part of a contract of sale freely negotiated between equal parties became more and more out of sync with reality. In fact, modern consumers have very little bargaining power as compared with the monolithic corporations that mass-produce our goods. Most frequently, the consumer is merely presented with a take-it-or-leave-it package deal. The drugstore patron is in no position to dicker with the manufacturer of a deodorant over its promise to keep him smelling like a "meadow in spring." For one thing, the buyer of a modern consumer product may be removed from the actual maker of a warranty by several layers of distributors. Thus, the manufacturer of a product may warrant it to be free of defects, but if the product passes through an intermediate distributor, the rule of privity will prevent a consumer from recovering from the manufacturer if the product does not live up to its warranty.

This harsh result, together with a long history of wildly confusing and treacherously deceptive warranties offered by the sellers of consumer goods, has led to many developments in the law of warranty in the twentieth century. One of the biggest has been the emergence of the concept of implied warranties. Essentially, the law now holds that there are certain warranties as to the quality of goods that arise automatically in any sale, independently of what the parties to the sale may actually bargain for. Ironically, the upshot of this development is to move the concept of warranty back towards the realm of tort law, where it originated. See **implied warranty of merchantability.**

Other recent developments in the law of warranty that benefit consumers have been a slow erosion of the rule of privity and a relaxation of the necessity to prove reliance in order to recover. See **privity of contract; reliance.**

Importance to Consumers

Warranties are a major source of legal rights for consumers to receive satisfaction from the goods they buy. Therefore, it is important to understand the different types of warranties and when they arise. Today, written warranties on consumer goods are subject to the provisions of the federal **Magnuson-Moss Warranty Act.** In addition, the provisions of the **Uniform Commercial Code** apply to warranties on goods in all states except Louisiana. Rules of the common law as well as other state laws may apply to warranties on the sale of services, real estate, and other transactions. The word *warranty* is frequently used interchangeably with *guaranty*. Although this is not technically correct, the mistake is now made so often as to have become acceptable. For more on the different types of warranties, see **express warranty; express warranty by description; express warranty by model; express warranty by sample; implied warranty of fitness for a particular purpose; implied warranty of merchantability; implied warranty of title.** See also **contract; damages; privity of contract; reliance; tort.**

WILEY, HARVEY WASHINGTON (1844–1930) Doctor, chemist, publicist, politician, and tireless campaigner for the cause of purity in **food** and **drug** products in the United States. From his post as Chief Chemist at the Department of Agriculture in Washington D.C., Wiley was the main architect and promoter of the 1906 Pure Food and Drug Act, a landmark in **consumer** protection legislation.

Born on an Indiana farm, Wiley went from a log cabin to Harvard by way of Indiana Medical College, from which he received his M.D. degree in 1871. After serving in a volunteer Indiana regiment in the closing days of the Civil War, Wiley taught public school in his native Indiana. He added a degree in chemistry from Harvard in 1873 before accepting a position teaching chemistry at the newly opened agricultural and mechanical university at Purdue in 1874.

Wiley had been interested in the relationship between food and health from his earliest days. At Purdue he pursued advances in analytical chemistry, which was just coming into widespread use. While at Purdue, Wiley accepted a joint appointment as state chemist for Indiana. His work at that post in exposing the use of glucose as an adulterant in sugar products earned him national recognition.

Wiley was recruited to the Department of Agriculture in 1883, becoming its Chief Chemist in the same year. From this position, he began a tireless crusade for purity in the nation's food supplies. Wiley created a special unit at the Department of Agriculture devoted to studying food **adulteration.** He published a series of bulletins based on the research of that unit that exposed fraudulent and dangerous methods by which food was doctored and disguised before sale to an unsuspecting public. Between 1887 and 1902, these publications served to keep the public's attention focused on food safety issues.

One of Wiley's major concerns was the increasing use of chemical preservatives in food products. In a series of experiments, Wiley recruited healthy young men to voluntarily dine on foods laced with increasing amounts of common chemical preservatives. The purpose of the experiments was to determine the extent to which these chemicals were deleterious to health. Nicknamed the "poison squad," the group met daily for their test meals at a special dining room set up in the Agriculture building. The health of the "poison squad" was the subject of regular and lively reports in the press of the day—also helping to focus public attention on the issue of food purity. Although Wiley's methodology in the study leaves much to be desired by today's standards, it was one of the first attempts to use a controlled study to determine the effects of diet on health.

In the waning days of the nineteenth century, the pressure on lawmakers to act to stem the flood of harmful adulterated food and drug products was increasing. Wiley, blessed with excellent political instincts and a talent for public speaking, threw himself into the fray. He was extremely effective at building coalitions among lawmakers and stirring up public agitation for reform at the same time. His alliance with the **muckrakers,** who were supplying the public with graphic descriptions of the evils of impure foods, was particularly effective in advancing the cause of pure food legislation. Wiley was among the first politicians to understand the great power of women as a lobbying force. Speaking at women's clubs throughout the country, Wiley even gave housewives rudimentary chemistry lessons on how to detect common adulterants in food by using substances on hand in their kitchens.

Passage of the 1906 Pure Food and Drug Act was a personal triumph for Wiley. He was appointed to head the new Bureau of Chemistry at the Department of Agriculture, the agency assigned to enforce the act. Unfortunately, bad drafting of the law made its enforcement difficult. Resistance to enforcement—not only from food producers, but from within the government itself—severely hampered Wiley's attempts to bring violators of the law to heel. He resigned his post in bitter disappointed in 1912, in favor of a position as professor of agricultural chemistry at George Washington University in Washington, D.C.

WOLFE, SIDNEY (1937–) Medical doctor, consumer activist, and cofounder and head of the Health Research Group, a subdivision of **Public Citizen.**

Wolfe grew up in Cleveland, Ohio. His father was an inspector in the Wages and Hours division of the Department of Labor and his mother was an English teacher in the inner city. He credits them with instilling in him an understanding of social injustice. At Cornell University, he studied to be a chemical engineer. However, one summer he took a job at a company that produced hydrofluoric acid used for etching glass. He left work every day with first-degree burns from the chemical. This experience led him to abandon chemical engineering in favor of medical school at Case Western Reserve University. There he studied under Benjamin Spock, the famous pediatrician whose books on child-rearing brought up an entire generation of Americans. Spock impressed on Wolfe the notion that it is not possible to understand people's health problems without understanding the circumstances in which they live.

Following medical school, Wolfe followed his ambition of doing medical research at the National Institutes of Health. While there in the late 1960s, he began consulting with Ralph Nader [see **Nader, Ralph**] about health issues. In 1971, the two sent a letter to the **Food and Drug Administration** (FDA) warning that bottles of an intravenous fluid were contaminated with bacteria, and that use of the substance had already caused 150 cases of infection and nine deaths. When the FDA merely proposed that a warning label be added to the bottles, Wolfe and Nader escalated their protest. Two days later, the FDA ordered a nationwide recall of the substance. The incident impressed Wolfe in two ways: First, the fact that two outsiders had to prod the federal agency to act in the face of clear danger indicated that the FDA was not doing its job, and second, the FDA's swift response to the activists' loud protest indicated that an independent, public watchdog over health issues could have a salutary effect.

In the same year, 1971, Wolfe and Nader founded the Health Research Group to be that watchdog. Wolfe left the National Institutes of Health and has been head of the Health Research Group since 1971. The organization focuses on six primary areas of activism: **food** safety, **drug** and **medical device** safety, occupational safety, women's health, consumer empowerment, and health care cost containment. The organization conducts its own research into the safety and efficacy of food additives, drugs, and medical devices. Some of the results of its lobbying activities before federal agencies charged with protecting the public health include the banning of Red Dye No. 2 as a food additive, banning the use of vinyl chloride as a propellant, removal of chloroform from cough medicines and toothpaste, establishment of zero tolerance in the workplace for ten widely used chemicals, and publicizing alerts about many other chemicals used in foods and drugs. The Health Research Group also publishes numerous books and pamphlets geared to the average consumer with advice about drugs, medical care, and dietary matters. Other publications expose unsafe drugs, doctors who have been disciplined but remain in practice, and unsafe hospitals. The latest crusade of Wolfe and the Health Research Group is to overhaul the nation's health care insurance system and replace it with a single-payer government insurer.

Admirers describe Dr. Wolfe as the physician with 240 million patients in his waiting room. Critics charge that he and his organization unnecessarily frighten the public and burden federal agencies with exaggerated health concerns about particular products. However, even his critics admit that Wolfe has been singularly effective in breaking new ground in health research and calling attention to matters of real concern.

For Further Reading

LEGAL TREATISES

These books are intended for lawyers and students of the law. Some of them are specifically to aid corporate professionals in keeping the corporation within the limits of the law. The material in them tends to be technical. Nevertheless, much of general interest may be gleaned from these books.

Freedman, Warren. *Products Liability for Corporate Counsels, Controllers, and Product Safety Executives.* New York: Van Nostrand Reinhold Co. 1984.
A brief primer on the law of products liability geared for lawyers representing the sellers of products. Some information will be of interest to general readers.

Katz, Robert N., ed. *Protecting the Consumer Interest: Private Initiative and Public Response.* New York: Ballinger Publishing Co. 1976.
General discussion of laws protecting consumers and how sellers can comply.

Kintner, Earl W. *A Primer on the Law of Deceptive Practices.* New York: Macmillan Co. 1971.
A well-written and interesting discussion of common business practices and how they can run afoul of consumer protection laws, especially in the area of advertising. Also discusses practices that result in unfair competition between businesses. Somewhat dated at this time, but still valid in its general points.

Le, Tang Thành Trai, and Edward J. Murphy. *Sales and Credit Transactions Handbook.* Colorado Springs: Shepard's/McGraw-Hill. 1985.
Mostly of interest to commercial buyers and their attorneys, this book nevertheless provides interesting information about sales law in an easy-to-read format that includes hypothetical "cases" and their solutions.

O'Reilly, James T. *Food and Drug Administration*, 2d ed. Colorado Springs: Shepard's/McGraw-Hill. 1992.
> A very technical and detailed analysis of the workings of the Food and Drug Administration aimed at lawyers practicing in the field. Discusses thoroughly the provisions of the Food, Drug & Cosmetic Act and outlines the procedural steps to be taken both by sellers wishing to comply with FDA regulations and by those defending against charges that they have not complied.

Prosser, William L., and W. Page Keeton. *On Torts*, 5th ed. Minneapolis/St. Paul: West Publishing Co. 1984.
> The classic textbook—or *hornbook*, as legal treatises are called—on the subject of tort law. Now in its fifth edition, this book provides an exhaustive, yet clear, explanation of tort theory as well as specific features of different types of private wrongs. A "must read" for anyone seriously interested in American law.

Scher, Irving, ed. *Antitrust Adviser*, 4th ed. Colorado Springs: Shepard's/McGraw-Hill. 1995.
> A very technical and detailed discussion of antitrust law aimed at lawyers practicing in the field. Nevertheless, some general information and historical background make this two-volume set a useful "browse" for general readers.

Sherman, Paul. *Products Liability for the General Practitioner*. Colorado Springs: Shepard's/McGraw-Hill. 1981.
> A concise summary of laws and legal theories under which sellers may be found liable for defects in their products that cause injury. Although geared for lawyers, the book is readable by laypersons as well.

Stern, Louis W., and Thomas Eovaldi. *Legal Aspects of Marketing Strategy: Antitrust and Consumer Protection Issues*. Englewood Cliffs, NJ: Prentice Hall Inc. 1984.
> An excellent textbook addressed to business people regarding the legality of common business practices. The book includes the text of actual court cases in order to illustrate points under discussion.

White, James J., and Robert S. Summers. *Uniform Commercial Code*. Minneapolis/St. Paul: West Publishing Co. 1980.
> A very good basic treatise on the meaning of the provisions of the Uniform Commercial Code. Aimed at lawyers, but sufficiently clear and concise for general readers.

GENERAL READING

These books are intended for a general readership.

Bishop, James, Jr., and Henry W. Hubbard. *Let the Seller Beware.* Washington, DC: The National Press. 1969.
A history of the 60-year battle to outlaw the anachronistic doctrine of *caveat emptor* that explains why the battle had to be fought.

Bollier, David. *Citizen Action and Other Big Ideas: A History of Ralph Nader and the Modern Consumer Movement.* Washington, DC: Center for Study of Responsive Law. 1991.
An extremely flattering view of Ralph Nader and the achievements of the organizations he has founded.

Creighton, Lucy Black. *Pretenders to the Throne.* Lexington, MA: D.C. Heath and Company, Lexington Books. 1976.
A history of the consumer movement in America with an explanation of the economic theories behind consumption and consumer behavior.

Freidman, Lawrence M. *A History of American Law.* New York: Simon and Schuster. 1973.
An excellent history of law in America, with lucid explanations of legal concepts and how they developed from the wider fabric of historical events.

Lieberman, Marc R. *Consumer Rights and Remedies.* Scottsdale, AZ: Makai Publishing Group. 1992.
A simple explanation of legal principles and consumer rights with practical advice about how to use them in particular situations.

McCarry, Charles. *Citizen Nader.* New York: Saturday Review Press. 1972.
A biography of Ralph Nader. Contains a useful timeline showing events in his life.

McCraw, Thomas K. *Prophets of Regulation.* Cambridge: Harvard University Press, Belknap Press. 1984.
A history of government regulation of industry as told through the stories of four great proponents: Charles Francis Adams, Louis D. Brandeis, James M. Landis, and Alfred E. Kahn.

Mayer, Robert N. *The Consumer Movement*. Boston: G.K. Hall & Co., Twayne Publishers. 1989.
    A history of the consumer movement, including an assessment of its accomplishments and outlook for the future in America and abroad. Discusses various consumer organizations, including their history and the people who founded them.

Nader, Laura, ed. *No Access to Law*. New York: Harcourt Brace Jovanovich, Academic Press. 1980.
    A case study of alternatives to the judicial system as methods of resolving consumer complaints. This book is more a litany of horror stories rather than a helpful guide for consumers with problems. Nevertheless, it provides an interesting study of the effectiveness or ineffectiveness of various routes to consumer satisfaction.

Sanford, David. *Me & Ralph: Is Nader Unsafe for America?* Washington DC: The New Republic Book Company, Inc. 1976.
    An unflattering look at Ralph Nader.

Classics

These books were very influential in effecting changes in the laws pertaining to consumers.

Caplovitz, David. *The Poor Pay More*. New York: Macmillan Co. 1967.
    Discusses the spending habits of the poor and how they are prey to unfair marketing schemes that result in their paying higher prices than more affluent consumers. This book influenced reforms in sales and credit practices.

Chase, Stuart, and Frederick J. Schlink. *Your Money's Worth*. New York: Macmillan. 1927.
    Classic exposé of marketing techniques and advertising claims that result in consumers paying inflated prices for inferior goods. A discussion of how the impartial, scientific product testing that was being undertaken by Schlink in White Plains, New York, led to a flood of consumer inquiries and the founding of the Consumers' Research organization.

Magnuson, Warren G., and Jean Carper. *The Dark Side of the Marketplace*. Englewood Cliffs, NJ: Prentice Hall, Inc. 1968.
    A laundry list of shady practices that cheated consumers in the late 1960s.

Most of them went unremedied despite the authors' attempts to rally support for legislation to outlaw the practices.

Nader, Ralph. *Unsafe at Any Speed.* New York: Grossman. 1965.
The book that made Ralph Nader a household name. An indictment of the American automobile industry, and in particular General Motors' Corvair sports car. The book describes how automobile design was not concerned at all with safety. Though interesting reading, it was the reaction of General Motors to the publication of the book—in hiring private detectives to discredit Nader—that accounted for its immense readership. The book and the reaction to it led to enactment of laws setting safety standards for automobiles.

Packard, Vance. *The Hidden Persuaders.* New York: David McKay. 1957.
An account of how modern advertising plays on consumers' subconscious fears and fantasies in order to induce them to buy products or support politicians or political causes.

Schlink, Frederick J., and Arthur Kallet. *100,000,000 Guinea Pigs.* New York: Vanguard Press. 1933.
An alarming description of how American companies were adulterating or dosing their products with chemicals whose properties had not been tested, then placing them on the market where the first testing would be done unwittingly by the American public. This book helped galvanize support for the Food, Drug & Cosmetic Act of 1938.

Sinclair, Upton. *The Jungle.* New York: Doubleday, Page. 1906.
The book that caused America's appetite for meat to falter. This novel, though fictional, drew on Sinclair's actual research of conditions at Chicago's meat packing plants. Although it was intended to promote support for socialist causes, the book resulted in outrage over practices in the meat industry. The uproar helped push through passage of the Pure Food and Drug Act of 1906.

Table of Cases

Listed below are cases mentioned in the text, with **boldfaced** page numbers referring to entries on that case.

Baxter v. Ford Motor Company, 168 Wash. 456, 12 P.2d 409 (1932), **27–28**, 130

Brown v. Kendall, 60 Mass. (6 Cush) (1850), 229

Cipollone v. Liggett Group, Inc., 112 S. Ct. 2608 (1992), **37–39**

Commercial Credit Company v. Childs, 199 Ark. 1073, 137 S.W.2d 260 (1940), **44–45**

Cunningham v. CR Pease House Furnishing Company, 74 N.H. 435, 69 A. 120 (1908), 216

Escola v. Coca-Cola Bottling Company, 24 Cal. 2d 453, 150 P.2d 436 (1944), 274–275

FTC v. Colgate-Palmolive Company, 380 U.S. 374 (1965), 104

FTC v. Sperry & Hutchinson Company, 405 U.S. 233 (1972), 151, **161–162**

Gardiner v. Gray, 4 Camp. 144, 171 Eng. Rep. 46 (KB 1815), 183

Greenman v. Yuba Power Products Inc., 59 Cal. 2d 57, 377 P.2d 897, 27 Cal. Rptr. 697 (1962), 9, **167–168**, 296

Grimshaw v. Ford Motor Company, 119 Cal. App. 757, 174 Cal. Rptr. 348 (1981), **168–170**

Hall v. Geiger-Jones Company, 242 U.S. 539 (1917), 30

Henningsen v. Bloomfield Motors, Inc. , 32 N.J. 358, 161 A.2d 69 (1960), **171–173**

Hogg v. Ruffner, 66 U.S. (1 Black) 115 (1861), 303

MacPherson v. Buick Motor Company, 217 N.Y. 382, 111 N.E. 1050 (1916), **203–204**

United States v. Aluminum Company of America, 148 F.2d 416 at 430 (2nd Cir. 1945), 219

United States v. E. I. du Pont de Nemours & Company, 351 U.S. 377 (1956), 220

United States v. Standard Oil Company, 221 U.S. 1 (1911), 316–318

Index

Boldfaced page numbers refer to entries on that subject.

Abnormal use. *See* Misuse
Absolute liability, **15**
Accountants, 216
Acquired immune deficiency
    syndrome. *See* AIDS
Action, **15–16**
Adams, Samuel Hopkins, 221
Adulteration, 2, **16–17**, 74, 154, 158,
    221, 290, 333
Advertising
    bait-and-switch, **25–26**
    of boycotts, 52
    for children, 151, 242
    of cigarettes, 147
    consequences of rise in, 4
    of contests, 68–69
    of cosmetics, 75
    as creating warranties, 6, 27, 75,
        130, 173, 253
    of credit, 84, 142, 151, 191, 307
    deceptiveness in, 95–100
    definition of, 96
    demonstrations in, 104–105
    of drugs, 114
    endorsements and, 122–124
    false, 64, **145–147**, 197, 226
    First Amendment protection of,
        95
    of food, 155, 237
    infomercials, 100
    of lease terms, 58, 78
    of medical devices, 211
    popular literature on, 63, 282
    price, 92–95

    of professionals' fees, 242
    regulation of, 13, 96, 122, 148, 155
    remedies for false, 146
    sellers' self-regulation of, 29
    state laws regulating, 250,
        314–315
    unsubstantiated claims in, 96–97,
        327
AIDS, 156, 303
Air pollution, 35
Alcohol, 35
Allergic reactions, 74, 76, 175
All-in-the-family loans. *See* Interlock-
    ing loan
Alteration of product, **17–18**, 297
Alternative dispute resolution, 13
American Civil War, 19, 287, 332
American Council on Science and
    Health, **18–19**
Antitrust law, **19–21**
    attempts to repeal exemptions
        from, 226
    consumer boycotts and, 53
    consumer product testing as
        enforcement of, 65
    exclusions from, 20
    Federal Trade Commission Act
        and, 150
    Federal Trade Commission and,
        148, 161, 241
    impetus for, 3, 19
    See also Clayton Antitrust Act;
        Division of markets; Exclusive
        dealing; Failing company

Antitrust law (*continued*)
  defense; Meeting the
  competition defense; Merger;
  Monopolization; Predatory
  pricing; Price discrimination;
  Price fixing; Refusal to deal;
  Resale price maintenance;
  Restraint of trade; Rule of
  reason; Tying agreement
Arbitration, 29
"As is" sales, 109
Assignment of wages clauses, 81
Assumption of the risk, **21–22**, 239,
  297, 325
ATM cards, 119
Attorneys, 216, 234
AUTOCAP. *See* Automotive Con-
  sumer Action Program
Automobiles, 11, 22, 65, 219, 271
  applicability of consumer
    protection laws to, 50
  crashworthiness of. *See* Enhanced
    injury doctrine
  Pinto litigation, 168–170
  Ralph Nader and, 224
  safety claims on, 297
  used, 320
  warranties on, 198
  *See also Baxter v. Ford Motor
    Company;* Enhanced injury
    doctrine; *Grimshaw v. Ford
    Motor Company;* Lemon law;
    *MacPherson v. Buick Motor
    Company;* National Highway
    Traffic Safety Administration;
    National Traffic and Motor
    Vehicle Safety Act
Automotive Consumer Action
  Program (AUTOCAP), **22–23**

Bad check lists, 62, 81, 82
Bait-and-switch advertising, **25–26**
Balloon payment, **26–27**
Bankcard Holders of America, 27
Baxter v. Ford Motor Company, **27–28**
Better Business Bureau, **28–29**, 147

Bill collectors. *See* Fair Debt
  Collection Practices Act
Blue sky law, **30–31**
Bona fide purchaser, 281
Boycott
  consumer, **51–53**
  group, 269
Brown v. Kendall, 229
Bulk supplier defense, **31**, 329
Bunyan, John, 221
But-for test, 255
"Buyer beware." *See Caveat emptor*
Buyers Up, 258

Carter, Jimmy, 225, 241, 243, 244
Caveat emptor, 7, 12, 28, **33–34**, 145,
  181–182, 183, 296, 330
Caveat venditor, 12, **34**
CCPA. *See* Consumer Credit Protec-
  tion Act
Center for Science in the Public
  Interest, **34–36**, 244
Center for the Study of Responsive
  Law, 224
Chase, Stuart, 11, **36–37**, 63, 282
Cigarettes
  common-law claims not pre-
    empted, 37–39
  criticism of, 19
  as inherently dangerous product,
    188
  labeling of, 147
  merchantability of, 185, 186
  unknowable defect defense and,
    319
Cipollone v. Liggett Group, Inc., **37–39**
Civil law
  in American legal system, 13, 45,
    39–40, 84
  in European legal tradition, **40**
Civil War. *See* American Civil War
Class action, **40–41**, 308, 309
Clayton Antitrust Act, 20, **42**, 127,
  150, 213
Close-connectedness doctrine, **42–43**
Cognovit clauses, 81

Collateral source rule, **43–44,** 87
Commercial Credit Company v. Childs,
    44–45
Common law, **45–48**
    criminal law and, 84
    distinguished from civil law, 40
    distinguished from statutory law,
      294–295
    history of, 1, 4, 5
    importance of precedent to, 46
    place in U.S. jurisprudence, 47–48
Comparative fault, **48–49,** 73
Concealment. *See* Nondisclosure
Confession of judgment clauses, 81
Conflict of warranties, **49–50**
Congress Watch, 258–259
Congress. *See* U.S. Congress
Consumer, defined, **50–51**
Consumer boycott, **51–53**
Consumer Credit Protection Act, **53,**
    125
Consumer credit transaction, **53–54,** 78
Consumer expectations test, **54–56,**
    159
Consumer Federation of America, 11,
    56–57
Consumer Information Center, **57–58**
Consumer Leasing Act, 53, **58–59**
Consumer Product Safety Act
    (CPSA), **59–60,** 251
Consumer Product Safety Commis-
    sion (CPSC), 8, **60–62,** 152, 171,
    214, 225, 244
Consumer product, defined, **59**
Consumer report, **62–63,** 138–140
Consumer Reports magazine, 64
Consumers' Research Magazine, 63
Consumers' Research, 37, **63–64,** 282,
    283, 327, 328
Consumers Union, 11, **64–66,** 163,
    244, 283, 327, 328
    criticism of, 65, 66, 327
    declared "subversive"
      organization, 327
    testing procedures, 65
Contest, **66–70**

Contraceptives, 114
Contract, **70–72,** 268
    as requirement for implied
      warranties, 184
    assumption of the risk and, 21
    in contests, 69
    damages for breach of, 87–89
    in development of consumer law,
      5, 6
    products liability and, 254
    rescission as remedy for breach
      of, 276–277
    in sales law, 281
    to buy land, 192
    warranties as part of law of, 6,
      199, 330–332
    See also Privity of contract;
      Rent-to-own contract
Contributory negligence, **72–74**
    compared with open and obvious
      danger defense, 239
    distinguished from assumption of
      the risk, 21–22
    distinguished from comparative
      fault, 48
    history, 6, 9, 72–73
    unavailability in strict tort
      liability cases, 297
Cosmetic, **74–76**
CPSA. *See* Consumer Product Safety
    Act
CPSC. *See* Consumer Product Safety
    Commission
Crashworthiness. *See* Enhanced
    injury doctrine
Credit, 7, 11, 27, 51, 103, 148, 174,
    271, 281. *See also* Consumer
    Credit Protection Act;
    Consumer credit transaction;
    Consumer report; Fair Credit
    Reporting Act; Credit card;
    Credit insurance; Electronic
    Fund Transfer Act; Equal
    Credit Opportunity Act; Fair
    Credit Billing Act; Fair Debt
    Collection Practices Act;

Credit (*continued*)
  Garnishment; Interlocking
    loan; Loan flipping; Time-price
    doctrine; Truth in Lending Act;
    Truth in Savings Act
Credit card, 27, **76–78**, 207, 307
  authorization services, 81, 82
  disclosure requirements, 137
  disputes regarding, 138
Credit insurance, **78–80**
Credit practices rule, **80–81**
Credit reporting agency, 62, **81–83**,
    138, 139, 142
Creditor, defined, **83–84**
Criminal law, 4, 39, 47, **84–85**
*Cunningham v. CR Pease House
    Furnishing Company,* 216
Custom specifications, **85**

Damages, 41, 43, **87–90**, 100, 138,
    260, 277, 278
  for breach of contract, 71
  for breach of warranty, 178, 180,
    183, 186, 188, 205, 206
  as common-law remedy, 48
  compensatory, 88
  consequential, 88
  under Consumer Product Safety
    Act, 60
  duty to mitigate, 87, 236
  under Electronic Fund Transfer
    Act, 121
  for emotional distress, 121, 127, 140
  under Equal Credit Opportunity
    Act, 127
  exemplary, 89
  under Fair Credit Reporting Act,
    140
  under Fair Debt Collection
    Practices Act, 144
  for false advertising, 146
  under Lanham Trademark Act, 197
  liquidated, 89
  measure of, 87–88, 195, 207, 210
  punitive, 10, 89–90, 140, 168–170
  special, 90

  under state laws, 315
  See also Private right of action;
    Restitution; Warranty
Deceit, 6, 13, 39, 48, 85, **90–92,** 100,
    124, 146, 161, 216, 270, 277, 305
Deceptive pricing, **92–95.** *See also*
    Advertising
Deceptiveness, **95–100.** *See also*
    Advertising; Deceptive pricing
Defectiveness, 54, 85, **100–101,** 115,
    158, 207, 321. *See also*
    Consumer expectation test;
    Design defect; Foreign-natural
    test; Manufacturing defect;
    Risk-utility test; State-of-the-
    art defense; Warning defect
Deferral charge, **101–102**
Delaney, James, 102
Delaney Clause, **102**
Delinquency, **103–104**
  in rent-to-own contracts, 273
Demonstration, **104–105**
DES. *See* diethylstilbestrol
Descriptions, warranty created by.
    See Express warranty by
    description
Design defect, **105–107**
  consumer expectations test for, 56
  distinguished from manufacturing
    defect, 208
  in negligence cases, 231
  risk-utility test for, 279
  where open and obvious, 239
Diethylene glycol, 299
Diethylstilbestrol, 209, 210
Disclaimer of warranty, **107–111,** 322.
    See also Express warranty;
    Implied warranty of
    merchantability; Implied
    warranty of title; Warranty
Discrimination. *See* Equal Credit
    Opportunity Act
Division of markets, 20, **111–112,** 288
Door-to-door sale, **112–113**
Drug, 8, 64, **113–115**
  adulteration of, 16–17

advertising of, 114, 242
for animals, 156
distinguished from cosmetic, 74, 75
distinguished from medical
    device, 210–211
efficacy of, 114
ethical, 114
FDA regulation of, 155–156
labeling of, 75, 214
over-the-counter, 114
patent, 221, 298, 299
premarketing approval required
    for, 75
safety of, 114, 226, 258, 332, 335
as unavoidably unsafe product, 311
warnings on, 114–115
See also Federal Trade Commission;
    Food and Drug Administration;
    Food, Drug & Cosmetic Act;
    Sulfanilamide tragedy;
    Thalidomide incident
Duty of care, **116–117**
as element of tort of negligence,
    230
role in tort law, 304

Eat, Drink, and Be Wary, 283
ECOA. *See* Equal Credit Opportunity
    Act
EFTA. *See* Electronic Fund Transfer Act
Electronic Fund Transfer Act (EFTA),
    53, **119–122**
Ellenbourgh, Lord, 183
Endorsement, **122–124**
by consumer protection
    organizations, 166, 226, 313
See also Advertising
England
legal history of, 1, 4, 33, 45, 183,
    195, 281, 330
Enhanced injury doctrine, **124–125**
Entire liability. *See* Joint and several
    liability
Environmental Protection Agency.
    See U.S. Environmental
    Protection Agency

EPA. *See* U.S. Environmental
    Protection Agency
Equal Credit Opportunity Act
    (ECOA), 53, **125–127**
Equitable remedies, 48. *See also*
    Injunction; Rescission
Escola v. Coca-Cola Bottling Company,
    274–275
Exclusive dealing 42, **127**
Express warranty, 33, 37, 77,
    127–133, 179, 198
advertising as creating, 27–28,
    130, 146
as affecting right to sue remote
    seller, 253
arising after sale, 132
"basis of the bargain" requirement
    in, 131–132, 270
on cosmetics, 75
disclaimer of, 108–109
distinguished from implied
    warranty, 183, 186
distinguished from puffery,
    128–129, 260
on drugs, 115
effect of multiple warranties on, 50
importance of, 132–133
necessity to prove reliance on,
    270–271
on services, 181
statements qualifying as, 128–129
statutes of limitations for, 293
under Uniform Commercial
    Code, 127–128
on used goods, 321
See also Express warranty by
    description; Express warranty
    by model; Express warranty by
    sample; Lemon law;
    Magnuson-Moss Warranty Act;
    Warranty
Express warranty by description,
    133–134
Express warranty by model, **134–135**
Express warranty by sample,
    135–136

Failing company defense, **137**
Fair Credit and Charge Card
    Disclosure Act (FCCCDA),
    137–138
Fair Credit Billing Act (FCBA), **138,** 225
Fair Credit Reporting Act, 53, 62, 83,
    138–140, 149, 225
Fair Debt Collection Practices Act,
    53, 80, **140–144,** 149
Fair Packaging and Labeling Act,
    144–145, 148, 225
False advertising, **145–147.** *See also*
    Advertising; Deceptive pricing;
    Deceptiveness; Demonstration;
    Endorsement; Lanham
    Trademark Act; Printer's Ink
    Model Statute; Unfair and
    deceptive acts and practices
    statute
FCBA. *See* Fair Credit Billing Act
FCCCDA. *See* Fair Credit and
    Charge Card Disclosure Act
FDA. *See* Food and Drug
    Administration
Federal Cigarette Labeling and
    Advertising Act, 37, **147,** 225,
    241
Federal Trade Commission (FTC), 36,
    42, 68, 80, 91, 112, 122–124, 127,
    140, **148–150,** 155, 161, 175,
    199, 207, 241–242, 308, 320
  in antitrust law, 20, 42, 213, 249,
    288, 310
  criticism of, 149, 224, 241
  history of, 8, 20, 148
  regulation of advertising by,
    95–100, 104, 237
  See also Pertschuk, Michael
Federal Trade Commission Act, 25,
    92, 96, 144, 146, 148, **150–152,**
    204, 208, 318
  FTC Improvements Act, 150
  history of, 20, 150
  as model for state laws, 9, 314
  unfairness doctrine, 162
  Wheeler-Lea Act, 148, 150–151, 161

Firearms. *See* Guns
Flammable Fabrics Act, 62, **152–153**
Food, 2, 3, 64, **153–154,** 242, 244
  additives, 102, 155, 166
  adulteration of, 8, 17, 155, 282,
    283, 288–290, 332–334
  advertising of, 97, 98, 123, 237
  distinguished from drugs, 114
  labeling requirements for, 145,
    214–215, 236–237
  merchantability of, 184–185
  privity requirement abolished for,
    172, 203, 252
  regulation by FDA, 155, 214–215
  safety of, 34, 35, 158, 166, 221, 226,
    258, 335
Food, Drug & Cosmetic Act, 8, 74,
    102, 113, 155, **157–158,** 210,
    214, 226, 236, 251, 298, 299,
    302. *See also* Cosmetic; Drug;
    Food; Medical device;
    Nutrition Labeling and
    Education Act
Food and Drug Administration
    (FDA), 8, 17, 35, 123, 145, 153,
    154–157, 158, 334
  history of, 154, 299, 302,
  regulation of cosmetics, 74–76
  regulation of drugs, 113–115, 299,
    302–303
  regulation of food, 153–154, 166,
    236
  regulation of medical devices,
    210, 214
  See also Fair Packaging and
    Labeling Act; Foreign-natural
    test; Nutrition Labeling and
    Education Act; Sulfanilamide
    tragedy; Thalidomide incident;
    Wiley, Dr. Harvey
Ford Motor Company, 27, 28, 168–
    170
Ford, Gerald, 243
Foreign-natural test, **158–159**
Foreseeability, **159–160**
Fraud, **160–161**

Fritsch, Albert J., 35
FTC. *See* Federal Trade Commission
FTC v. Colgate-Palmolive Company, 104
FTC v. Sperry & Hutchinson Company,
      151, **161–162**
Furness, Elizabeth Mary, **162–163**

Game. *See* Contest
Gardiner v. Gray, 183
Garnishment, 53, 142, **165–166**
General Motors Company, 224
Generally recognized as safe, 153, **166**
Good faith purchaser, 281
Gramm-Rudman-Hollings deficit
      reduction law, 259
Great Depression, 11, 236, 298
Green Seal, **166–167**
Greenman v. Yuba Power Products, Inc.,
      9, **167–168,** 296
Grimshaw v. Ford Motor Company,
      168–170
Guaranty, **170**
Guns, as inherently dangerous
      products, 188

Habitability, implied warranty of.
      See Implied warranty of
      habitability
Hall v. Geiger-Jones Company, 30
Hand, Learned, 219
Hazardous Substances Act, 62, 153,
      171, 244
Henningsen v. Bloomfield Motors, Inc.,
      171–173
History of the Standard Oil Company,
      221, 302, 318
Hogg v. Ruffner, 303
Holder-in-due-course doctrine, 42,
      43, 162, **173–175**
Hypersensitive consumer defense,
      175

Implied warranty 9, 33, 34, 72, 77, 134,
      as affecting right to sue remote
      seller, 253
      consumer expectation test and, 56

disclaimer of, 109
distinguished from express
      warranty, 127
need for, 9, 33–34
as remedy for nondisclosure of
      defects, 234
under Magnuson-Moss Warranty
      Act, 205
See also Implied warranty of
      fitness for a particular
      purpose; Implied warranty of
      good and workmanlike
      performance; Implied
      warranty of merchantability;
      Implied warranty of title;
      Notice in warranty;
      Limitations of warranty
      remedies; Warranty
Implied warranty of fitness for a
      particular purpose, **177–179**
      breach requiring proof of reliance,
      271
      disclaimer of, 109
      effect of multiple warranties on, 50
      importance of, 178–179
Implied warranty of good and
      workmanlike performance,
      179–181
Implied warranty of habitability,
      181–183
Implied warranty of merchantability,
      134, 172, **183–186,**
      compared to implied warranty on
      services, 180
      disclaimer of, 109, 173
      effect of multiple warranties on, 50
      on food products, 154
      importance of, 186
      necessity that seller be merchant,
      131, 184
      no proof of reliance required, 271
      standards for determining breach,
      184–186
      under Uniform Commercial
      Code, 184
      on used goods, 321

Implied warranty of title, **187–188**
Industrial Revolution, 1, 2, 5, 6, 72,
    229, 252, 329
Infomercials. *See* advertising
Inherently dangerous product,
    188–189
Injunction, **189**
Instructions. *See* Warning defect
Insurance, 43–44, 51, 56, 58, 62, 64, 89,
    113, 242, 265, 266, 273, 315, 316
    exclusion from antitrust laws, 20,
        226, 242
    See also Credit insurance
Interlocking loan, **189–191**
Interstate Land Sales Full Disclosure
    Act, **191–192**
Intervening cause, **193–194**. *See also*
    Foreseeability; Proximate
    cause

Jacobson, Michael F., 35
Johnson, Lyndon B., 162, 163, 243
Joint and several liability 10, 12,
    195–196. *See also* Enhanced
    injury doctrine
The Jungle, 221, 288–290

Kallet, Arthur, 63, 282, 283, 327
Kelsey, Frances B., 300, 302

Labeling. *See* Fair Packaging and
    Labeling Act; Hazardous
    Substances Act; Misbranding;
    Nutrition Labeling and
    Education Act; Warning defect
Labor unions, 20, 42, 51
Land. *See* Real estate
Lanham Trademark Act, 146, **197**
Latent defects, 73, 106, 182, 233, 239.
    See also Disclaimer of
    warranty; Nondisclosure;
    Open and obvious danger
Latent-patent rule, 239
Law merchant, 281
Leasing, 58–59, 112. *See also* Rent-to-
    own contracts

Legal cause. *See* Proximate cause
Lemon law, **197–199**
Lender. *See* Creditor
Limitations from exemption clauses,
    81
Limitations of warranty remedies,
    172, **199–202**. *See also*
    Disclaimer of warranty;
    Express warranty; Warranty
Limitations, statute of, **292–293**
Loan flipping, **202**
Loans. *See* Credit
Lotteries, 66–68, 262
Louisiana
    as civil law jurisdiction, 40, 45
    Uniform Commercial Code in,
        315

McClure, S. S., 301–302
MacPherson v. Buick Motor Company,
    203–204
Magnuson, Warren, 241
Magnuson-Moss Warranty Act, 108,
    111, 127, 149, 151, **204–207**, 241,
    242, 309, 332
Mail-order rule, **207–208**
Manufacturing defect, 101, **208**
    distinguished from design defect,
        106
    in drugs, 115
    See also Consumer expectations
        test
Market share liability, **208–210**
Medical device, **210–212**
Medicine. *See* Drug
Meeting-the-competition defense,
    212–213
Merchant. *See* Implied warranty of
    merchantability; Strict tort
    liability
Merchantability, implied warranty
    of. *See* Implied warranty of
    merchantability
Merger, 137, **213–214**
Misbranding, 74, 155, 171, **214–215,**
    299

Misrepresentation, 13, 39, 48, 91, 161, 192, **215–217,** 305
  in advertising, 100, 146
  fraudulent, 161, 214
  intentional, 214
  necessity to prove reliance on, 270
  negligent, 214–215, 231
  nondisclosure as, 232–234
  rescission as remedy for, 276, 277
  See also Deceptiveness; Deceit
Misuse, 49, 73, 76, 194, **217–218,** 297.
  See also Alteration of product;
  Foreseeability; Reasonable
  person test; Strict tort liability
Mock-ups. *See* Demonstration
Models, warranty created by. *See*
  Express warranty by model
Monopolization, 214, **218–220,** 287, 288, 316–317. *See also* Antitrust
  Law
Moynihan, Daniel Patrick, 224
Muckrakers, 10, **220–222,** 223, 290, 301, 333

Nader, Ralph, 8, 10–11, 66, 222, **223–226,** 241, 258, 327, 328, 334–335
National Consumers League, 10, 167, **226–227**
National Highway Traffic Safety
  Administration, 8, **227–228**
National Traffic and Motor Vehicle
  Safety Act, 225, **228,** 241
Negligence, **228–231**
  abolishment of privity
    requirement in, 203–204, 252
  comparative. *See* Comparative
    fault
  contributory. *See* Contributory
    negligence
  distinguished from strict tort
    liability, 296
  duty of care and, 116
  history of, 4–5, 9–10, 228–230
  intervening cause and, 193
  misrepresentation, 216

  place in common law, 48
  products liability and, 254
  in providing services, 180
  proximate cause and, 257
  reasonable person test and, 266
  res ipsa loquitur and, 273, 274
  sealed container defense and, 284
  standard of care and, 290–291
  state-of-the-art defense and, 291, 292
  as unintentional tort, 305
  waiver of liability for, 326
Negligence *per se,* **231–232**
Nixon, Richard, 243
Nondisclosure, **232–234**
  under Real Estate Settlement
    Procedures Act, 265–266
  See also Deceit; Fraud
Notice in warranty, 168, **234–236.** *See
  also* Express warranty; Implied
  warranty; Magnuson-Moss
  Warranty Act; Warranty
Nutrition Labeling and Education
  Act, 35, **236–237.** *See also* Fair
  Packaging and Labeling Act;
  Food and Drug Administration;
  Misbranding

Open and obvious danger, 73, **239–240,** 297. *See also*
  Reasonable person test
Ordinary useful life, **240,** 294, 297
OSHA. *See* U.S. Occupational Safety
  and Health Administration

Parole evidence rule, 108
Pertschuk, Michael, 149, **241–242**
Peterson, Esther, **243–244**
Pharmacists, 115
Physicians, 114, 115, 123, 212, 299, 335
Pilgrim's Progress, 221
Poison Prevention Packaging Act, 62, **244**
Predatory pricing, **244–245,** 317
  and rule of reason, 280

Predatory pricing (*continued*)
defenses to, 212
See also Antitrust law; Sherman
Antitrust Act
Preemption, **245–246**
under Electronic Fund Transfer
Act, 122
under Federal Cigarette Labeling
and Advertising Act, 37–38
under Food, Drug & Cosmetic
Act, 212
under Interstate Land Sales Full
Disclosure Act, 192
under Truth in Lending Act, 308
Preservation of defenses rule, 191,
246–247. *See also* Holder-in-
due-course doctrine
Price discrimination, 18, 42, **247–248.**
See also Antitrust law; Clayton
Antitrust Act
Price fixing, 212, **248–250**
per se illegal under antitrust laws,
20, 280
resale price maintenance and,
275–276
under Sherman Antitrust Act, 288
See also Clayton Antitrust Act
Pricing. *See* Deceptive pricing
Printer's Ink Model Statute, 146, **250.**
See also False advertising
Private right of action, 40, 154, 158,
215, 250, **251,** 266
under Consumer Product Safety
Act, 60
under Equal Credit Opportunity
Act, 127
under Fair Credit Reporting Act,
140
under Fair Debt Collection
Practices Act, 144
under Interstate Land Sales Full
Disclosure Act, 192
under Lanham Trademark Act, 198
under Magnuson-Moss Warranty
Act, 149, 151, 166, 206
under Sherman Antitrust Act, 288

under state laws, 100, 146, 315
under Truth in Lending Act, 308
See also Statutory law
Privity of contract, **251–254**
abolished in personal injury cases,
28, 203–204, 252, 253
history of, 5, 9, 116, 251–252, 331
in warranty cases, 130, 172, 180,
186, 252–254
See also Disclaimer of warranty;
Seller
Products liability, defined, **254–255**
Proximate cause, **255–257**
in contributory negligence, 73
intervening cause and, 193
in joint and several liability, 195
in market share liability, 209
in negligence, 230, 232
requirement of *cause in fact*, 255
role of foreseeability in, 159–160,
256
in strict tort liability, 297, 320
in warning defect cases, 330
See also Alteration of product; *Res
ipsa loquitur*
Prudent manufacturer test, **257–258.**
See also Consumer expectations
test; Reasonable person test;
Risk-utility test
Public Citizen, 11, 225, **258–259,** 334
Puffery, **260–261**
demonstrations as, 105
opinions as, 91, 96, 128, 270
trend to construe as warranty,
129, 146
Pure Food and Drug Act of 1906, 8,
221, 226, 290, 332
Pyramid sales, **261–263,** 314

Reagan, Ronald, 225, 242
Real estate
exclusion from consumer protection laws, 50, 59, 316
express warranties for, 127, 332
implied warranties for, 181–183,
184, 332

See also Interstate Land Sales Full Disclosure Act; Real Estate Settlement Procedures Act
Real Estate Settlement Procedures Act, **265–266**
Reasonable person test, **266–267.** *See also* Assumption of the risk; Contributory negligence; Duty of care; Foreseeability; Negligence; Standard of care
Recalls, 17, 157, 228, 299, 334. *See also* Consumer Product Safety Commission
Referral sales, **268,** 314. *See also* Pyramid sales
Refusal to deal, **268–269.** *See also* Antitrust law; Consumer boycott
Reliance, **269–271**
    as element in tort of deceit, 91
    as element in tort of misrepresentation, 216
    as element of express warranty, 131, 134–135, 331, 332
    as element of implied warranties, 177–178, 183, 186
    See also Puffery
Rent-to-own contract, **271–273.** *See also* Consumer Leasing Act
Rental transactions. *See* Leasing
Repose, statute of, **293–294.** *See also* Ordinary useful life; Limitations, statute of
Res ipsa loquitur, **273–275**
Resale price maintenance, 20, **275–276**
Rescission, **276–277**
    in contracts for housing, 183
    in credit transactions, 308
    in door-to-door sales, 112
    in sale of land, 192
Restatement (Second) of Torts §402A, 319
Restitution, **277–278**
Restraint of trade, **278,** 287, 317, 318
    consumer boycott as, 53

See also Antitrust law; Clayton Antitrust Act; Sherman Antitrust Act
Ribicoff, Abraham, 224
Risk-utility test, **278–280**
    in design defect cases, 107
    in determining defectiveness, 101
    related to prudent manufacturer test, 257
    See also Consumer expectations test; Subsequent remedial measures rule; Unreasonably dangerous condition
Rockefeller, John D., 317
Roosevelt, Franklin D., 37, 298, 300
Roosevelt, Theodore, 221, 290
Rule of reason, 20, **280,** 287, 316–318

S. E. Messengill Company, 299
Sales Act of 1906, 184
Sales law, 33, 254, **281–282,** 330
Samples, warranty created by. *See* Express warranty by sample
Schlink, Frederick J., 11, 36, 37, 63, 64, **282–283**
Sealed container defense, **283–284**
SEC. *See* Securities and Exchange Commission
Second collision doctrine. *See* Enhanced injury doctrine
Secondhand goods. *See* Used goods
Securities and Exchange Commission (SEC), 262, **284–285**
Securities Exchange Act, 30
Securities. *See* Arbitration; Blue sky law; Mediation; Securities and Exchange Commission
Seller, defined, **285–286**
Services, warranties on, 179–181
Sherman Antitrust Act, 8, 13, 20, 42, 53, 111, 150, 212, 248, 249, 278, 280, **286–288,** 302, 316. *See also* Antitrust law; Clayton Antitrust Act; Federal Trade Commission
Sherman, John, 287

Sinclair, Upton Beall, 221, **288–290**
Specifications
as creating warranty, 50, 133
deviation from as manufacturing
defect, 208
as voiding seller liability, 85
Standard of care 153, 180, **290–291**
and reasonable person test, 267
for sale of inherently dangerous
products, 189
in tort of negligence, 230, 231
See also Duty of care; Proximate
cause
Standard Oil Company, 301, 302,
316–318
State-of-the-art defense, **291–292**,
319. *See also* Design defect;
Reasonable person test
Statute of limitations. *See*
Limitations, statute of
Statute of repose. *See* Repose, statute of
Statutory law, definition of, **294–295**
Stocks. *See* Blue sky law; Securities
and Exchange Commission
Strict tort liability 17, 34, 39, 50, 217,
231, 273, 291, **295–297**, 311
applicability, 286, 319
comparative fault in, 49
defectiveness and, 101
distinguished from fault-based
liability, 296, 306
history, 4, 9–10, 167–168, 295–296
intervening cause and, 193
open and obvious danger and, 240
in products liability, 254
prudent manufacturer test, 257
used goods and, 321
waiver of liability for, 326
See also Absolute liability;
Ordinary useful life; Proximate
cause
Subsequent remedial measures,
297–298
Sulfanilamide tragedy, **298–300**
role in passing Food, Drug &
Cosmetic Act, 157, 283

See also Drug; Food and Drug
Administration
Sullivan, James B., 35

Tarbell, Ida Minerva, 221, **301–302,**
317
Testimonial. *See* Advertising;
Endorsement
Thalidomide incident, **302–303**
Time-price doctrine, **303–304**
Title, concept of, 281. *See also* Implied
warranty of title
Tort, **304–306**
damages for, 88
of deceit, 90–92
distinguished from crime, 39, 84,
304–305
forseeability and, 159
of interference, 52
of misrepresentation, 215–217,
232–234
of negligence, 228–230, 305
origins of warranty as, 330
as part of common law, 48, 72
privity and, 252
products liability and, 254
strict liability in, 295–297, 306
Truth in Lending Act, 53, 54, 58, 225,
306–308
balloon payments and, 26
credit cards and, 77, 137
credit insurance and, 78
FTC enforcement of, 148
real estate transactions and, 266
rent-to-own contracts not
included, 272
Truth in Savings Act, 53, **309**
Tying agreement, 206, **309–310**

Unavoidably unsafe product, **311**
distinguished from inherently
dangerous product, 189
drugs as, 115
See also Hypersensitive consumer
defense

Underwriters Laboratories Inc., 122, **311–314**
Unfair or deceptive acts or practices statute, 9, **314–315**
   deceptive pricing and, 92
   Federal Trade Commission Act as model for, 152, 314
Uniform Commercial Code, **315–316**
   conflict of warranties and, 49–50
   disclaimer of warranty and, 107, 109, 200
   express warranties and, 127–133, 270, 332
   implied warranties and, 184, 332
   limitations periods and, 293
   notice in warranty and, 234
   referral sales and, 268
   sales law and, 281
U.S. Congress, 27, 38, 56, 102, 154, 157, 227, 236, 241, 259, 295, 298, 299, 318, 327
   House Un-American Activities Committee of, 327
U.S. Constitution
   Commerce Clause, 8, 20
   common law and, 47
   First Amendment, 52, 95
   Supremacy Clause, 245
U.S. Department of Agriculture, 155, 333, 334
U.S. Department of Health and Human Services, 155, 158
U.S. Department of Justice, 42, 150, 213, 288
U.S. Environmental Protection Agency (EPA), 225
U.S. Occupational Safety and Health Administration (OSHA), 225
United States Rule, **316**
U.S. Supreme Court, 37–39, 52, 105, 147, 150, 151, 161, 162, 246, 302, 316–318
United States v. Aluminum Company of America, 219
United States v. E. I. du Pont de Nemours & Company, 220

United States v. Standard Oil Company, **316–318**
Unknowable defect, **318–319.** *See also* State-of-the-art defense
Unordered merchandise, 208
Unreasonably dangerous condition, 188, **319–320**
   as element of strict tort liability action, 296
Unsafe at Any Speed, 11, 222, 224
Used car rule, 199, **320**
Used goods, **320–322**
   implied warranty of merchantability on, 321
Usury, 102, 103, 143, 202, 272, 273, 303, 304, **322–324**

Waiver of defense clause, **325.** *See also* Holder-in-due-course doctrine
Waiver of tort liability, **325–326.** *See also* Assumption of the risk
Warne, Colston E., 64, 238, **327–328**
Warning defect, 175, 217, **328–330**
   bulk suppliers and, 31
   cosmetics and, 75–76
   drugs and, 115, 311
Warranty, 13, 16, 23, 33, 34, 217, 260, 282, 293, **330–332**
   advertising as creating, 27, 146,
   defectiveness of product as issue in breach of, 101
   by description. *See* Express warranty by description
   disclaimer of. *See* Disclaimer of warranty
   disclosure of terms of, 204–206, 320
   distinguished from guaranty, 170, 332
   express. *See* Express warranty
   federal law on. *See* Magnuson-Moss Warranty Act
   of fitness for a particular purpose. *See* Implied warranty of fitness for a particular purpose

Warranty (*continued*)
full, 205-206
of good and workmanlike
performance. *See* Implied
warranty of good and
workmanlike performance
of habitability. *See* Implied
warranty of habitability
history of, 5, 9, 330–332
implied. *See* Implied warranty
importance of, 332
lifetime, 293
limitations on remedies for
breach. *See* Limitations of
warranty remedies
limited, 205–206
Magnuson-Moss Act, 204–207
of merchantability. *See* Implied
warranty of merchantability
by model. *See* Express warranty
by model
multiple. *See* Conflict of
warranties

necessity to give notice of breach.
See Notice in warranty
necessity to prove reliance for
breach, 269–271
as part of common law, 48
place in law of contract, 72
remote buyers or bystanders as
beneficiaries of, 252–254
requirement of privity of contract
for, 5, 9, 28, 251–254
by sample. *See* Express warranty
by sample
state law on, 314
of title. *See* Implied warranty of
title
who may claim benefit of,
252–254
See also Lemon law; Puffery
Wiley, Harvey Washington, 8, 155,
332–334
Wolfe, Sidney, 258, **334–335**

Your Money's Worth, 11, 36, 37, 63, 282

Lauren Krohn is a graduate of Stanford Law School (1979). She has written extensively on legal topics for lawyers and is presently employed on the in-house author staff at Shepard's/McGraw-Hill, a publisher of legal materials. This is her first work for readers who are not lawyers. Miss Krohn is also a scholar of the Russian language and specializes in the translation of legal documents from Russian to English. She resides in Colorado Springs, Colorado.